Byways of Baldwin

The Baldwin Times office on the north side of the Baldwin County Courthouse Square in the 1920s and 1930s.

BYWAYS OF BALDWIN

Its People, History, Scenic Attractions and Growth from 1936

More *Mumblings* by

Jimmy Faulkner

NewSouth
Montgomery

Library of Congress Cataloging-in-Publication Data

ISBN-13: 978-1-60306-019-6
ISBN-10: 1-60306-019-7

Design by Randall Williams.
Printed in the United States of America

Second Printing, 2007

Order from:
Barbara Mitchell
1304 Forest Park Ave.
Bay Minette, Alabama 36507
Telephone: 1-251-937-9382
E-mail: stevemitchell@bellsouth.net

On the Cover: Modern Baldwin County Courthouse
facilities have spread extensively within Courthouse
Square and across the street on the north and northwest
areas of the square in Bay Minette. This is a 2005 view
of the main entrance to the courthouse. (Photo by John
C. Lewis of The Gallery)

Jimmy Faulkner

CONTENTS

Jimmy and Karlene Faulkner, 2006.

Acknowledgments

To James G. Walther, group publisher of Gulf Coast Newspapers, *The Baldwin Times, The Onlooker, The Fairhope Courier, The Independent, The Islander, The Bulletin, The Lillian Ledger*, and the *Spanish Fort Sun,* goes my sincere appreciation for publishing my **Mumblings** column. Also to Site One on the Internet for making each weekly column available online. I further wish to thank various other writers and media which I have quoted or made reference to in **Mumblings** over the years. My executive assistant, Dorothy Martin, and her staff receive my very grateful thanks for their research and assistance in preparing **Mumblings** for publication each week. Further, may I recognize former editor Steve Mitchell, and his wife Barbara, for compiling and preparing the columns for this book, and John C. Lewis of The Gallery for providing vintage restoration pictures of the old Baldwin County Courthouse, and a picture of my coffee club friends. And to my wife, Karlene; to my sons, Jimmy Faulkner, Jr., and Dr. Wade Faulkner; to my grandchildren and other members of my family, and to my readers, who for more than half a century have encouraged me with compliments about **Mumblings** and offered suggestions of subjects they would like to read, go my very deepest appreciation. You have been and are my inspiration to continue writing **Mumblings**.

— JIMMY FAULKNER

Baldwin County Courthouse Square circa 1920. The old *Baldwin Times* building is shown to the right and behind the courthouse, the Masonic building is to the left, and the county jail is on the far right near the windmill. (Restored vintage photo by John C. Lewis of The Gallery)

INTRODUCTION

STEVE MITCHELL

A young journalist arrives in Baldwin County, buys half interest in *The Baldwin Times*, and begins evaluating Bay Minette, the county and its unique attractions, plus its needs. He expresses positive thoughts for Baldwin County, envisioning what it is and what its future holds.

The above paragraph is a 1936 capsule view of future Mumblings columnist James Herman "Jimmy" Faulkner, then age 20.

The scenario began at his home in Vernon, Alabama. He had just returned with a Journalism Degree from the highly renowned School of Journalism, University of Missouri. Eager to launch a media career, Faulkner heard of a newspaper for sale in Alabama's largest geographical county, Baldwin, a county with a land area of some 1,596 square miles.

It was a time when America was striving to emerge from the depths of the Great Depression, the greatest economic devastation the country had ever suffered. Teachers' salaries were less than $1,000 per year, county commissioners were earning only $150 per month, and thousands of people could not find employment, literally surviving by growing their own food.

But the woes of that era, although stressful, did not phase the desire of young Faulkner to buy his own newspaper, nor dampen his optimism that he could be successful. Franklin D. Roosevelt had been elected president of the United States in 1932 and had launched a package of "New Deal" programs everyone hoped would revive the national economy.

Faulkner was just 12 when his father, Henry Lanier Faulkner, died from burns October 24, 1928, two days after a tragic fire at their home. He had an older brother, Thurston Lanier Faulkner, attending the University of Alabama at the time.

Now, eight years later, Jimmy and his brother Thurston, were on their way from Vernon to Bay Minette in Baldwin County to meet R. B. "Bob" Vail, owner of *The Baldwin Times* weekly newspaper. Arriving, Faulkner was told by Vail that he was interested in selling *The Times* but he would have to let him know later.

Within a few weeks, a letter from Vail offered to sell him half interest in *The Times*.

Jimmy and his mother, Ebbie Faulkner, a school teacher, arranged with a bank to borrow money for his venture by mortgaging her home for a $1,500 down payment. He bought half the newspaper August 15, 1936, for $3,750, with Vail saying he would consider selling the other half later.

The first public announcement of the sale of half the newspaper was a Page One story October 1, 1936, written by Vail. In part, he wrote,

> "Believing firmly in Bay Minette and Baldwin County and that a new era of great prosperity is coming on apace, and realizing that during the past few years *The Baldwin Times* has not measured up to its proper place in the Baldwin sun, the management has taken some long steps toward correcting the shortcomings of the past and prepare for that greater usefulness that is coming with improved business conditions and a more abundant prosperity and a large degree of human contentment.
>
> "And so, we introduce J. H. "Jimmy" Faulkner—the new editor of *The Baldwin Times*. Jimmy is a native Alabamian, having been born in Vernon, Alabama. He attended Alabama public schools and is a graduate of the School of Journalism of the University of Missouri. He is an experienced, though young, newspaperman of ability and high ambition. Jimmy is unmarried. He is energetic, anxious to meet the people of Baldwin County and from here on out will be seeing you."

Vail also wrote that a new typesetting machine had been purchased for the newspaper, that more local news than ever would be published, and "As heretofore, *The Baldwin Times* will be militantly Democratic in its policies."

He concluded, "Under the firm of Vail & Faulkner, owners of *The Times*, the undersigned will serve as publisher. Thanks for all the kindnesses of the past and with high hopes for the future _ truly yours, R. B. Vail."

Faulkner immediately expressed his support of the Democratic Party, writing in the October 1 edition that President Franklin D. Roosevelt should be re-elected. He also told of U.S. Rep. Lister Hill visiting Baldwin County the previous Thursday and is "a man who is fast becoming a prominent national figure."

He further wrote of Hill, "Naturally Baldwin County is proud of the position the congressman from our district is taking in national affairs, for his position and ability are not only serving this county and state but the entire nation. We feel that his record in the coming months and years will loom larger and larger in public attention and service."

Three weeks later, Faulkner congratulated Baldwin County Democrats after being informed by County Democratic Chairman Judge G. W. Robertson that county Democrats "and other friends of the President have subscribed 47 percent more than their quota to the Democratic campaign fund. In fact, they have oversubscribed by $350."... "Judge Robertson, like *The Times*, now hopes that the citizens of Baldwin County will not fail to vote all their numbers for the President (Roosevelt) on Tuesday, Nov. 3."... "Certainly we can go to the polls and show our appreciation for THE GREATEST PRESIDENT OF MODERN TIMES."

In the same edition of *The Times*, Faulkner and Vail came out strong for improving the appearance of Bay Minette, citing the cemetery as a point of beginning and calling upon the city council to take the lead.

"Bay Minette's cemetery is one place that needs attention more than any other in town. It is absolutely a disgrace to any town, regardless of how small the town might be. It is grown up in weeds, there is no shrubbery to speak of, or anything else that a well kept cemetery should have. A few people have pride enough to keep their lots cleaned."

They told the city council "the citizens of Bay Minette are looking for you to do something about this disgrace," pointing out that Councilman Leslie Hall was the only one who had sought to do something about the cemetery. The editorial concluded, "We know that you realize something must be done about the situation, we also believe that you can and will do something about it. But please, for Bay Minette's sake, stop procrastinating!"

Keeping a constant eye on state and federal governmental actions, Faulkner on December 24 that same year called attention to the work of State Sen. Robin Swift. He wrote, "We thoroughly agree with *The Foley Onlooker's* editorial about Senator Robin Swift. No truer statement could be made than, 'The people of Baldwin County have no more true nor loyal friend than a native son, Robin Swift, who at the present time so ably, intelligently and honestly represents this senatorial district in the Legislature.'

"Senator Swift fought an intelligent but losing fight against the present administration's pie eaters to prevent further taxation for the citizens of Alabama. He continually argued for economy instead of more taxes in the present legislative session."

Just six months after Vail announced the sale of half interest in *The Times* to Faulkner, he elaborated about the sale of the other half to him when he wrote on March 4, 1937, "As announced in last week's *Times*, we have sold this tower of journalistic virtue, erudition and hope to Mr. James H. Faulkner, who has youth, ambition, training, ability, a high sense of journalistic values and ethics, and keen appreciation of and rapidly growing faith in Baldwin County and its future, to recommend him.

"And we recommend him to you. Since last August, he has been among us improving *The Times* and building it back to the place it occupied before the depression and a multiplicity of other outside interests offered us a satisfying alibi for our own shortcomings in permitting it to fall far away from its wonted position as one of Alabama's stoutest hearted, most fearless and service-rendering weekly newspapers. We predict that, under Jimmy's guidance, *The Times* will soon be back, yes, and far beyond its past peak of highest value to its people."

Reminiscing, Vail recalled many who had been significant in building Baldwin County.

"The day we moved into Bay Minette was the very day in June, 1922, when they buried J. D. Hand, whose name looms largest on the horizon of Bay Minette's history. Dr. Dahlberg was the first to welcome us and offer the hand of fellowship. (Thanks, Doc!) Soon our acquaintanceship was vastly enriched by those salty characters who contributed so much to the prosperity and happiness of our fine little town. There were Frank and Norborne Stone, Dr. Lambert, Judge J. H. H. Smith, Judge Anderson and Judge Chas. Hall, John M. Green, Capt. C. S. Tompkins, Henry Moorer, Rowe Watson, Roland Heard, Orrie Hall, Tom Gilmer, Judge Hearin, Dr. Stallings, "Tramp" Irwin, "Major" Leak, Howell Hall, G. W. Burns, and many others too numerous to mention.

"Over the county, we were happy to add to this distinguished list, such stalwarts as Pat Cooney, Bill Stoddard, Jack Randall, "Farmer" Scott, Bob Greenwood, Oscar Johnson, Hilary Herbert Holmes, Harry Bill and many others, builders all, all of whom have now laid down their working tools forever. To them we extend a silent salute; they were men."

Now in full ownership of *The Baldwin Times*, Faulkner looked at the positive in everything he encountered and wrote editorials acclaiming the good things happening in Baldwin County, recognizing those helping make it so.

Germany's Adolph Hitler was causing conflict in Europe in the late 1930s, invading many different countries and bringing concern to all Americans. Japan also had taken five northern Chinese provinces, was having skirmishes with Russia and showing disregard for American property and rights in China.

It was the hope at the time that America could remain isolated from war with these countries and continue to rebuild its economy and infrastructure destroyed by the depression.

In early 1939, J. C. Burns was mayor of Bay Minette; Natalie Feulner, town clerk; and councilmen were L. D. Owen Sr., M. M. McMillan, John P. Beebe, Leslie Hall, and O. J. Manci. J. B. Blackburn was town attorney; J. L. Barrow, chief of police; and, A. A. Ray, fire chief.

Holding county government positions were Probate Judge G. W. Robertson, Tax Collector Jesse M. Smith, with M. H. Wilkins tax collector-elect to take office October 1, Circuit Clerk R.S. Duck, Tax Assessor E. S. Tunstall, and Sheriff W. R. Stuart. There were approximately 500 county, state and federal employees working in Baldwin County at that time. Newport Industries in Bay Minette was the largest industry in the county, with about 250 employees.

Soon after launching his journalistic career with his own newspaper, Faulkner met Bay Minette's young Evelyn Irwin and they were married April 15, 1937. Their first son, James Herman Faulkner, Jr., was born May 31, 1938, and their second son, Henry Wade Faulkner, was born January 29, 1941.

The world of politics opened for Faulkner in 1940 when he was persuaded to run for mayor of Bay Minette after Mayor J.C. Burns decided to not run for reelection. Faulkner won and at age 24 was soon said to be the youngest mayor in America. He served as mayor until early March 1943, when, with the United States immersed in World War II, he entered the Army Air Corps. L. D. Owen Sr. succeeded him as mayor.

Returning from military service in the summer of 1945, Faulkner was elected to the Alabama Senate and later, in 1954 and again in 1958, made two close but unsuccessful campaigns for Governor of Alabama.

From the beginning of his journalistic career in 1936, Faulkner wrote editorials from time to time on national and world problems, but mainly focused on Baldwin County's people, its treasures, and goals.

His first Mumblings column, called Mumblings in Black and White, was published August 8, 1940. After returning from the Army Air Corps, he continued Mumblings in Black and White in October, 1945, but also added a more personal column, Byways of Baldwin. Still later, on April 7, 1960, he changed the name of his column to Mumblings, which he continues writing and is published in *The Baldwin Times* and seven other Gulf Coast Media newspapers to the present time.

Faulkner's career accomplishments have grown from being a newspaper editor and publisher to serving as a mayor, a state senator, twice a gubernatorial candidate, radio executive, founder of Loyal American Life Insurance Company, and affiliated with the David Volkert & Associates, Inc., architectural and engineering firm since 1958. Named in his honor are Faulkner University, a private college in Montgomery, and Faulkner State Community College in Bay Minette.

He has received numerous awards during his career, including the "Person of the Century" award in 2000 from the North Baldwin Chamber of Commerce, the "Ageless Hero" award in 2000 from Blue Cross and Blue

Shield Association, and the "Lifetime Achievement Award" in 2003 from the Alabama Press Association.

He has visited every state in the United States and more than 100 countries worldwide.

His columns have provided readers with a vast amount of information about interesting people, unusual and beautiful places, political leaders, and historical facts about Baldwin County, Alabama, the United States and many countries of the world.

Byways of Baldwin

EDITORIAL COMMENTS BY JIMMY FAULKNER, 1937–1943

⁓

After buying *The Baldwin Times* in 1936, during the coming months of 1937 through 1943, the following excerpts and dates of publication are from editorial subjects about which Jimmy Faulkner wrote.

March 11, 1937—Baldwin To Get Rural Electricity

"Baldwin County has been successful in getting $200,000 appropriated by the national government for rural electrification. . . .

"We predict a small boom for the county as a direct result of this.

"The importance of rural electrification is recognized by all who are interested in the further growth and development of this wonderful county.

"The cooperation of the farmers of the county has made this appropriation possible. Our Congressman, Lister Hill, was quick to see that Baldwin farmers wanted electricity and to see the many advantages that it would bring to them. It was largely through his support of the project in Washington that Baldwin has been able to receive this money."

July 1, 1937 —Opening of Fort Morgan Park

"The opening of Fort Morgan highway and parkway on July 4 means more to Baldwin County than merely the completion of another link in the public highway system, for it recalls to the attention of America and the world the historic battles of which that extremity of Baldwin's Mobile Point was the scene.

"Fort Morgan, still in a good state of preservation, is made a patriotic shrine, with guns replaced as nearly as possible as they pointed when they menaced the Federal Fleet of Admiral Farragut who, lashed in the rigging of the Hartford, gave the deathless command: 'Full speed ahead, Damn the Torpedoes,' and steamed, his vessels lashed two abreast, through the withering fire from the fort to a position in the bay that doomed the fortification to defeat."

August 19, 1937—Bill Beebe Of Baldwin
"Important political moves are being made in Alabama this week, moves which may give Baldwin County a chance to furnish its first representative to the Congress of the United States.

"This chance, which would mean much to Baldwin County and the whole second district, lies in none other than W.C. (Bill) Beebe, attorney of Bay Minette and former state representative.

"This grand opportunity may come about in the event our present Representative, Lister Hill, becomes a candidate for the United States Senate to succeed Senator Hugo Black. We have every reason to believe Lister Hill will be elected to succeed Senator Black.

"The opportunity is also dependent on whether the friends of Mr. Beebe can persuade him to make the race. It is known that he is 'seriously considering,' but naturally can make no announcement until a vacancy occurs in the office."

Sept. 16, 1937—Baldwin County Bank
"During the darkest days of the depression and at the time when the future of Bay Minette was not so certain, a man came up from Mobile with a desire to reorganize the Baldwin County Bank, a bank that had disastrously gone broke on the brink of the depression, leaving men and widows alike practically penniless. Bay Minette was at a low ebb, the business men were discouraged and the majority opinion said that a bank could not be revived in this town.

"However, a few of the business men looked far into the future and believed that the bank could be reorganized, realizing of course the importance of a strong bank to the well-being of a community. Frank Holmes, who had a good position in one of the Mobile banks, was obtained to direct the difficult task.

"On November 1, 1932, the old bank was reorganized with a structure that wasn't strong but with a president and board of directors who were determined to give Bay Minette a strong bank as soon as possible.

"After struggling for almost five years—President Holmes received a telegram last Friday stating that the Baldwin County Bank had been admitted to the Federal Deposit Insurance Corporation, thus making the local institution as strong and safe as any in the entire country." ...

"Frank Holmes deserves the largest slice of this credit. His untiring effort during the time when things did not look so bright are no doubt largely responsible for the achievement. J.B. Blackburn, one of the directors, as attorney for the concern, worked hard and long and with genuine wiseness to bring the institution to a level that could render service to its fine community. Too, the directors played a big part in this important role."

June 30, 1938—Let's Restore Old Blakeley

"Elsewhere on this page, we have reproduced an editorial from *The Montgomery Advertiser* about Baldwin's Fort Mims. The article is interesting and the *Advertiser's* Mr. Hall naturally comes to the conclusion that the historic scene has not received enough publicity and that it should be restored as a national park.

"As a matter of fact, much publicity has been given Fort Mims. Some six years back, *Liberty* magazine had a serial story, 'The Hussy and the Rake,' written by Rex Beach, which thoroughly covered the historical background of the old fort. The story was fine and an effort was made to get Warner Bros. to make a movie of the novel, but to no avail. Beside this, Baldwin and Mobile papers have often taken the Indian battleground as a subject for writing.

"This paper has a particular interest in the old fort because Red Eagle's great, great, great grandson is a printer in this shop.

"Baldwin appreciates the *Advertiser's* interest in having the place restored into a national park, but at the present time we feel that all efforts should be turned to restoring Old Blakeley. For many reasons.

"This historic spot where the last battle of the Civil War was fought, one week after the war was supposed to be over, is pleasantly situated on the east bank of the Tensaw River, at about equal distance from the seas with Mobile, and perhaps more readily approached by vessels, whether from the rivers or from Mobile Bay.

"At one time Blakeley had a population of about 3,500 and was the largest town in this section. She had her cotton factories and storekeepers and newspapers. It was a port of entry, the locality of a steamboat company, and exported considerable quantities of cotton and lumber. But because of the high price of property, malaria and yellow fever, its decadence was rapid. Many of the houses were moved to Mobile, and its stores and warehouses gradually decayed."…

"… Blakeley may yet and should be rebuilt—though not as a commercial rival to Alabama's Seaport, but as a national park with good roads that would encourage tourists from all over the country."

Nov. 3, 1938—Benjamin F. McMillan, Jr.

"Benjamin F. McMillan, Jr., member of one of Baldwin's most prominent families and who had been an outstanding lawyer in Mobile for 30 years, died last Friday in a Mobile infirmary.

"Although he had not lived in Stockton for many years, he claimed it as his home and paid frequent visits there to see his beloved relatives and his many other friends. He loved Baldwin County and the people of Baldwin County had high regard for him. He was widely known and well liked, not only in his home county but throughout the state.

"Proving the high respect held for him, the *Mobile Register* had the following to say: 'His death was unexpected and his professional associates and many personal friends are shocked and grieved at the untimely end of a man who had proven of such sterling worth in his work and his activities.

" 'Mr. McMillan was active in social, civic, church and fraternal affairs of the community and in his profession his opinions were sought and greatly respected.

" 'Those who knew him feel a great sense of personal loss in his passing, yet they feel as well that his integrity and worth to the community will be remembered long as a memorial to a man who ran the good race and finished his course without cause for shame or regret.' "

Dec. 8, 1938—Dr. S. A. Y. Dahlberg

"An old landmark has been removed.
It stood for many a year.
It was a guide to passers by,
With laughter or with tears.

"It set the weary traveler on
The road that led to light.
It never led the wanderer wrong,
But always led him right.

"Altho' the sign was bright and plain,
It was wrongly read by few
Who could not see the gold beneath,
As some will always do.

"But, the Savior died for men,
That others might yet live.
'For greater love hath no man.'
Than his life for others give."

These lines were written and contributed to *The Times* by a friend of Dr. S. A. Y. Dahlberg and they, to a great degree, typify the 'landmark' which passed into history last Friday night. He had been a resident of Bay Minette since 1905.

"Dr. Dahlberg got much out of life because he put a lot into it. He lent his moral and physical support to almost every worthwhile move and was the leader in many of them. Besides being a dentist, his activities were many.

"Typical of the respect held for him throughout the county, he was elected and reelected as secretary and treasurer of the Baldwin County

Democratic Executive Committee. For many years he was a leader in the Masonic Temple. He was a church and civic leader. Because he had two of his own, he was especially interested in boys and at one time was the leader of the Boy Scouts in Bay Minette and continued interested in their behalf until death.

"Among his chief hobbies were hunting and fishing. He was a member of the Baldwin County Hunting Club and was a true sportsman.

"In his passing, the editor of *The Times* feels a deep personal loss but we pleasantly remember a recent incident that few people knew about, which might be considered typical of his endeavors to aid his fellow man. Dr. Dahlberg recently had an opportunity to get a position that, in the course of a few years, would have meant much to him financially, but one of his friends also wanted the job. And because of this friendship and because his friend was in financial difficulty at the time, he withdrew his application, knowing that it would probably mean his son would be deprived of an education that he so much desired him to have. Small men do not do such things.

"Dr. Dahlberg was a great character. Bay Minette does and will miss him."

Dec. 8, 1938—Bob Duck Raising Winter Pears

"We thought R.S. (Bob) Duck, popular county clerk, had been taking a rest because of illness for the last few months, but we found out this week he has been experimenting in raising winter pears.

"Whether he has been experimenting with winter pears or not, he has some ripe on the tree now, in December, 'believe it or not.' We don't know how he does it, but he has the pears and the tree to prove that he does."

Feb. 2, 1939—God's Gift To Baldwin County

"No newspaper could be starting on its fiftieth year of publication in Baldwin County without being thoroughly convinced of the bountiful natural advantages bestowed upon this great geographical sub-division of Alabama by our Deity. ...

"Land is always important, and this county was given plenty of it—good land with fine soil. Being endowed with a moderate climate and fertile soils, this was bound to become the most diversified farming county in Alabama. Almost any crop, including fruit, can be raised here.

"Timber is another thing that was made to flourish here and it now contributes well over a million dollars annually to the income of Baldwin citizens. Pine trees grow faster in this section than in any other in the United States, according to government surveys. From the pine comes turpentine, lumber and paper wood. And in the vast bottom lands also may be found hardwood timber in abundance. ...

"Although the county has developed rapidly in recent years, as yet it has not even scratched the surface. Advantage has not been taken of many of the natural resources. The major part of Baldwin's history will be written about the future and not about the past. Baldwin is so large in area and its land potentialities are so varied in scope that it is impossible for a human to predict accurately what may develop. ...

"... it has a population of less than 35,000. Less than 10 percent of its fertile lands are in cultivation. Miles of its waterfront property is undeveloped. Parks could be made of many historic battlegrounds. Some day these things will come into their own. ...

"Industries will some day see the advantage that the county offers and then our farms will be supplemented with factories. With the progressive citizenship that it has, Baldwin is destined for great things.

"And God will continue to be good to Baldwin County."

May 4, 1939—Foley Publisher Dies

"Death came to Frank Barchard, Sr., publisher of *The Foley Onlooker*, Monday morning and removed from Baldwin County one of its pioneers and prominent citizens. Since his arrival in this county 35 years ago, he has seen wonderful progress made in this section, much of which was speeded and boosted by him and his paper. He played an important role in Baldwin during the active part of his life and he was active except for the past few months.

"The publisher's political affiliation was with the Republican Party, and he was always active in its interest. He served as chairman of the Baldwin

County Republican executive committee and as a state delegate to the G.O.P. Convention at Kansas City in 1928, as well as other positions in the party at different times. His friends admired him all the more for his loyalty to the Republican Party in a Democratic county and state.

"With the death of Mr. Barchard went the last active pioneer publisher of Baldwin County. A little over a year ago, E.B. Gaston, founder and for over 40 years publisher of *The Fairhope Courier*, died. Mrs. Abner J. Smith, who assisted and edited *The Times* for a number of years, is still living in Mobile but she retired from newspaper work in the early twenties. This leaves the County's Fourth Estate in younger hands, hands who must work all the harder trying to uphold the fine reputations built by the ability of their predecessors.

"This week Baldwin County and her citizens lost a friend."

May 18, 1939—New Telephone System

"The citizens of Fairhope and Bay Minette are fortunate that the Southern Bell Telephone and Telegraph Co. is going to install dial systems in these two cities.

"The dial telephone system is much faster, more accurate, and it will be possible to hear much better than is possible over the present telephone. The dial system is modern and up to date and *The Times* believes that users in general will be well pleased after they become accustomed to using the new method when it is completed seven or eight months from now.

"Progress of this kind is always welcomed."

July 6, 1939—The Produce Market

"Friday night farmers from all over Baldwin County will gather at Robertsdale to organize so they can put over a valued project, a produce market.

"The Baldwin County Chamber of Commerce, with the cooperation of the county agent's office, has announced plans for the formation of such a market. The chamber of commerce, along with the county agent, has spent considerable time and effort getting information about how markets have been working in other parts of the state.

"It is calculated that if it is operated similar to those now run in Evergreen and Mobile, this project will prove an aid to farmers raising produce not shipped in car load lots. ...

"It offers an opportunity for Baldwin County farmers to increase their cash income. *The Times* hopes that everyone will cooperate and help put the project over for the advantage of the county as a whole."

July 13, 1939—4-H Club Honors

"Baldwin County has long been proud of the splendid records her farm boys and girls have been making in 4-H Club work. Clothing, food preservation, home improvement, poultry—these are but a few of the varied phases of 4-H Club work in which Baldwin's own youths have shown superiority.

"This week Homer Garner of Fairhope, Marion Rhodes of Summerdale, Frieda Koehler of Foley and Roy Simms of Fairhope are in Auburn representing the county because of their leadership activities in 4-H Club work this past year.

"Just a few weeks ago, Mary Guarisco, Daphne, won a trip to Washington to represent Alabama at the national 4-H Club camp. She was chosen for outstanding club work. She has also won trips to Chicago and other places and has received outstanding recognition for bread making. ...

"Better 4-H Club work today means better farms of tomorrow."

August 17, 1939—Hampton D. Ewing

"Last week *The Times* carried the story of the death of Hampton D. Ewing, a person who wrote much of the history of Bay Minette and was a leading factor in making the town what it is today.

"Indicative of his high esteem and importance to this county seat town, the town council in a meeting Tuesday night passed a resolution deploring his death and praising his service to the town and county. Few people are honored thus by a governing body.

"In 1906, with other associates, he purchased 40,000 acres of land in and about the town of Bay Minette, and in 1907 the Bay Minette Land Company was organized with Mr. Ewing as president. For many years he was deeply interested in and contributed much to the building up of the town.

"It was through his influence the land company gave the land for the Baldwin County High School and the site for the public library, which was named for Mr. Ewing. Being a man of profound learning himself, he contributed much to the building of the library.

"Coming from noble heritage, he led a life that indicated his superior training. During the prime of life and almost until the last, he led an extremely active life, not only contributing much to his own native state, New York, but to Bay Minette and Alabama as well.

"Bay Minette was fortunate in having such a father."

August 24, 1939—The World, Especially Great Britain, Is On A Spot

"The agreement between Germany and Soviet Russia to a non-aggression pact that was announced in Berlin Monday night, and aggressive action since that time by Germany, apparently leaves the European nations on the brink of war.

"All the events point somewhat to a showdown almost any hour now. Before the week is over we may know whether or not there will be war. The Germans seem determined now to make a decisive thrust in the direction of Poland. A quarter of a million German troops with big guns and ample other military supplies are massed on the Polish border. ...

"With Japan making trouble for her on one side and Hitler on the other, Great Britain is in a tough spot. Between letting Hitler take Poland and war, world sentiment seems to favor war.

"America's cousins, the British, and the rest of the world are facing a grave crisis at this time. But of vitally more importance locally is what the United States will do about it if there is war."

Oct. 5, 1939—Congratulations

"We feel in a 'congratulating' mood today, but there's so many things deserving praise ...

"Softball has enjoyed a successful season in Bay Minette. And much credit should be given the Lions Club for sponsoring the project for the entertainment of local sports loving citizens.

"Cooperation between several parties stands to the front in making the project a success. But if one man is singled out to receive credit for really putting softball over, that man is Clint White. Appointed to head a three-man control board to run the league, he has given his time and effort to make it a success.

"Credit is also extended Cly T. Smith for his assistance in announcing the schedule and seeing that collections were made, L.J. Hooper for taking care of the grounds and Ort Ertzinger for supervision of the umpires."

Jan. 23, 1941—Tragedies Occur In Baldwin

"Tragedy hit Baldwin County again over the weekend … Accidents happened that have made many unhappy … Mrs. Clyde O. Weekley of Perdido was killed in an automobile wreck Saturday morning on the Bay Minette-Atmore highway just a few hundred yards from the place where four weeks previous her cousin, Roy Weekley, was also killed in an automobile … But, if possible, even more tragical on the same day was the accidental shooting of 14-year-old James Denny Hatchell by his young playmate while they were dove hunting … The shot of the .410 gauge gun landed in his back and proved fatal … Thus the life of a fine young man is gone … And equally as sad is the reaction sustained by his companion whose gun accidentally went off … Of course no one blames him, but none the less the 12-year-old is a nervous wreck and probably will be for some time to come … These accidents should serve as warnings to other parents and boys and automobile drivers … However, experience is a dear teacher."

March 13, 1941—Proud Of Daphne Postmaster

"Gordon G. Stimpson, postmaster of Daphne, is a citizen of which Baldwin has a right to be proud. Although having a full time job that keeps him busy as postmaster, Mr. Stimpson takes time to aid in many outside activities that have no remuneration other than the pleasure of helping other people. He has long been active in American Legion work and is probably responsible more than any one man for the success and accomplishments of the Baldwin County Post.

"His latest honor comes from the American Red Cross. He is chairman of the Central Baldwin Chapter which is one of the most active in Alabama. Last week his chapter received an honorary certificate 'for distinguished achievement' in connection with the 1941 Red Cross Roll Call. He had a lot of help getting 555 members to enroll but he was the guiding spirit behind the efforts. His efforts to help his fellowman in any way possible is a living example of unselfish American patriotism."

March 27, 1941—Angelo A. Corte

"Angelo A. Corte, since 1896 a leading citizen of Baldwin County, died Thursday night, March 13.

"In his 74 years of active life, Mr. Corte contributed as much or more to the development of this county as any other man. Coming to the Belforest-Daphne district in 1896, he started farming in a meager sort of way on a 40-acre tract of land. Since then, by hard work and intelligent planning, and with the aid of six sons, he has built an agricultural empire.

"Corte and Irish potatoes have long been synonymous terms to many people because of the leading role that family has taken in developing potato production in Baldwin County.

"Yes, this county is greatly indebted to such families as the Cortes, Bertollas, Mancis and others. They have done much to bring it as far as it has come in the agricultural world.

"In the passing of A. A. Corte, Baldwin has a great loss. But of the many things for which we have to thank Mr. Corte, one of the most important is the fact he left a fine heritage in his sons and daughters who will carry on the fine work he started way back in 1896."

April 17, 1941—A Leader Passes

"An interesting character was lost to Baldwin last week with the passing of Brog Nard Van Nette of Daphne at the age of 91. Mr. Van Nette followed his wife who died only a few months before.

"To those who knew him, Brog Nard Van Nette was a rare individual. Twenty-seven years ago his search for a home amid peaceful surroundings in which to spend his declining years was rewarded upon the discovery of somnolent Daphne on the shores of Mobile Bay.

"Here cloistered among his books, flowers and gardens, he and his wife found contentment. Active almost up until the time of his death, Mr. Van Nette was a keen student of economics, history and current affairs.

"The many friends who visited his home were charmed by his cultured manner. Here they received food for thought from his almost inexhaustible supply of facts about almost any subject, which he had retained from his reading and travel.

"Daphne and the surrounding community have been extremely unfortunate during recent months in the loss of some of its founders and most prominent citizens.

"Baldwin has been saddened in the passing of her leaders but the work they have begun and the influence on the lives of those with whom they came in contact, will be perpetuated."

Sept. 4, 1941—Millions Being Slaughtered

"Seven million men have already been killed in the present world conflict, according to news articles ... And still no end is in sight for stopping this slaughter of human beings .... And yet we call this a civilized world ... The whole thing seems so foolish, so unnecessary ... Yet, not but one human being can stop it ... That being the beast who started it ... And we also know he has no intentions of stopping it until he gets what he wants, the price in human beings being no consideration to him ... As he has no intentions of stopping the horrible war, it is up to the rest of the world, which includes us as individuals, to stop him ... Thus the casualty list is apt to double, or more, before we see peace ... Through it all we must not lose our optimism and hope for final victory and peace."

Dec. 10, 1941—The Four Horsemen

"The four horsemen are on the loose once more.

"War, disease, hunger and death.

"It is easy for many to remember their ravages of the great World War No. I.

Remember the suffering, the broken bodies, the broken lives, broken homes? The pestilence, breaking of friendships, and the many lesser horsemen that rode with the mighty four?

"Japan has attacked America (Dec. 7, 1941, Pearl Harbor). Japan has started the four horsemen to work again in this great country.

"But because of Japan's cowardly stab in the back, America is united. United for any and all eventualities. We Americans love peace. But we know what to do in case of war. Our forefathers have left us a heritage of bravery and loyalty. We fight hard. We fight to win. We fight, not merely for victory over our enemies, but for peace and to conquer the four horsemen that ride so hideously with all wars.

"All out for VICTORY. ...

"Now what we need in this country is action and more action and less talk. So we stop the latter, time being."

Dec. 10, 1942—From The Defensive To The Offensive

"Monday was a year after Pearl Harbor ... And we hope a year or less before victory ... We were in World War No. One 19 months, but we can hardly expect as good luck this time as this country has a much bigger job to perform than in 1917-18. But a year of war has seen America and her allies go a long way on the hard road to victory ... We have changed from the defensive to the offensive ... Now we carry the ball and will keep lugging it until the goal of Tokyo and Berlin is reached."

April 8, 1943—Will We Succeed?

(Ford Cook edited The Times while Faulkner was in the Army Air Corps.)

"The second War Loan Drive is the largest war financing campaign in the world's history. It will start April 12 and run for approximately three weeks. The national goal is 13 billion dollars, a gigantic sum, which no individual can actually conceive the full meaning. If this drive is to be successful it must reach into every home in the land, because the money must come primarily from the individual American.

"Baldwin County's campaign to raise its part in the 13 billion dollar Second War Loan Drive will be directed by J.R. Wilson of Bay Minette,

District Chairman of the War Savings Staff; S.F. Holmes, Bay Minette, District Chairman of the Victory Fund Committee; Howard Ruge of Fairhope, District Chairman of the War Savings Staff; and Kirby Wharton of Fairhope, District Chairman of the Victory Fund Committee. These men are giving much of their time to make the goal and more if possible. However, they can never succeed alone. They must have the help and support of every man, woman and child in Baldwin County.

"To make the amount conceivable, we'll break the goal of the nation into quotas for the many states. After dividing it all around, Alabama gets an allotment of $50,287,500 to spread over the sixty-seven counties within her boundaries. This state quota is still so large that we can hardly imagine such amount. But, after breaking it into various county quotas, we get it to a more reasonable figure. Baldwin's quota will range way up in the hundreds of thousands of dollars for the April campaign."

May 10, 1945—On to Tokyo

"The long-awaited collapse of Nazi Germany has finally come … With the victory in Europe an accomplished fact, it is fitting that all of us—freedom loving people of the allied countries of the world—pay tribute to those gallant people who have made this victory possible for us. Back through the days of war that have passed, we recollect the gruesome task that they must have experienced to subdue the enemy to make our life here more livable and lovable.

"This Victory, which we all are so proud to see, is not the accomplishment of any one Nation or any one group of select people, but is the Victory which is realized through the efforts—physical, mental and moral—of thousands upon thousands of men and women, young and old, of many Nations.

"The coming of the announcement of the end of German resistance is to the peoples of the Allied Nations as a life belt to a tired swimmer. It is food-energy to further the advance on Tokyo. It gives us further inspiration to help those guys in the Pacific in their trek on the 'Road to Tokyo.'"

MUMBLINGS
THROUGH THE
NINETEEN-FORTIES

∾

October 4, 1945

FORD COOK ABLY PRODUCED *The Times*

APPRECIATION . . . Three years ago this month we washed our hands of printers ink and started drawing a slight stipend from our Uncle Samuel. It is good to be back. We sincerely appreciate those who continued to patronize *The Times* in our absence. We will always be grateful to Ford Cook, who ably carried on while we were away.

DIFFICULTIES . . . Ford kept ye ole family journal coming out every week in spite of many hardships and difficulties. Labor was difficult to get and for several weeks back in '44, he had to print the paper by himself. He worked many nights until daybreak in order to get the paper out on time. That he served his country well during these war times is obvious. We feel confident that the people of Baldwin appreciate his diligence too.

MANY CHANGES . . . Three years makes for a lot of changes, particularly in ever-changing Baldwin. We are meeting hundreds of new people who have come to our fine county to live. These we welcome. But it is sad to admit many faces are absent from the scene. Happily most of our boys in the armed services are returning home.

WILL NEVER RETURN ... But during the three weeks we have been out of the Air Corps it has been impossible for us to get use to the fact that many of our old friends have passed on. We could write columns about each but to indicate "the changing scene" we'll just mention some of their names for the present. Among them are three ex-probate judges; Judge Voltz, Judge Humphries and Judge Robertson. And a few others are Dr. E.A. Moore, brothers G.H. and J.C. Burns, Mrs. L.T. Rhodes, C.M. Northcutt, Sr., W.M. Richerson, W.A. Alexander, George Perrin, and all too many others.

MAY RETURN ... Others have taken positions elsewhere and left our fair county, we hope some day to return. One of the most outstanding characters Baldwin has ever had pulled up stakes almost three years ago and went to California. B.D. Hendrickson, known by many and respected by all, was the efficient AAA man in the county agent's office and was president of the Baldwin County Chamber of Commerce for two years. Also to leave for an important position with the Alabama Farm Bureau was E.E. Hale. But he returns occasionally for a short visit and we'll have more to say about him from time to time.

BALDWINITIS ... Saw several old friends at the court house here Monday ... Bill Dryer of Daphne; Carl Bloxham of Fairhope; Mr. Gulledge and Olds of Rosinton; A.B. McPhaul of Robertsdale and Seminole; Paul Kaiser of Elberta, etc. First Lt. Charles Byrne, son of George and husband of Winifred Robertson Byrne, B-29 pilot instructor, arrived home from the Air Corps Monday ... His brother-in-law, Jack Robertson, expects to get out of the same organization this week. Hector Smith told us we would never regret being a civilian. Dr. Stacey's son, Johnny, wrote him from Germany that if he ever got out of the Army, he'd never sign another contract as long as he lives ... Many another G.I. feels the same way Johnny.

October 25, 1945

It's good to see S.W. Pickens
healthy again

HEART ATTACK . . . Had the pleasure of seeing S.W. Pickens at his home "Contentment" in Daphne recently and it was good to see he is in a healthy condition again. "Pick," as he is known by hundreds of friends, had a narrow escape recently. He was driving from Mobile when he felt himself getting dizzy after he had reached the Bridgehead. Fortunately he had good judgment enough to pull along the side of the road and stopped his car. Immediately he lost consciousness. After staying there about an hour, he regained enough consciousness to start his car and drive home. Afterwards he could not remember driving home, did not remember driving through Daphne or anything.

LUCKY . . . But he got home safe and sound and he spent the next few weeks giving his ole ticker a chance to rest up. Now he is up traveling around over the country for Uncle Sam again. He looks good as ever and seems friendlier and happier than before, if possible.

ANOTHER WRITER . . . Saw Carl Boseck here last week and it was good to have a chat with him after about four years. Mr. Boseck is 71 years old but his mind is still bright and a young fellow can learn plenty by listening to some of his sage advice. He is a writer, too, and doesn't hesitate one minute to say what he thinks. Once in a while he favors us with a personal letter that is always appreciated.

OLD PAPER . . . It is sometimes difficult to read what he has to say because he has the habit of writing on anything at hand, some of which is so dim it makes reading difficult although he writes a good hand. And it is surprising how much information he has about what goes on over the county.

FUNERALS . . . We heard a person remark recently that now since election time is nearing you can always tell when a funeral is to start by noting when the politicians arrive.

BACK HOME . . . Lt. Commander T.J. Mashburn, Jr., arrived home last Saturday and is ready to set up law practice again in the Bank Building here. The county still has two other lawyers in the service, Cecil Chason of Foley and Orvis M. Brown of Robertsdale. Telfair was the first of the three to get into the service and he is the first to return.

TAYLOR WILKINS . . . Another young man who has seen considerable service overseas and in Army hospitals, is arriving home in about two weeks. He is Taylor Wilkins, who is well known throughout the county. Taylor worked with the United States Employment Service before entering the service. He was injured in Europe last winter and has had to spend most of his time since then recuperating in hospitals.

PRIZES . . . The Elberta Farmers Club sent a few exhibits over to the Pensacola Fair last week and walked away with 10 first prizes and about $25.00. You can depend on those Elberta farmers to put things over in a big way. They are now building a $40,000 quick freezing locker plant, which will be the first in the county. Those people know the meaning of the word cooperate.

PUT OFF . . . We intended to have something to say about our county postmasters this week in the column but we have run out of space, so we'll save them and work them over later. They can stand a little special attention, don't you think?

November 1, 1945

A look at some of the best people in Baldwin

POSTMASTERS . . . Ever stop to think about the stamp pushers in Baldwin County? Of course you have quite vividly when you didn't get that letter you just knew you were going to get or that package from the mail order house that didn't show up. But we mean thinking in our calmer moments about what a fine lot of people they are. We actually believe you could pick the county clean and you would be unable to find a better lot of men, as a whole, than the men, and ladies, incidentally, that run our mail service for us.

SECOND CLASS . . . Take the men in charge of our largest post offices in the county for example. Start with Charlie Boller of Foley, as he is perhaps the oldest in years if not in service. Can you think of a finer man anywhere than Mr. Charlie? Then there is Clayton Baldwin of Fairhope who is certainly one of the best known and liked postmasters in Alabama. Mr. Clayton is active in anything for the betterment of Fairhope and Baldwin County. And Harry Wilters of Robertsdale. Harry's (he'll have to get a little older before we'll call him Mister) post office just grew into a second class office this year and it expanded largely because of the fine service he gives. As someone said about him, he may run a second class post office but he is a first class postmaster.

ROOKIE SMITH . . . Possibly there is no one in Baldwin liked better than Cly T. Smith of Bay Minette. He picked up the name of "Rookie" years ago as a rural mail carrier and most people still give him that handle although he has been postmaster here for about six years. And we can vouch for the fact that he runs a jam up good post office. Only last week he got a letter from the federal post office inspector commending him for his fine work. And most any postmaster will tell you those boys are slow to hand out commendations.

MANY OTHERS . . . We could go on writing about the fine qualities of the above four gentlemen, but they aren't the only good postmasters in the county, not by a long shot. We could also say lots of nice things about such people as: Roy J. Ellison of Loxley, Roy Underwood of Summerdale (his wife, Sybil Davidson Underwood, has been Summerdale postmistress while Roy is serving in the armed forces), L. Lindoffer of Elberta, Albert Phillips of Silverhill, and where would you go to find a better gentleman and scholar than G.G. Stimpson of Daphne?

POSTMISTRESSES . . . And don't think for a minute that all the good postmasters are men. In fact, we imagine there are many who would tell you that the most efficiently run offices in the county are run by women. On the whole, the ladies are in charge of the smaller post offices but they are doing good jobs. Off hand we can't remember all of their names, but here are a few; Mrs. Frank Taylor of Stapleton, Mrs. Roy Underwood of Summerdale, Mrs. Pearl Stanton of Stockton, Mrs. Weekly of Perdido, Mrs. Earle of Blacksher, Mrs. Amelia Wakeford of Bon Secour, Mrs. Eddie Myles of Little River, and we know there are a few more in the county but they slip our mind at the present.

MRS. MCKENZIE . . . And while we are on the subject of ladies, we met a fine character in Barnwell last week in the person of Mrs. Georgiana McKenzie. You couldn't guess it by looking at her but she was 81 years old last April. She is still active, both physically and mentally. In fact, she has a very alert mind for a person her age. She likes to discuss several topics but perhaps her proudest achievement is the fine family she raised. And she enjoys her big family all the more because they all live near her. She has five living sons and three daughters. One son died in 1909.

THE FAMILY . . . Her five boys, who have been men for several years, are, in order of seniority, J.W., Fred, Raleigh, Elroy and Frank. J.W. and Raleigh live near Magnolia Springs, Elroy at Fairhope, while Fred and Frank are successful farmers at Barnwell. All of her daughters live in Barnwell. They are Mrs. Iola Henderson, Mrs. G.W. Henderson (yes, they married brothers), and Mrs. Georgia Nolte. Mrs. McKenzie lives with Mrs. Nolte, who is her baby daughter.

STRONG COMMUNITY . . . Now you can see why the McKenzies

have so much influence in Barnwell and Baldwin County. Mr. Frank is president of the Barnwell Farmers Club which is one of the most active in the county. Barnwell has a strong club and one of their chief interests at this time is an improved farm to market road, leading from their community to Fairhope. And we pity the county commissioner who says they don't deserve one because they really mean business.

November 8, 1945

IT TAKES A LOT OF FAITH TO DO ANY JOB

FAITH . . . It takes a lot of faith to run a newspaper. There are so many things to try one's nerve. As this is being written there isn't enough newsprint in *The Times'* office to dry your hands on. Yet we have faith that we'll get enough to print this paper as we're taking new subscriptions and preparing copy for it.

SQUIRRELS . . . We do like to hunt the bushy tailed squirrels with a 22 rifle. But we haven't found the shells or the time to go this year. But thanks to Rudolph Cromartie, who just retired from the Army to hunt and fish a while before taking up his old job in the tax assessor's office, we had some to eat last week. And he brought them to us already cleaned. It's like we always say, a cleaned squirrel in the hand is worth two in the other hand not cleaned.

TOO MANY . . . It really is a pleasure to see all the fellows getting back from the armed services and into civilian clothes again. We want to mention every one in *The Times*, but it is impossible for us to know about all of them. Many separation centers send us notices but others do not. So, if you have a son, friend or relative returning home, drop us a card so we can let his many friends know about it.

BILL HOOPER . . . Bill wrote his parents, Mr. and Mrs. L.J., the other day from Treasure Island, California, where he is stationed in the Navy. We have long thought that Bill was one of the finest looking young men in Bay Minette and now we get rewarded for our kind thoughts toward him. He wrote his parents: "There may be some great pieces of literature in the world but none we appreciate more than *The Times.*" Thanks, Bill. It is a pleasure to send it to you, but hurry home, we had rather mail it to you here.

HENRY . . . We feel like we have lost our right arm. Ford Cook, who had been with *The Times* for almost five years, left last week for northern California, where he has a job in some hick town, only about twice the size of Bay Minette, running a weekly newspaper with perhaps an opportunity to buy it. We miss him here but wish him well in his new locality. We were in California recently but prefer Baldwin.

BOB VAIL . . . Word has reached Bay Minette from Washington that Bob Vail is in serious condition. He has had to undergo an operation. His present condition is not known but latest reports will be carried elsewhere in this issue. Mr. Bob for nine years has been one of our very favorite people. Although we have not been privileged to see him much in the past few years, it is great comfort to know he is still a great friend. All reports are that he has made Congressman Grant a wonderful secretary, and we know he has. We trust that he will survive this physical setback because he has overcome serious ones before. In the meantime, there will be hundreds hoping for the best.

HARD WORKER . . . Possibly no person has returned from the armed services back to his old job and taken over in as fine fashion and as little fanfare as has W.H. Johnson, assistant county agent. Herbert is a tireless worker but it is difficult to get him to talk much about it. He has one of the biggest and best 4-H Club programs of any county in the state and Baldwin is fortunate and glad to have him back doing his good work. He is one person who is far better off now than when he went into the Army, he now has two fine baby boys.

November 15, 1945

FRANK EARLE, GUST RIEMER
PUBLIC-SPIRITED MEN

OLD MULE . . . One for "Believe It or Not" is a mule named "Black" owned by Frank Earle of Blacksher. While we admit the mule isn't so much to look at, it isn't every day that you run across one that is 41 years old. Of course all "Black" is good for is to eat a little of Mr. Frank's corn and hay. He said the mule has been drawing unemployment compensation without perspiration for several years. The aged beast of burden was bought from L.T. Rhodes of Bay Minette and Mr. Earle said he knew he was 41 years old because Mr. Rhodes admitted him to be 12 years old when he bought him 29 years ago. Since mule traders have never been known to add to the age of a mule, we have no doubt but what "Black" is about the oldest in these parts.

THE OWNER . . . Frank Earle is a renown man in Baldwin County and Alabama and, incidentally, he didn't get that way by owning old mules. He became renown by being one of the most devoted, unselfish, non-paid workers for mankind it has ever been our privilege to know and ever expect to know. It is a conservative statement to say that he devotes at least 80 percent of his time for the good of humanity and the 20 percent he devotes to his own interests is for the benefit of other people in the long run.

FORTUNATE . . . Baldwin has been unusually fortunate for years to have such a public spirited man as Mr. Frank. He is a rare combination of man that is all too seldom found. Fortunately he is financially able to devote much time to affairs outside his own business but it is most unusual to find a man financially able who is willing to do it. Frank Earle is not a young man, he is almost 60, but the only thing we know of that he has lost of his youthfulness is his teeth. He is energetic, intelligent and has youthful optimism, saged and mellowed in years with good common sense.

MANY JOBS . . . To give some idea of how much time he devoted to public causes, we'll list some of them; there are so many we can't remember them all and if we could we don't have the space. He is president of the Baldwin County Electric Membership Corporation, chairman of the county Board of Education, president of the Baldwin County Farm Bureau, chairman of the board of the Bay Minette Production Credit Association, member board of trustees of Birmingham Southern College, president of the Alabama Marketing Association, a director of the Alabama Farm Bureau Federation, a Methodist, a farmer, a cattle raiser, a timber grower and the owner of so much land he got lost on it while hunting last week. About the only thing we have ever heard him criticized for is that he lives so far up the road, he has no telephone and when you go to see him you have to get out and open a gate to get to his house because he has refused for years to build a stock gap.

FARM LEADERS . . . And while on the subject of farm leaders, we would like to challenge any other county in Alabama to produce as many able farm leaders as we have in Baldwin County. This is an agricultural county and, as it should be, many of our most able men and leaders are farmers. We could name them by the dozens, and intend to mention various ones from time to time, but only one other today. Seventy-five miles from Mr. Earle is another good leader and gentleman. One of the soundest thinkers it has been our privilege to learn things from is Elberta's Gust Riemer. He doesn't talk so much but he is a deep thinker and when he does talk people sit up and take notice.

PROFOUND . . . He has long been an active farm and civic leader. When the Baldwin County Chamber of Commerce was active, he was one of its most able and cooperative directors. It was largely through his perseverance and insistence that the Lillian bridge was finally freed of tolls. Many consult him for his sage advice and he is one of the county's most successful farmers.

POLITICS . . . Several have wondered why we haven't written more about politics. We intend to later on. Right now the only ones in the county interested in politics are those who want to run for some office next spring. Incidentally, that is quite a few.

22-SHELLS . . . We were fortunate enough to find two boxes of 22 rifle shells this week. … Anybody got any squirrels needs killing?

November 22, 1945

W. M. RUPLE GROWING TALL SUGAR CANE

TALL CANE . . . W.M. Ruple, hard-working and successful farmer of Hurricane, brought us the longest stalk of sugar cane Saturday afternoon we have ever seen and he says he has plenty more just like it. This stalk had 22 joints and was 10 feet and 10 inches tall. Although we haven't "chewed" it yet, we can vouch for the fact it is fine cane because Mr. Ruple was kind enough to bring us some fine syrup made out of the same patch and a sopping good time has been had at our house with the luscious biscuits we have taught (ahem) the wife to make.

DIFFERENCE . . . Who can tell us the difference between ribbon cane and sugar cane? We were yanked up on a farm in Lamar County where we had ribbon cane patches from which molasses were (or was) made. Perhaps the reason it was called ribbon cane was because much of it was striped, looking like blue and white ribbons. But this Mr. Ruple brought in, admittedly much taller than the ribbon cane, was a white variety of sugar cane. We frankly don't know too much about cane varieties but believe this to be one of the new kind recently developed that has a number for a variety instead of a name. Anyway it isn't ribbon cane and if it was we don't know what difference it would make but Mr. Ruple said he had never been so successful in growing such fine tall cane before. And coming from him that is something, because he has been highly successful at growing most everything, even a good big family.

BIG HOGS . . . Yes, things are done big in Baldwin County. Last Thursday C.E. Garrett, county sheriff, killed off one of his shoats. This pig has been his pride and joy for several months, and rightly it should be because it weighed 790 pounds. And that kind readers, is a lot of pork.

FEAST . . . And if you want to know where a lot of the hard-to-get lard is you can readily imagine it is in Mrs. Garrett's pantry, because most of that pig went into lard. But about the best thing concerning the whole thing is the fact that Sheriff Garrett saved the chitterlings and invited a few friends in for a feast.

BIG 'TATER . . . And not to be outdone and to prove that he is a farmer, Bruce Beveridge, ex-Bay Minette merchant, brought to town a "field-run" sweet potato—weight, 9 pounds and 11 ounces.

GETTING HOME . . . Several young men have learned most of what they know about running a weekly newspaper working for *The Times*. Four have been in the Armed Service, evenly divided between the Army and Navy. The two that were in the Navy have been discharged and already have their hands in printers' ink. Paul Corwin is back helping us out for a few weeks until a "hanging business deal" develops about the first of the year. Paul sold his Fayette *Northwest Alabamian* to join the Navy but hopes to get another paper soon. He not only received his initial newspaper experience in Bay Minette, he got his wife here too, the former Miss Lauda Leak.

LT. FOREMAN . . . The last time we heard from Bill Foreman a few weeks back he was on Okinawa until the other night he called by phone and now is back at his old job as editor and publisher of *The Atmore Advance*. With many months overseas duty behind him, Bill is in good health and happy to be back at his newspaper job. Bill Stewart and Eugene Thomley broke their journalistic eye teeth on *The Times* and both are still in the Army. The last time we heard from Gene, he was in Europe, but when he will arrive home is unknown by us. Bill Stewart was the last to work with *The Times* before Ford Cook and he plans to return to his old job here about the first of the year, we hope.

November 29, 1945

W. R. COOPER MAKING LOTS OF SYRUP

LOTTA LASSES . . . *Life* magazine could keep a photographer busy full time in Baldwin taking pictures of people doing outstanding jobs and accomplishing unusual things. W.R. Cooper, prominent farmer and farm leader of the Rosinton community, has five acres in sugar cane this year and is making 4,000 gallons of syrup from it. Some of his cane was so fine it yielded a thousand gallons to the acre, which is a lot of molasses from one acre of land.

GOOD PROFIT . . . Naturally Mr. Cooper wouldn't admit it, probably, but you don't lose money on syrup when you get that kind of yield from your land, particularly when it sells for a dollar a gallon and over. Mr. Cooper has a big syrup mill, one that he thought up and had specially made. We don't know whether it is the mill or him, mostly him we suspect, but his syrup certainly makes the wife's biscuits taste good. He makes all his own syrup and can make as high as 200 gallons a day, if he doesn't have too many people around drinking his juice.

PATRIOTISM . . . Many boys fought in the firing lines and other undesirable places during the war but none served more faithfully and patriotically, nor deserve more credit, than the six men who composed the membership of Baldwin's two draft boards. They deserve the praise of everyone. Our hats are off to them.

THREE VETERANS . . . While all deserve credit, three members of the two boards have served continuously from the time of their appointment in 1940, when Frank Dixon was Alabama's governor and Pearl Harbor had not been dreamed of by us. These three men are J.H. Stacey of Bay Minette, Ed Tietgen of Summerdale and Bill Cooney of Foley. Possibly no board in the U.S. has had two members who were as sincere and devoted to their non-compensated-for work as Ed Tietgen and Bill Cooney. Ed is Mayor of Summerdale and has been working at Brookley Field for four years. He was in Bay Minette last week for the first time in three years.

OTHERS . . . Others who have served faithfully upon the resignations of original members who found it impossible to serve for various reasons are Ben Sims of Belforest and C.L. White of Bay Minette. They took the places of G.K. Page and Joe Garrett on the Bay Minette board. Arthur Corte took Guernsey Clark's place when he resigned on the Foley board. Few people realize the trials and tribulations these men have gone through in doing an excellent job drafting in excess of 3,000 Baldwin boys into the Armed Forces.

RATIONING . . . Others in the county have also served faithfully on such as rationing boards, civilian defense, war bonds, etc. All of them played an important part in winning the war. We'll try to mention some more names in the future.

GOOD HUNTER . . . To prove he was a good hunter and that it was unusual for him to let a deer get away, Wallace Killcrease killed one last Thursday afternoon. Almost before the ink had gotten dry on the unusual story of his deer getting away between two dogs after he had been shot down last Tuesday morning, Mr. Wallace went out and displayed his marksmanship again. However, most of those who lost their shirt tails last week have as yet not proven that it was an accident they missed their shots. Mr. Wallace is a veteran hunter and from all reports one of the best. He is also the veteran bookkeeper of Bacon-McMillan Veneer Co., of Stockton.

SOAKING . . . If he weren't such a good friend of ours, we wouldn't dare tell about George Stough tipping over his boat and falling in the lake while hunting last Tuesday. Naturally these double-enders turn over easily. George is the able and popular AAA administrator in Baldwin. Although from the Black Belt, he is full of praises for Baldwin and its people. But he does admit our water gets cold in November.

December 6, 1945

HALL, MASHBURN KNOW FARMING AND THE LAW

DIRT-LAWYERS . . . We have often heard of, and know many dirt farmers, but dirt-lawyers are few and far between. Bay Minette is distinguished by having two such citizens. Hubert Hall was a farmer before he became a lawyer and has chosen to live his bachelor's life on a farm. Hubert has one of the best farms just north of Bay Minette that can be found anywhere. He is proud of his farm but his real pride and joy is his pure bred strain of Hereford cattle. He really has some beauties. And if you want to get his mind off prosecution (he is the county prosecuting attorney, you know) just mention a big cattle show or anything about fine cattle and you have his immediate attention.

A NEW ONE . . . Now, as of about two weeks ago, we have another dirt-lawyer in Telfair Mashburn. He has just purchased a dandy little farm about three miles out of town in Pine Grove. And he lives on it and feeds the chickens, hogs and milks the cows (or cow). Telfair has just reopened his law office in Bay Minette after an absence of about four years in the Navy. So in the future if you can't find him in his office, you might drive out to Pine Grove and see him looking at his cow, chickens and pecan trees. One big advantage about his farm is that you don't walk yourself down looking at it, you can just stand in one place and examine it. But at that he has a great advantage over many of us town dwellers; he can at least scratch his ear without poking his neighbor's eye out with his elbow.

CLERK DUCK . . . All indications are that popular Bob Duck isn't going to have any opposition for his post as circuit clerk in next Spring's primaries. Possibly there are two reasons for this. One of the more important of course is that Bob is about the most universally liked public official we have in the county. And another is that his office doesn't pay much money, less by far than any of the full time county posts. You know if he had opposition we couldn't say these nice things about him because then *The Times* would be accused of playing politics and having favorites. But since he will most likely be unopposed, we feel confident no one will have such thoughts and will thoroughly agree with us about Bob.

FAMOUS PEOPLE . . . Of Alabama's famous people, possibly the colored ones have brought us the most publicity. Proof: Booker T. Washington, George Washington Carver, Joe Louis, Hazel Scott and now Baldwin comes forth for her just share of the Negro great. Perhaps many of you saw the picture of the 7-year-old colored piano playing Honey Chile in *Life* magazine about three weeks ago. This youngster with a MGM movie contract in hand has his heritage in Blacksher. Honey Chile is the grandson of old Frank Bracey, 85-year-old colored school teacher of Blacksher. Uncle Frank's daughter, Elizabeth, who is now dead, married Clarence Robinson and to them was born the now famous Honey Chile.

ORGANIZATION . . . Possibly no small community in America has accomplished more through cooperation and community spirit than has Elberta. This squibbler had the privilege of attending their tenth annual celebration of their Farmers Club Monday night and their achievements through community effort are nothing short of amazing. Practically every citizen, well over 90 percent of the families, belongs to the strong farm organization and work together under strong leadership for the greatest good of all.

GUIDING LIGHT . . . Naturally every such organization must have a strong and capable leader. Fortunately Elberta has this, several in fact. But their guiding light and untiring leader is young 28-year-old bachelor John Gottler. Naturally John could not accomplish so much if he did not have able and intelligent assistance, but it is his ability to lead and organize that has made the organization what it is today. Ten years ago the club organized and besides the officers, had two members. Now they have 245 and a list of accomplishments a mile long. Of the ten years, John has been president eight and as an indication of what his community thinks of his efforts they made him a present of $200 Monday night.

December 13, 1945

Echo Café is coffee drinkers haven

COFFEE DRINKERS . . . The British may drink their tea but they'll have to go some to beat the business men of Bay Minette drinking coffee. The reputation of Bay Minette's Echo Café has grown far and wide for the fact that local citizens crowd in there at periodic intervals to drink coffee, visit, trade, talk business, politics, hunting or what ever may be the topic of the day.

HANDY . . . Mac Hodgson is a hard man to find any time, as he is out of town so often. When he is in town you will most likely find him at the Echo. You might assume he had a special table reserved there but if he does it is used a lot by other people too. Mac thinks the fact that most of Bay Minette's business men crowd in there around nine-thirty or ten o'clock every morning is fine because he says it makes it easy to find the people you are looking for. Just go in there and set down, he says, and sooner or later the person you want to see will come in for his coffee and you can transact your business with him and enjoy the coffee at the same time. Mac is of the opinion that most important business transactions in this section are agreed on there.

HABITUAL . . . Some of us are amateurs at this coffee drinking and only go in occasionally but we can name several that hit there at least twice a day, in fact their drinking habits are so punctual that time pieces can be set by their daily arrivals. In most cases however the departing schedule is not run by a time table because often a five-cent cup of coffee will be lingered over for an hour or more, depending upon the topic of conversation and so on. This column isn't long enough to name all of them but there are at least 20 people in town, and out, that get there on an average of a dozen times a week. Virgil McMillan, for one.

CONTAGIOUS . . . This coffee drinking is contagious too, because when new citizens come into town in a few weeks they have been led into the old grind by one of the local veterans. We have observed that the people who move in from the Black Belt are the most easily led into the habit, in fact they are led into it so easily one might think they had the habit before arriving here. Frank Turner and George Stough are good examples. Other things have been observed about the Bay Minette Coffee Drinkers Association. One of these is that the quality of the coffee has nothing to do with whether a member does or does not show up. Even during the extreme shortage of sugar when some of the members absolutely could not drink the java without sugar they would be seen sipping away. Some of the members went to the extent of bringing their own sugar, J.R. Wilson and Grey Cane, etc. Another observation is that the people who laundry the table cloths for the Echo get plenty of business because everyone seems to think that buying a five-cent cup entitles him to do his figuring on the table cloth.

NOT EXCLUSIVE . . . The coffee drinkers are not necessarily an exclusive group, as anyone with a nickel and the urge can join in, and in Bay Minette that only excludes those who have no nickel. Although 90 percent of the membership are men, a few ladies have the habit. Of course the regular members will give you a hard look if you intimate that the time spent at the coffee shop is wasted, in fact they will soon prove to you it is absolutely necessary for the proper functioning of their business. But this we do know, if all the man hours spent in a week drinking coffee in Bay Minette were paid for at union rates, with time and one-half for all over forty, it would run into a heap of greenbacks. Also it is fairly well agreed that the three musketeers of the coffee club are G.K. Page, Doug White and Cly T. Smith.

BALDWINIAN OF THE WEEK . . . Truly one of Baldwin County's most valuable citizens is Emanuel Davidson. He is an untiring worker and always for anything that is for the betterment of the county or community. Emanuel has probably gotten more people to join the American Legion than any other person in Alabama. He has held practically every office in the Legion and he still works almost day and night for it. As president of the Bay Minette Chamber of Commerce, he is a wheel horse for the development of the community. One of the jobs he does best, and hates the most, is collecting money for a worthy cause. He can really rake it in and the reason he can is because he goes after it and the people have confidence and respect for him. Any community and county could use many citizens just like him.

December 20, 1945

PROFESSIONAL MEN WORK FOR OUR TOWN, COUNTY

PROFESSIONAL MEN . . . This writer was discussing problems with a prominent citizen over a cup of coffee last week in the presence of a professional man, at which time the prominent citizen politely but definitely raked the professional man over the coals for lack of community spirit and cooperation among the professional men of the town. He, referring to the doctors and lawyers, took the theme that they made more money than most anyone and did least to cooperate in the progress of the town and county. Perhaps we agreed at the time, at least his argument was convincing for the moment. But since then we have thought of the matter and wish to come to their defense, not that they need it particularly.

BUSY . . . During the war years the ranks of the professional men were hit hard and those left in civilian clothes had their hands full, particularly is this true in the case of doctors. Take Dr. McLeod. Although still active, he is certainly beyond the crusading age and if he wasn't he hasn't had time to devote to anything other than his practice. He works day and night for his patients and about the only relaxation he gets is by going to church, which he does regularly. Also this writer knows a number of people, widows in particular, that he has doctored for years and always forgets to send a bill. And what is more important than health in a community?

COOPERATE . . . And most of the lawyers can be depended on to cooperate in any worthwhile civic enterprise, contributing both their time and money. Although only two of them are members of the Chamber of Commerce, they often work with the organization for the betterment of the town. John Chason is very progressive and if you don't think he is, just get in a conversation with him and you'll see quick that he is interested in seeing this town and county grow and prosper. He has been active in the bond campaigns and has really done yeoman service as head of the local volunteer fire department.

EAGER . . . Telfair Mashburn is also aggressive and eager to help out in anything he is called upon to do for the general welfare of the people. He has accepted the chairmanship for this section of the American Red Cross, even though he has just returned from the Navy. It would be difficult to find a more civic minded person anywhere than Telfair. W.C. Beebe and J.B. Blackburn were both active during the war for necessary non-paying war agencies. Mr. Beebe organized the county as chairman of civilian defense, spending much of his time and money in so doing. Mr. Blackburn for several months devoted practically all of his time as chairman of the local ration board. Hubert M. Hall has been interested enough and had confidence enough in Bay Minette to build two of the town's finest buildings. Of course it has been to his own interests to build them, but none can say they aren't assets to the town. Also Mr. Hall is interested in the industrial and agricultural development of this area. A few years ago he took the lead in attempting to bring a textile mill here; although unsuccessful, he can be counted on to try again.

MERRY CHRISTMAS . . . To the boys overseas and to our readers at home, we wish a sincere Merry Christmas.

December 27, 1945

DOZENS OF CAMELLIA LOVERS IN THIS AREA

JAPONICAS . . . Fancy prices have taken hold of one of Baldwin's age old hobbies which includes many fancy names. Although Bay Minette and Baldwin has been a center in the cultural art of raising camellias for years, the old timers in one of the most cherished and fascinating hobbies say never before have the cuttings and plants changed hands at such a fast pace and good prices. And this in a field of flower fanciers that have always had a yen for an additional cutting of some new variety. Possibly no other hobby, even including all other flowers, can hold a light to the enthusiasm and devotion given by those who play with the never-ending wonders and miracles of the camellia-japonica. And another good thing about the hobby is that it is often profitable financially although most do it for the love of the blooms and many wouldn't sell their favorite plants for any price.

OLD HANDS . . . Bay Minette has many who have grown japonicas for years and new enthusiasts have developed so fast there are few homes that do not have at least a few plants. In fact most citizens in this area know what you are talking about when they hear such words as Professor Sergeant, Purple Dawn, Empress of Russia, Marchioness of Exodus, Victor Emanuel, Pin Perfection, Pope Pious, Hermie, etc. and etc. for dozens of varieties. Some individuals have more than a hundred varieties. There are a few people in Bay Minette whose names are almost synonyms of camellia. Mrs. Ned Noonan, Mrs. Florence Irwin, Miss Leola Cain for three and there are many more in the county. Mrs. Noonan's father, Dr. Campbell, was one of the first persons to bring the japonica to this section and she has been working with them ever since. Now she has one of the most cherished selections in this section.

FIVE HUNDRED . . . Many, many years ago Uncle Joe Blackburn rooted a little cutting and his daughter, Mrs. Florence Irwin, still has the now huge plant and at least 500 others to keep it company. She has developed new varieties and calls one of the favorites the Ann Blackburn, after her little granddaughter. Mrs. Irwin really knows her camellias and if you think she isn't fond of them just try to buy one. Miss Leola Cain's big and valuable selection was also started by her father years ago and she has followed in his footsteps in her fondness for them.

MANY OTHERS . . . There are so many local ladies interested in camellias it would be impossible to name them all but some of the more enthusiastic are: Mesdames L. D. Owen, Claudia Dahlberg, J.D. Crosby, Anne Gilmer, Cly Smith, Joe Still, John Chason, J.H. Stacey, Bruce Beveridge, J.R. Wilson, Grey Cane, Clint White, L.J. Hooper, Lee Smith, E.S. Tunstall, Jim Hervey, G.H. Burns, Charlie Hand, H.T. Crumpton, R.A. Carlisle, Ethel Calhoun and we apologize to the dozens we have left out. The men are fewer but non-the-less enthusiastic and their interest has arisen, no doubt, because their wives were smart enough to get them started.

HARD CASH . . . Dr. Stacey will talk to you hour on end about his and Mrs. Stacey's camellias. He knows the varieties well and likes to discuss their advantages and disadvantages. And he'll back his likes with hard cash if he finds a new plant he wants. The same goes for Bruce Beveridge and J.R. Wilson. Grey Cane, Clint White and Cly Smith also know something about camellias and have many choice varieties along with L.J. Hooper. And the way Hubert Hall and John Chason can talk about them you would think they studied camellias in college along with their law.

RESENT . . . And many of these authorities resent Greenville calling itself "The Camellia City," claiming that city has only a few of the very fine varieties. They also claim that no other section can grow such fine specimens as this immediate Gulf Coast area. Perhaps Greenville can prove they have one or two good varieties though. Of course proving and claiming are two different things.

ENDING THE YEAR . . . The year began with a worldwide war; now we have ended most of it and what better subject for such a column as this than ending the year with the subject, peaceful camellias.

January 3, 1946

COL. FARIS UPDATES US ON THE HENDRICKSONS

REPORT . . . Lt. Col. T.M. Faris was in Bay Minette Sunday and Monday of this week and it was a real pleasure to see him after several years of absence. Col. Faris is well known in Baldwin County, particularly among the farmers. Before he went into the Army, he was agricultural agent for the L. & N. Although he lived in Atmore, much of his time was spent in Baldwin. He was in England during hostilities but for the past several months he has been in various Army hospitals trying to get his left foot back in condition so he can resume his good game of golf. Col. Faris expects to be released in February and hopes to return to his old job. It will be of particular interest to our readers to know that he visited B.D. Hendrickson in California about a month ago.

DOING WELL . . . The Hendricksons are fondly remembered in the county. For many years, he was the popular and efficient Triple A director and possibly held the affection and admiration of Baldwin farmers as well or better than any other man in the county. But he up and left about three years ago and few have heard from him since. Now Col. Faris comes forth with a full report on the Hendricksons, and naturally it is good. They live in Culver City, California, which is a suburb of Los Angeles. B.D. is assistant general manager of a plastic manufacturing concern, Mrs. Hendrickson is working in Hollywood, Virginia is a Junior in UCLA and Jeane is a senior in high school. He and Col. Faris saw Southern California play a big game while there and the Colonel wasn't so impressed with their team.

DEAR DEER . . . It seems that never before have so many deer been killed than this year. Successful hunts are being pulled right and left. Always one of the best hunts of the year is the one given by Jewel Smith and Henry Bryars on the Old Island Hunting Club land. And this year was one of the best of all, according to every one we talked to that was privileged to attend.

However, the old hunters were put to shame by the younger generation. Of the five deer killed, three were downed by young boys. Grey Cane, Jr., Henry Bryars, Jr., and Gerry Rodgers, son of Mr. and Mrs. Ed Rodgers, were the successful young nimrods at the annual hunt on the day after Christmas. Other successful shooters were J.C. McDavid, Bay Minette, and Winthrop Hallett of Mobile.

BEST YET . . . And speaking of the plentiful supply of deer here is something that maybe hasn't happened for many a day, at least not in broad open daylight. Last Saturday Wallace Killcrease and son, Roland, were driving from Stockton to Bay Minette. When they got in the city limits of this county seat town, a doe deer was seen by them along about Grey Cane's house and Grey only lives about six blocks from the court house. They circled the block to see if dogs were running the doe. Since there are no tame deer around, this proves our deer are getting civilized or Bay Minette is getting closer and closer to the back woods like Clarke County.

MARRIED . . . Many people will be interested in the fact that L.T. Rhodes and his long-time secretary, Miss Pearl Erskine, were married recently. Both are well known throughout the county. Mr. Rhodes has been in the produce and farming business in Bay Minette for many years and Miss Pearl has been an able assistant. They are vacationing in Fort Myers, Florida, and will be there for several weeks, it is understood. Mr. Rhodes is one of the most civic minded men for his age it has ever been this writer's privilege to know. He is always active in support of anything that is for the good of the community and is a charter member of the Bay Minette Chamber of Commerce. It is hoped he won't stay in Florida too long as his presence is needed in Bay Minette.

January 17, 1946

COMING ELECTION STIRRING POLITICAL RUMORS

POLITICS . . . With the County Democratic Executive Committee meeting definitely set for Tuesday, January 29, one can hear more and more political rumors floating around the county on who is and who may run for this and that office. Although many politicos have definitely made up their minds to toss their hats out in the ring for size, others are still considering only, and by the time the deadline for qualifying comes six weeks from now, on March 1st, the scene on many of the locally pitched battle fronts will no doubt have changed.

SHERIFF . . . One of the most sought after offices in Baldwin during the coming spring primaries will be that of Sheriff. There are several reasons for this. The fact that the office can be made to pay good money hardly keeps people from wanting the position nor does the fact it offers a person a wonderful opportunity for service. Each reader can judge for himself which has the greatest force on the aspirants. Too, several people have had an eye on this office for years but W.R. Stuart, long-time popular sheriff, but who now holds the office of probate judge and will be out to keep it, kept opposition down to a minimum. But now that he is out of the way, these would-be gun-toters see a chance to achieve their ambition of high service and a fat pocketbook. Despite the number of aspirants this race seems to be crystallizing faster than the other county offices that will be sought after this year.

GARRETT . . . Naturally the present Sheriff, C.E. Garrett, who obtained the job through appointment of Governor Sparks, is expected to ask the people to let him have it for a full term. Mr. Garrett is a well liked gentleman and has raised one of the finest big families to be found anywhere.

KUCERA . . . Good natured Ben Kucera of Robertsdale and Silverhill is expected to be ready with his fee and qualification papers when the starting whistle blows after January 29. Ben is experienced, having served as deputy under two sheriffs, and is present Marshall of Robertsdale.

BARROW . . . And J.L. Barrow has long made it publicly known he will be a contender for the highest law enforcement office in the county. Chief Barrow is another man with plenty of experience. He has been police chief at Bay Minette for years and has also served as deputy under more than one sheriff. He also takes an active part in Legion affairs.

DURANT . . . Norman Durant is one of those who has long been ambitious to be Baldwin County Sheriff. And he has chosen the coming Spring primaries to make the attempt. Norman is past commander of the Legion and has gotten himself well-known over the county. Although some have rumored he will not run, he makes no bones about the fact that he definitely will be a candidate.

WILKINS . . . Tall Taylor Wilkins, son of ex-sheriff M. H. Wilkins, also makes it clear he will without fail be a contender for the office at the proper time, and he thinks the proper time to announce will be about February 1st. Taylor has just recently been released from the Army, where he had to spend most of his time in hospitals after getting severe frost bite in the trenches of Europe.

OTHERS . . . Still others are known to be considering the post but to this writer's knowledge, they have not made definite statements about their intentions. But time will tell and the run-off will indicate the two high men, no doubt.

WELCOME VISITORS . . . J. N. Shambo of Shambo Station, on Daphne Route, is *The Times'* oldest subscriber. Calling by last week to renew his subscription for two more years, he told us he started taking the paper 56 years ago in Daphne when it was *The Daphne Times*. Celebrating his 50th wedding anniversary last summer, he promised to send a picture of himself and Mrs. Shambo. It was also good to see our old friend A.B. McPhaul this week. Mr. Mc is getting old in years but not in mind and thought. He lost his wife recently and he tells us he is going to move from Seminole to Robertsdale soon. Long active in politics himself, he says he is going to sit on the sidelines this year and let'em fight.

February 14, 1946

BALDWIN HAS 10 LAWYERS READY TO SERVE YOU

LAST LAWYER . . . Lt. Cecil Chason, son of Mrs. John Chason, Sr., Bay Minette, has been discharged from the Navy and will resume his law practice in Foley soon. Cecil is one of four Baldwin lawyers who entered the service and is the last one to get out. With overseas service to his credit, he will have his shingle out again in Foley just as soon as he can find suitable office space, he says. Two of the four lawyers have already resumed practice, T.J. Mashburn, Jr., in Bay Minette, and E.G. Rickarby, Jr., in Fairhope. The other one, Orvis M. Brown, got out of the Navy but did not resume practice in Robertsdale. He is now working for the Veterans Administration in Montgomery. So if you are interested in having a little litigating done, we have 10 lawyers in the county ready to serve you. Foley has two, Fairhope three and Bay Minette five. Incidentally, this is fewer than has been in the county, except during the war, within the last ten years or more. But each of the ten thinks ten is enough. Welcome back to the bar, Cecil.

LETTER . . . We have just receive a much appreciated and interesting letter from a friend in Japan. He is Pfc. Harry J. Wilters, Jr., son of his parents by the same name in Robertsdale. All in all, Harry seems to think he has a fairly good deal there considering he can't be at home, but is a little disturbed over the slowness of the mail service. It does seem that his postmaster father would do something about this. Young Harry writes a good letter and makes some wise observations; listen to his idea about the draft: "I think they should keep up the draft. Draft a man for a year, give him six months overseas. That way you will have men in the States and men over. Of course, there will be a need for regular army men to occupy the key positions both in the States and over. I really don't believe in drafting men over twenty-five or married men . . ."

MORE STANLEY . . . "Here's Jimy Faulkner again. (We purposely omitted one 'm' in his name because he omits one 'n' from ours. But we have finally taught him how to spell 'camellia,' even if he doesn't know anything else about the flower.) We located, with no effort at all, several Gloria de Nantes in Greenville, but the owners laughed at the idea of 'cuttings' from this rare variety. Propagation is done with scions in a process of grafting in the newer and rarer varieties. One man was just about to take a scion when he learned it was going to Bay Minette. Then he refused quite firmly. He said if the people of that community don't appreciate the Pride of Greenville, they wouldn't appreciate the Gloria de Nantes, but would probably chop off the top in a few years to graft a single red. Yes, Jimy, we have Gloria de Nantes here, and the Magnolia Queen, the Conflagration, the Marion Mitchell and even the finest of all the rare camellias—the Beauty of Greenville—as well as hundreds of other varieties. Come on up to the Camellia City and learn about camellias." You're right, that was Glenn Stanley talking again.

BREWTON LADY . . . We got our hands slapped by a lady from Brewton last week. We were informed that we shouldn't take unfair advantage of Greenville's camellias, because "really the people of Greenville have done quite well with their camellias considering they haven't been interested in the plant for so long and they actually have quite a few, small of course, but naturally you can't expect them to have so many big fine plants like Bay Minette and other towns in Baldwin County in so short a time . . ." Well, now isn't that interesting! In as much as this lady was born in Greenville and visits there quite often, we can rightly assume she knows whereof she speaks.

UNFAIR . . . Perhaps we have been a bit unfair with Greenville. Maybe if we would wait about 20 years and give them a chance to catch up, it would be more sportsmanlike. But what would our camellia lovers be doing in the meantime but grafting more "scions" and keeping our age old lead over the so called "Camellia City." And the idea of us going to Greenville to learn about camellias! That would be like a farmer going to town to learn how to pick cotton . . . and besides, there is already one editor too many in that town.

A THREAT . . . And who else but a Greenville editor would spell his name, Glenn, with two "n"s? And the next time he questions our questionable spelling ability, we're going to tell folks how good Butler County didn't do in the recent Victory Bond Drive.

April 18, 1946

STAPLETON BARBECUE ATTRACTS 20 CANDIDATES

BARBECUE . . . Jesse Baggette of this city went with us to the barbecue last Saturday at Stapleton. Mr. Jesse is well known and liked in this area. For the past two years he has been suffering so badly from arthritis and rheumatism that he is confined to his home almost constantly. He walks only with the greatest of difficulty and pain. He used to be a great fisherman and says one of the greatest drawbacks to his ailments is that he can't go fishing because he can't sit in a boat. He can eat barbecue though and we both thoroughly enjoyed the fine beef and pork the Stapleton Civic Club had prepared for the visiting guests and politicians. The affair was well arranged and everything apparently clicked with perfection.

SPEECHES . . . H.V. Harrell was the master of ceremonies and introduced each of about 20 candidates to the audience and gave them five minutes each to express their views. Fortunately for the crowd, most of the office seekers were thoughtful and said their pieces in short order. Jesse M. Smith, candidate for probate judge, was the orator of the group but all did well and most speeches indicated they had been prepared before they arrived at Stapleton. We believe everyone, including the candidates, appreciated the efforts the Stapleton citizens went to for the occasion.

CHARLIE HEAD . . . After the barbecue and speeches, Mr. Jesse and this writer drove by to see Mr. Charlie Head who has been confined to his bed for over a year. Mr. Charlie is one of the oldest cattlemen and farmers in this section . . . 81 will be his age this August. For years he has been a member of the county democratic executive committee and at a recent meeting, where he was absent for the first time, other members were full of praise for him and his long service to the party. In spite of his present physical handicaps, his mind is just as alert and bright as any time we have ever talked to him. He is well informed on county affairs and still has a great interest in politics. He has 10 children, five of each gender, and most of them live near him, which he says is a source of great comfort. Two sons, Lambert and Perry, are veterans of World War II. It was good to see you again Mr. Charlie and we look forward to seeing you up and around before long.

DENTIST . . . Bay Minette has another dentist. Dr. J.M. Reed has opened his offices here and is associated with Dr. S.F. Crook in the Arcade Building. Dr. Reed (Mac to most people around here) was born and raised in Bay Minette and it is good to see him return home to follow his chosen profession. He was recently discharged from the Navy. We can recommend him because last week he extracted one of our favorite jaw teeth with the greatest of ease.

TOM'S TOM . . . Tom Mitchell was all smiles the first of this week. The main reason being that he killed a 21-pound gobbler last Saturday.

April 25, 1946

GOOD PIES, GREAT SINGING
ENJOYED BY ALL

PIES . . . OPA ceiling prices did not prevail at the Bellefountain school last Saturday night when county candidates started bidding for pies the patrons of that school had baked to auction off to the highest bidders. We don't know how many pies they had there but the ones they had brought top prices, many selling for as much as $3.00. And the candidates were not the only ones bidding; others too, recognized a good pie when they saw one.

SINGING . . . The school house was packed with local citizens, candidates and other visitors for the Saturday night affair. Alec Pittman was the toastmaster and allowed each one of them a minute to tell why he should be elected to a certain office. Most of the candidates were kind to their audience and did not take the full minute. Easily the most enjoyable part of the program was the singing rendered by the Gulledge Quartet. Many people in the county have had the privilege of hearing this fine quartet but those who have not have missed much. The quartet is composed of two brothers and three sisters; Carl, Otis, Louise and Lillian Gulledge and a married sister, Mrs. Ruby Calvert. Charlie Hobbs, president of the Baldwin County Singing Convention, played the guitar for the quartet. This Sunday the convention will hold an all-day singing with dinner on the ground and coffee in the pot at Gateswood.

NEED . . . It is always good to go to Gateswood. Some of the finest people in the county live there. About all they need in that area is a paved road. And this they are determined to have some day.

FARIS . . . His many friends in this area will be glad to know that T.M. Faris is back on his old job as L. & N. agricultural agent. He was stationed at Atmore before spending five years in the Army but will now live in Mobile and will be the horticultural specialist for "Old Reliable" in the Gulf Coast Area. He was called into his Uncle's service in 1941 and rose from the grade of captain to Lt. Col. He saw foreign service in Europe and South America.

HELPED OUT . . . Faris started working with the agricultural program of this area in 1931 and one of his first contributions was to the potato industry. He worked with the Fairhope Experiment Station to bring about better certified seed potatoes for the county. He also helped materially in improving the relationship between South Alabama and the seed experts of the Northwest, where the seed potatoes are bought. E.E. Hale and Otto Brown, who worked with Faris in the early beginning of the potato disease work, say that he more than any one else, is responsible for starting the work on controlling the various potato diseases, particularly in getting cooperation of the Northern seed producers.

HOBBY . . . Faris is a big, jolly fellow, well liked by all who know him. He particularly likes to play golf but it is doubtful if he will be able to resume his old pre-war hobby because of a foot ailment obtained while in the Army. At any rate, it is good to have him back from the wars and once more doing important work for the farmers of this section.

JUST LISTEN . . . Read the comments of Herve Charest, Jr., in his popular column, "Folks & Facts" in *The Alabama Farmer's State*: "The noise you will hear from the southern tip of the State in about a week will be the annual movement of Baldwin County Irish potatoes. This is big business in Baldwin and the folks down there have little time for anything else when the shipping season is under way. This is the only time of the year when they probably don't read Jimmy Faulkner's readable *Baldwin Times* from cover to cover. As a matter of fact, they probably recruit Jimmy from his shop to help get the spuds started on their way to tickle the palates of the rest of America." You're right Herve. Our busy season is just getting underway but our good farmers know better than to try to get the editor to help with the potato harvest. It takes brains as well as brawn to raise spuds, you know. But we're confident you could qualify, so come on down and grab a hamper.

NICE . . . Last week we ran a story about Mr. and Mrs. L. Glendinning of Robertsdale who are among the most popular and loved old couples in the county. And now we know why. Anyone who is thoughtful and kind enough to write us the following is bound to have thousands of friends . . . "I enjoy your paper very much. I sure have been missing something, it is a real paper." Thank you sir, and may you have many more wedding anniversaries.

January 2, 1947

RECORD NUMBER OF DEER KILLED AROUND TENSAW LAKE

SAFE NOW . . . Since the deer season is over January 1st we presume it will be safe for us to tell about the number of deer killed last Thursday on the annual hunt of the Old Island Land Company, up around Tensaw Lake. No doubt, however, the game thirsty hunters of Clarke County will make a note for next year's hunting expeditions down into Baldwin. The hunt was the most successful of the year in this section and many old timers, remembering back as far as 30 years, said it resulted in more game killed in one drive than any they could recall. Seven deer were killed in the drive that lasted about three hours. This hunt is always one of the best of the year, but last Thursday everything was perfect (except to those who missed shots) including the weather and the results.

DINNER . . . The hosts to this annual drive were Henry and A.B. Bryars, John and Jewel Smith. They own about 1500 acres together and protect it the year around, allowing only one hunt on it a season. The hunt is always well arranged and ends up with a big dinner, given by the hosts.

THE MOOSE . . . J.D. Crosby killed one of the biggest deer that has been seen in this area, according to the old hunters. He had 16 points. Several of the hunters figured it must have been the moose the Montgomery hunter thought he saw on a Thanksgiving hunt on Thomas Earle's lands. Cly T. Smith, Bay Minette postmaster, had the first opportunity at the big buck. He said he never saw anything with such big horns. Mr. Smith hates it because he missed the deer and also hates it 'cause he lost his shirt tail.   Then the 16-pointer came in gun range of Mr. Crosby. He shot at it a couple of times and the deer jumped in the lake. After it swam to the other side, Mr. Dougald shot him three or four times at a distance of about 100 yards. Evidently dazing him with one of his shots and because a dog came up on him, the buck jumped back into the lake and swam back to

Mr. Crosby, who then ended his misery. Few people have seen a 16-point buck, and still fewer have every killed one.

OTHERS . . . Others who were successful on the hunt were J.C. Mc-David, Tom Bryars, Taylor Wilkins, Joe Still, Carl Slaughter and Henry Miller. Several admitted missing shots, others didn't admit it as 53 shells were fired on the drive. Shirt tails were cheap. Bruce Beveridge also learned what the treatment is for those killing their first deer. Kiddingly, he told some of the boys to tell J.R. Wilson that he killed one of the deer. Trouble was some of them took him seriously and before he could make a satisfactory explanation they had covered him with the deer's blood. So much fun was had by all.

SUCCESSFUL . . . Several other bucks were killed over the holidays but it was impossible for *The Times* to have reporters on every hunt and we don't have a record of them. Judge Childress of Loxley killed a fine 10-pointer Saturday up on the Baldwin County Hunting Club. He came through town with two on his car but we failed to learn who got the other one. With the season at an end, we believe this has been one of the most successful in recent years.

BALDWINITIS . . . Reports are that a group from Gateswood are leasing the Southern Kraft lands for a hunting preserve. His many friends will be glad to know that R.B. Vail has been released from a Washington hospital where he underwent his second operation of the year recently. George K. Page of Robertsdale writes that he passed through Greenville, a small town up the L.&N. from Bay Minette, recently and saw some pretty homes and their new sign proclaiming "The Camellia City," but that he saw no camellias to back up the claim of the sign . . . George, Greenville has a few camellias, but most of them are just out of sight, in the back yards, no doubt. Fairhope is staging her camellia show soon . . . Greenville citizens would profit by attending.

January 9, 1947

Two bucks killed in one shot and two dozen oysters eaten

TWO-IN-ONE . . . We thought we could hush up about Baldwin's deer hunters when the season closed last Wednesday. But this happened before the season was over and it's too good to keep from Clarke County and the rest of the state. We don't have the official record but we will wager this feat hasn't been duplicated many times, if ever. P. Grey Cane, Jr., was on a deer hunt Christmas week above Stockton. Young Cane is no novice at hunting deer, as he killed a fine buck last year. But he had never killed two bucks with one shot. Now he has. While on his stand, which incidentally was on the one next to the state game warden, Mr. Wharton, a fine five-pointer came within reach of his gun and right along with him was a smaller spike buck. Grey took a bead on the biggest one, pulled the trigger and two deer fell to the ground. Well, the marksman knew the game laws well enough to know they say a hunter can only kill one buck a day. And instead of being jubilant over a feat that any older and more experienced hunter would have given his right arm to accomplish, it was with fear and trembling that he reported the incident to the game warden. Naturally the warden knew it hadn't been done on purpose, so all was well.

THICK . . . It is evident that when deer get so thick you can't shoot one without killing two, they are plentiful.

NO BACK TALK . . . We could brag all day about Baldwin's bountiful supply of game and not get a peep out of Greenville's Glenn Stanley. Because Glenn knows he can't compete with us on fish and game facts. And he won't admit Baldwin's superiority in camellias. We are grateful to him though for sending us a printed program of Greenville's 1947 Camellia Show, which is to take place Saturday and Sunday of this week. We are proud to know that they can get enough camellias together by including Brewton, Evergreen, Andalusia, Luverne and other neighboring towns to have a show. We would like to attend but feel slighted because Mr. Stanley didn't insist that we be called in as one of the judges.

OYSTERS . . . Baldwin also has some fine oysters, although not as many as we could have with the proper development. We are grateful to Jack Taylor, popular merchant of Bon Secour, for bringing us some of the fine oysters that community is famous for last week. They were fine. We accompanied J.H. Stacey, J. Bruce Beveridge and Clint White down to Cooper's Fishing Camp last Friday to see C.P. Taylor, who has just sold the camp, on some business, mainly camellias. Business completed, we decided to look up Charley Wakeford and get some oysters, fresh and on the half shell. We drove to his old place to find he had sold out to Melvin Plash and had opened a new business on the canal. But the Plash Oyster Company had the oysters and we had the appetite. Dr. Stacey didn't think he would like them served in the raw but ate two dozen and the rest of us devoured smaller amounts before we could drag him away. Mr. Plash took them right off the boat, opened them and they were the biggest we had seen in a long time. Our appetites being whetted sharply, we proceeded to Fulford's and bought a gallon to bring home. Dr. Stacey said he had never been to Bon Secour before but now that he knows what they have to offer he's going more often.

TRADE . . . We have traded subscriptions for many things but never for a camellia. Mr. Taylor put an end to that. He pointed to a nice Chandleri Elegans and said he would give it to us for a year's subscription. We agreed but said the bush was worth more than that. To which he very courteously said: "But your paper is also worth more than $2.00 a year." Bon Secour certainly has fine people, as well as oysters.

February 6, 1947

LOCAL FAMILIES CELEBRATE SUCCESSES

VISITOR . . . An appreciated visitor last week was Lt. Col. Ira B. Thompson of Luverne. Col. Thompson was visiting his mother, Mrs. Laura Thompson, and other relatives here. He is a native of Bay Minette and is well known in this section. He served in both world wars with honor and distinction. In 1915, Col. Thompson served Baldwin County in the Legislature. A lawyer by profession, he moved to Crenshaw County and was elected to the legislature there, but resigned to go back into the Army in 1942. He was re-elected for this session and holds a high position in the legislative circles under the Folsom administration. His many Baldwin friends will wish for him continued success.

HAPPY . . . About the happiest man in Bay Minette Wednesday was Judge W. Ramsey Stuart. Reason: a son was born on Tuesday to Mr. and Mrs. Ramsey Stuart, Jr. He, the grandson, has been named W. Ramsey Stuart, III. From all accounts all three are doing fine but "Grand Pa" is wearing the biggest smile.

BALDWINITIS . . . Several people expressed surprise that Governor Folsom appointed S.F. Holmes, Bay Minette, to the county jury commission this week . . . We know Mr. Holmes was surprised too . . . Naturally he will do a good job and it is obvious the present administration thinks considerable of him, if not he would not have been offered the position in Montgomery as head of the State Banking Department . . . Fortunately for Bay Minette, he turned it down. E.E. McMillan of Hurricane is one of our most faithful subscribers . . . Looking in fine health he came in the other day and planked down five bucks for a three year renewal . . . When his present subscription expires he will be 78 . . . We like people that aren't pessimistic. H.E. Smith, Jr., University student of Stockton, may bring renown to Baldwin some day . . . Some of his art work was placed on display at the University recently . . . Incidentally, the great artist of Montgomery,

Major Harold Sims, who has gained world-wide fame for his drawings, is the brother of *The Baldwin Times'* Linotype operator, C.T. Sims. Earnest Hawkins, son of Mrs. W.H. and the late Judge Hawkins, of Bay Minette, has made an outstanding record with Autry Greer & Sons in Mobile . . . Mr. Hawkins has risen to a position of major importance with this large grocery house . . . His boss, Barton Greer (who is himself one prince of a fellow), speaks highly of the Bay Minette boy "who has made good in the city."

CREATIVE . . . George Carleton of Grove Hill fame is a good newspaper man. He also claims to be a hunter and fisherman. We only give him credit for his editing ability. He is so good if he can't find a news story to his liking he sets down and creates one. Recently when we had something to say about J.D. Crosby killing a 16-point buck, the next week the *Clarke County Democrat* had a story about someone killing a 16-point buck, (a few years back). Then we printed the very factual information about Grey Cane, Jr., killing two bucks with one shot. Then what—you guessed it—George claimed a Clarke County man did the same thing. These creative writers make it difficult for people, like us, who stick to facts.

VERSE . . . Here's a verse, not mine: "He passed a cop without a fuss, He passed a load of hay; He tried to pass a speeding bus, And then he passed away!"

February 13, 1947

ALICE DUCK APPOINTED COUNTY AND CIRCUIT COURT CLERK

AMEN . . . Judge F.W. Hare must be a Gallop Poll all in himself. At least he knew the sentiment of the citizens of Baldwin County when he gave the full term, (six years), appointment to Mrs. Alice J. Duck as clerk of the county and circuit courts. If there have been any objections to Mrs. Duck, we haven't heard them and we hear a lot of objections in the course of a day's work. Since her late husband, R.S. (Bob) Duck, Sr., was one of the most popular men in the court house at the time of his death, his many friends must be grateful to Judge Hare for giving her the appointment. If she doesn't continue to make a top notch public official, we're a bad misjudge of character and ability.

ED . . . Baldwin has many outstanding citizens. Of course most of them still live in the county but now and then one is so outstanding his ability is demanded elsewhere. One such is Ed N. Rodgers. He left Baldwin four years ago where he served as highway engineer to become assistant director of the State Highway Department under Senator Swift. Later, he was promoted to acting director. But, he didn't vote for Jim Folsom, along with a few others of us. Although he did have an opportunity to stay on with the new administration he accepted another position, and wisely we think. Monday, he took over as executive director of the newly organized Alabama Road Builders Association. And if you happen to be one of his many friends you'll be glad to know that his salary is considerable.

CONTACTS . . . We have been asked on various occasions, who in Baldwin County has the most state-wide contacts. Not claiming to be an authority on the subject we would say, judging from comments heard over Alabama, the following men have the most contacts over the state, in just about this order: W.C. Beebe, Dr. W.C. Holmes, W.M. Hodgson, Frank Earle, S. M. Tharp. In the immediate surrounding counties it would be harder to say but certainly Judge Stuart, Jim Gaston and Fred Griffin would be close to the top of the list. Of course, we know naming such a list is bad business for a writer. The above gentlemen may not appreciate being mentioned and dozens who could easily be named resent being omitted.

ATTICUS . . . We had long considered Atticus Mullin of the *Montgomery Advertiser* one of Alabama's most accurate reporters. Our faith has been dimmed. In his Monday's column he had this to say: "Greenville proudly calls herself the Camellia City and is entitled to it. There are more camellias in Greenville than any other city of the same size in the country." No doubt Mr. Mullin realized when he made the above statement that Bay Minette is not the "same size" in population as Greenville. Neither is Mobile. But both towns have several camellias.

BALDWINITIS . . . Dr. P.M. Hodgson, Stockton, celebrated his 82nd birthday Tuesday . . . He is still active physically, mentally and in the practice of medicine . . . Although saddened last year by the loss of his wife, he still has an optimistic mind, looks to the future . . . Dr. Hodgson is another of Baldwin's rich characters. Paul Corwin, secretary to the local chamber of commerce, is fast proving his worth to this area . . . Because of his personal friendship to a man, Bay Minette is able to announce the addition of another post-war industry this week . . . This will be the fifth new industry for this area since the war and two more are strongly interested in locating here . . . And still a few people say, "What does the chamber of commerce do?"

CHECKER PLAYER . . . A.G. Hinshaw, Summerdale, is a checker fan. We saw him in the courthouse last week and he was looking for Deputy Sheriff Duckworth then for a game. Tuesday, we had a letter from the retired school teacher, who is now farming, telling us about the checker tournament, which is to be held in Mobile on February 22 and 23. This is to be a statewide affair and Mr. Hinshaw is going to enter in class B, "as I am hardly good enough for class A." The tournaments will be conducted on the "Double Knock Out" system. Mr. Hinshaw has played for over 50 years "for the pleasure of the game." He urged all county players to enter the contest and will be glad to give them further information upon request.

February 20, 1947

CONCERN OVER TUNG OIL PRICES

TUNG NUTS . . . Talked to C.D. Sweat, Robertsdale, this week and he was quite concerned about the tung oil situation at the present time. Mr. Sweat and his partner, C.L. Matthews, bought several tons of the tung nuts this year at their Hub City produce market and are disappointed with the price. It seems the price of the oil has fallen from over 38 cents a pound to about 34 cents within the past few weeks. Naturally the tung growers feel like blaming somebody, so they are blaming the government—and small wonder if what they say is correct. The story is that Uncle Sam allowed China to repay part of her lend lease by shipping tung oil into this country at a price in excess of 40 cents per pound. The producers claim the government cut the price of the oil she owned to 34 cents, thus forcing down the price all over the country.

THREE BROWNS . . . Lyle Brown, commercial horticulture marketing specialist of Auburn, was down visiting his brother, Otto, at the Fairhope experiment station Monday. Lyle has worked with Auburn for 27 years and is quite a farm expert, particularly with horticulture. On the side he hobbies with camellias and knows considerable about them, too. Knowing this, the Fairhope Camellia Club invited him to talk to them Monday night on the subject. This he did. Lyle and Otto are the oldest of three brothers who are engaged in agricultural work in Alabama. We don't care to mention ages, but Baldwin prides itself in having the oldest of the three, with each being born five years apart. The youngest is Julian, 44. Being employed by the Farm Security Administration for several years, it is reported he is going to Washington to take over a big job soon.

SHERIFF . . . Taylor Wilkins, sheriff for a month, must be taking his job seriously. At least we hardly ever see him around and reports are that the jail is feeding more people here of late.

BALDWINITIS . . . We're always glad to get good news about Baldwin boys and girls in school . . . Harry West, Jr., Bay Minette, is doing graduate work in physics and chemistry under a fellowship at Auburn . . . He has just been honored by being selected as a member of the national honorary scholastic fraternity, Pi Kappa Phi. O.J. Manci, Jr., Bay Minette, who is a cadet at Annapolis, was a guest at the White House recently. Robertsdale merchants really fight for business . . . If you don't believe it just observe their ads in this week's paper. Grand Hotel at Point Clear is scheduled for reopening in April.

ANSWER . . . Recently we accused George Carleton, of Grove Hill, of creative writing. Now just listen to him: "Suggestion IS a wonderful thing, isn't it, Jimmy? The story of Leo Dorman, of Jackson, killing two bucks at one shot was carried in the *Democrat* a full two weeks before *The Times* carried an account of a similar feat by a Baldwin hunter. And although Joe York, of Thomasville, had killed a 16-point buck last fall, we didn't trouble to mention the fact as such a feat is hardly newsworthy in Clarke. However, when Jimmy began bragging about some hunter down there killing a 16-pointer buck, we mentioned the fact that York had duplicated the feat. We could have told him—but didn't—of the point buck, we mentioned then a 19-point buck the season before. If Jimmy doubts this story, we will send him the horns for inspection." O.K., send them down. We want to see 'em.

February 27, 1947

OUTSTANDING RED CROSS WORKERS

WORKERS . . . Attending meetings and such is nothing new to this scribe, but we manage to enjoy and are benefited by most of them. It is always a pleasure to attend Red Cross gatherings because you can rest assured that those present are there for purely unselfish reasons—being anxious to help in a good cause. Baldwin has many outstanding workers in the Red Cross, both men and women. We could name dozens, all of which would be fine examples. Present at the meeting here last Friday night at the annual fund drive kick-off dinner for the Central and North Baldwin Chapters were many who have devoted hours and hours of work to the Red Cross. Martin Timberlake, local chapter chairman, was in charge of the meeting and made quite a hit with the audience.

TYPICAL . . . One of these outstanding workers, and one of the best known and most respected citizens in Baldwin County, is Gordon G. Stimpson of Daphne. Mr. Gordon devotes a lot of time to many worthwhile causes but we believe his favorite extra-curricula activities are the Red Cross and the American Legion. He makes a living by being postmaster of Daphne, a position he has held for 13 years. He is always at the forefront in Red Cross drives and his interest and enthusiasm is equaled by Mrs. Stimpson. The beloved gentleman has held virtually every position in the county Legion Post and was adjutant for years. Because of his outstanding service with this organization, he was honored several years ago by being selected as a member of 40 and 8, honorary society of the Legion. Yes, Gordon G. Stimpson is a typical example why Red Cross drives are always successful in Baldwin County.

ALWAYS THE SAME . . . The same thing happened during the war. Also it's the same with camellias. During 1946 many Baldwin County citizens continued the purchase of series E. U.S. Savings Bonds to the tune of $528,066. During the same period Butler citizens bought $257,126. In district No. 13, which includes Baldwin, Butler, Conecuh, Covington, Crenshaw and Escambia, this county led the group with the above figure. Second was Covington with $463,292.

DETERMINED . . . P.M. Stephenson, county highway engineer, is a determined person, which is a fortunate thing for Baldwin County. About six months ago, when everyone was screaming about the terrible condition of the roads, he gave serious consideration to accepting two or three other attractive jobs offered him, and leaving us with our road troubles. But he decided to stick it out and get Baldwin out of the mud. And it looks as if he is going to make good at it. At least, he is on his way. He has drained more ditches and roads in the county than have ever been drained before and finally, with the able assistance of the County Commission and the fact that the Maritime Commission decided to store more ships in the Tensaw River, he is getting equipment to really go to work. It is probable that the county now has more good road equipment than ever, although they still need some specific pieces. He says if the weather will just be considerate and the people will bear with him a little longer, the road situation in every section of the county is going to be much improved six months from now. That's good news and we believe that if anyone can get the job done, it is Jim Gaston as highway commissioner and Paul Stephenson as engineer.

ENVY . . . Incidentally, Baldwin with its new road equipment is the envy of every county in Alabama. The reason the county got 13 new pieces of equipment, including 8 four-yard trucks, was because the Commissioners were able to persuade the Maritime Commission to give them priority to buy it to build the roads to the two Tensaw landings. Naturally when these roads are completed, the new equipment will be diverted to use elsewhere in the county. The Maritime Commission wanted to rent the equipment to the county but the Commission refused and held out for the privilege of outright purchase, which they finally obtained.

April 17, 1947

Birthday and Golden Wedding
anniversary celebrated

MEETINGS . . . No doubt an editor is expected to attend more meetings and public gatherings than any other individual. Naturally there are so many it is impossible to get around to them all. But two events occurred

Sunday that we really wanted to attend. Rev. A.D. Duck had another birthday celebration at his home near Cross Roads and Rev. and Mrs. R.T. Coleman held their golden wedding anniversary at Perdido. Although it would have been difficult, we had ambitions of attending both events. But a person isn't always able to do what he plans. A meeting of the Alabama Press Association was called in Birmingham over the weekend and we felt that business, in this case, must come before pleasure.

OCTOGENARIAN . . . Rev. Duck observed his 84th birthday Sunday and had his usual big crowd of children and grandchildren and admiring friends around him during the day. Old Brother Duck is one of the most respected and loved individuals in this county. His long record as a Methodist preacher and service to his neighbors and fellow man would make a fit subject for any biography writer. The occasion was somewhat saddened over some of the previous ones because, since his last birthday, one of his sons had died—the late R.S. Duck.

SEPTUAGENARIAN . . . Another respected and honored preacher is Rev. Coleman, 70, of Perdido. He and Mrs. Coleman were greatly honored Sunday afternoon when a big crowd of descendants and friends were present at their golden wedding anniversary. A native of Spanish Fort, he has been an active minister in this area for 45 years. Naturally, he is well known and respected. Like Bro. Duck, he has also raised a big family. They now have 10 living children, most of whom live in and around Perdido. We congratulate Rev. and Mrs. Coleman on their long life of usefulness and trust they will live to serve humanity many years to come.

CATCH RIDE . . . At the press meeting in Birmingham Sunday afternoon, we were standing in the lobby of the Tutwiler when in walks Dr. P.A. Bryant. Dr. Percy had just driven from Bay Minette alone and we had ridden the train alone, both arriving there at about the same time. He was there to attend the convention of the Alabama Medical Association. On our return trip we didn't have to ride the train, at least not all the way. Bill Brooks of the *Brewton Standard* was kind enough to ask us to ride back with him in his shining new automobile. He also picked up Charlie Dobbins, *Advertiser* editor, who rode with us to Montgomery.

MR. MAX . . . Charlie, his son Peter, and Mrs. Dobbins have a beautiful

Dalmatian dog. Several months ago we admired her so much they promised us one of her pups. He made delivery on the promise Sunday. Bill kindly agreed to let the 30-pound, five months old, Mr. Max ride in his new car to Brewton, where he would put us both up for the night. To say that Mr. Max is a fine and beautiful dog is to be modest. So far as canine beauty is concerned, we don't think we have ever seen the beat of this Dalmatian pup. White with very distinct small black spots, it can truly be said he is "as pretty as a speckled pup."

TROUBLE . . . The two editors and the dog arrived in Brewton in fine style. But Mr. Max raised a continuous howl when placed in the basement for the night. Although it was obvious Bill had grown attached to the pup, he didn't particularly enjoy having his delayed sleep disturbed. As we dozed off we faintly remember that the dog quieted down. Next morning we learned why. Bill had let him in his room, preferring to sleep with the pup to not sleeping at all.

MORE . . . We had to catch a train for Bay Minette the next morning and left the pup with Bill. However when we got on the train we ran into our old friend, Sherman Gideons, who was brakeman on the run and he kindly told us we should have brought Mr. Max aboard. But we learned this a little late. Bill assured us the dog would be no trouble, but it worked out differently. About 9 o'clock a strange speckled dog was seen on the Escambia County courthouse lawn by Dr. McCreary, Brewton vet. Dr. Mc-Creary thought he knew all the Dalmatians in Brewton so he reported the stranger to the sheriff's office. Eventually word got to Bill about the stray and he immediately surmised his guest pup had broken out of the basement. Naturally Mr. Max didn't stay around the courthouse so the local editor instigated a city-wide search for the culprit. A few hours later a gentleman returned to *The Standard* office with a big arm full of dog.

HOME . . . Yes, Mr. Max was a lot of trouble but the little boys on East Fifth St. don't care. They are proud of their fine new dog.

May 22, 1947

Chamber of Commerce
groups outstanding

FINE . . . Baldwin has several fine organizations. Two of these are the Robertsdale and Silverhill chambers of commerce. B.B. Larrimore is president of the Hub City group and makes them a splendid leader. Although he has only been in the county a few years he has taken to it like a duck to water. He really believes in Robertsdale and Baldwin and is making both a good citizen. His organization is working on several worthwhile projects, including a cow coliseum for the county to be located there.

SILVERHILL . . . For the size town, Silverhill probably has the biggest chamber of commerce in the county. With 34 members to back him, Axel Rundquist is making the group a good president. This community has a civic spirit of progressiveness that is unique and fine.

SUPPORT . . . It might be expected that these two communities, being inland from the bays and Gulf, might not be interested in the development of tourist business in Baldwin. But such a thought is far from the truth. In a joint meeting of the two organizations Monday night, both groups' representatives unanimously and enthusiastically voted to support some kind of county-wide organization to promote the recreation field here.

UNUSUAL . . . Baldwin is finally awakening to her opportunities in the tourist and vacation world. Out of six meetings held in every section of the county, not one person has opposed the establishment of such an organization as mentioned above. This unanimity is unusual.

CHALLENGE . . . George Carleton, who edits the fine *Clarke County Democrat* as a hobby and fishes and hunts with a vengeance, would have people believe he is an expert fisherman. Considering the fact he does most of his fishing in Clarke County, he does do fairly well, sometimes. This editor enjoys fishing but doesn't seem to find time to go very often. Evidently, though, *The Times* has in its employ several good fishermen. Although it isn't necessary to be an artist to catch a good string of fish in Baldwin, it does help if you know how to put a worm on a hook. As mentioned here before, one member went with his mother and brother Saturday before last and caught 75. (If we knew Game Warden Fred Smith wasn't looking, we could tell how many they really caught.) Last Saturday three more members of the staff went and brought in 70.

SIZEMORE . . . A few people still seem to be doubtful that the reserve fleet is actually moving into Baldwin County. A trip down to the Sizemore Landing should convince most anyone that the Maritime Commission means business. Tons and tons of dirt have already been moved to build a road down the high cliff to the wharf on the river. The $200,000 construction job is well under way. Besides the wharf and road, two buildings are being built along with other work.

WELL . . . There is a bored well on the banks of the river at this landing which is somewhat mysterious. Although the bank is about 50 feet above the river's water line, water in the well stands within a few feet of the top of the ground at all times. And there seems to be no ground around the well that is higher than it.

ODDITIES . . . A sow owned by Mr. and Mrs. Edward Quinley, Bay Minette, played a trick on them this week. She gave birth to six pigs. This isn't unusual, but the pigs are. One didn't have any hind legs at all, while the others had more than their share of toes. Some of them had from four to six toes, and looked more like dog's feet than pigs. Mrs. D.M. McKinley, also of Bay Minette, found a petrified rock which looked for the world like a petrified chicken . . . Not satisfied with this oddity, she picked up a 5-cent piece made in 1835 . . . It is smaller than a dime and she has already been offered $5.00 for it. Her daughter, Mrs. Annie Nichols, didn't want her mother to get ahead of her in the unusual field, so one of her hens laid an egg that looks exactly like an ordinary peanut.

July 31, 1947

CAMPAIGNER FULFILLS UNUSUAL PROMISE TO LOXLEY JUDGE

PROMISE MADE . . . During the governor's race last May, Handy Ellis, one of the leading candidates, was making speeches in Baldwin. He had made four talks in the county and was returning from Foley to Bay Minette when he stopped in Loxley at Judge Childress's filling station to buy some gas and do a little politicking. Mr. Ellis and Judge Childress got together on their politics in a hurry and then started talking about a subject that, if possible, they liked even better—coon hunting. The Lieutenant Governor had to tell the judge about his fine pack of coon hounds and right off he wanted to give the Loxley Justice of Peace a pair of coon pups. The Judge was willing.

PROMISE KEPT . . . This writer heard the promise made and couldn't help but wonder if Mr. Ellis would remember the coon pups after the heat of the campaign was over. Several times during the past year I asked the Judge if he had gotten the pups. The answer was always, "No, but I will. Handy won't forget, give him time." Last Thursday the Judge had a different story to tell. He had just received three fine coon pups from Mr. Ellis. One was a red bone pup and the other two were black and tans. Judge Childress and I still don't think we voted for the wrong candidate for governor in 1946.

ANGUS CATTLE . . . Baldwin has a lot to brag about, not the least of which is Aberdeen Angus cattle. Last Thursday this county and area received its fair share of recognition as a wonderful place in which to raise fine livestock. The occasion was the meeting of the Alabama Aberdeen Angus Cattle Breeders Association at Corte's farm in Belforest. About 300 guests saw some of the finest Angus cattle in the entire South and many of the cattlemen from other sections seemed to be amazed that such excellent quality beef could be raised here on the Gulf Coast.

CORTE BROS. . . . . Hosts of the cattlemen were the six sons of the late A.A. Corte, Arthur, Ernest, Albert, Ferdinand, Julio and Teel. Hard workers all, they have followed and added to the training of their father and have made a huge success in producing about everything that will grow out of the soil in Baldwin County. They are best known, perhaps, as potato growers and shippers. But they know their way around at other things too, particularly cattle. This spring they won first, second and third places at the Montgomery fat stock show with a carload of Angus cattle. It was proclaimed the best car lot of cattle ever sold in the Southeast.

SUCCESS . . . The history of the Corte family runs like a story book. Their father came to Baldwin years ago from Minnesota. He didn't succeed at first but finally got a toehold by raising sweet potatoes. A toehold was all he needed, from there on he was in. The fact that his sons now live in fine brick homes and drive Cadillac automobiles has nothing to do with their success . . . but is rather a result of it. Some day this scribe would like to write a book about this family . . . only thing the story deserves better handling.

HOSPITALS . . . Read the *Greenville Advocate*: "*The Baldwin Times*, always claiming wonderful things for Baldwin and Bay Minette, resents the fact that Greenville has so many more camellias—and only on one occasion broke down and acknowledged it. Last week, while making a rash claim about Bay Minette camellias, Jimmy Faulkner added, 'Greenville has it over Bay Minette in one respect, however. She can refer to her hospitals in the plural. Bay Minette can't even refer to one in the singular.' Now that's bad. Alabama is far behind in the hospital program, Greenville being one of the very few cities in the entire state with adequate hospital facilities. However, we of Greenville can't brag too much about it, for the citizens as a whole had nothing to do with it. Our hospitals were constructed and are operated by our progressive physicians and surgeons, not by the community."

SUGGESTION . . . Foley, Fairhope and Atmore can say the same thing about their "progressive physicians and surgeons." Dr. Holmes has made a success for himself and his community at Foley with his hospital. The same is true for Dr. Jordan at Fairhope and Dr. Lisenby at Atmore. These towns are also close to Mobile, but that didn't bother these doctors. Bay Minette has some fine doctors, too . . . but they could serve better with a small hospital.

January 1, 1948

BIG ANNUAL DEER HUNT
MOST SUCCESSFUL EVER

NEW YEAR . . . 1948 has done a lot already . . . it has brought a lot of varied predictions . . . if all of which happens it will be the strangest year in history . . . of course anything can happen during an election year, and usually does . . . I might make a few predictions about 1948 but it seems to me too many have been made now . . . I do predict this, however—come Thursday, 1947 will be history . . . In Alabama, 1947 will be remembered as the year the Big Boy was inaugurated Governor . . . In America, it will be remembered as the year of flying saucers and high flying prices . . . In the world, it will be remembered as a year of hunger, strife, civil wars and a struggle with Russia for peace . . . In Baldwin, the predominant thing to remember will be progress, growth and prosperity . . . this country has had "growing pains," which we all have learned to enjoy throughout the year . . . Baldwin sportsmen are apt to refer to 1947 as the year of the big deer hunt.

BIG HUNT . . . Almost always the best annual deer hunt in these parts is the one held the day after Christmas at the Old Island Hunting Club with Henry and Brown Bryars and Jewel and John Smith as hosts. The one last Friday was no exception, in fact, it was the most successful ever and more deer were killed on the drive than on any the old timers can ever remember. In about three hours 10 bucks were killed and from 12 to 15 shirt tails were lost. Right after the drive, when the hunters were coming home, Rudolph Bryars killed another one, making a total of 11 for the hunt.

CRACK SHOTS . . . Those who didn't miss and received a buck for their reward as good shots were: Lloyd White, Bay Minette; A.L. McCue, Fairhope; J.O.Cox, Satsuma; Ben Hastie and H.E. Smith, Stockton; Jesse Slaughter, Tensaw; Homer S. Waters, game warden; E.N. Rodgers, Jr., Monroeville; J.C. McDavid, Jr., and G.K. Page, Bay Minette. Embree Smith killed the biggest one with 12 points. All deer killed were pronged and the hunters were asked not to kill spiked bucks or turkeys. On the hunt last year, a 16-point buck was killed but only seven were bagged in all. The usual big dinner was given the 106 guests.

January 8, 1948

OLD DEED SIGNED BY PRESIDENT MARTIN VAN BUREN

OLD DOCUMENT . . . Mrs. W.A. Boone, Little River, brought in an interesting old land document last week. It is a deed to Thomas Saunders for 40 and 40/100 acres of land near Little River which was signed personally by President Martin Van Buren and dated January 5th, 1841. Later the land was willed to Mr. Boone's great-grandfather, "Major" Dreisbach. Then it was handed down to Mr. Dreisbach's daughter, Mrs. I.T. Staples, who was Mr. Boone's grandmother. The land is now owned by Mr. Boone.

TAXES . . . In 1893 Mrs. Staples paid taxes on the property, plus additional land and other property. According to the tax receipt, which is also preserved by Mr. and Mrs. Boone, 147 acres of land was assessed at $175. Other assessments on the receipt was, "Guns, pistols, etc.", $3.00; two head of cattle, $14; and two horses, $75; or a total assessment of $267. Obviously the state and county tax rate in 1893 was $1 per hundred, or 10 mills, plus a "special" county and state tax of one mill, because the total bill paid was $3.43 and 7 mills.

TERMS . . . A new term to me was one on the old tax receipt. The total value of the personal property was $92. And the costs were itemized on this as follows: "State Tax on Personality"—46c; "County Tax on Personality"—46c. Evidently the word "personality" referred to the personal property. Incidentally, the receipt was signed by H.W. Slaughter, Sheriff and Tax Collector of Baldwin County, and T.A. Booth, deputy sheriff. In those days, the sheriff did the tax collecting. Mr. Slaughter was the father of the late H.W. (Boy) Slaughter of Tensaw. Mr. Booth became sheriff the following term when the tax collector and sheriff's office were separated. He was elected to two terms.

INTERESTING . . . Mr. Booth's home at that time was also in Tensaw. His widow, Mrs. T.A. Booth, now lives in Mobile. She is M.H. Wilkins' sister, who is the present tax collector and who was also sheriff for one term. And now her nephew, Taylor Wilkins, is sheriff. So Mrs. Booth has been interested in the sheriff's office, off and on, since 1894 through her husband, then her brother and now her nephew.

ANOTHER . . . Speaking of old papers, next week this column will try to copy "Frank Stone's Recipe Barbecue Stand." It should also bring a lot of interesting memories to some of Baldwin's old timers.

VOTING . . . Didn't many people vote in Tuesday's amendment election but at least three more opportunities will be presented this year. Two Spring primaries and the general election in November. I predict plenty people will be voting in them.

"NOTABLE STATE LEADERSHIP" . . . Baldwin has several citizens who are outstanding throughout the state; men and women who have contributed to the general welfare and progress of Alabama. Many times, these men render fine service in various organizations without their neighbors realizing the significance of their efforts. His many friends will be pleased to know that Bay Minette's W.M. Hodgson is getting state-wide recognition for the splendid job he is and has done with the Soil Conservation Service. An indication of this is found in an editorial under the above heading in *The Montgomery Examiner* of recent date. We quote:

"The State Association of Soil Conservation has made no mistake in electing W. (Mac) Hodgson, of Bay Minette, as president of their respected organization. Mr. Hodgson has been a wheelhorse in Alabama's great soil conservation program and is a worthy successor to Pearson Compton, of Gallion, the retiring president, who made a great leader.

"The American public is rapidly becoming aware of every day's battle to protect our God-given natural resources. We are learning that prosperity rests not just on peace and productive labor, but on the factor of material resources within the nation.

"After years of prodigality, it is heartening to note that farmers and business men are working shoulder-to-shoulder for the preservation of our un-spent resources. In the long pull, history may record that men like Compton and Hodgson did bigger jobs for their state than the captains of industry and politics."

January 22, 1948

BALDWIN VOTERS CAN EXPECT 75 OR MORE CANDIDATES

THE YEAR . . . For a lot of ambitious souls, this is the year. At least 75 people will seek favors from the voters of Baldwin by trying to be elected to some political office within the next few months. There will be five county offices to be filled, two circuit posts, five councilmen and one mayor from each of the six incorporated municipalities in Baldwin. On the state level, you will have the opportunity to cast a ballot for one congressman, one senator, two district delegates to the National Democratic Convention and eight from the state at large, National Democratic Committeeman and a Committeewoman. And in the Fall general election, you will have the chance to vote for a president and vice-president. And probably some other things. Certainly, if you pay your poll tax, on or before January 31, you'll get your buck and a half's worth.

CITY . . . The city elections won't come up until July or August. This will be after the state and county arguments are settled in the two Democratic primaries. Plenty of time left to talk about the city fathers.

CIRCUIT . . . Two new offices to be filled in the county this year are the circuit judge and circuit solicitor. The recent legislature made Baldwin a separate judicial circuit. Although the officers will be elected this year, they will not take office until January 1st, 1949. Until that time, Judge Hare of Monroeville will continue to be in charge of the circuit court here. There was some opposition in the county to making Baldwin a separate circuit. Since both the system and the officials will be eyed closely after they are elected, it is but natural for the citizens to be very interested in knowing for whom they will have the opportunity of voting.

JUDGE . . . Practically every lawyer in the county has been mentioned either for the judge or solicitor's post. However, the prospects for the judgeship has narrowed down to the point where a fairly accurate picture can be given as to who will be in the race. E.G. Rickarby, Jr., Fairhope, was considering running but I have heard from reliable sources, although not from him, that he has decided against it. Hubert M. Hall, present county solicitor and Bay Minette attorney, was the first to make known to his friends that he would definitely be a candidate. He can be expected to qualify soon after the Democratic Committee sets the fees. It is also definite that Telfair J. Mashburn, Jr., Bay Minette, will be a candidate, and will announce soon. He is a veteran of World War No. 2 while Mr. Hall is a veteran of the first. I have been told that W.C. Beebe, ex-member of the state legislature and county attorney, is still giving serious consideration to making the race. Some of his friends say he will be a candidate although I understand he has not made a statement one way or the other. Mr. Beebe and Mr. Hall were law partners for several years. So the picture reveals itself with at least two candidates in the race, with a 50-50 chance of it being a three-way affair.

SOLICITOR . . . The job of solicitor pays $4800 a year but there seems to be few lawyers interested in the position in spite of its importance. I understand, however, that Robert S. Mundine of Robertsdale is willing to make the race. He hasn't been in the county many years but has made a lot of friends and is considered a good lawyer by his professional brothers. At this point, it seems that he may get the job without opposition unless Kenneth Cooper, major in the army and son of W.R. Cooper, Rosinton, gets out of the army in time to make the race. The last information I had was that he is to be home the last of February. It is definite that he is interested in making a race for some office and that it will probably be for solicitor. However, he is still in Italy and probably won't make up his mind until he arrives home.

MORE . . . Prospective candidates for the other offices will be taken up at a later date, next week, perhaps.

February 19, 1948

FOLKS IN BALDWIN VERY ACTIVE IN VARIOUS ENDEAVORS

LEGAL . . . If you live in Baldwin and expect to have any legal work done soon, I suggest you get about it now. You know six of our attorneys are going to be engaged in the profession of politics for the next several weeks and probably won't have too much time to spend at their legal profession. Four are running for Circuit Judge, one each for County and Circuit Solicitor. Those that aren't running will be busy trying to take care of their own practice plus the overflow from the contestants.

KEENEY . . . Had a pleasant visit from R.C. Keeney, well known Fairhope Realtor, recently. I always enjoy seeing him as he is forever full of ideas about Baldwin County and other things. Usually he, and H.C. Peterson, Robertsdale, can give me the latest information, if any, on oil development in the county. Mr. Keeney has been active in Boy Scout work for a number of years and recently was awarded the Silver Beaver badge for "Outstanding Service to Boyhood" at an area Scout meeting at the Battle House in Mobile. This is the highest award that can be obtained for service to Boy Scouts and he is to be congratulated for his fine service.

CAMELLIAS . . . Paul Corwin, popular secretary of the local Chamber of Commerce, got Bay Minette and Baldwin County a lot of favorable publicity last weekend in Birmingham at the annual meeting of the Alabama Press Association. Local citizens gave Paul about 200 beautiful camellia blooms, which he took to Birmingham where he gave them to all the ladies attending the main banquet. Naturally it was made known from where they came. One disappointing thing about it though was that Glenn Stanley of the *Greenville Advocate* wasn't present to see the beautiful flowers. Perhaps it's just as well because he might not have enjoyed the banquet.

BALDWINITIS . . . A trip to the Gulf will acquaint you with the fact that the area is developing . . . several new cabins and other tourist accommodations are being constructed there . . . Mr. and Mrs. Romeo, famous restaurant operators of Birmingham, are erecting several fine cottages and a beautiful restaurant at Gulf Shores . . . The Gulf Shores Lions Club had a charter night recently at the Gulf State Park . . . it was a grand affair . . . President Wingate Pickett and his members deserve a lot of credit for such a progressive organization . . . The oil situation is looking up in Baldwin . . . Rumors have it that an 8,000 foot well is going down near Lottie . . . and it's a fact that several hundred acres of land was leased recently around Loxley and vicinity for $5.00 per acre . . . Land at Mexia, in Monroe County, is leasing for $20.00 an acre . . . and the beauty part about it is the oil companies are anxious to strike pay dirt . . . Harry Still, Bay Minette, has become one of the most popular young business men of the county . . . Harry has been having a hard time of it with spinal meningitis, in fact he had the kind that is supposed to be ungetoverable . . . but Harry, with his strong constitution and modern medical science, is making the grade although he will have to stay in bed for several more weeks.

I WOULD . . . Listen to the sage of Grove Hill: "While in Grove Hill last week Bonnie Overstreet stated that members of his hunting club—the Community Hunting Club of Choctaw Bluff—killed 50 bucks during the past season and didn't start hunting until the latter part of December. Sixteen were bagged on the last four days of the season. There are other good hunting clubs, as well as private hunting preserves, adjoining the Community Hunting Club land. It would be interesting to know—especially to Jimmy Faulkner—just what was the total kill in bucks during the past season." Mr. Carleton is well acquainted with the fact that 11 deer were killed on the one short hunt of the Old Island Hunting Club. Until he can beat this in Clarke, I won't gather any more vital statistics.

February 26, 1948

CORTE HEADS BALDWIN POTATO TOUR ASSOCIATION

POTATO TOUR . . . Revival of the annual Potato Tour was the purpose of a meeting held at the Malbis Restaurant Tuesday night. Arthur Corte, general chairman of the Baldwin County Potato Tour Association, called the meeting of the directors to make plans for staging the annual popular event that was postponed during the war. It wasn't held last year because plans were started too late, but unless something unforeseen happens the event, which probably brought Baldwin more favorable and profitable publicity than any other single thing will go off this year.

LESS . . . Potatoes aren't as important to the economy of Baldwin as they were when the annual tour was started several years ago, but they are still important. Besides timber, spuds still bring in the most cash money to county farmers. Ten years ago the Irish potato was undisputed king of Baldwin's farm crops. It may still be king but its monarchy is weakening in relative influence as other crops, such as soybeans, gladioli, cattle, dairying, corn, etc., have continued to grow in importance. While acreage of these other crops have increased, the potato acreage has declined. Nevertheless, Baldwin is still proud of her potatoes. It was this crop that started the county on its way to agricultural greatness. So Mr. Spud will always have a tender spot in the hearts of our farmers. Hurrah for the return of the Potato Tour.

CREDIT . . . Possibly no other crop requires the credit that potatoes do. Baldwin's fine banks supply most of this money. The Bay Minette Production Credit Association furnishes a lot of it, too. Which brings me to the point. Jesse Hearin, president of the Production Credit Association at New Orleans, was a visitor in Bay Minette Saturday. Visiting his sister, Mrs. S. A. Y. Dahlberg, he dropped by to chat awhile with Thomas E. Mitchell, secretary to the BMPCA. I was supposed to see him but missed connections, which makes me the loser. Mr. Jesse is one of Alabama's favorite sons. An astute politician, he knows what's going on and retains a great love for his fellow man. Mr. Tom said complex problems of state and world affairs simplify themselves in Mr. Hearin's great mind.

STOCKTON . . . *The Times* took the opportunity to congratulate the citizens of Stockton last week on the construction of their country club. Last Saturday, I had the privilege and pleasure of visiting it. The building would be a credit to any community, but the gracious and hospitable nature of the Stockton people can't be excelled anywhere.

REPORTER . . . Ford Cook can do most anything there is to do around a newspaper office. He has worked on several papers from the editorial department to the composing room. Recently he took a job with *The Mobile Register* as a staff reporter. Until then, he took pictures around these parts. Best of luck Ford. And while you are working around those daily newspaper fellows, tell all of them who dream of some day owning a weekly and taking life easy that the weekly field is no bed of roses either.

SWAP . . . While Ford went to Mobile to work for the *Register*, one of their men, J.L. Glover, started work at *The Times* this week. Jimmy is a native of Daphne and has had varied newspaper and printing experience himself. He is a topnotch composing room man. C.T. Sims, who has worked here off and on since the Vail days, found the pastures greener in Montgomery. Mr. Glover's fine experience is needed to help Frank Taylor, Albert Martin, George France and Norman McReynolds get *The Times* out on time (they say they'll do it as soon as the boss gets a folding machine to go with the new press), get all job printing orders that our fine customers wanted yesterday finished without delay, and the thousands of other chores that go with running a newspaper. Anyway, if something goes wrong, blame Mr. Glover. I'm tired.

June 10, 1948

Baldwin's Gulf Coast in greatest tourist season

BOOM . . . It is quite obvious to the visitor that Baldwin's beautiful Gulf Coast area is having its greatest tourist season this summer. Recreation seekers by the hundreds are visiting the Gulf, bays and rivers in the county. There are several reasons for this increased tourist business. First, more and more people are learning about the fine fishing, swimming and other opportunities for fun, frolic and rest on Alabama's Gulf Coast. Next, the people of the county and other investors are getting better prepared day by day to take care of the crowds coming into this playground area.

ROMEO'S . . . Several new restaurants have been built along the Coast during the past year. An outstanding one is Romeo's at Gulf Shores. Mr. and Mrs. Romeo moved down from Birmingham last year where they had been successful in the restaurant business for several years. They wanted to put up a business on the beautiful Gulf of Mexico and take life a little easier. They wisely chose a site at Gulf Shores. They have a beautiful restaurant and several very modern cabins. Although he has been open for only a few months, his reputation for serving good meals has spread far and wide. He served me one of his special steaks last Friday night and when I picked up a knife to cut it, he was insulted. "Just use your fork," he explained. He was right, it melted in my mouth.

OTHERS . . . I mention Mr. and Mrs. Romeo because they are good examples of the progress that is coming into the county to help boost our tourist business. A number of others could be named. Lex Fullbright is a good story all in himself. He is a newcomer to the Gulf area and a fine asset, along with his wife. He has several nice cottages near Pop Messerole's place and is building others. He told me that 84 new cabins have been built in that area since last season. Growth is also fast over on the Mobile Bay side of the county.

BOOSTING . . . And another important thing which makes the recreation and tourist business of the county have a bright look is the co-operative and optimistic spirit of the citizens along the coast. Through the Gulf Shores Lions Club, they are doing much to take advantage of this fine spirit and turn it into cash assets. While in Romeo's, W.E. Steele, secretary of the Lions Club, came in with a big bundle of auto bumper placards which invites readers to visit Gulf Shores. They don't have money to pay for the placards so they sell them to the various business firms who in turn tie them on to out-of-county cars. Mr. Romeo took the big bundle and asked Mr. Steele to bring him some more.

BASEBALL . . . While on the subject of recreation, baseball comes to mind. Saw John Evans in Romeo's and he was telling me about the new lighted baseball field that has just been built at Foley. John said it is really a dandy. And I don't doubt him. He knows the flower business, having made a big success in it, and no doubt he knows a good baseball field when he sees one. I agree with John that such a field is a credit and asset to any town. South Baldwin has a splendid baseball league and the interest is spreading over the entire county.

PHIL BRADY . . . Saw another baseball fan this week, Phil Brady of Fairhope. Phil wants to see Bay Minette and Fairhope get into the county league next summer. He says there are already three lighted fields in the county, Fairhope, Robertsdale and Foley, and if Bay Minette will get one by next year most of the league games can be played at night. I think Phil has a good point.

PLAYERS . . . Although Bay Minette is not in the league, she has a dandy team and is winning games right and left. In fact, we have two winning teams. The last account Douglasville hadn't lost a game this season. Too, Bay Minette furnishes several players on the league teams. Five play on the league-leading Robertsdale nine and two or three on the Rosinton team.

August 12, 1948

RUMOR ABOUT NEW
CIRCUIT SOLICITOR CLARIFIED

COOPER . . . Rumors are like crops in Baldwin County—they grow fast. People have been spreading the word around that Kenneth Cooper, local attorney who was recently elected circuit solicitor, has been called back into the Army, is headed overseas and another man will have to be appointed solicitor. Part of the story is right, and perhaps explains how the rest got started. He has been called back for 60 days of active duty but will return to Bay Minette long before his new duties start in January. He is going to Washington for duty in the civil affairs, or military government duty, for the Army. Lt. Col. Cooper was stationed in Trieste for several months after the war and is considered an expert on economic affairs for that area of Europe. He doesn't expect to go overseas.

INTERESTING . . . Reports from some of the towns in Baldwin about city politics is interesting—but not encouraging. Like here in Bay Minette, a lot of people are interested in getting good people to run for the various city offices but they want the other fellow to run—they don't have time themselves. This is serious. The next four years will be important ones for this county and every town in it. Plenty of good business men should make themselves available to serve their towns even though the criticisms are great and the pay small.

AUTO GROWTH . . . A good indication of a county's growth and prosperity can be obtained from the number of automobiles registered in it. From this standpoint, Baldwin looks good. According to figures released in the *Birmingham News*, comparing the automobile registrations during the first three quarters of 1948 with registrations during the corresponding period of 1946-47, Baldwin has jumped from 17th place among the 67 counties to 12th. During the same period a year ago 6,253 automobile tags were bought here at Bay Minette while this year the figure has jumped to 8,908, for perhaps the biggest percentage increase of any county in Alabama.

COMPARE . . . This means that only 11 counties in Alabama have more motor vehicles than Baldwin. Take a county that had almost the same number of cars as Baldwin in 1947—Covington, for example. Covington had 6,105 but increased to only 6,926 a year later while Baldwin increased from 6,253 to 8,908. Escambia jumped from 4,530 to 5,114. Mobile from 38,265 to 43,341. Houston, which has just 20 more cars registered this year than Baldwin, had 7,807, but had 1,554 more than Baldwin one year ago. So if automobile registrations can be taken as any indication, and they certainly can, Baldwin is one of the fastest growing counties in Alabama.

HOOPER . . . I always enjoy reading the *Auburn Alumnews*, a fine monthly publication sent to the school's alumni. But June's issue particularly interested me because one of the feature articles of the magazine was written by a local Auburn student, Leonard J. Hooper.

AUTHOR . . . The magazine runs a picture of Hooper and gives the following information about the eldest of four sons of Mrs. L.J. Hooper, Sr., Bay Minette: "Leonard Hooper, the author of this interesting history of Auburn's famous landmark Langdon Hall, hails from Bay Minette, Ala. Leonard has been interested in journalism since his high school days, and the B.S. which he will get from Auburn next August (this month) will have an English-Journalism major engraved upon it. Leonard served for three years in the Army during World War II, one and one-half years of which time were spent in Germany. Right now, he's on the staff of the *Plainsman*, the *Glomerata*, and Auburn's handbook, to be published in the fall. After he graduates, Leonard plans to go into the advertising phase of magazine work." Congratulations Leonard on a fine record. It is also good to know you believe in advertising. So do I.

BIG MELON . . . Watermelons even grow big in the city limits of Bay Minette. Uncle John Baggett plucked a 50-pounder out of his garden patch last week. He weighed it to be sure. He said he wasn't sure what variety it was but thought it was a "Florida Giant." Anyway, he said it was round, dark green, big and delicious. Now a 50-pound melon isn't any record for big melons in Baldwin but they certainly don't grow in every hill.

August 26, 1948

MAYORAL RACES ATTRACT 10 GOOD CANDIDATES

MAYORS . . . One thing is sure, following the elections Monday, September 20, Baldwin's municipalities should continue to have good mayors. At least plenty of good men are running. If good men aren't elected, it'll be the voters' fault for not electing the right one in each town. This writer personally knows each candidate for mayor in the county's six incorporated towns. There are 10 candidates.

BAY MINETTE . . . L. D. Owen, Sr., mayor of Bay Minette for the past six years, is not seeking re-election. Mayor Owen is popular but said he is ready to turn the town over to other hands. As mayor, he never had opposition in an election. Eight years ago he ran for council and was high out of a field of 10 candidates. He was named mayor pro tem by the council and when the mayor (me) volunteered into the Army Air Corps, he took over as mayor and served out the remainder of the term of about two years. He was elected four years ago without opposition.

REID . . . Although there are 15 running for council here, M.D. (Max) Reid is running for mayor unopposed. This is a tribute to his popularity in

Bay Minette. If there had been overwhelming opposition to his candidacy, he would have had an opponent because it has been known for several weeks that he was going to make the race. So he has no opposition and his hands are free to make the town an excellent mayor. I sincerely believe he will. Max was appointed to the council to take Mayor Owen's place when he became mayor. He was re-elected to the post four years ago without opposition. Being on the council twice and now to be mayor without opposition is certainly an accomplishment in a town the size of Bay Minette. Head bookkeeper at the Newport Industries, he is also active in civic affairs here and is interested in the town's progress. He'll take over his new duties in October.

ROBERTSDALE . . . Dr. Amos Garrett, who has been Mayor of Robertsdale, and a good one, for ever so many years—18 I believe—decided not to seek re-election. Many people in Robertsdale have told me he could have been re-elected had he chose to run. Be that as it may, for his good work he deserves a rest.

LARRIMORE . . . There are two candidates to succeed Dr. Garrett. One is B.B. Larrimore, hardware man and civic leader of the town. A graduate of Howard College, he has had considerable experience which qualifies him for the post of mayor. As president of the Central Baldwin Chamber of Commerce, he already has a program worked out for Robertsdale. He says he doesn't intend to put the town in a big debt but he wants to pave the street to the school right away. Also the side walks with the cooperation of the town, county Board of Education and possibly others. He wants sanitation for the entire town and intends to improve the public park. One thing he makes clear, and I understand he and his opponent are in agreement on this point at least, he says he intends to keep Mrs. Florence M. Higgins on as town clerk. With this move I am sure everyone will agree.

SELLERS . . . The other candidate is J.D. (Josh) Sellers. He is proprietor of a sundries store in Robertsdale. One of his great loves is baseball. He helped to organize the Robertsdale Baseball Club and is its manager. Popular with his players, he has made his team a big success in the Baldwin County League. If elected, he is anxious to bring new industries into Robertsdale area to offer payrolls to the local citizens. A great believer in Robertsdale and Baldwin County, Mr. Sellers is of the opinion that county and city officials can do much for the continued development of the county. He says if he is elected, he will give his efforts to this end as well as routine city affairs.

DAPHNE . . . His many county friends will be glad to know that J.M. (Matt) Broadus is running for Mayor of Daphne without opposition. About a year ago when the municipality had to go to the courts to get the town's government straightened out, he was appointed mayor. It's a credit to him that he will be elected to a full term unopposed. Mr. Broadus is an electrical contractor and several years ago lived in Bay Minette where he still has scores of friends. Both Daphne and Mr. Broadus are to be congratulated.

SPACE . . . When I started this column, it was my intention to write something about each of the 10 candidates. Since I know too many good things to say about each one, my space has run out this week. But next week I'll have something to say about W. Max Griffin and John G. Evans, Foley candidates; Emery Johnson, who is unopposed for Mayor of Silverhill; Howard Ruge, T.J. Klumpp, Sr., and W.L. McWhite, Fairhope candidates.

ALSO COMING . . . I have been wanting to devote this column to the Bacon-McMillan Manufacturing Company of Stockton for a long time. This fine old company and the grand people behind it make an interesting story. Too many people in Baldwin know too little about Bacon-McMillan as well as some of our other industries. With mental notes already made, you can watch for the story soon. Because of the subject matter (only), it'll be good.

September 2, 1948

SIX MUNICIPALITIES TO ELECT MAYOR, COUNCILMEN

MORE MAYORS . . . Several people have agreed with this column that Baldwin's six municipalities have some fine citizens running for mayor. Last week a brief sketch was given about M.D. Reid, only candidate for mayor of Bay Minette; J.D. Sellers and B.B. Larrimore, candidates for the same office in Robertsdale; and J.M. Broadus, only candidate in Daphne. The other three towns have good men running too—and in each the incumbent is seeking re-election.

SILVERHILL . . . If I remember correctly, Emery Johnson has been mayor of Silverhill since 1936. And he'll be mayor for at least four more years because he has no opposition. In fact, if Mr. Johnson has any opposition anywhere I have never heard about it. He is one of Baldwin's most civic minded and sincerely honest citizens. With these fine attributes, coupled with the love of hard work, it is natural for him to be a leader. And it is encouraging when a community like Silverhill recognizes and honors its able leaders.

FOLEY . . . The mayor of this fine agricultural and tourist town has one of the most responsible jobs of any public official in the entire county. The town of Foley owns and operates the Riviera Utilities which furnishes electrical service to the biggest portion of the population in that end of the county. Of course the utility has a manager, but in the final analysis the responsibility of efficient service rests upon the mayor and town council. Foley and Riviera's customers are fortunate in having Sherman Lemler as the able manager of the utility. He is hailed far and wide for his ability. However, this is beside the subject.

GRIFFIN . . . Seeking re-election for a second term as mayor of Foley is W. Max Griffin, genial and successful oil distributor and business man. He has been keenly interested in civic affairs and believes his area of Alabama should be one of the greatest tourist and recreation spots in the South. The record indicates he has made a good mayor. The people will say what they think about it two weeks from next Monday when they vote.

EVANS . . . The other candidate for the highest office Foley has to offer is John G. Evans. John has made a success at growing flowers. Owning farms near Foley and in Florida, he has become one of the most successful glad producers in the area. Although he has been in the county only 12 years, he has a lot of friends and knows his way around. Two years ago he ran for the State Legislature and although he hardly moved out of his tracks to obtain support, he still received over 1000 votes. Being a great believer in Foley, John is anxious to be mayor so he can put some of his policies into effect.

FAIRHOPE . . . Possibly the hottest city election in the county is the one now in full swing in Fairhope. An organization has been formed called the Better Business Bureau which is opposing the present administration. The opposition is chiefly over the present system of traffic enforcement, according to information received from both sides. Anyway, this is one of the biggest issues.

RUGE . . . Mayor Howard Ruge has been mayor for 14 years and is seeking re-election on his record. I could write at length about Mayor Ruge but have just read what Ed E. Reid, efficient and intelligent Executive Director of the Alabama League of Municipalities, has to say about him in the current issue of the Alabama *Local Government Journal*: "He is one of the finest and most conscientious officials we have ever known. He's been in office a long time and done a great job—but sometimes that is not what the voters want. If they want a good job continued, they'll re-elect Smick Ruge in Fairhope."

KLUMPP . . . Endorsed by the Better Business Bureau for mayor is T.J. Klumpp, Sr. If elected, and he makes as good a mayor as he has been successful in his various business enterprises, he'll do all right by Fairhope. He owns automobile agencies in Fairhope, Robertsdale and Foley. He is also a successful pecan grower, farmer and dairyman. A native of Point Clear, he has previously served on the town council and is well acquainted with the duties and opportunities the mayor of Fairhope has. Having lived there practically all his life, he has seen Fairhope grow into one of the most beautiful small cities in Alabama and it is natural for him to be anxious to see it continue to progress.

McWHITE . . . An independent candidate for mayor of the Eastern Shore town is William L. McWhite. He has never sought public office before. He retired from the Navy in 1945 as a result of combat injuries incurred in World War II. Receiving valuable training in the Navy, he has traveled widely and is vitally interested in his chosen home, Fairhope. He is a member of the Gaston-Lee Post 5660, Veterans of Foreign Wars; also Baldwin County Post 99, American Legion, as well as several other organizations. He is the only World War II veteran running for mayor in the county.

SIX . . . Those six who are elected Monday, Sept. 20, will take office in October.

September 9, 1948

Stockton's Bacon-McMillan company
HIGHLY RATED

STOCKTON . . . People south of Bay Minette know very little about the fine little village of Stockton. And many of the county's best citizens live there. Its citizens never apologize for being from Stockton. They don't because they are proud of it. And people who know Stockton don't blame them. The community has an aristocratic air about it which attracts comment. Many things cause people to visit Stockton, most important of which is perhaps the fact some of the best fresh water fishing anywhere can be found to the west of her. For a rural community, her citizens are prosperous above the average. There are several reasons for this but they all revolve around the Bacon-McMillan Manufacturing Company, Ltd.

VENEER . . . The big furniture factories in Grand Rapids, Michigan, and other   parts north probably know more about Stockton, Alabama, than many citizens in this county. The reason is because of the high grade veneer produced by Bacon-McMillan out of the gum trees that come out of Baldwin's swamps. Yes, Stockton's "Veneer Mill" is known far and wide and it means meat and bread, candy and cake for about 200 families. And many other families receive financial benefits indirectly.

OLD . . . Bacon-McMillan Veneer Company, as it was called until recent years, has been an institution for a long time. It was established by the late "Captain" John McMillan and operated by him for many years, or until he turned it over to the present management before the turn of the last decade. During the war, the plant operated full speed, with much of its machinery and equipment out of date.

NEW . . . Months ago a modernization program was started. Several days ago Paul Corwin and I had an opportunity to look at some of the new equipment. It interested and amazed both of us. They have a new automatic lathe that'll do everything to a gum log including chewing it up into veneer and spitting out the bark. I could fill the rest of this column telling what this lathe will do—but if you ever get the chance go and see it then you'll know as much, or more, than me about it. But the object of the new machine is to make veneer of a better quality, faster and cheaper. It does.

PLYWOOD . . . They also operate a plywood mill. And own a few thousand acres of land. In fact, the operation takes in three main divisions, veneer, plywood and timberland. Under a limited partnership basis all three divisions are under the same management. And rather able management at that.

McINNIS . . . Norman McInnis is the general manager. Under 40 years old, Norman is every inch a hustler—a go-getter if you prefer. He got his experience the hard way, working around saw mills. He beats his men to work every morning and apparently doesn't mind working all hours. A devout church worker, he seems to have a sincere interest in the people working under him. I have been in the plant with him several times and he can call all of the workers, which number about 150, by their first names. And if you ask him about one of them, he seems to have a file of information on each in his mind. Although a comparatively newcomer to the community, he has the respect of all. I think this is because he is honest above question, a hard worker and interested in the welfare of those around him. But he has one bad habit. He never cleans his pipe.

KILLCREASE . . . To Bacon-McMillan, as well as Stockton, Mr. Wallace Killcrease is an institution. He has been bookkeeper, secretary and treasurer for the organization much longer than the 12 years I have known him. He was there for the years Captain John ran the business and judging from his apparent good health, he'll be around many more years. At least everybody hopes so. No one is more devoted to the firm than he is. One of the partners, I believe he thinks of Bacon-McMillan first and himself last. A perfect gentleman, he is a person to whom you enjoy talking. He is too kind to disagree with you, yet you have the feeling he knows much more about any given subject than you do. Unlike the general manager, he has no bad habits.

HASTIE . . . You might go to the plant 50 times and never see Ben Hastie but you can rest assured that if anything goes wrong he'll soon be there. Titles don't interest Ben but he is in charge of the woods and logging which is a big operation in itself. One of the major partners and managers, his advice carries great weight around the place. Comparatively quiet, he isn't the man to waste words but gets good results with those he does use. I have never heard of a person who doesn't like Ben Hastie.

GAUSE . . . Warren D. Gause, known by all his friends as "Bubba," is in charge of sales, as sales manager. And he is ideally suited for the position. He knows his merchandise and has a personality that sort of melts sales resistance. Actually he hasn't had too much selling to do since the war because of the high demand for the quality product they produce. But he keeps up his contacts just the same, ready for a possible rainy day. He was wounded in the right arm in the South Pacific during the war but doesn't complain or let it interfere with his many duties.

OTHERS . . . There are many others who are important in the operation of Bacon-McMillan. But if you get the above four to okay something, you won't need to go further.

December 2, 1948

LITTLE RIVER HUNT GOOD IN SPITE OF HEAVY RAIN

PLENTY . . . Every person I have talked to enjoyed Thanksgiving. They had plenty to eat, lots of them enjoyed plenty of hunting and killed plenty of game. The Bay Minette followers of the local football team had plenty of thrills at the Atmore ball game which we "won" 7 to 7, and certainly every person had plenty of rain. Worst since 1916 Jesse Smith tells me. At least he said the water in the swamps will be higher than at any time since that date. He ought to know. Anyway that's too high for water to get, especially if you are interested in a cabin that wasn't built high enough off the ground on Stiggins Lake.

BUCKS . . . There have been more successful hunts held in past years on the opening of the deer season, and there have been years when far less game was killed. Several of the big hunts had to be called off because of high water. This was the case of the annual hunt of the Baldwin County Hunting Club, which is the oldest of the county hunting clubs. But Warren Gause, Stockton, killed one buck on this preserve, in the Tensaw swamps, just walking along without a drive going on. The Tensaw Hunting Club also had to call off their hunt. These two clubs always kill a number of bucks on their annual hunts.

COUNT . . . It's difficult to get a list of all deer killed during the first few days of the deer season. Several people were kind enough to bring in the names of a few and I ran down the names of other successful hunters with the aid of a few friends. As I write this column Tuesday night, I have the names of 21 who have killed bucks so far this season. This is probably not over one third of those killed in the county but it is most likely more than have been killed in Clarke County. I'll know when I read *The Clarke County Democrat* this week, maybe.

LITTLE RIVER . . . One of the most successful hunts was held on the

Little River Hunting Club which was just organized this past summer. This was their first hunt. The following men aimed straight on this hunt: Thomas E. Phillips, 6 points, Little River; E.L. Phillips, 7 points, Little River; N.M. Mabry, 3 points, Little River. Two were killed on Dr. Fiest's hunt at Tensaw but so far I haven't been able to get their names.

EARLE . . . Thomas Earle had his usual good luck on his hunt at Blacksher. Three of his guests were in luck. J.F. Barnes, manager of Ray E. Loper Lumber Company here, killed his first buck on his first deer hunt. Needless to say he really got a kick out of it. We north Alabamians usually learn a lot by coming south. W.J. Hardin, Bay Minette, and Mr. Higgins, Birmingham, also bagged a buck each.

BAY MINETTE . . . C. LeNoir Thompson gave me the following names of nimrods who killed bucks on the Bay Minette Hunting Club lands on Thanksgiving Day. Three were 8 pointers and one 4 pointer. Oscar Mixon, White House; Alton Tenant, Atmore; Charlie Frank Williams, Hurricane; and a Mr. Ward of Mobile, who was a guest.

LOCAL HUNT . . . One of the successful hunts was held close to town by A.G. Weaver, W.H. Fail, J.B. Beveridge, Wallace Killcrease, and Jesse Smith. Those killing a buck were: A.G. Weaver, George Duck and Andrew Crysell, all local hunters. Crysell also killed another a day or so later on the same lands. Out Rabon way, William Lee Dean killed a 10 pointer on Thanksgiving Day and Woodrow Latham, Perdido, killed a 7 pointer.

BIGGEST . . . To date, the biggest buck I have heard of being killed was a 13 pointer. He was killed by Coby Hall, Rabon, Monday in the fork of Hall's Creek and Little Creek.

January 13, 1949

EMANUEL DAVIDSON TO WORK BACK IN BALDWIN

FINALLY . . . For years friends of Emanuel Davidson, one of Bay Minette and Baldwin County's most popular citizens, have been urging him to retire from his pace killing job of selling groceries for a wholesale concern of Mobile. But his comment was always something like this, "They gave me my start when I had nothing and I'm going to work for them as long as they want or need me." So he stuck on for 30 years. But last week he made it known that in about two months he is going to quit and devote a whole lot of time among the pine trees which belong to him and Leslie Taylor of Robertsdale.

REASON . . . It has been known that it would take a miracle to make him quit, and the miracle happened. His company, Taylor-Lowenstein & Company, has decided to get out of the wholesale grocery business.

AUTOS ON 31 . . . Riding with him to Loxley last Thursday night to attend the More Trees for Baldwin Committee meeting, he was telling of his long service with his company and how he would miss seeing all his friends over the county. It is natural for people to take up habits. One of the unusual habits Emanuel took up while traveling over the county was counting the number of automobiles he passed between Bay Minette and Stapleton. Even while we were talking he was keeping count of the passing cars. Seventeen, he said, when we had only gone about four miles down the road. He said during the depression he would pass only six or seven between here and Stapleton. Now, he said, it will average 34 or 35. So time marches on and Baldwin continues to grow.

COURT . . . Speaking of growth, beginning next Monday Baldwin will have its own circuit court. On that date, at 10 o'clock a.m., the court will have its formal opening here at the courthouse court room. The public is invited to witness the brief but important ceremonies. Although the success of the court will depend mainly on the officials, it will proceed under great difficulties without the wholehearted cooperation and well wishes of the public.

LIGHTS . . . This editor appreciates the many compliments upon the general appearance of *The Times* building since the flood lights have been installed in front to reflect the whiteness of the structure. It was done for several reasons. And, incidentally, I do not object to the many questions being asked about it. S.F. Holmes is the main reason the lights were installed, I guess. Over a year ago, he made himself a committee of one to get Bay Minette better lighted, claiming the town was much too dark at night. He set the example by purchasing an imposing neon sign for the bank. Several others followed suit. He approached *The Times* to do something about this side of town. It's funny how a banker can get results better than other people at times.

DONE . . . We decided to be different and at the same time take advantage of the fact our building is white (It should be, the front has been painted no less than six times). So the lights were ordered eight months back. They were installed last week, at a slight cost. (A friend in Robertsdale happening along while they were being installed said he had two reflectors just like them rusting away in his yard he would have given us had he known—such is life.) And another reason why they were installed. *The Times* not only advocates advertising—she practices what she preaches. Hope you like it, the lights that is.

January 20, 1949

TELFAIR J. MASHBURN, JR., FILLS NEW
CIRCUIT JUDGESHIP

NEW COURT . . . Those who attended the brief ceremonies here Monday morning marking the beginning of Baldwin's new circuit court were impressed. And there was a good attendance. It is unfortunate that all the citizens of the county were not present to hear what was said concerning the new court. If they had been present, they would have gone away with a better understanding and a deeper appreciation of the court and its officials. The desire of the officials to make good and serve the people fairly and intelligently was very much in evidence.

JUDGE . . . The new judge is a strong character. Although he is often referred to as a young judge, Telfair J. Mashburn, Jr., is actually in his early forties. This isn't old to be sure, but a person should be able to get around by that time. Deeply honest, Judge Mashburn prides himself in being just what he is and nothing more. He speaks his mind and lets the chips fall where they may. But when he is wrong, he doesn't mind admitting it. He may not make the most outstanding jurist on earth but if honesty of heart and sincerity of purpose will get him such an honor, he'll have it.

CREDIT . . . He may be the boss on the judge's bench but he readily acknowledges and gives credit to the power behind the bench. In concluding his brief talk at the ceremonies, he said: "I want to introduce the person without whom I wouldn't be here—Ida Bell." Mrs. Telfair J. Mashburn, Jr., quietly stood up.

SOLICITOR . . . The new circuit solicitor is Kenneth Cooper, of the Rosinton Coopers. Kenneth hasn't had much opportunity to practice law because just at the time he graduated from the University of Alabama, Uncle Sam needed his services in the Army. He stayed in during the war and after until last March, making an outstanding war record and coming out a Lt. Colonel. What he lacks in experience he'll get in hard work and determination. And he has the character and background to make a good law-enforcing solicitor.

OTHERS . . . The two others who will, in an official capacity, help make the court a rapid dispenser of justice are Mrs. Ora S. Nelson and Mrs. Alice J. Duck. Mrs. Nelson is the court reporter and you can rest assured she'll keep the court notes and records straight. Mrs. Duck will hold the same job with the 28th Judicial Circuit she did with the 22nd, circuit clerk and register. So she already knows what it is all about.

LeNOIR . . . Assisting in the prosecution in the new court will be C. LeNoir Thompson, the new county solicitor. A native of Baldwin, LeNoir really enjoys practicing law. And he should because he got through law school the hard way, attending school and studying at night while earning a living for himself and family during the day. A holder of many jobs, I believe he prides the one he has just taken over above them all.

March 24, 1949

Baldwin County Hospital Association
NAMED

IMPORTANT . . . Last week the County Commission named the members of the Baldwin County Hospital Association. Since the citizens of the county are vitally interested in better hospital and health facilities, they will be looking to this group of men for action and intelligent leadership in finding ways to get the new hospitals built. And looking over the names of the 15-man association, a person can readily assume Baldwin citizens have every reason to be optimistic about the hospital development. The group as individuals have considerable influence in their various communities and the people will listen attentively to any and all recommendations they make.

MEETING . . . The association will have its first meeting next Thursday afternoon in the courthouse to organize and begin formulating plans to solve the hospital problems of the county. Naturally the citizens will anxiously await action.

ACQUAINTED . . . The association is of such importance it will probably be a good idea to give a little information about each member of the group. Of course most of the men are known widely but it is likely there are some people in the county who are not acquainted with some of the members. Following is a brief, very brief, sketch on each of them. A man was named from each precinct.

NAMES . . . Representing Precinct 1 is Frank Earle, naturally, of Blacksher. If there is a person who has been in Baldwin County over a month and hasn't learned who Mr. Earle is all he has to do is ask his neighbor. You can't be brief in writing about him as he has so many titles, so we won't even start here. Robert A. Smith of Latham is a timber and sawmill man, successful too. Y.A. Cox, Stockton, has a number of interests including a directorship of the Baldwin County Bank. His main interest centers around his mercantile business in Stockton, however. The same thing applies to Emanuel Davidson of Bay Minette as to Mr. Earle. He is also well and favorably known.

PERDIDO . . . Harold T. McGill, Perdido, also has a number of interests besides being a leader in his community. His main business is running his store. M.G. Harrison, Stapleton, may not be so well known as some of the others but those who do know him say he is a fine person. He is woodsman and timber buyer for Ray E. Loper Lumber Co., here. Peter Morris, Gateswood, is a successful community leader, farmer and school bus operator. A.A. Trione, Daphne, is well known over the county and is in the general mercantile business in Daphne. Walter Hammond, Sr., Robertsdale, is well known, has a wide variety of interests, including operating what is perhaps the biggest grocery business in the county.

FAIRHOPE . . . Carl Bloxham, Fairhope, has been a civic and business leader for a few more years than I can remember. He is in the real estate and insurance business in Fairhope. H. Kennedy, Summerdale, is a successful shipper, farmer, produce buyer, seed and soybean man. C.S. Faircloth, Lillian, is a timber and turpentine man and is well known in that field. J.A. Pilgrim, Sr., Elberta, has more interests than I can mention. He deals in real estate, is a timber operator, inventor, moving picture owner, etc. Max Lawrenz, Foley, likes to talk about his timber and seafood businesses, but he works the hardest at operating one of the biggest hardware stores I have ever been in. Lee Calloway, Canal, or Ft. Morgan road, also has a number of businesses, including fish, tourist cottages, grocery and real estate.

OBVIOUS . . . There are a few definite conclusions that can be drawn from the above list. 1. They are all successful in their line or lines of activity. 2. Land owners predominate, which means they will think twice before suggesting a raise in ad valorem taxes to build anything. 3. Being hard businessmen, when they recommend something you can rest fairly well assured it will work. 4. They have a hard and important job to do for Baldwin County.

April 21, 1949

HUNDREDS GATHER TO HONOR BROTHER A.D. DUCK

BRO. DUCK . . . One of the most honored and beloved old men in Baldwin County is Brother A.D. Duck of Cross Roads. Sunday, people, lots of them, gathered to pay him tribute on his 87th birthday. Celebrating his birthday has been a custom for several years and annually his hundreds of friends gather for the occasion. Naturally he isn't in as good health as he was several years ago but he still looks fine and was able to enjoy seeing his many admirers Sunday at the Cross Roads Church.

FIFTEEN . . . Bro. Duck has 15 children and he told me Sunday that 12 of them are still living, most of them in Baldwin County. He is one of those fairly rare persons who had sons in both World Wars. T.V., the oldest of the 15, and the late R.S. (Terry and Bob, that is) participated in the first war while Horace was involved in the second one.

KINDNESS . . . Nothing but good is ever said about Bro. Duck. A preacher for years and years, he has spread joy and kindness throughout this area. An humble man, it is little wonder so many people admire him. One of his admirers is Ort H. Ertzinger of this city. Ort has been sick for the past several weeks but he felt good enough to compose a poem about Bro. Duck. *The Times* policy is not to print poetry (because most of it isn't poetry) written by amateurs. But because of our respect for both of these two gentlemen, an exception is being made right here. Following are three of the five verses:

POEM . . . Today we meet to honor one
Who lowly paths has trod;
Who spent his life in Christian works
And followed close to God.
From early youth unto this day
He sought not wealth or fame,
But gave himself, without reserve
To serve in Jesus' name.
So while he lives, we honor him,
And wish him world's of luck,
This grand, good man, our saintly friend,
Beloved Brother Duck.

RETURN . . . As of right now we go back to our long standing policy of not printing poetry. Please don't ask us to make exceptions.

GLADS . . . We are hearing lots about our potatoes but glads have also started moving from the county. At least two Foley growers have started shipping. John Evans, who has become one of the most successful growers in the section, is expressing glads all over the country. John says so far he has been fairly well pleased with the price but doubts if it will stay satisfactory. Top flowers are bringing as high as $2.00 per dozen and he sold a few of his early ones for as much as $2.50. The growers have sold a lot of glads for 25 cents per dozen and, as John says, probably will again this year.

SUCCESS . . . There is a lot to growing glads which doesn't meet the eye. One of the biggest parts of the business is selling bulbs. John works hard and has succeeded where many others have failed.

ATTICUS . . . One of Baldwin's best boosters is Atticus Mullin, old warhorse of *The Montgomery Advertiser*. During the past several weeks he has written many fine articles about our farming operations. Thanks Atticus. We appreciate your fine publicity.

June 9, 1949

NEW HOMES ARE GOING UP THROUGHOUT BALDWIN

HOMES . . . It is pretty much the same way all over Baldwin County. But it's more so in Bay Minette right at this time. Many new homes are going up. New homes have been built fast here ever since the war but the type going up now are a bit unusual for Bay Minette. One thing has always impressed me about homes here, most of them are average in size and cost. Few are big. None you would call mansions like it takes $50,000 to build. This means of course that most citizens here are just average—what money there is here is fairly evenly divided, no one person owns the town. This is in contrast to a lot of towns this size, in fact, most all of them.

COMPARE . . . Take Fairhope, Foley, Atmore and Brewton. In these towns you can find any number of "very expensive" homes. Probably Brewton is the outstanding example of all small cities which has so many mansions. There are any number of homes there which cost as much as any two here.

SLIGHT CHANGE . . . But this situation is gradually changing. More big fine homes are now being built, or have been built within the past few months, than since the town became the county seat back in hectic 1901. Of course most of the homes built here have been in the five to ten thousand dollar class. But I can name at least nine that will go above $10,000 which will have been completed in 1949. The Tax Equalization Board has already said I don't know anything about tax values so naturally they won't pay any attention to what is said here.

THE NINE... Houses in this class recently completed are those belonging to: Dr. and Mrs. W. Bruce Nelson, Dr. and Mrs. P.A. Bryant, Mr. and Mrs. N.P. Beasley, Mr. and Mrs. L.P. Tucker, Mr. and Mrs. W.H. Oswell. Those a-building are: Mr. and Mrs. G.M. Lambert, Mrs. G.W. Robertson, Mr. and Mrs. Doug Bullington, Mr. and Mrs. Lee Smith. Even so, still the biggest home here is the one belonging to Mr. and Mrs. L.T. Rhodes, Sr., which was built while Mr. Hoover was president.

LOOKERS... And judging from those who go from house to house on Sundays looking at and criticizing the new homes, a lot more people here are dreaming of new homes. Easily 200 have been built since the war. You would think that the shortage would soon be over. But try to find a house for rent. You'll be lucky to find an apartment. Of course other towns in the county are the same way. The 1950 census figures are anxiously awaited to see which towns have made the fastest growth during the decade. Wanna bet?

LOST... Seems the older you get the more friends you lose via the way of the grim reaper. Last week saw the loss of two friends and two splendid Baldwin citizens. They were J. Shambo of Daphne and J.B. McGrew of Elberta. Mr. Shambo didn't get to town often but when he did he usually came by this office, and it was always good to see him. Mr. McGrew of course was well known all over the county. He served as a member of the County Commission and was a member of the Tax Equalization Board at the time of his death, having served on it a number of years.

FULL COLONEL... Friends of T.M. Faris, popular agricultural agent of the L. & N. R.R., will have to pay him a mite more respect now. Uncle Sam has just given him the permanent rank of a full Colonel in the transportation corps. Tom Faris went into the last war from the reserve in 1941 as a captain. He served as a commander of troop transports in the Caribbean area during the early part of the war and then later went to England. He got out of the army with bad feet and the rank of Lt. Colonel. Congratulations Col. Faris. I just hope we don't have another shooting war in which case this First Lt. might have to bow and scrape to you.

HAY FEVER . . . Got hay fever? Me too. Just discovered the discovery of a new medicine for it, the 1647th such discovery during the past few months. My fingers are crossed—so far it is working good, thank you.

June 23, 1949

Many bankers are being overworked

BANKERS . . . I am about convinced that most people (myself included) have had the wrong idea about bankers all along. Even with all their holidays and what appears to be short working hours they still must have to work awfully hard. Obviously the 9 'til 2:30 banking schedule does not include their entire working day. At least many of them are overworked, according to health statistics. No doubt it is the worry of bad loans along with the thousands of other details of running a bank which eventually gets many of them.

OVERWORK . . . Of course people around these parts have known for a long time that the local bank's president, Frank Holmes, has been working too hard. His friends, which are legion, have warned him about it. But he enjoys hard work. He never knew anything else. As it always does, it finally caught up with him. He is going to have to take things easy for several weeks, part of which will have to be in the Mobile hospital where he was taken last Friday. In the meantime the customers of the Baldwin County Bank will have to get along without one of the most popular bank presidents in Alabama.

You can travel far and wide, let them know you are from Bay Minette and someone in almost any crowd will say, "How is my friend, Frank Holmes?" And now all his local friends are asking the same question.

OTHERS . . . And Kirby Wharton, one of Alabama's younger bank presidents, of the Bank of Fairhope, found out that a person can't work day and night always. He has been told also to take life a little easier. Although he keeps well in touch with things, he has been spending fewer hours in his office. Alfred Neumann, of the State Bank of Elberta, has been a human dynamo at work for a number of years. And he still hasn't eased up much but manages to get off fishing nearly every Thursday afternoon. And other county bank heads, Frank Sanders, Farmers & Merchants Bank of Foley, and Mr. Ellis, Central Baldwin Bank of Robertsdale, also know what long working hours are.

STRONG . . . Guess hard work is one thing that accounts for the fact that Baldwin has five of the strongest rural banks in Alabama, with total assets of 11 to 12 million dollars. Strong banks are fine. And so are strong, healthy bankers. Slow up men. Go fishing because most of us will pay our notes anyway.

BROTHERS . . . There are so many things for a country editor to learn. Have been knowing Charles W. Snyder, who lives near the Stockton-Perdido road just north of Rabun, for 13 years. And have been knowing Alford W. Snyder of Spanish Fort for several years, too, but didn't know the two men were brothers until this week. Mr. Charlie, who is about 75, has been in poor health for a few years and doesn't get down as often as he used to. But I was talking to his younger brother, Mr. Alford, Monday and he tells me Mr. Charlie is still doing a little farming and that he has some of the tallest corn this year he has ever seen. He said he measured one stalk, which was about average for the field, and that it was 13 ½ feet tall. He has about four acres in this one field. And that is tall corn even in Baldwin County. At 75, Mr. Charlie is young as Snyders go. He lost his mother in Michigan last week. She was 97 years old.

????? . . . It's hard to understand. I think the Stanley boys of Greenville and George Carleton of Grove Hill have gotten together after all these years of feuding and fighting. Week before last Webb and Glenn, of *Greenville*

Advocate fame, went over to Clarke County to go fishing with George. This was surprising enough but when the Stanleys go back to Butler County and run a picture of George on the front page of the *Advocate* with a big string of fish they claim they caught in Clarke County, I am amazed no end. Maybe it is a diabolical scheme to try and equal the many fine fishing stories which come out of Baldwin County.

July 7, 1949

J. D. Hand owned much of Bay Minette town site

HAND . . . There is no other as significant as the name "HAND" in the history of Bay Minette. The town's chief street is Hand Avenue. Abstractors, lawyers and others who have reason to look at land titles read about Hand's Addition to the Town of Bay Minette, and this addition takes in most of the town now. There is a significant reason for all of this—mainly because of the late J.D. Hand.

HELP MATE . . . Another important factor in Bay Minette's indebtedness to the Hand family was caused by the above Mr. Hand's wife, Mrs. Mattie Hand Crockett, who is visiting here from San Antonio, Texas, this week. She had a great influence in the early planning of the town. Her husband laid out the town and no doubt it was largely through her influence that all the streets in Hand's Addition are 100 feet wide, making Bay Minette one of the most perfectly laid out towns anywhere. She wanted wide streets for several reasons, one of which was so there would be plenty of room for oak trees to grow. And it was through her leadership that many of the fine oak trees now living in this town were planted around 1900 and later. She was also the main leader in getting the present Baptist church building erected.

ORT . . . Ort H. Ertzinger has written some of the highlights of this couple's endeavors for Bay Minette. Let him tell you some of the rest of the story: Mrs. Mattie Hand Crockett of San Antonio, Texas, is visiting with friends and relatives in Bay Minette for a short time, spending most of her time with the Charles C. Hand family and with Mrs. Belle H. Wooley, her relatives.

PIONEER . . . Mrs. Crockett is truly a pioneer in Bay Minette. She came here as the bride of J.D. Hand who had purchased some 10,000 acres of land before the present town site of Bay Minette was laid out. J.D. Hand is the founder of Bay Minette as it is now known and laid out the Hand Land Company addition to the town; which includes the place where the court house now stands and all the land north of the railroad which is divided into lots. Mr. Hand built the lovely home on Second Street where Judge W.D. Stapleton now lives and Mrs. Hand, (at that time) presided in the home with grace and charm and through her many courtesies to the people of Bay Minette, endeared herself to all. Mr. Hand operated a large sawmill about two miles west of Bay Minette at a place then known as D'Olive, but now almost completely abandoned. Mr. Hand in laying out the town of Bay Minette, donated the present cemetery site, the various church sites and the present playground square north of the Presbyterian church, and had several squares set aside for hospital, industrial school and other public purposes. He later died and is resting in the upright vault in the center of the present cemetery.

LEADER . . . Mrs. Mattie Hand was at one time Worthy Grand Matron of the Order of Eastern Star of the State of Alabama and is the only Grand Matron ever provided by Bay Minette. She was always extremely interested in making Bay Minette a lovely place and headed the Civic Club for many years and was instrumental in "cleaning up" the streets, court house square and unsightly places around town, while it was being built up. After Mr. Hand's death, Mrs. Hand kept her lovely home open to the social needs of the entire town and few were the weeks when some social event did not take place in her home. Many of the older residents of the town recall most pleasantly her hospitality.

TEXAS . . . Mrs. Hand later married W.S. Crockett, who came to Bay

Minette about the year 1914, and with him moved to Texas where she has resided ever since. Mr. Crockett has two sons who went with them to Texas and after Mr. Crockett's death, some years later, Mrs. Crockett remained in Texas to be near her stepsons Robert and Gibson. Mrs. Crockett, during her stay in Bay Minette, will be given many social courtesies by her friends, many of whom are having happy times recalling the "old days" in Bay Minette while she was its leading lady.

October 6, 1949

Baldwin well represented at Alabama State Fair

STATE FAIR . . . Baldwin is being well represented, and presented, at the Alabama State Fair in Birmingham this week. This is fine. It is a good way for Baldwin to get a lot of good, profitable advertising because a lot of people attend this annual event in the big city. I didn't have an opportunity to see the exhibit before it left here last Saturday but those who did say it is a credit to the county. The county chambers of commerce and other organizations are sponsoring the exhibit and Bay Minette's Bootsie Noonan designed and prepared the exhibit—then took it to Birmingham and set it up. Of course he had some help but County Agent Frank Turner said Bootsie furnished most of the ideas—and work.

PICTURE . . . *The Times* has been promised a picture of the exhibit. If we get it, we'll present it to Baldwin citizens in the columns of this newspaper next week. Also a report on the reception it received while in Birmingham from Mr. Turner, who is attending the fair this week.

SUGGESTION . . . Why not return the exhibit to Baldwin and put it on display for our own people. Plenty of Baldwin's own citizens don't know all the things we do have in this county. Am sure the citizens of Elberta would like to have it in their annual Elberta Community Fair which is coming up soon.

GOTTLER . . . Speaking of Elberta and the fair always reminds me of John P. Gottler because he has been one of the main springs behind the success of the fine fair for years. That community's postmaster had a vacation recently and took a trip to Philadelphia and other points North. Several months ago it was reported in this column that sometimes this Fall the nationally circulated magazine, *Country Gentleman*, was going to publish an article about Elberta and Baldwin County. While in Philadelphia, John paid a visit to Curtiss Publishing Company and *Country Gentleman* to check up on the article. They let him read the article and see the pictures that will appear eventually in the big magazine. They told John that the article is of such nature that it can be published anytime—or "time copy" as we newspapermen call it. But he did say the article is excellent and will be a big boost to big Baldwin.

BROTHERS . . . E.H. Brothers, formerly assistant county agent of Baldwin and until recently associated with Riemers Farm in Elberta, has a job as supervisor on a big farm near Philadelphia. John said he went by looking for him. Brothers was out somewhere on the big vegetable farm and to locate him the girl in the office just called him by two-way radio. I'll agree with John that this is farming in class when you can call all over the place via radio. He said Brothers was in charge of 900 acres of vegetables, which included about 200 acres of spinach. John said he likes his work but misses Baldwin.

MANY FARMERS . . . Don't think I have ever seen more Baldwin farmers gathered at the same time as attended the annual meeting of the Silverhill Farmers Association in Silverhill Saturday. And they had good reason to be there. The some 1100 members all had a slice of the big $27,000 dividend coming to them and many of them were there to get it.

SUCCESSFUL . . . This is one of the most successful farmer co-ops in Alabama, or anywhere else for that matter. Under the able management of Harry Marker, the cooperative did over $700,000 worth of business last year. Although selling to the farmers on a small margin of profit, they still rebated the members the above amount. A. Anderberg is president of the association.

November 10, 1949

Brother A. D. Duck lived
WHAT HE PREACHED

GOD FEARING MAN . . . Loved and respected by all who knew him, Baldwin lost one of her oldest and finest citizens last week when Brother A.D. Duck died at the age of 87. An humble, God fearing man, many are the tales of his kind deeds and Christian living. He was one person who always lived the way he preached. We never heard a critical word about this fine old gentleman and he always had an encouraging word for the thousands who loved him so well. There will be stories of Bro. Duck's goodness for years to come.

WINTER . . . The days are getting shorter . . . that's a sure sign winter is on the way . . . most everybody thought it was here a few weeks ago, but the cold weather just stayed long enough for the garages to do a thriving business in anti-freeze . . . anti-freeze does wonders for an automobile, but a lot of humans bring on highway tragedies, broken homes, business bankruptcies, etc., by trying the same idea on themselves . . . solutions with alcohol bases don't mix at all with traffic and business.

Mr. Plunkett says the British treasury and American women have a lot in common . . . they're both having trouble with their poundage . . . which prompts us to ask why the British haven't followed the example of a lot of American women and squeezed themselves a little tighter . . . the answer is simple . . . Uncle Sam still has plenty of money and we like the British . . . the British know it, too . . . after all, King Arthur and Sir Gallahad are our ancestors as well as theirs.

Speaking of Uncle Sam, he always helps those in distress . . . except the Russians and they haven't realized yet just how distressing their situation is . . . Stalin and Vishinsky haven't let them in on the secret . . . but the Germans reaped the results of Hitler's thinking he could get along by alienating the whole world, so someone ought to pass along to the Russians the well-known Biblical verse, "As ye sow, so shall you reap" . . . the world is currently missing Hitler in a very pleasant manner.

Tomorrow is Armistice Day and it reminds us that, in 1918, they fought a war to end wars . . . just another case where the statesmen were wrong in their assumptions . . . that wasn't any plaything we were embroiled in from 1941 to 1945 . . . guess politics and wars will always be with us unless, of course, the world chooses to adhere more closely to the Golden Rule . . . there are several million persons who talk the Golden Rule much better than they practice it . . . talk is usually cheap but actions speak louder than words . . . somebody ought to remind Joe Stalin of that.

This is American Education Week. If you haven't already visited your local school to see what's going on, you ought to . . . the advances in education since you last answered the roll call will probably be an education to you . . . however, if you just can't get there, the best way to keep up with educational progress—and every other kind of progress—in Baldwin County is by subscribing to this newspaper . . . we like Baldwin County more than any other newspaper alive . . . read our paper and prove it to yourself . . . see you next Thursday, probably.

December 29, 1949

Resolution: Work less but more
effectively

1950 . . . I have little reason to complain about 1949. One thing it has done to me that I don't like is 1949 has made me a whole year older than I was at the end of 1948. Older people may slow up some but it appears to me that time passes a lot faster as you put distance behind you. So my main resolution for the New Year is—not to work harder, but more effectively and less.

GOOD HUNT . . . Went on my first hunt of the year Monday and while there I enjoyed it so much it occurred to me that I should be a little more sensible and go more often in the future. Considered by all who are privileged to attend, the best hunt held in this county every year is that given by the Old Island Hunting Club. It is always a successful hunt. Mr. Jewel Smith and Mr. Henry Bryars are the hosts at the event and they always put it over in a big way. Fewer deer were killed this year than usual but it wasn't the hosts' fault, nor the deer.

SHOTS . . . Once the drive got underway, the guns shooting sounded more like a dove shoot than a deer hunt. Emanuel Davidson said he counted over 60 shots that he heard. But out of all this shooting five bucks were brought in. At least two others were knocked down but got away, which is one of the more unfortunate things of a deer hunt. The successful hunters were Dr. P.A. Bryant, George Stuart (George also killed one last Saturday), Buddy McDonald, Leroy Ruple and Hamilton Catrett. I won't name the long list who lost their shirt tails as a result of bad shells, or perhaps poor aim. Three of the above gentlemen got their faces bloodied because it was the first deer they had ever killed.

GOOD EATS . . . Besides the bountiful supply of deer, another thing that makes this one of the best hunts each year is the fact that the hosts feed the guests at the end of the hunt. And I mean they really feed you.

JOSH SELLERS . . . Ed E. Reid, executive secretary of the Alabama League of Municipalities, knows a good city mayor when he sees one in action. Listen to what he says about one of Baldwin's good mayors: "We've pointed out so many times in this column that a very real community service is being performed every day in a dozen ways by the officials of our small towns. We are always impressed with this fact when we go into the smaller communities. Right in line with this thought, we were thinking a day or two ago about the fine job that Mayor J.D. Sellers is doing for his people in Robertsdale. No official in Alabama has been more interested in doing constructive things than Josh Sellers. Recently we had a note from him telling us about his municipal paving program. Before that, he was working on plans to buy the local electric system. He's always doing things to improve the community life of Robertsdale. We salute men like Josh Sellers who are rendering a real and unselfish service for the betterment of Alabama communities."

MUMBLINGS
THROUGH THE
NINETEEN-FIFTIES

∾

January 19, 1950

MIKE KAISER AND SONS BIG OPERATION

VEGETABLES . . . Winter vegetables are coming to the forefront in Baldwin County, thanks to a few aggressive farmers and citizens in the Foley-Elberta area. This is particularly true with two new crops, broccoli and cauliflower. And because of these two crops this county's farmers are receiving another wave of good publicity.

WORTH SEEING . . . This writer had been getting a lot of information about the fine work being done by Mike Kaiser and Sons, Elberta, and Gulf Frosted Foods, Foley. However, it wasn't until Tuesday that I had the opportunity to see the big operations first hand. It was at a meeting called by the Extension Service and the State Department of Agriculture at which buyers from over the entire country were invited to offer their suggestions and advice to the local growers and processors on how to sell their products to the most people. But you can read about this meeting elsewhere in *The Times*—I want to tell you a little about the personalities involved in the venture.

FORESIGHTED . . . Mike, Jr., and John Kaiser are the two enterprising brothers who are putting the Elberta end of the deal over. Showing they have great faith in what they are doing, they have made a big investment in machinery, equipment and buildings to grow, properly process and package their vegetables. They are developing the idea of cooling vegetables to about 35 degrees within a few minutes after they are harvested. By doing this and keeping them at this temperature they will stay at their fresh best for days. They will tell you that if the vegetables are allowed to stay hot very long after they are gathered they will deteriorate in food value and taste.

COUSIN . . . John and Mike's first cousin, Paul, Jr., is associated with W.M. Carmichael of Gulf Frosted Foods. Paul is on the production end and Bill takes care of the processing. Both concerns have learned that putting the vegetables in attractive packages is important in getting people to buy them from the grocery stores. In order to get the packages over the country in good shape, they use refrigerated trucks and airplanes. So you can see what a big business this is getting to be. To give you another idea, John and Mike employ about 60 people. Besides this, many other farmers have put in smaller acreages of vegetables that will be processed through the above concerns. And the variety of vegetables which can be properly grown is almost unlimited in this county.

ADVERTISING . . . And one of the things we like best about the deal is that all the packages have the Alabama addresses on them. This will furnish us good advertising for the many other products that Baldwin has to put on the buyers market.

NEWS . . . Sunday's *Birmingham News* had a full page of pictures and a story by Jack House, state news editor, about the above new developments. This is just one of the many papers which has given the idea wide publicity.

TYPICAL. . . A letter just received from Paul Corwin, director industrial division, Montgomery Chamber of Commerce, and former manager of the Bay Minette Chamber of Commerce, typifies the reception the Baldwin vegetables are receiving. Listen to Paul: "I could not help but drop you a line to tell you of the superior quality of the Baldwin County grown broccoli. John Kaiser, of Elberta, was kind enough to send me several packages by a friend of mine who was in his office recently, and without a doubt it was the best I have ever eaten. You know it is with a great deal of pleasure that I note Baldwin's moving ahead with the fine crop." Thanks, Paul.

January 26, 1950

The Times WILL BE FAIR AND NEUTRAL

HAT IN RING . . . This writer, as you may have learned by now, qualified for the office of state senator this week.

FOR FREE . . . Of course I could tell you why, the reasons you should vote for me, etc., right here in this column. It would cost me a lot less and be much easier than using other methods. But other candidates for this office don't have a newspaper and not desiring to take unfair advantage of any person—even an opponent—I hereby want it publicly known that *The Baldwin Times* is going to be fair and neutral in this race. Even though the editor and publisher of *The Times* is prejudiced in the senate race, he has instructed his two assistant editors to have the paper treat all state senatorial candidates just alike.

COLUMN . . . So just to make sure I do not use this column to my own advantage during the race it is going to be written by someone else during the next several weeks of the campaign and Bob Morrissette will write the editorials.

ROUGH . . . It's kinda bad for me to have to buy advertising from my own newspaper to help get my story across to the people. But that's just what I'm going to do. Other candidates have the equal privilege.

FAIR . . . Now could I be any fairer?

THANKS . . . I'm going to miss writing this column. And I hope you'll miss it a little too. But I'll be writing it again soon.

May 4, 1950

SIX SENIORS IN BALDWIN COUNTY HIGH SCHOOL BAND

(This week's Byways guest columnist is George "Bootsie" Noonan, owner of the Noonan Advertising Service and leader of the Baldwin County High School Band.)

I was asked to write this column about bands in general, however, since it's almost graduation time, I would like to single out the six graduating seniors that are in our band. I am very proud of these young people for their work in the band as well as their other activities. Each one has made one or more outstanding contributions to their school.

GAYNELL McELHANEY . . . is one of our oldest and most dependable trumpet players, is an "A" student and has always carried an overload in school work with ease. She plays piano, is active in Girl Scout work and school clubs and plays trumpet in the orchestra. She also was selected to work with the Blood Testing unit that is in the County.

SUE HARRIS . . . (She is the red head that works in Hardy's Restaurant). Sue is a charter member in the present band, playing clarinet. She keeps up with our money and usually keeps everyone in line—all ages, boys and girls. She was one of the hardest workers on the Annual staff this year, too. Mr. Daniels recognized her ability and had her working in the office one period each day. In addition to all of this, she usually catches a shift at Hardy's.

SABRA STOUGH . . . has been one of our drum majors since the band was organized. She has always done an outstanding job with the band. She has been selected Miss BCHS of 1949-50, May Queen and has won a number of other honors. Always polite and friendly and usually on time, usually that is, she is a credit to our band.

FREDDY POSTMA . . . joined the band as a bass drummer—soon decided to play trombone. Six weeks after he started, he was playing with the band, an unusual feat. He is president of the Band Club and has done a fine job. He is always willing to help in any way. One week during football season when our bass horn player was going to be absent, Freddy volunteered to play it. In two days he learned to play the saxophone and appeared with the band that week. He also "lugged" that same horn 28 miles during Mardi Gras to help us out of a tight spot. You can't forget things like that.

BROOKS McDILL . . . is one of our best saxophone players. He is an outstanding member of our newly formed high school dance orchestra. Brooks is known all over the state for the fine 4-H Club calves he raises. Every time he enters a calf show he comes home with a ribbon. He is a member of the Glee Club and Camera Club, having taken a leading part in both of these organizations. Incidentally, he is going to Troy next fall to study music. He is planning to be a band director.

JOHNNY WILSON . . . is another charter member of the band, playing saxophone. Johnny has always been a worker in the band. You could depend on him to do his part and several others. He is another Camera Club fiend, doing a lot of picture work for the school Annual for the past several years. Probably his biggest contribution to the school is the fine Annual that he and his staff have just completed. One look at that and you can tell that he has been a busy man the past year, and on top of this, he makes good grades, very good in fact.

Won't you agree that these young people are "tops"? It has been a pleasure for me to have been associated with them and the band and school will miss them next year. But we would like to wish them the Best of Luck.

May 11, 1950

RUNOFFS IN THREE BALDWIN COUNTY RACES

By Bob Morrissette, Jr.

POLITICS . . . This is a subject that has grown rather cold in the past few days after some eight weeks of intensive campaigning in both county and state elections. We predict it will get hot again after folks have had a breathing spell. Naturally there were some disappointments over the first primary results—among both voters and candidates. There always are. However, it must be remembered that one of the primary requisites of a democracy is majority rule. Anyway, there will be other elections—for both candidates and voters.

RUNOFFS . . . As most of you know, all county races were decided on May 2nd, with the exception of three offices. The State Representative race will see incumbent L. W. Brannan, Jr., Foley attorney and turpentine operator, against Jameal Kahalley, Bay Minette businessman. Taylor Wilkins, of Bay Minette, is seeking a second term as Sheriff against Norman Durant, veterans training coordinator and Bay Minette councilman. Running it off for Second District County Commissioner are Green Jordan, Bay Minette businessman, and R. J. "Jack" Robertson, Bay Minette farmer and cattleman. Biggest problem facing some of the candidates will be getting voters back to the polls in numbers—especially if there is no runoff in the governor's race.

NEW CLUBHOUSE . . . Robertsdale VFW Post 5226 members received a nice boost in their drive to raise funds for a new clubhouse this week. Post Commander Mike Giuliani of Loxley informed us this week that A. Bertolla & Sons had donated an Angus calf to the group. The calf will be auctioned Monday at the Robertsdale Livestock Auction sale.

APPRECIATION . . . We would like to express our thanks to the guest writers of this column while Editor Jimmy Faulkner was "politicking."

You supplied us and *Times* subscribers with many interesting facts in your varied fields. Jimmy is still recuperating from his successful Senate race but promises to be back at his post next week.

May 18, 1950

WRITING A COLUMN EASIER
THAN SOME THINGS

"REST" . . . It's good to be writing my column again after a number of weeks "rest." At least I was resting from writing this column. Incidentally, writing this column is much easier than some things I have done. I refer more specifically to activities participated in about three months before May 2nd. It's a funny thing though, while I wasn't writing the column hundreds of things popped into my mind of what I would like to write about. But, like talking, some things are best unwritten.

THANKS . . . Want to thank all the guest writers who filled this column for me each week. They did a fine job and I appreciate it. In fact, most of them wrote such good columns they sort of showed me up.

HAPPENINGS . . . So many things have happened during the last few months that it is difficult to know which are the most important. Of course the elections of the first primary took place. The first primary was the climax to politics in Alabama for this year. By May 2nd both the candidates and the voters were so tired of politics that few people seem to have much interest for the runoff races. Another important development, one which comes every year instead of every two like elections, is the potato digging season. And that is always a busy time in Baldwin. It's the time of year when farmers' tempers are short, shippers' shorter and bankers go through sleepless nights.

BLACK GOLD . . . Perhaps the most important recent development of all though is the discovery of oil right across the line from Baldwin in Clarke County. I have talked to a number of oil people during the past few weeks and they seem to be in agreement that Baldwin will soon have several producing fields. A number of wells are in prospect of being drilled. One is almost completed three miles north of Stockton. Another is planned across the river from the Clarke well in Baldwin. And another two or three miles south of the well dug at Lottie several months ago. This well is supposed to have had some oil in it but not enough for production. And a number of other wells are in the rumor stage. Better watch out Texas.

OFF SET . . . An oil man explained to me the other day that sometimes a well is dug at an angle. I believe he called these "off set" wells. The more I think about this type of well the more I am convinced that this is the type that is producing in Clarke County. The people from that county are all time coming to Baldwin to catch our fish and kill our game. They liked what they get in Baldwin so good they just angled them an oil well under the Alabama river and started pumping up our oil. And I'll bet George Carleton gave them the idea.

PICTURE . . . Come to think of it, the picture at the top of this column is slightly out of date. Personally I like it better than the ones that are up to date.

June 15, 1950

LIVESTOCK TOUR BEING HELD IN BALDWIN

NEW TOUR . . . Congratulations to Hubert M. Hall, Bay Minette lawyer, cattle raiser and president of the Baldwin County Cattlemen's Association, and others who are responsible for the idea of having a livestock tour in Baldwin. With the first tour being held today and with the fine program arranged, it is bound to be a success. Baldwin is known far and wide for its potatoes and annual Potato Tour, and since cattle has become such an important part of our economics it is just a natural to invite citizens into the county to see what we are doing in the way of livestock production.

FINE MAN . . . It's good to have such an outstanding man as O.J. Henley of Tuscaloosa as the main speaker of the first livestock tour. Cattle is a subject Mr. Henley knows well. He is president of the Alabama Cattleman's Association, vice president of the Sumter Farm and Stock Company, which operates a chain of 40 stores as well as a huge livestock farm at Geiger, Alabama. In addition, he is a director of the First National Bank in Tuscaloosa, director of the Alabama State Chamber of Commerce and a number of other things which keep him busy and makes him an outstanding Alabamian.

EXCUSE . . . It's hard to get such a busy man to drop what he is doing to make speeches and attend such things as livestock tours. But I have a hunch Mr. Henley was glad of an excuse to come to Baldwin County. He has a daughter living in Bay Minette, Mrs. Bob Morrissette. And the Morrissettes have a little daughter, Martha Bacon. Well, this is the only grandchild the Henleys have—and you have heard about people and their grandchildren. Anyway, it's good to have Mr. Henley visit the county.

DOUBTFUL . . . It's always good to see all the college students returning home. Had an interesting talk Monday with Harry Wilters, Jr., Robertsdale, who is studying law at Cumberland University in Tennessee. Harry has been doing a good job selling the Tennessee folk on Baldwin County. However, he said so far he has not been able to get them to believe the fact that we have "Fish Jubilees" on the Eastern Shore of Mobile Bay. This is a phenomena that is hard to believe, but it is true. Of the many strange things that happen in this great county, I believe this is about the strangest. And until this date no one has been able to give a satisfactory explanation of what causes the fish to go crabby and try to crawl out on the banks. So you shouldn't be discouraged Harry, because many people refuse to believe less strange things than our fish jubilees.

ADVERTISING . . . Apparently more people than ever before are flocking to Alabama's Gulf Coast for fun and rest. A unique way to advertise the coast was used last weekend. The citizens of the Foley, Pleasure Island area raised $500 and hired an airplane to fly over Mobile, Montgomery and Birmingham with an advertising streamer trailing the plane. On one side it said, "Visit Alabama's Gulf Coast," on the other, "Visit Gulf Shores, Pleasure Island." Pat McKinnis flew the plane. We all agree that we need to advertise our fine coastal area more and more.

GOOD ADVERTISER . . . One of Baldwin's best boosters is Atticus Mullin of *The Montgomery Advertiser*. Read what he had to say about our Gulf Coast last week in his column, The Passing Throng:

"One Montgomery couple switched to the Alabama Gulf Coast this year and liked it. It has been my belief all along that those who go to the Florida beaches, especially the North Florida beaches, would enjoy the Alabama beach just as well if they would try it. There is no prettier beach anywhere in the world than the Alabama Gulf Coast from Fort Morgan to Perdido Bay pass.

"Mr. and Mrs. Edgar McKay are back from a short vacation and this year they went to the Gulf Coast instead of to their usual haunts on the North Florida coast.

" 'And we liked it,' said the McKays of Montezuma Road. 'While our stay was not as long as we wanted, we had a mighty good time at our own Gulf beach. The only trouble with ours is that it has not been built up like the North Coast of the Gulf in Florida.'

"And that is true. But the Alabama Gulf Coast is coming forward every year. There is a teaming settlement at Gulf Shores. It is true that there is not the variety of entertainment on the Alabama Gulf beach as on the others but as the population grows, the entertainment opportunities will grow.

"This is not written for the purpose of knocking or belittling the Florida Gulf beaches. They are beautiful and built up far beyond ours, but the climate is the same, the breezes are the same, the sand is the same. All we need is more time and growth to rival them in every way. We need a little more faith in our own and a little more Panama City spirit."

July 6, 1950

George 'Bootsie' Noonan
'Citizen of Year'

'CITIZEN OF YEAR' . . . The naming of George "Bootsie" Noonan as Bay Minette's outstanding citizen of the year came as surprise to no one but the very modest recipient of the local Rotary Club's first annual award. The Rotarians choice was a very wise one, for we know of no other individual who has devoted as much interest to civic affairs than "Bootsie" Noonan. In making the award for the Rotary Club, retiring president Clyde Steele made special mention of his untiring efforts with the youths of this area. Foremost among his many achievements is his work in directing the Baldwin County High School band. He has built this musical organization into one of the top bands in the state. Heading drives, an active worker in local veterans organizations and participating in dozens of other projects are also included in the long list of civic accomplishments of this young man.

RESERVE . . . The stock question when one War II veteran meets another these days is, "Are you in the reserves?" And this veteran's stock answer is, "Yes, are you?" Of course, I have been on the inactive list. And that continues to be my preference. Of course my wish is one among millions.

WELL REPRESENTED . . . In the current issue of *Alabama Today and Tomorrow*, monthly publication of the Alabama State Chamber of Commerce, Baldwin County is well represented. Recently the State Chamber set up several statewide committees. This month their magazine had write-ups and pictures of two of these committees. On the Tourist and Recreation Committee, we had two representatives out of the 15 members. Dr. W.C. Holmes of Foley and J.E. Gaston of Fairhope adorned the picture of this committee. On the Forestry Committee picture was Bay Minette's E. Davidson.

IMPORTANT . . . And if two subjects are important to Baldwin County, it is these. All will agree that the county is well represented on these committees. Jim Gaston and Buddy Holmes have long been boosters of Baldwin's recreational opportunities and if any person can bring to the attention of the rest of Alabama the importance of taking advantage of these opportunities, these two men can—and will. And Baldwin's pine trees are our biggest money crop, year in and year out. This county's 800,000 acres of timberlands bring in at least one-third of Baldwin's annual income. And if every citizen in the county will listen to Emanuel Davidson, our forests will continue to grow in importance. Alabama was lucky when they got him to serve on this statewide committee.

RAIN . . . A trip through south Alabama will make you appreciate the fine crops we have in this county—even if corn and watermelons aren't bringing a good price. Was in southeast Alabama Monday and Tuesday and the lack of rain has really played havoc with crops there. Their corn is all swiveled up and most of the stalks won't even make good nubbins. Their cotton is in full bloom and most of the stalks look too small and weak to hold more than two or three bolls. Their peanuts look a little better. Of course, the farmers in this county have suffered considerable from the lack of rain but nothing in comparison to the rest of the state. This is one time we all can be happy that Baldwin's annual rainfall is so much higher than it is in most of Alabama. And if you don't think it high, just hang around a few months.

WELL DO YOU? . . . Do you know of another town in Alabama with as many as 3742 people in it which doesn't have a hospital? And Bay Minette isn't going to do without one always, no doubt.

OIL . . . The oil well being drilled between Perdido and Lottie is going right on down. Hope it goes into pay sand. There are many small landowners in that area a few oil wells would really benefit. And another permit has been issued for a well near Latham on Mr. Henry Bryars' land. Mr. Henry's neighbors tell me he is a lucky man and this well will probably be "it." Hope so.

August 24, 1950

Owen, Noonan and band going to national VFW meet

51st. VFW . . . Ordinarily the annual national Veterans of Foreign Wars meeting wouldn't mean much to Bay Minette. But this year it does. The 51st. VFW Encampment will be held in Chicago beginning Sunday and Bay Minette will be well represented. First, because L. D. Owen, Jr., who is a prominent local citizen, is the Alabama VFW Commander and will lead the Alabama delegation in the Windy City. Second, the Bay Minette High School Band, under the able leadership of Bootsie Noonan, will be in Chicago at the head of the parade of 48 states with Commander Owen. Also several other citizens will be there from here. So Chicago may just proclaim a "Bay Minette Day" since we will be there in such strong and creditable force.

MARSH . . . Timber land owners and his many other friends will be glad to know that George Marsh is back in Baldwin County as the area manager of the State Forestry Department. George was here until March, 1948, at which time he left to join the woodlands division of the Masonite Corporation in Laurel, Mississippi. But he had Baldwin County sand in his shoes and he couldn't stay away. He made a lot of friends when here before and did a good job in keeping down forest fires. Now that he is back, he'll do another good job and perhaps this time the county will be fortunate enough to keep him. His area includes Washington, Mobile and Baldwin Counties—which is a lot of good timber territory.

REYNOLDS . . . While everyone is glad to see George return, it is bad to have to give up the person who took his place and has been here since—H.T. Reynolds. He is also a hard worker and will be missed by the many friends he made while here.

GROVE HILL . . . It is particularly bad to see Reynolds leave since he is going back to Grove Hill. He was there before he came here. Now I can understand his leaving there to come to Baldwin but it is impossible to see why he is going back there. If he hadn't done such a good job here with the forestry department, I might think they are sending him to Grove Hill as punishment. Anyway, there has to be a first time for everything. Dozens of people here come from Clarke to Baldwin County but this is the first time I have seen a person who had lived here a year or so return there. No doubt the state gave him a big increase in salary as consolation for going back. Just hope all those wild animals George Carleton dreams about don't get him.

September 14, 1950

OVER 100 IN NATIONAL GUARD
LEAVE FOR ARMY

BAY MINETTE . . . This county seat town was sad and heart broken last Friday. The reason, over 100 men from this area who were members of the National Guard left for the Army. It was quite natural for many eyes to be wet with tears. And when you take that many men out of a town the size of Bay Minette, it really makes a dent in practically all activities as well as most of the hearts. But the men should have been pleased with one thing about their departure. Practically the whole town turned out to see them off and to show their respects. Also local citizens pitched in and gave each member of the guard a nice cigarette lighter as a small token of esteem and appreciation.

SINGLE SHOTS . . . While it was bad for all these men, many of them married with children, to have to leave, I could hardly help but think of all the boys who are being drafted and quietly inducted into the Army without fanfare or notice. Of course it can't be helped and I feel confident if the citizens of the county could, they would gladly pay tribute to each man who leaves for the service. But it just can't be done.

HOMETOWN . . . It is interesting to think about all the boys who have gone and all those who will go and wonder what they think about their hometowns. For the boys who left last Friday, most of them claim Bay Minette as their hometown. And if you think about it in the right spirit you can't help but feel a keen obligation to these men. Surely we people who are still at home should do everything we possibly can to make these boys proud of their hometown. Make it a place for them to be anxious to return when they complete their jobs. A place where they can make a good living with good churches, schools, municipal and health facilities, as well as many other things.

PROGRESS . . . Of course these men know that their hometown has made much progress in the past few years. This is bound to be a source of pride to them. But it also makes them more aware of the fact that Bay Minette needs a number of other things, many of which can be obtained if the hometown citizens will all work together for their accomplishment.

PROUD . . . These boys can be proud, along with the rest of us, that within the past five years at least 750 additional jobs have been made available here. That the population has gained 105 percent. That the gas, sewage and water systems have or are being expanded to serve practically all citizens in the town. That the cemetery for the first time in history is beginning to look decent. That the town as a whole looks neater, more prosperous and better.

NEEDS . . . And like most military men's hometown, Bay Minette has growing pains and needs a lot of things. I am sure though we can all agree that our greatest present need is for the present crisis to be over so all who want to can return home. Naturally this is something local people can't do too much about except do our part. Next, I think Bay Minette's greatest need is a good hospital. Certainly no one can intelligently argue against this. Do you know of another town in Alabama with a population of 3742 without some sort of hospital? Efforts are being made to get one but immediate success looks discouraging. And we need a modern hotel. (Two people are now considering Bay Minette for a 50-room hotel.) We need more paved streets but this is also being worked on and by next Fall should be solved in the main. Another great need is city planning. Too many shacks and other unsightly buildings are going up without any attention from the city fathers. The city is supposed to do something about this soon. Some of the local church buildings are too small. And on and on.

THE POINT . . . There is plenty for us all to do. Let's work together and get as much done as possible. What applies to Bay Minette applies in a similar way to every town in Baldwin County, although the details may be somewhat different.

December 21, 1950

LEON BIGGS WRITES FROM TOKYO ARMY HOSPITAL

LEON . . . It hasn't been many weeks ago I was at my typewriter writing this column when in walked Leon Biggs for a chat. I was glad to see him because he had long been one of my favorite young friends. When Leon was attending high school here he was interested in photography and journalism. His parents, Mr. and Mrs. J. Henry Biggs, Lottie, are also good friends and it was my desire to help and encourage him as much as possible. Then he decided to join the Army. And when he dropped in for the chat he was home on furlough, at which time he figured he'd be on his way to Korea within a few weeks. He calculated right.

LETTER . . . Leon liked the Army when he was talking to me but still had dreams of being a writer. That pleasant talk with him seemed only yesterday when Monday I received a letter from him—written from Tokyo Army Hospital, Tokyo, Japan. Before opening it I figured he had made it to Korea. He had. But he didn't get to stay long. I believe you will be interested in reading a part of what he had to say:

"NOT SERIOUS" . . . "I wrote several articles for you while I was in Korea and also got several photographs, all of which I had to leave in Korea when I was wounded. I was wounded on November 30, 1950, near Pyongyang, Korea. I was removed to the rear area and then flown to the Tokyo Army Hospital. The wound is not serious, just a couple of holes in the back as the result of small arms fire. I was awarded the Purple Heart and all that stuff . . ."

HOME . . . thus once again, although thousands of miles away, the fighting in Korea is brought home to us. Leon isn't complaining because he was one of the lucky "casualties." Thousands of others didn't get back to the rear area and to a hospital.

REMEMBER . . . So while we at home are enjoying Christmas, let's think about and pray for those who can't be with us. Let's hope that before long they will be.

SINCERELY . . . So, MERRY CHRISTMAS AND ABOVE ALL, PEACE ON EARTH . . .

March 29, 1951

CORTE, BENIK AT MONTGOMERY
CATTLE SHOW

BALDWIN CATTLE . . . Couldn't resist the temptation last Wednesday morning to go out to the Union Stockyards in Montgomery to see Baldwin's cattle exhibited there at the Fat Cattle Show and Sale. As usual A.A. Corte & Sons, Loxley, had the prize winning car lot at the show. And I don't think I have ever seen 10 finer head of beef in my life and that was the sentiment of the people there who really knew something about beef cattle. Every one of the 10 Black Angus graded Prime, which is something. It looked to me as though any of the 10 could have been taken and entered into any individual competition with excellent chances of walking off with the Grand Champion prize. After taking the show honors, they were later sold for 41 cents per pound. I never did see the weight but they must have weighed about 1400 pounds each. That times 41 runs into a little money. But I believe they would have sold for that much at our own weekly sale in Robertsdale.

SHORTHORNS . . . Also saw Al Benik of Silverhill. Al bets on Shorthorns and he had two fine ones at the sale. It is real interesting to an amateur to hear the cattlemen give you the fine points of their favorite breed of cattle. And Al can make you feel that anyone is foolish raising any kind other than his favorite, Shorthorns. Anyway it made me feel proud of the fine reputation Baldwin has gained in raising beef cattle. And I get considerable kick out of kidding the Blackbelters about us having the largest weekly cattle sale in Alabama at Robertsdale.

RELUCTANT CANCELLATION . . . The present national emergency has played havoc with Baldwin County's traditional Potato Tour. This colorful event which is anticipated annually by thousands in Baldwin and other counties, will not be held this year. Arthur Corte, president of the Baldwin County Potato Tour Association, reluctantly announced this week that because of the intense desire of Baldwin farmers and association members to cooperate with the national emergency, the 1951 tour, which would have been held in about a month, is being cancelled. The colorful event was interrupted one time before when a national emergency arose before the last World War. However, it was resumed in 1947. We, too, fervently hope that we can return to a normal situation soon. Then Baldwin will be able to resume the traditional tour that pays homage to the county's number one cash crop—the Irish potato.

ANOTHER AUCTION RECORD . . . Results of the weekly cattle auction at Robertsdale Livestock Auction held Monday were startling with the announcement that 1100 cattle and over 400 hogs sold for a total of over $162,000. This was the largest number of cattle to ever go through the Robertsdale yard and the receipts broke the previous record of $146,000 set three weeks ago. Top prices paid at the weekly auction are spurring the livestock industry in Baldwin County and we predict that Baldwin will be right up at the top among cattle raising counties within the next 10 years. Horace Driver, president and manager of the Robertsdale Auction, and other officials are to be congratulated for their fine handling of the sale which has gained statewide recognition as Alabama's leading cattle market.

WOMEN ON JURIES . . . It is high time that Alabama discarded the old fashioned idea that women should be secondary to men in the full rights and duties of citizenship. The legislative interim committee now has under consideration a proposed bill which would permit women to serve on juries. Let us hope this bill will be acted upon by Alabama legislators in the summer session. Our fair sex is granted the privilege of voting and paying taxes like male citizens, so why should sex prevent their being drawn for jury service if they meet the necessary qualifications as good citizens.

July 5, 1951

NEW HOSPITAL ATTRACTS DOCTORS

(Publisher Jimmy Faulkner is vacationing this week on one of Baldwin's sunny beaches.)

By Bob Morrissette, Jr.

HOSPITAL . . . Work on the Bay Minette Hospital is proceeding nicely. Dr. James B. "Jimmy" Thomas hit town over the weekend and is helping supervise the job. His partner, Dr. Philip Hitchcock, is expected to join him by the middle of the month at which time they will open an office in the hospital until construction work is completed.

THUMBNAIL SKETCH . . . An interesting pointer or two on Dr. Thomas . . . He is married and the father of three fine children, two boys and one girl. The oldest son and daughter are twins. Dr. Thomas graduated from the University of the South with an engineering degree and worked at this profession for four years before entering the Navy. While in the Navy, he decided to become a doctor and upon discharge he entered the University of Alabama Medical College. He has just completed his residency at Jefferson-Hilman Hospital in Birmingham.

FOOTBALLER . . . Incidentally, Thomas was a star athlete while at Sewanee. He lettered three years at end and had the honor of serving as captain of the team the last year Sewanee was in the Southeastern Conference.

SMALL TOWN . . . Several persons have asked Dr. Thomas how he thinks he and his family will like living in a small town after residing in Birmingham. He said he reminds them that he is a native of Faunsdale, Ala., and that his wife, Lucille, hails from Billingsley, Ala. Most anyone will tell you that these places are far from being metropolitan areas.

PARTNER . . .The other half of the hospital's staff, Dr. Hitchcock, should easily be Bay Minette's most educated man. He holds a list of degrees a mile long. They are: B.S., A.B., M.A., Ph.D., and M.D. He received his B.S. at 18 and by the time he was 23 he had a Ph.D. in Pharmacology. An interesting sidelight is he taught Bay Minette's Dr. Charles Sherman Pharmacology at Tulane and says he was one of his top students.

NURSE . . . Dr. Hitchcock's wife is a registered nurse and will serve on the hospital staff. They have no children. It is a pleasure to welcome both doctors and their families to Bay Minette.

FURLOUGH . . . Home on furlough from the Army before being assigned to overseas duty are two popular young Bay Minette men, Jimmy Owen and Bruce Beveridge, Jr. When I first saw Jimmy, I patted him on the back for getting such a nice leave until he reminded me that a 30-day leave in these times means only one thing—you are about to be shipped out. Jimmy and Bruce have both amassed fine records as officers in their units and we wish them the best of luck.

July 26, 1951

FRANK HOLMES DESERVED TITLE
'MR. BAY MINETTE'

FRANK HOLMES . . . Bay Minette lost one of the best citizens she or any other community ever had Sunday when S. Frank Holmes died. If any man deserved the title of "Mr. Bay Minette," he did, because he really believed in this town and area. He came here during the depth of the depression in 1932 and with a few dollars and lots of faith took over the Baldwin County Bank which had been closed for several months. Many people, local and otherwise, ridiculed him for his action but he never lost faith in this county and lived to see his bank grow from almost nothing to one of the biggest in southwest Alabama, outside of Mobile.

OPTIMIST . . . I liked Mr. Holmes for a lot of reasons but I most admired him for his enthusiastic and progressive spirit. He was full of energy and spent it to the advantage of the community and his fellow man. He was seldom pessimistic about anything, not even his health which hadn't been good for several months. It would be impossible to mention all the things he did, and caused others to do by his enthusiastic leadership, for Bay Minette. He was active in his church, was awarded the highest honor attainable for service to Boy Scouts of America, was president and one of the organizers of the local Chamber of Commerce, and active in many other organizations including Alabama State Chamber of Commerce and the Alabama Bankers Association. Besides his work in various organizations, he carried on many private campaigns of his own for the benefit of this community. He waged a one-man campaign for a better lighted town, including street and business lights. He helped get more houses built here following the war. He was the first man notified of the possibilities of getting the Reserve Fleet near here and worked to see it become a reality. I could write a page about his many such achievements.

WELL KNOWN . . . I doubt if any country banker in Alabama was better known than Frank Holmes. Everywhere I went people would ask, "How is my good friend Frank Holmes?" It's a little unusual for me to devote this column to a person following his death. But it's the best way I know to pay tribute to a man who also meant much to me. He was always a friend, financial and personally. He had faith in me when few others did. He encouraged me when I needed it most and furnished me money when others would not. Of course I was just one among many he treated the same way. Because of all things he liked most, it was people. And people by the thousands liked him. As I often stated when he was alive, "Frank Holmes is a fine citizen." He won't be replaced but life has been made finer for many people because of his 61 years on earth.

October 4, 1951

HE DIED FOR THE FLAG AND COUNTRY HE ALWAYS LOVED

ALLEGIANCE . . . Some 12 or 13 years ago a little incident happened while I was attending the local picture show that has stuck in the back of my mind all these years. It was while a news reel was showing a group of American soldiers marching. One was carrying the flag of the United States and the Star Spangled Banner was being played by the band. A group of small boys in the row just to the front also looked at the scene. But one of the small fellows was impressed more than the others. He popped up out of his seat, saluted the flag and stood at attention until the music of Uncle Sam's song stopped. Then he sat down with a slight look of disgust toward his playmates who hadn't been so attentive to "his flag" and "his Star Spangled Banner." Of course, technically speaking, his actions weren't necessary but I thought it was a fine act of respect for his country and proved he was an excellent young American.

SAME FLAG . . . During the ensuing years the youngster grew up. Rather rapidly it seems now. He got in the Army at the last of World War II, proudly marched for and saluted the same flag he loved so well as a little boy. He got out of the Army and went to school a while before being recalled to service. Only a few weeks ago he was here visiting his parents and friends. He was on his way to Korea. Just a few days after he left, he was on the battle front. Then on September 8th, along with several buddies, he was killed. He died for the flag and country he always loved and respected.

HIS NAME . . . Thus John Bruce Beveridge, Jr., acquitted himself well. He has also brought the terribleness of the Korean war close to home. Perhaps it will cause us to see our flag with more pride, as did he, and not so dimly "as the manner of some is."

WHY? . . . Several times a day I ask a question which to me is unanswerable. "What's going to happen in Korea?" is the question. It seems that more and more people are wondering what is it all about. Others seem not to give the "police action" much consideration and go along in life as though nothing of importance is happening. In fact, all of us are guilty of this to a certain extent. To those who have sons, brothers, husbands or fathers over there, the thing is quite serious. And frankly, who can blame them for wondering "what's it all about?" I doubt if there is anyone who really knows what is going to happen in Korea. How long it is going to last or how it will end.

PURPOSE . . . As to what it is all about, there should be a little clearer conception in all of our minds, perhaps. The whole purpose is to stop communism from engulfing the world. No doubt there should be a better, and perhaps more direct, way of stopping communism. But until our leaders find a better way, or until peace is declared, it would seem we are destined to struggle on in Korea. And our casualties shall continue to rise. But through it all we shan't become destitute unless all of us lose faith in America. Certainly this will never happen.

October 18, 1951

NAME FUTURE BAY MINETTE ARMORY FORT BEVERIDGE

JIMMY OWEN . . . I have just received a letter from First Lt. James R. Owen. Jimmy is the second son of Mr. and Mrs. L. D. Owen, Sr., of Bay Minette, and is on the battle front in Korea. His older brother, L. D., Jr., likewise is overseas. Jimmy was wounded in action recently but recovered and returned to the front. However, he didn't mention any of this in his thoughtful letter. It had to do with one of his former buddies, Lt. John Bruce Beveridge, Jr.

EXCELLENT THOUGHT . . . I quote from his letter: "I am writing you about a matter in which I am sure you will concur with me. You have no doubt heard of the tragic death of Lt. Bruce Beveridge, Jr., here in Korea. I do not know the exact procedure that you go through in a matter of this kind, but I would like to suggest to you that if and when the National Guard Armory is erected in Bay Minette, that it be named "Fort Beveridge" in his honor. He was the first guard officer to be killed from Bay Minette and his fidelity and devotion to duty have been approached by few in the military service. I would appreciate it very much if you would take steps to see that this proposal meets with approval by the proper state authorities . . ."

WILL DO . . . Jimmy you can rest assured your suggestion will be followed. No one knows at this time when Bay Minette will get an armory. But a few things point in our favor. First, and most important good news, is that most of our National Guard boys will be back home some time after the first of the year. Certainly after the fine service they are rendering their country they are entitled to a good armory when they return. Also the recent session of the legislature made a conditional appropriation (which means that if the money is available) to erect four or five armory buildings in Alabama during the next two years. If Bay Minette is not near the top of the list in deserving one of these, every effort should be made to get us there. And, Jimmy, I am sure every person in this area will think your suggestion for a name is tops.

STOCK LAW . . . During the recent session of the legislature a statewide stock law was passed. The law will go into effect one year from the date of passage but will only affect five counties since all the others already had such a law. One of the counties with open range is Escambia. It has been interesting watching the citizens of that county get ready for the day when their cattle must be put behind fences. Two big companies, T. R. Miller Mill of Brewton, and Alger-Sullivan Lumber Company, Century, own a big proportion of the county's land. Strange as it may seem to some people both of these companies are bending over backwards to cooperate with the cattle owners. T. R. Miller is really going all out to be helpful to the small farmers so they can have some place to graze their cattle.

BUILDING FENCES . . . T. R. Miller is giving an excellent example to other big land owners in this area of good public relations and the old idea of living and letting live. This Brewton concern is not only letting the farmers who live close to their lands graze their cattle on their property but in addition is giving the farmers wire and posts to build fences. As I understand it, the farmers in a community get together and organize themselves, decide how many acres of land is needed to take care of their cattle, let T. R. Miller Company know and they are given enough material to fence in that many acres.

All the farmers have to do is put up the fence and help protect the forests from fires, etc. It will be interesting to see how this spirit of cooperation works.

November 1, 1951

Danny Hall—Pave the road to Fort Mims

JUNIOR SENATOR . . . Next week Baldwin County will have as a visitor the person who is probably Alabama's most popular public official. Senator John Sparkman will be in this section of Alabama and has accepted two invitations to speak in the county Wednesday, November 7. He will talk to the Fairhope Rotary Club at noon and to the Bay Minette Chamber of Commerce Wednesday night. Last year Alabama's junior senator was a delegate to the United Nations. He is better posted on international affairs than most Americans and is considered an authority on many domestic subjects, including housing, small business, etc. His standing is such in the nation that he has been considered by many as fine presidential material and has been prominently mentioned as a possible vice-presidential nominee for the Democratic Party next year.

HONOR. . . The last time Senator Sparkman visited Baldwin was about two years ago when he spoke to the Baldwin County teachers at Summerdale and at the annual meeting of the Fairhope Chamber of Commerce. Baldwin is honored to have her outstanding junior senator visit any time. He is interested in Baldwin's progress and is always helpful when called upon in giving us assistance in Washington.

DAN HALL . . . We have many fine citizens in Baldwin who have pet projects they have long wanted to see completed. One of these gentlemen is Danny Hall, Tensaw. His pet project, along with the general progress of Baldwin County, is to get a paved road into the site of the Fort Mims Massacre. From the present paved road at Tensaw down to the monument is only about two and one-half or three miles. A good road into this historical site would certainly boost its popularity as a tourist attraction. I doubt if the road is paved within the next 12 months but I would bet even money that Danny succeeds in getting it done before three more years pass. Wanna bet?

MASSACRE . . . Last week Danny called our attention to an editorial in *The Montgomery Advertiser* which had something to say about the Fort Mims Massacre. Here is the part of the editorial in which he was interested: "The Fort Mims Massacre occurred in Alabama more than a hundred years ago. But it remains a fresh event in the minds of Alabamians to this day because of its horror. The Indian savages swooped down on the fort, filled with men, women, children and a detachment of troops. Only about 36 escaped the tomahawks and blazing arrows of the savages. Five hundred thirty-three were mercilessly murdered. Such Indian attacks were the peril of the Alabama wilderness of that day. Yet the 533 Alabamians slaughtered in the Fort Mims Massacre was less than the 836 Alabamians who were slaughtered on Alabama highways last year. In other words, the highways today are more deadly to Alabamians than were the Indian savages in wilderness Alabama."

GOOD POINT . . . The above makes a good comparison. The Fort Mims Massacre will never be forgotten. But the 836 killed on our highways won't go down in history books. At least it should serve as a strong warning to those living today.

January 3, 1952

NEW HOSPITAL TO OPEN IN BAY MINETTE

HOSPITAL . . . Sunday will see the formal opening of Bay Minette's fine new 30-bed hospital. An open house will be held from 2 to 6 p.m. so the public can take a look at their hospital. Although there is still some work to be done, mostly outside, it is ready to receive patients. I am confident that all those who go to see the hospital Sunday will be delighted with it. Without a doubt, it is one of the most complete and modern hospitals that can be found anywhere in a community of comparable size which has been built with private funds. It is completely furnished with the most modern medical tools and equipment. It is well laid out and attractive. It would be a credit to a town of any size.

WORK . . . The completion of this hospital is the climax of a long story. A story in which the citizens of this community have cooperated far in expectations of what might be expected. It is a 10-year dream, finally come true. Baldwin County is noted for its efforts and accomplishments of progress caused by hard work and cooperation of its citizenship. I believe the completion of the hospital will equal or surpass any cooperative movement that has ever been undertaken in this section. It has simply been a case where the people realized a great civic need, put their shoulders to the wheel and pushed hard. The result is a hospital that would ordinarily cost $300,000. Only about $35,000 is still owed on the entire project. All of the money has been raised by individual contributions. Not one cent has come from any government agency, local or otherwise.

CREDIT . . . It would be impossible to select any one individual or group entirely responsible for the success of the hospital project. The Chamber of Commerce has worked on it for several years and has spearheaded it. *The Times* has tried to keep the need of the hospital before the people. Several individuals have contributed a lot of time, energy and thought to the project. Almost every person who has been called on has put money into the hospital. I would guess that out of several hundred seen in this area, less than a half-dozen have said no. Which in itself is remarkable. The nine directors of the Bay Minette Hospital Corporation, of course, have been in direct charge of raising the money and completing it. Among those who have devoted the most time and thought to the important job from the beginning are Norman McInnis, J.R. Wilson, E. Davidson, P. Grey Cane, J.B. Beveridge and Hubert M. Hall. Several others have also been active and available when called upon to help.

HEALTH . . . The whole purpose of the hospital naturally is to make the health facilities in this area better. The first requirement for this is good doctors. Doctors to practice the best medicine must have good facilities. The hospital is available for the use of all doctors in this area and most of them have already indicated their desire to take advantage of it. Bay Minette is fortunate in having four excellent medical doctors. Without the doctors, the hospital would be of little use.

HITCHCOCK . . . Dr. Philip Hitchcock is purchasing the hospital from the local citizens and has his offices in the building. Bay Minette is extremely fortunate in getting a doctor of his ability. Although young, 35, he is exceptionally well trained and already has considerable experience. He has several degrees, B.S.; M.S.; Ph.D. in Chemistry; and his M.D.; with additional training in surgery which qualifies him as a surgeon. He attended school at Tulane's Medical School and got his M.D. at the University of Alabama's Medical School. He has also taught at both places. Out of a class of 50 at Alabama, he graduated No. 1 in his class. In fact, his dean told me that he is probably the most brilliant young doctor ever to attend school there. He predicted that within five years he would have a wide reputation as a successful doctor and surgeon. He further stated that Bay Minette is extremely fortunate in getting him.

COME SEE . . . Be sure to visit the hospital Sunday afternoon and see if you don't agree with what I have told you.

January 17, 1952

J. D. Sellars, Robertsdale getting
ATTENTION

ROBERTSDALE . . . Mayor J.D. (Josh) Sellars and the other city officials of Robertsdale are getting wide attention over the state because they have paid their city out of debt. Recently they redeemed $14,000 in electric revenue warrants. After which they still had a cash balance of $18,000 in the treasury. Judging from this, a person who doesn't know the facts might think the city fathers of Robertsdale are just a bunch of misers opposed to progress. This is a long way from the truth. Obviously they are interested in saving money but they also believe in making their city a better place in which to live. Proof of this is the fact they have paved all of the town's streets within the past several months. New sidewalks have been added as well as other municipal developments.

NO PRAISE . . . This reminds me of the time in 1941 when I was mayor of Bay Minette. This town had been in debt for years and about six months after we had taken office enough money was accumulated to pay the last of the old bonded indebtedness. Naturally the councilmen and I felt proud and expected a little praise. As I recall not one person in town congratulated us. On the contrary, the local people wanted to know what we were going to do for the town in the way of municipal improvements. To cap it all off, the late Oscar Duggar of the old *Andalusia Star* criticized Bay Minette's debt free status in a long editorial. He said he had been driving through this county seat town for years and during that time hadn't seem any improvements—hence since the town hadn't done anything it should be out of debt.

TOOK NOTE . . . Following his suggestion we put the town in debt to the tune of $50,000 to build a natural gas system. The same people who weren't interested in the town being out of debt liked the gas system. As a result of that debt, the city has been able to extend the gas system, build a new sewage system and pave a lot of streets. Bay Minette still owes a lot of money but we have a lot to show for it and the people are enjoying the modern conveniences. I imagine if Mr. Duggar were still living, he would be pleased if he saw the old town now.

SAME . . . Josh and his fine councilmen did somewhat the same thing. They bought their municipal light system and from the profits paid their debts and improved Robertsdale. Now that the public knows, and they have a right to know, their city has some money in the bank you can rest assured the citizens of that Hub City will make plenty of requests on how to spend it. So congratulations, you progressive, frugal city fathers of Robertsdale.

BRANNAN . . . Baldwin's popular representative, L.W. Brannan, Jr., talked to the Rotary Club here last Friday. He told the members something about the recent legislative session. While he was talking here, I was bumping my gums before the Rotary Club in his hometown. I would like to have heard his talk as several people told me he made a good one. Come back again, Louie, maybe next time I'll be at home.

BOOKLET . . . E. Davidson, president last year, and A.C. Mott, secretary of the local Chamber of Commerce, are to be congratulated on the fine booklet they have just gotten out on Bay Minette. The local organization has received several letters praising the pamphlet. Robert D. Hays, general manager Mobile Chamber of Commerce, wrote: "Congratulations on your very attractive new folder describing Bay Minette as 'the gateway to good living'." Jefferson D. Henry, director, industrial division, Alabama Chamber of Commerce, said, "This is an excellent folder . . ." R.E. Bisha, general industrial agent, Louisville & Nashville Railroad Company, Louisville, wrote, "Thank you very much for sending me a copy of the very attractive pamphlet which you have issued covering Bay Minette." All wanted additional copies to distribute. The booklet was gotten up to help advertise Bay Minette and if you haven't seen one, do so and resell yourself on this fine town.

April 10, 1952

LOWERY, WHARTON WERE GOOD FRIENDS

FRIENDS . . . One never has enough friends to lose any. Nevertheless, I lost two last week. Both through death. J.S. Lowery, Bay Minette, first, and then Kirby Wharton, Fairhope. *The Times* has already commented on Mr. Lowery. He was called "Simp." But, as I had told many people, it was just a nickname—it didn't mean anything. He was a successful businessman in a quiet sort of way. He owned considerable property, mostly timberland. He told me considerable at various times about his holdings, not in a boasting manner but confidentially. Over the years, he had accumulated several thousand acres of land, in Alabama and Mississippi. He had a heart as big as all get out. You could never do him a favor but what he would do twice as much for you. All the office girls around Bay Minette will miss him. He probably gave away more candy than any ten men here.

WHARTON . . . Fairhope's popular bank president has been one of Baldwin's leading citizens for years. At the time he became president of the Bank of Fairhope, he was the youngest bank president in the United States. Only 46 at death, he died much too young. I had been associated with him in many matters of a civic nature. He was always interested in things that would contribute to the progress of this area. He was also active during the recent war in the sale of War Bonds. Because of his health, he had to slow down during the past several months—perhaps because he didn't slow down enough earlier in life. But he was the type of man that made Baldwin County the fine place that it is. We can ill afford to lose them.

SNAG . . . Lawrence K. (Snag) Andrews, Union Springs, was in Baldwin Monday and Tuesday pushing his candidacy for the important position of associate justice, Supreme Court of Alabama, Place No. 1. He is no stranger in this county as he has been here many times. He not only has a lot of friends here but business property as well. So it's natural for him to be interested in the continued progress of this area. I have had the pleasure of knowing him for a long time and at present am serving in the State Senate with him. He is able, full of grit and integrity. He'll make a good judge.

EDUCATION . . . Have been kept busy working on matters pertaining to education the last couple of weeks. Went to the AEA convention in Birmingham last week. If you could have seen all the teachers there you would know why it takes so much money to run schools in Alabama. We have about 22,000. So you see, each time you give them all a raise of $100 per year, it takes over $2,000,000 to do it. This week our special education committee is holding hearings in Montgomery to let citizens voice their opinions on various phases of education—tenure and the minimum program act in particular. If anything exciting happens, I'll tell you about it.

CONGRESS . . . People are hearing much more about the congressional race in District One than they are in District Two this year. We are in District

Two, of course, and George Grant is our congressman. Boykin represents the First District. One reason we haven't heard much about Grant's race is because it is generally conceded he doesn't have much of a race. He should win hands down. I don't know whether he is even campaigning or not but imagine he will be in the county before voting time. On the other hand, Boykin seems to have the race of his life before him. All reports indicate he'll be re-elected, however. Certainly if the people of Baldwin could vote for the genial Frank Boykin, they would. He has a world of friends over here.

June 19, 1952

New missionaries going to Japan

TRIBUTE . . . The First Baptist Church of Bay Minette paid tribute last Sunday to one of Bay Minette's native sons, Virgil O. McMillan, Jr., and his wife, Donnabel, who are sailing August 2 for Japan to serve as Missionaries for the Southern Baptist Mission Board. We would like to join this church and other friends in paying tribute to this fine young couple who have dedicated their lives to carrying the message of peace and goodwill toward men to a nation who so recently was our enemy in battle. So long as our youth is still willing to sacrifice in order to put the forces of Christianity against the forces of evil, there is still hope that peace may yet prevail upon the earth.

POTATO DEAL . . . I wish I had a full-length book written on the Baldwin County potato deal this year. It would certainly be full of interesting and valuable information. Of course, most of the things our potato growers had to say about OPS couldn't be printed—Harry came in for his share of unprintable words also. Some of the deals that took place and some of the incidents that happened are gems. I have heard several of the stories and we'll all be hearing others for several years to come. In fact, 1952 will probably go down in history as a very special year so far as potatoes go in this county. Instead of saying before the flood or after the flood, a.d. or b.c., we'll probably be saying before the "big potato steal" or after the "big potato steal" in referring to time, henceforth.

TOO BAD . . . John Kaiser, one of Elberta's better farmers, told this one. He was standing on the shipping shed watching the potatoes go through the grader into the sacks without thinking too much about it, and said, "Just think, every time a potato goes into that sack it's another dollar." A colored man working nearby kept right on working but mumbled, "When did dey go down?" Of course, every person has heard about the potato buyers having to hire their trucks pulled out of the fields by the farmers at rather high prices. One prominent citizen at Foley said he sold all of his potatoes at legitimate ceiling prices but if the government didn't do something to those who didn't, he had been a "d--n fool." One buyer with a lot of the folding green in his pocket walked up to a man leaning on a truckload of potatoes in Loxley and made a cash trade with him for the potatoes. In a few minutes he came back to get his potatoes and found out the fellow leaning on the truck had left—and didn't own the load of potatoes in the first place.

SAD . . . As is well known by now, the ceiling price was removed from potatoes last week, just as Baldwin was through digging. The ceiling price had been under $4.00 per bag, which is what the farmer who bent over backwards to be honest (and get double-crossed) received. The few farmers who had not sold their potatoes when the ceiling went off got as high as $10.00 per hundred for their potatoes. Of course the growers in other sections will get the same high price until the supply gets more plentiful. Obviously the government has been very unfair to our honest farmers, which most are and have been.

August 21, 1952

Ben Hastie a man of strong character

BEN . . . This section lost another valuable citizen last week when Ben Hastie of Stockton died rather suddenly. He was a nephew of the late John McMillan, one of the founders of the Bacon-McMillan Veneer Company of that community. He became the first of the second generation who is presently operating the veneer company to die. Ben was a strong character and had a great stabilizing influence with people in all walks of life. He was well liked and respected by those who were privileged to know him. Although a little old for it, he was a veteran of World War II and took an active part in the African campaign. Fine old Stockton has lost another fine citizen.

LITTLE GREEKS . . . George Marinos, Loxley, took a trip back to Greece a few years ago. He saw the conditions of the country and was sadly impressed. The thing that particularly impressed him was the number of orphaned children there. They had been dealt with harshly by the ravages of war, worst of which was to separate thousands of children from their parents through death or other reasons. George doesn't brag about it but he has done well in the United States. He reasoned that he could well afford to take care of some of those orphan children if he could just get them over here. He started working on getting them sent to the U.S. about three years ago. He thought he would be glad to take care of about ten anyway. He soon found that having a big heart wasn't all that it took to get the unfortunate children.

TWO HERE . . . He worked through and with almost every person from Washington on down trying to get the children. He kept in almost constant touch with Congressman George Grant, who helped him all he could. After three years he had partial success. Tuesday George proudly brought the two children he finally succeeded in getting about two weeks ago to Bay Minette. He brought them by *The Times* office and I was delighted to see two such fine looking, and now happy, children. One was a boy, eight, Jimmy

Staurou, and the other a girl, 10, Petrolou Vemopama. When they came in they held out their hands and said: "Hello Mr. Jimmy!" They are having to learn to speak English and can already count to 10 and say their ABCs. George arranged for them to fly over in TWA to New York. But they lost their papers and had to be retained on Ellis Island until they were found.

GOOD . . . I am sure all of Baldwin County will join *The Times* in welcoming these two fine youngsters in our midst. I am confident they, like 42,000 others, will find this a wonderful place in which to live. They can be sure of two things. Here in the U.S. they can grow up with the greatest freedoms on earth and in Baldwin County they should never go hungry.

BIG MONEY . . . While Baldwin has suffered some from the lack of rain, we have been very fortunate compared to most of Alabama and the South. You might be interested in knowing that the hard-working farmers of the county have already sold over $10,000,000 worth of produce this season and have a $3,500,000 soybean crop almost made. Corn is not what it was last year when the average yield was 50.9 bushels per acre but it is still good. Our pine trees are still growing, too.

September 25, 1952

CITY OFFICIALS READY
FOR NEXT FOUR YEARS

CITY GOVERNMENT . . . Now that the city elections are over, I believe it is time to say something about city governments in general. I don't believe this statement can be intelligently contradicted: "Taxpayers get more for their money in city governments than in any other." I have often wondered why this is true. Perhaps the best reason is, as a rule, you have higher type city officials than you do, for example, county officials. Naturally this isn't always true, but it often is. You seldom read in the newspapers about city officials being brought before the grand jury on charges of misusing public funds. Few months go by that you don't read about some county officials being charged for just this. Why is this? Your answer would probably be better than mine. For one thing, county officials with few exceptions are much better paid than city officials. Perhaps the real reason is that the general public is closer to their city government and watch it so closely that their officials are afraid to do anything wrong. But the whole subject is worth thinking over.

OURS . . . For one thing, city governments under Alabama law have much more freedom than county governments. City fathers can do just about anything the state laws don't forbid them to do where as county officials can only do what the law says they can do. It may be these many restrictions that cause some county boys to go afoul of the laws. I believe most people will agree with me that Baldwin citizens who live in municipalities enjoy as good city government as anyone.

BAY MINETTE . . . Most local citizens wanted our present popular mayor, Max Reid, to run for a second term. He could have been re-elected easily. But he decided not to for several reasons. Certainly the $50.00 per month salary he has been getting wasn't enough to compensate him for all the worries and time he devoted to the job. The job should pay at least $200.00 per month. County commissioners, who aren't overpaid for their responsibilities, get $250.00 per month. The mayors in the county's four larger towns devote at least three times as much time to their jobs as does the average county commissioner.

FOUR TOWNS . . . Speaking of these four towns, they all have popular and good mayors for the coming four years. Julian Bristow has acted as mayor-protem for four years in Bay Minette and knows the city's problems. Besides, he has a store right up town where people can (and will) get at him easily. He has a very good council and this town should see four more years of real solid progress. As I have often said, you can't find a better city official anywhere than Josh Sellars of Robertsdale. He wants to give the credit to his city council, and they are good, but Josh has shown the leadership. Foley and Fairhope have two of the county's most successful businessmen as their mayors. Foley has Max Griffin and Fairhope Tony Klumpp. Those towns enjoy exceptionally good government. The progress they are making proves this.

MAYOR COOPER . . . Speaking of popular mayors, this month's *Local Government Journal* has an interesting story about Mayor Roland Cooper of Camden. Roland, who hails from Robertsdale, is Kenneth's brother and a son of Mr. and Mrs. W.R. Cooper, Rosinton, also went to Chicago as a delegate to the Democratic Convention. He is strong for Stevenson and Sparkman. He was almost run our of Camden one time, along with his council, for passing a city sales tax. But he used the money so wisely and improved the town so much that he was re-elected without opposition. Thus another Baldwin son makes good.

SHOULD PROGRESS . . . Since Baldwin has good government, both city and county, good farmers, good civic clubs and other organizations, good schools, good churches, the best natural resources, the best people, good newspapers, good climate, excellent representation in the state legislature (could it be I'm prejudiced?), a highway system that is rapidly becoming the best in Alabama, etc. and etc., why shouldn't we continue to grow and prosper?

November 20, 1952

Fine old citizens deserve recognition

TOO MANY . . . Old age and death has caught up with too many of our fine old Baldwin County citizens. I can't mention them all but two or three were good friends and had such a wide acquaintance throughout the county that some recognition should be given them. Mr. Sam Martin, 86, died in Bay Minette recently. He had lived here since 1890 and was one of the last living citizens who actively participated in the historical incident which resulted in bringing the court house from Daphne to Bay Minette. He was a fine citizen and delighted in reciting early Baldwin County history to this writer as well as other people.

TRIONE . . . Undoubtedly one of the staunchest Democrats in the entire county was Angelo A. Trione, Sr., who died recently. He had lived in Daphne over 60 years and was a successful businessman there. He also served as postmaster one time and at death was a member of the county Democratic Executive Committee. On the morning of the election, November 4th, Mr. Trione got out of bed to call me that Daphne would vote for the Democratic candidates and for me not to worry. I never had a chance to talk to him after the Democrats lost nationally but it must have been a heavy blow for him. Daphne did go Democratic, as he said. So the Democrats lost a great advocate and Baldwin a great citizen.

SHARRETTS . . . Another prominent Baldwin citizen died in Summerdale last week. He was Harlow S. Sharretts, Sr., who was a former county commissioner and postmaster of Summerdale. Mr. Sharretts was a good citizen and was extremely interested in the good welfare of this county. The last time I talked to him was in Robertsdale a week or so before his death and it appeared he was in better health than usual. He was a good friend and a good citizen.

OIL . . . Drove down to see the wildcat oil well being drilled near Orange Beach about one-half mile north of Cotton Bayou. Originally, a few months back, a well was sunk to about 3,000 feet at this location by Dr. Amos Garrett and associates. The prospects looked so good it was decided to raise more money and go down 8,000 feet. The new test was started last week. Strangely enough, they didn't use the old hole. They started a new one within about 35 feet of the old one. Think the old one had caved in. Monday night they were drilling away in shale at 6,700 feet. They hope to hit oil producing sands Friday or Saturday at around 7,300 feet. If no oil is found, they should be down to the 8,000 feet the drilling contract calls for by Sunday or Monday.

COSTLY . . . Digging an oil well takes considerable money although it is my understanding this one was contracted for at a little under $40,000.

There is considerable interest in the well although there has been no widespread leasing in the area. But if they hit, watch out Baldwin County. Some of the people putting money into the well figure they have about one chance in four to hit since there was some show of oil in the original hole. Looks like a good business risk to me—I hope. Of course, if they get a producer the people putting up the hard cash, which included Gulf Oil Company, will be brilliant. If they don't hit, people will say, "They should have known better." One thing is sure—before Baldwin becomes an oil producing county somebody must do some gambling. Keep your fingers crossed for the next few days.

IN THE NEWS . . . Thanks to R.C. Keeney, Realtor of Fairhope, Baldwin made the front page of the *Wall Street Journal* last week. In an article about the high price of farm land in the U.S., the *Journal* also said this: "Down in Baldwin County, Ala., says R.C. Keeney, of Fairhope, Ala., smaller farms from 40 to 160 acres, are selling for $400 to $500 an acre, a 300% rise since the end of World War II. Most buyers, he says, are city people picking up land as a hedge against the future. The outsiders, Mr. Keeney says, are willing to pay more for the same land than professional farmers. He recently sold one 900-acre piece to a commercial potato-raising outfit for $65,000, or a little over $70 an acre." (This same piece sold for $5,500 in 1935 and over $60,000 in timber was cut off it before selling this year).

December 4, 1952

ARCHIE M. McMILLAN WAS GOOD
FRIEND, CITIZEN

McMILLAN . . . This writer, Stockton and Baldwin County lost another good old friend and citizen last week in the death of Archie M. McMillan.

Mr. Archie was an interesting character and an excellent person. I never had the good fortune of knowing him well until about four years ago. For the past two of these, he was a good friend. I always liked to talk to him about current and past events. He had his own ideas about things. You might not agree with him but you never doubted but that he meant what he said. The lifelong Stockton resident left a lot of friends.

STILL NO OIL . . . One thing is sure about Baldwin citizens. They are interested in oil news. Just wish *The Times* could print more good news about the black gold. Tuesday night the news was still sad from the Cotton Bayou well. Sunday they were down to 7,600 feet. The contract called for 8,000. Imagine before you read this they will be that deep. As said last week, no news when it comes to oil wells is usually bad. However, rumors are spreading in that area that leases are being signed up near Lillian and another wildcat well is to be tested in the near future. This is strictly in the rumor stage. Don't buy land in that area on the strength of it. I believe there is oil in Baldwin County. To date, this belief is based on faith, not sight.

McGOWAN . . . I don't believe any person would argue the fact that the job of Baldwin County Superintendent of Education is the most important and responsible job in this great county. The fact that he handles and is responsible for the spending of over $1 million a year is just one item. More important is seeing that all our school children get the best possible education. Unless it is the churches, nothing is closer to the people than their schools. So the person in charge has a great responsibility. Last Friday the most significant news to happen in a long time in this county did happen. The county board of education selected W.C. McGowan, Foley school principal, to be the next County Superintendent of Education. Fortunately for all, they selected a responsible man for this responsible position.

THARP . . . After next July 1, Mr. McGowan will step into the very large shoes of S. M. Tharp. For 34 years Mr. Tharp has run the schools of Baldwin County with a firm, intelligent hand. He has long been recognized as one of the outstanding county superintendents of education in Alabama. Also he has received national recognition. About 10 years ago, the Baldwin County school system was selected as one of the 10 best in the United States. This selection was made by *Look* magazine after a nation-wide survey. I could write a full page in this newspaper about the fine qualities of this grand old man of Baldwin. And I probably will between now and the time he retires from his present position. Time being, let's talk a little more about his successor.

UNITE . . . Surely we will all agree that W.C. McGowan should know the schools of this county. He has taught in them for a long time—and in every section of the county, from Lottie to Foley. Perhaps the best recommendation for him is the success he has made in the jobs he has held. School patrons in the Foley area swear by him. His teachers admire and bet on him. His students love him. He has a good education, holds many honors in his profession, has a good personality, apparently is in good health. With these fine qualities, it appears to me the only other thing he needs to make a good superintendent is the wholehearted cooperation of the people of Baldwin. This writer and *The Times* promises their.

December 18, 1952

S. J. IRWIN A FINE OLD-TIMER

ANOTHER . . . Baldwin lost another of its fine old-timers last week when S. J. Irwin, Gateswood, died. He had been sick for a long time. Dropped by to talk to him several weeks ago and although seriously ill at the time he seemed to enjoy talking. He was a loyal member of the Baldwin County Democratic Executive Committee for years. He had the respect of his neighbors and was often spoken of as "a good man." It seems the county is losing an unusual number of these good old citizens lately. Hope he is the last for a long time.

OIL . . . Still no good oil news for Baldwin. The well at Orange Beach was abandoned as dry at 8,007 feet. There is some talk about taking it on down to 10,000 feet but this is still in the indefinite stage. Dr. Jones, state geologist, says Baldwin has oil but is not in the "hot area" at this time. That means they are not working real hard to find it now. According to him, Escambia and Monroe are the "hot" counties in this area. Many wells are scheduled to be drilled in those two counties in 1953. Baldwin will probably have two or three. Still can't find out why the oil companies don't go ahead and develop Baldwin's lone oil field, which has a total of one producing well. That is in the extreme northwest section of the county and is part of Clarke's Carleton field. There has been a lawsuit pending between one of the landowners and the oil company and some say this is what has held it up. Whatever the trouble, wish it would get settled because it is thought that that field extends a considerable distance into Baldwin.

LABOR . . . Just in case you might have thought there is a shortage of women wanting jobs in the Bay Minette area, you may be surprised to know that the labor survey shows 1600 wanting work. The survey is being conducted by the Alabama Employment Service and the local Chamber of Commerce. The number will probably run more by the time all names are in. If the entire county was included, it would probably run at least twice this number. Surely some good company will take advantage of this rich labor supply before long.

POTATOES . . . Talking to one of the county's potato shippers Tuesday. He says the potato growers are optimistic about next season and more acreage will be planted than last, perhaps as many as 15,000. In times past, before World War II, the acreage went as high as 24,000.

PUBLICITY . . . The *Progressive Farmer*'s current issue gives Baldwin considerable publicity. This magazine has over 1,000,000 circulation. An excellent picture shows County Agent Frank Turner and Rube Childress watching the latter's pasture being irrigated. Also, Harry West, Bay Minette agricultural expert and writer, has another article published. Same with this writer's brother. And Baldwin was mentioned in several places. It all helps.

ROADS . . . Didn't finish writing about county road developments last week. Will try to get back on the subject right after Santa Claus time. Several projects are in the process of development and perhaps more definite information can be had soon. Contrary to the oil news, the road news continues to be good in this county.

January 15, 1953

EDUCATIONAL APPOINTMENTS
GOOD FOR COUNTY

BACK HOME . . . When James H. Bennett moves to Bay Minette to take over his new job as supervisor of maintenance and transportation for the county school system, it will really be like coming home for him and Mrs. Bennett. He was school principal here at one time and has a bunch of friends in Bay Minette as well as other places in Baldwin. He has been principal in Fairhope for a long time and although they will hate to give him up, they shouldn't mind too much sharing him with the rest of the county. The Bennetts have been among my favorite people for a long time and it is good to know I'll get to see them more often.

GOOD . . . Things are happening in the educational setup in Baldwin these days. Recently popular W.C. McGowan, principal of Foley schools, was selected to succeed S. M. Tharp as county superintendent of education next July. Now McGowan and the county board of education come forth with the excellent idea of getting Bennett to be his assistant. Looks like things are working out well for our children educationally in Baldwin. Congratulations to all concerned and responsible.

FOSTER . . . Another good county citizen has died. Price L. Foster, editorial writer and production manager of the *Foley Onlooker* died Sunday night. I hadn't had the privilege of being with him very much but always enjoyed talking to him when the opportunity presented itself. Like myself, he moved into the county from elsewhere. He learned to love, praise and promote its interests more than many natives. He was a good newspaper-man and citizen.

HECK . . . There just isn't enough time to go around. I had a kind invitation from John Snook and others to attend the Alabama State Fox Hunt in Foley this week. I intended to go but couldn't. Understand they put over the hunt in a big way, as they usually do. This is a big event for Baldwin and is worth considerable in advertising and publicity for the county. Those who make it possible for the hunt to be held in Foley deserve great praise.

SORRY . . . Elsewhere in this issue you will see a picture of E. Davidson, chairman of the Baldwin County Democratic Executive Committee, handing a watch to the former chairman, W.C. Beebe. The watch was give to Beebe by other good Democrats in the county for his years of loyal and faithful service to the Democratic Party. The fine watch is inscribed "W.C. Beebe—a loyal Democrat." But the purpose of mentioning the picture here is to explain why the third party is looking on. Of course, I am secretary and treasurer of the county committee but *The Times* has a rather definite rule about not printing pictures of its publisher. It happened this way. Our photographer, Morgan Little, took one shot of Beebe and Davidson alone. This was to be run in *The Times*. The other shot with me looking on was just for posterity, or something. Morgan did a good job on both pictures but Emanuel blinked his eyes at the wrong time on the first one. After much deliberation among the editorial staff, it was finally decided it would be easier to break a rule than to take more pictures—hence the trio instead of the pair.

January 22, 1953

PROGRESS IN BALDWIN MOVING WELL

MORE PROGRESS . . . The old saying that nothing succeeds like success is being proven correct in Baldwin right now. A few weeks back the fine announcement was made that Newport Industries, Inc., is expanding here to the tune of $2,500,000. Right on the heels of this announcement was the news about the new pants factory for Bay Minette. The building for this should be started within two or three weeks. Several new school buildings are going up in all parts of the county, or are to be started soon. Road improvements are going on all over the county. Now comes the announcement from Lt. Jimmy Owen that Bay Minette is to get a National Guard armory. Work on this should start within a few weeks and will cost about $75,000.

LOCATION . . . The armory will be located on Highway 31 just west of the courthouse across from Manci's Nursery and in front of the present National Guard truck shed. The building will be about 14,000 feet in size and the drill hall will be more than large enough for a basketball court, with room for spectators. Adjutant General "Crack" Hanna has already told us that the building can be used for the benefit of the general public. This will offer a big boost in the recreation facilities of this area. It will be the second armory in Baldwin as Foley has had one for several years. At present, there are no other Guard units in the county but I have been told Fairhope is working for one.

BIG PARK . . . Another big recreation development is the one which will be started soon by the Alabama Department of Conservation near the foot of the hill at Spanish Fort. It will be a big state park. To be known as Meyer Park because the Meyers of Mobile are giving the land. It will be located south of the Causeway between the Blakeley and Apalachee Rivers. Conservation Director Earl McGowin has been working on this important project for many months.

PLANS . . . He showed me the plans and blue prints for it in Montgomery recently and they are something. The park is to be built in about four or five steps, as the money becomes available. Bids for the first step are being asked for now and is expected to cost in the neighborhood of $400,000. If and when the project is completed according to present plans, it will cost in excess of $4,000,000. The park will have a basin for boats, bath houses, concessions, swimming beaches, etc. The Bay will be deeper there by dredging the sand and at the same time making the land area larger. The eventual completion of the entire project will depend on several factors, including money being available, public demand and usage.

PROBLEMS . . . One of the many problems facing Alabamians in education is that of our retired teachers. Most of them have not made enough to live on after they are forced to quit teaching when they become 70. And for those who have already retired, or expect to soon, the pension is rather low. There are 14 retired teachers in Baldwin at present, having an average of 32 years of total teaching service. Their average monthly pension allowance is $40.77. Ten receive less than $50 per month and four get from $50 to $75.

March 19, 1953

New National Guard unit planned for Fairhope

GUARD . . . Fairhope is getting a new National Guard unit. This makes the third for Baldwin as Foley has had a unit for years and Bay Minette since World War II. The citizens of Robertsdale have shown a little interest in a unit but not much. The new group at Fairhope will be in the Infantry, or so we are told. They have been working for this a long time and I want to be among the first to congratulate them. Fairhope has a good Chamber of Commerce and they are getting things done down that way. The organization's popular president, Larry Blatchford, was in Bay Minette Tuesday in the company of Fred Wood, architect and good Baldwin citizen. Fairhope is also getting a fine new school building which is being built by Bay Minette's up and coming young contractors, Mitchell and Nall. They are vitally interested in getting a gymnasium and community house and have a livewire committee working on it. Fact is several more communities could use a gymnasium in the county. The guard unit at Fairhope is going to drill in Cummings Hall until they get an armory.

ARMORY . . . They tell me in Montgomery that Bay Minette's new armory should be started within a few days. It was caught in President Ike's general order to hold up on all military construction until reviewed. But National Guard officials say they hope the contract will be released this week. Hope so too. The $85,000 building will look good and serve a useful purpose as a recreation and community center on Highway 31 just west of the Court House.

BUSY . . . Nelson Gallahan, superintendent of the Bay Manufacturing Co., Inc., Bay Minette, (pant's plant if you please) had a busy day Monday. He announced he was going to take applications for workers in the new plant Monday and he was swamped. Over 250 signed up for work and he can only use 75 for the first several weeks. However, he seemed to be pleased with the fine people wanting work and pledges to do his best to be hiring 200 or 300 within a few months. He believes the number will be up to 150 within three months after the building is completed.

NIGHT . . . Mr. Gallahan is making a hit in Bay Minette from all accounts. Naturally some of the ladies are going to be disappointed because he can't give them all work. He is trying to be fair to all. He is giving them a chance to show what they can do. He is forming classes in which 20 hours of sewing training on the machines will be given. Naturally he will take the best ones first. To make it convenient for those ladies who can't take the training in the daytime, he is having night classes three nights a week. Understand women who are qualified will be hired from in or outside Bay Minette. In fact, several applied for work as far away as Silverhill, Uriah and Brewton. Derrill Stuart who has the contract for the factory building, has 90 days to complete it. If the weather holds up, he may cut that time in half, which will suit everybody. By the way, about $6,000 more is needed to completely finance the building, air conditioning and all. Have you done your part?

COURT HOUSE . . . Speaking of new buildings, I have heard talk about a new courthouse building for the county. Read in the *Clarke County Democrat* last week where Clarke County is going to build one in Grove Hill. Both counties need one. Baldwin has far outgrown the present structure which has been serving its purposes for 52 years. The county doesn't have room to house all its agencies and is having to rent additional space for some of them. The Commissioners got an engineering estimate of what it would cost to restore the present structure to good condition. The estimate was $180,000. This would not add any new space but would just stop the leaks, refinish the insides, replace the rotten foundation, etc. Many feel this would be money thrown away as the space would still be inadequate. Too, the old jail is no credit to any county, much less Baldwin. The recent grand jury investigated the entire situation and strongly recommended a new courthouse. They have been recommending a new jail for years.

SHOW WINDOW . . . Baldwin is the fastest growing rural county in Alabama. Many people passing through the county see the old courthouse and that furnishes them a lasting impression of Baldwin. I am sure every person will agree that this county is much more progressive than the old courthouse building looks. The county is certainly financially able to finance a new building. At least the Commissioners should get some plans and investigate the cost. Something is going to have to be done it seems as the county insists on keeping on growing.

April 2, 1953

S. M. THARP HONORED AT EDUCATION CONVENTION

THARP . . . A great tribute was paid to S. M. Tharp, county superintendent of education, at the annual Alabama Education Association convention in Birmingham last week. Mr. Tharp is retiring from the job he has held (34 years) longer than any other man in Alabama has held a county superintendent's job. He will retire in July. He has been recognized as one of Alabama's leading educators for many years. At the annual dinner of the Alabama Association of School Administrators Dr. H.H. Hadley, Tuscaloosa city schools superintendent, native of Baldwin and former teacher here, gave the address of tribute to Mr. Tharp. It was good. I am supposed to get a copy of it but haven't so far. The school administrators also gave him a present, a large sofa bed, as a token of their esteem.

AEA . . . Not many of our school people attended the meeting in Birmingham. Did see W.C. McGowan, J.H. Bennett, C.F. Taylor, Mrs. Dixie Johnson and Miss Carolyn Day. Mrs. Johnson was installed as vice-president of the AEA which is a fine honor for her and Baldwin County. As you would expect she is very popular among the school people over the state. With a little help from the home folk, maybe she will be president. She would make a good one. All in all the education people in Alabama are a great group and would be a credit to any state. They render an indispensable service for which they probably deserve more credit and support than they receive.

JENKINS . . . *Coronet* magazine has sent a man into Baldwin to write a story about the Jenkins family who live on Daphne Route on Highway 90. This colored family has already been given statewide recognition for their successful farming practices. Amelia Jenkins is the mother of 10 children, seven boys and three girls. Together they have a huge farm operation in the county. This year they have planted about 350 acres of potatoes. Recently Hilliard Jenkins, one of the older boys who lives in a nice home near his mother, was honored by Tuskegee Institute for his achievements and leadership among the Negro race. This is an annual award this famous old school makes each year to a deserving person in Alabama. It was for this reason that *Coronet* editors in New York took note of the Jenkins family and figured that a success story on them would make interesting reading throughout the nation. The story is being written by a Southern writer, a resident of Montgomery.

AUTOMOBILES . . . Baldwin evidently is going to have more automobile registrations this year than any other county in South Alabama, other than Mobile. Tax Assessor E.S. (Big Ed) Tunstall told me Tuesday that to date about 14,000 auto licenses have been issued. Before the year is over the number may go as high as 17,000. If so, this will be about 3,000 more than last year, which up to that time was the highest in history. As late as 1946 Baldwin only had 5,000 cars and trucks. Naturally this affects the tax income for the county. Besides the ad valorem taxes, the county and incorporated cities get 63 percent of the tag license money. This means that for every car registered in Bay Minette, the city gets 63 percent of the money. Same for a truck. If the car is registered outside of a city, the county gets 63 percent. In 1949, the county got from this source $36,402.94. In the same year the cities got $10,677.53. So far this year, the county has gotten $54,860.38 and the towns $13,857.43.

SIGNIFICANCE . . . Baldwin County is growing.

April 23, 1953

JENKINS FAMILY SUCCESS
GETS NATION-WIDE RECOGNITION

RANKIN . . . Again I am letting Allen Rankin, of *Alabama Journal* fame, write my column. This appeared in the *Journal* recently:

LOXLEY, ALA.—Hilliard Jenkins did not gross $130,101 last year—and win Tuskegee Institute's annual National Farm Family Award—by standing still.

To interview the 31-year-old Negro dynamo, I sometimes had to break into a jog as he would race across the 1,000-acre plantation here at Loxley.

Since Jenkins looks vaguely like Joe Louis, the Brown Bomber, is 219 pounds of gristle, and wears boxing shorts to do his farm sprinting, it occurred to me that he fights through every minute of his 14-hour day as if he were in the prize ring.

But when you see him in action with his three brothers (the Jenkins' operation is a family affair) it looks more like a commando attack, the objective being to take a potato field instead of a beachhead. I have not seen such an organized hustle, bustle and race against time since the building of B-29 strips in the Pacific.

The urgency is explainable when you learn that the Jenkins this year have about $65,000 worth (350 acres) of potatoes planted, and are taking this gamble against sun, rain and time. What they no longer have to gamble is their reputation as successful big-scale farmers and solid citizens in their community. Their successful up-grade fight for 18 years has made this reputation secure.

"Your daddy had big plans," Amelia Jenkins told her 10 children just after her husband died suddenly in 1935, "and we're going to carry them out."

Though her eldest son, John Wesley, was just 15 and Hilliard just 13, Amelia assumed a $10,000 debt her late husband had contracted to purchase some uncleared timberland he had planned to clear into a "dream farm."

"You're going to make something of this land and of yourselves," the widowed Amelia convinced her sons. Meanwhile, until they could grow up, she hired a few laborers and pitched in with them to clear timber and carve from it a farm. She joined her field hands in chopping cotton, riding mules, snaking timber out of the woods, and slowly edging out from under the $10,000 debt.

"Amelia Jenkins' word is as good as gold," a Foley banker told me. "Any of the Jenkins' words are."

Today, at 58, Amelia, still the farm's "big boss," drives a new Lincoln. "It's not my Lincoln," she says. "It's all of our Lincoln. We don't have any private belongings here. Everything anybody's got—trucks, tractors, everything, belongs to all of us."

Son Hilliard, physically the most powerful of a strong family, who quit after high school to send four of his seven brothers through college, does claim as private his new $16,000 home "The Jenkins Pine Nest." He is married and lives there with his young wife and three children. His mother Amelia now lives in a spacious, pine-paneled house in the plantation's center. The old unpainted shack in which she brought up 10 children is now part of one of several barns.

The plantation's "board of directors" still meets, as always around Amelia's family breakfast table each morning. Each "conference" begins with the reading of the Bible and a prayer. Then Amelia gives what she calls her "instruction," advising each member of the family how he can carry on his particular operation for the day in accordance with the wishes of the All Mighty.

The set-up is this: Amelia is "big boss." Hilliard is farm boss and general manager, John Wesley is bookkeeper, Shelly assistant manager, and Samuel labor chief.

But all Jenkins men work in the fields at every job that needs doing, and with a gusto that would prove fatal to men not in the peak of condition. They're up every morning at 4. All day the now well-to-do brothers work harder than any of their field hands, with Hilliard speeding around in a pick-up truck barking orders like a field general. Often, 16 hours after their pre-dawn start, their tractor lights are still blazing in the night. Except on dress-up occasions, the Jenkins brothers live in dusty overalls and heavy work shoes, like their hired hands, which sometimes number as many as 45.

I asked Hilliard if he wasn't condemning himself to a sort of self-imposed slavery. "Slavery," he answered, "is when you have to work for somebody else. But for yourself, you can work three times as hard and enjoy it. I enjoy, too, competing. I enjoy showing people that if a man has a chance given him, like we have, he can deliver the goods—on a quantity and quality basis equal to anyone."

Hilliard attends weekly farm meetings of his race and otherwise helps neighboring farmers by extending them advice and credit each year. Neighbors white and black are proud of the Jenkins' accomplishments.

One small farmer across the way told me: "Until I saw the Jenkins do it, I never did think I could ever make that kind of money farming. Now I'm trying and they're helping me compete with them."

May 7, 1953

THARP TRIBUTE CITES 35 YEARS PROGRESS, GROWTH

HIGHLIGHTS OF SERVICE . . . The program honoring Baldwin County Superintendent of Education, S. M. Tharp, on the football stadium here last Friday night was one of the finest I have ever seen. Hundreds of school students took part in the program which high purpose was to honor the man who has led the county's schools in 35 years of growth and progress. School bands, both white and colored, paraded before a crowd of 3,000 who had come from all over Alabama to pay their respects to Mr. Tharp. Beautiful floats depicted progress from the little red schoolhouse to the modern day school building. It was a great show.

THARP . . . The fine old man of education was born in Clarke County in 1883. He graduated from the University of Alabama in 1909 and came to Bay Minette the same year as principal of the local school. He was appointed superintendent of education in 1918. Now serving in his 35th year, he is the oldest superintendent in point of service in the state of Alabama. He will retire from his present job July 1st as Alabama law requires this when a person reaches 70.

AUTO . . . He was presented with several gifts of appreciation. Perhaps the one he will appreciate and enjoy the longest was a book of bound letters written to him in praise of his fine accomplishments over the years. Of course this was a surprise as he didn't know the letters were being written. The book contained about 250 letters, many from very prominent people through the state including Gov. Persons, Senator Lister Hill, Congressman George Grant and others. But the highlight of the program and the biggest surprise to him no doubt was the gift of a new automobile. The new car was given by the Baldwin County teachers in appreciation of his long years of fine service to education.

JOB . . . Although Mr. Tharp has already lived 70 useful years, he isn't yet thinking of the past. He is thinking of the future and wants a job where he can continue to serve humanity. It is a pleasure for me to join with the thousands of others who congratulate him for his many years of superior service and who wish him many more years of good health and happiness.

THIS COLUMN . . . It takes a lot of time to be a good writer. More and more of my time is being taken other places these days. There just isn't enough to go around. I sincerely hate for anything to take me away from *The Times* because it means much to me in many ways. It has gotten to the point where I seldom have time to write an editorial. Only recently I had to ask Bill Stewart to write my "Mumblings In Black And White" for a few weeks. I intend to keep up this column even while the legislature is in session. Not that it is so important to you—but I like it. But if I keep on writing it, I agree with you that it is about time to modernize the picture in the sketch above.

June 4, 1953

FINE EDUCATION TEAM CONTINUES TO GROW IN BALDWIN

KEEPING UP . . . Spending so much time in Montgomery these days, it is hard keeping up with what is going on at home. I do manage to keep in touch fairly well but it is not to my liking when I don't have time to go around and visit with the county people more. A lot of friends drop by to see me at home or in Montgomery. Others call or write. This I appreciate. But it is always interesting to note that good ole Baldwin continues to grow. Unfortunately, if you talk to the potato farmers you immediately get the idea the county isn't prospering so much right now.

TAYLOR . . . Talked to W.C. McGowan, superintendent of education to be (July 1st) Saturday and he gave me some interesting and important information. He said that C.F. Taylor, long-time principal at Robertsdale, is going to be the new supervisor of instruction for the county schools. This is the job held by Mrs. Hayes until she left for a similar position in Florida. Mr. Taylor probably has more college degrees than any educator in Baldwin. Besides his bachelors and masters, he also has a degree in law. Long considered an outstanding man in Alabama education, he is going to add a lot to the fine education team Mr. McGowan is assembling. He has already recruited J.H. Bennett as supervisor of transportation and buildings. He was principal at Fairhope High. I know Robertsdale isn't going to like losing him, but Baldwin is gaining a good man in Mr. Taylor.

DEAN DANIELS . . . Scheduled to take over is Virgil Buck. He has been teaching in the Robertsdale schools for some time and will be able to take over the No. 1 position there with ease. He is popular among the patrons and well liked by the students. C.V. Daniels, local high school principal, until recently, was the newcomer among the principals of the county's four white schools. Now he is the dean as McGowan, Bennett and Taylor retire to higher fields. Obviously we can still expect to see great things from Baldwin schools.

WHEP . . . Baldwin's first radio station, WHEP at Foley, opened Sunday. I was well pleased with the reception here in Bay Minette. The station has a tone and fine volume. I have had the pleasure of knowing Howard E. Pill, owner of the station, for a number of years. He is one of Montgomery's outstanding citizens and has long been one of the South's leading radio executives. His son-in-law, Ralph O. Howard, is the station's general manger; James E. Stewart, director of programs; and Wm. L. Rowland is sales manager. This is a strong team and WHEP will serve an important link in communication and entertainment in this great county. Congratulations and lots of luck.

BAY PANTS . . . Our local pants factory building is nearing completion. If you haven't been by lately go and have a look-see. The building is fine and the new machinery being installed looks good. E.J. Pleet, president of Well Made Pants Company (the parent company of Bay Pants), Baltimore, was down last week and was well pleased with the building and other progress. They expect to have 75 people working in about two weeks and already have the machines on order to put 75 more to work in another 60 days. Talk is now being heard of the plant eventually employing up to 400. Success at last.

June 11, 1953

FORT MORGAN GETTING OVERDUE FACELIFT

JAMES . . . Saw a fine old friend of Baldwin County Saturday. H.T. James is able to be up and around again after several weeks of sickness. He worked with the Soil Conservation Service here for several years. He then resigned and went into business locally. Later he sold out and went back with

SCS in Atmore. He has a lot of friends here and in Atmore and I am sure all of them will be happy to learn he is rapidly improving. Good luck "H.T."

FORT MORGAN . . . Historic Fort Morgan is getting a facelifting that is long overdue. Thanks to Conservation Director Earl McGowin and State Highway Director W.G. Pruett. Prison Director J.M. McCullough is also lending a helping hand by assigning 10 convicts down there to keep the place clean. A lot of sand had piled in on the old fort and work has been going on for several months cleaning it out. Restoration plans include brick preservation work, cleaning rooms inside the fort, landscaping and care of the lawns, construction of a shelter for the hotshot furnace and an access walkway to it, development of a museum in Battery Decortail headquarters room and directional signs at strategic points.

SIGNS . . . Eight signs made of bronze are about ready to be delivered by the Alabama Historical Society which are to be placed between Foley and Fort Morgan. The signs will relate historical data about the area and should do much to help interest the tourists.

FORT MIMS . . . Clarke County Representative Dave Mathews has introduced legislation in Montgomery to help restore and put up markers at the site of old Fort Mims. I have been informed that if this is done, a paved highway will be put to the site.

PROGRESS . . . So you can see progress is being made in many lines in Baldwin. Unfortunately the drought, low prices, etc., are causing many of our farmers to make financial progress in reverse. Undoubtedly brighter days are ahead—I hope.

LEGISLATION . . . As you know, the State Legislature is still in session. The current session is about one-third over and many important bills have already passed. Many others are up for consideration. I promise to try to give you a summary of some of these in the near future.

July 23, 1953

FRANK MANCI CAME TO BALDWIN IN 1890S

PIONEER. . . *The Times* this week pays tribute to the memory of Frank Manci—Pioneer. Born in Italy 86 years ago, Mr. Manci came to Baldwin in the nineties. That was when there were no roads, no markets, nothing but cutover pine land. He was one of a group of Italian settlers who came to Daphne just as the Germans came to Elberta, and other nationalities settled other Baldwin communities. His life was strictly that of the farmer on the farm. He remained active until a few years ago when he turned over the running of the farm to the boys, or we should say the "farms" as there are now many more acres than in the beginning. A few years ago, he was able to make a return visit to Italy. Like so many people who go back after a long time, things were not the same. Frank Manci typifies the European who came to this country so many years ago, who saw opportunities in this American land, who raised his family in this country. These are the people who have made America. Again, *The Times* wishes to pay tribute to the memory of Frank Manci—Pioneer.

SOYBEAN CONTEST . . . Soybean growers in Baldwin this year have an opportunity to see what yield of beans they can make and get paid for it. The production contest of the Baldwin Oil Mill is the first contest of its kind ever held in Alabama. These contests are common throughout the Corn Belt and keen interest is shown each year to see who can be tops. In Iowa, the top yield was 61 bushels. Indiana has had numerous yields of 50 bushels and better. The Delta country of Mississippi hit the 50 bushels last year.

At present, there are enough entrants to assure the success of the movement but Mr. Purvis is anxious to get as many as possible in it. There is one problem that presents itself and that is harvesting. All it takes is the total yield on a measured five-acre block. This may be in any part of the field. The beans from this block are then loaded and sent on to the oil mill. It is going to be interesting to see just what combination of crop rotation and fertilizers are going to pay best. We may not come up to the 50 bushels but we should get many in the 40-bushel class. If you have not registered, be sure to do it before August 1. The telephone will do it.

PLAY SAFE . . . More persons are killed in accidents while farming than in any other major industry. The tragic outlook for 4,000 deaths and a million and a quarter injuries in farm accidents during 1953 is the reason for observance of National Farm Safety Week, July 19-23. It is not just another "week." More appropriately, it is a time when all of us should reflect upon our own safety habits, whether we work and live on a farm or elsewhere. The National Safety Council lists 10 commandments for farm safety which should be heeded if, in the words of Secretary of Agriculture Ezra Taft Benson those who "'Farm To Live' will continue to 'Live To Farm.'"

November 12, 1953

DR. HODGSON TENDED THE SICK 63 YEARS

OUTSTANDING CITIZEN . . . Baldwin lost one of its outstanding citizens last Thursday when Dr. Philip Morton Hodgson, 88-year-old Stockton physician, passed away.

Dr. Hodgson had retired last year after administering to the ills of the people of this section for 63 years. For years he was the only doctor within a 100 square mile area.

Besides his tireless efforts in tending the sick and injured, Dr. Hodgson took a great interest in public affairs and once represented Baldwin County in the State Legislature. He was an elder in the Presbyterian Church, taught Sunday School and was a member of the Stockton Masonic Lodge for 60 years. He was also the first public health officer in Baldwin County.

His death takes one of the last of the old beloved country doctors who played such an important part in the lives of all of us. We shall always treasure having known him.

TEACHERS DO IMPORTANT WORK . . . This is American Education Week . . . can you think of any special week that should be more important to you, your children or the future of this nation? . . . our teachers do some of the most important work on some of the least pay of any profession in this good old country . . . a fellow who wants to learn gets his basic training during his grade school days and, thereafter, he's usually on his own . . . trouble with most of us is we stop too soon—learning, that is.

Politics is interesting, isn't it, or aren't they? . . . grammatically speaking, we never did know whether to treat the subject singular or plural . . . however, the facts in the statement are indisputable . . . first, Mr. Brownell says it's so, then Mr. Truman says it ain't, while the others just say they don't remember . . . when asked if he'd be willing to testify before a congressional investigating committee, Harry said he was a former President . . . guess you might term his answer as hiding behind the whole Constitution rather than the Fifth Amendment . . . however, Mr. George Washington Plunkett allows as how some sort of investigation, minus the dramatics of McCarthyism, ought to be instituted to determine whether the Republicans or the Democrats are lying about this reported Red spy being allowed to hold high government positions back when Harry was at the helm . . . friend Plunkett, since we mentioned McCarthy, wonders whether the Wisconsin senator's new wife will wear the pants in the McCarthy family . . . sensationalism, to a limited degree, is all right in newspapers but out of place in government.

Guess maybe you like this cold weather as well as we do . . . seems like the summers are getting longer all the time . . . we can remember one winter when it snowed in South Alabama but then our memory is getting longer all the time . . . "Newspaper Held Fine Ad Medium" reads headline . . . we always thought as much . . . the average American works one-third of the year just to pay his taxes—Uncle Sam lets him have the other two-thirds for himself and his other creditors . . . according to notices received this past week, we need a mite more of the year for ourselves and others . . . if you're the same way, we might advise that the psychiatrist says it's best to forget your troubles . . . may we suggest you let this favorite newspaper of yours and ours help you forget them? The charge so very small—the enjoyment so very great . . . if you don't believe us, subscribe anyway and prove us wrong . . . bye now, 'till next time.

March 18, 1954

HUNTERS IMPATIENTLY AWAIT GOBBLER SEASON

CLEANING GUNS . . . Baldwin hunters this week are cleaning their guns as they anxiously await the opening of spring turkey season which opens Saturday and continues through April 15th . . . not so enthusiastic are the many wives who will be awakened at unearthly hours either to cook breakfast or by their husbands preparing their own breakfast. Probably Baldwin's most enthusiastic turkey hunter is Tom Mitchell of Bay Minette. He had two sacks of yelpers when we saw him Wednesday. They included: cedar box yelpers, lead frame variety, slate and corncob, and the old turkey wing bone yelper.

Mr. Tom's favorite, he declares, is the slate and corncob but he has been experimenting with a new yelper sent to him by a friend from Monroe County. It is a cocoanut hull with a piece of slate.

City clerk Rudolph Cromartie, another authority on big gobblers, is in bad trouble due to circumstances beyond his control. During past seasons he used a lead frame yelper which fits into the roof of the mouth, but this year he will have to use a cedar box. Reason—new false teeth.

Other expert turkey hunters who can't wait for Saturday to roll around are Wilbur Richerson, John Young, J.T. Bradley, John Chason, and Robertsdale's Bob Hooks. Note to George Carleton, editor of the *Clarke County Democrat*, at Grove Hill, who also sells turkey callers. You can reach all Baldwin turkey hunters through the classified section of *The Baldwin Times*.

BIG RODEO . . . We hear they had quite a large crowd at Rosinton Sunday for the Rodeo. Among those going down from Bay Minette were Jack Robertson, Ray Reed, and Billy Robertson, formerly of Bay Minette.

MARKETING SCHOOL . . . R.C. Frederick of Foley, head of Baldwin's on the Farm Training Program, attended the Swift and Co. marketing school in Montgomery recently.

FASHION SHOW . . . Doing a wonderful job of modeling "Styles of Yesterday and Today" in the Avondale fashion show last week were B.C.H.S. Home Economics and F.H.A. girls. Sponsored by the S. Kahalley Store, the girls modeled styles of the late 1800s and early 1900s, borrowed from local persons, and new spring fashions by Avondale.

HONORARY . . . Among those initiated into Phi Eta Sigma, national freshman honorary for men, was Frank LeNoir of Magnolia Springs, who is a student at A.P.I.

SPORTSMEN . . . Baldwin sportsmen and conservationists are making plans to observe National Wildlife Week next week. Art Stenzel, president of the County Sportsman's Association, says his group will discuss water pollution cleanup and other conservation goals at the meeting in the Rod and Gun Clubhouse at 8 o'clock Monday night at Fairhope. The 1954 theme is "Water Pollution Control."

VISITORS . . . Miss Eva Waters and Mr. John Waters of Pensacola were welcome visitors to *The Times* office Tuesday.

September 23, 1954

BALDWIN LOSES PROMINENT CITIZEN

The death of Jesse M. Smith Friday night came as a distinct shock to his many friends as he had apparently been in good health recently.

Prominent in Baldwin civic and political affairs for many years, Mr. Jesse was tax collector for some 14 years. He was appointed to the office by the governor in 1926 when the late Judge G.M. Humphries was elected Probate Judge. He was reelected to the office three times.

A deeply religious man, he was a member and former elder of the Presbyterian Church in Bay Minette. Mr. Jesse was widely known throughout Baldwin County and was ever radiant with good cheer and a natural friendliness that embraced everyone. Baldwin has lost a fine man and a good citizen.

DIM YOUR LIGHTS

We do a great deal of driving around here, trying to keep in contact with this great big county of ours, and making an occasional jaunt home to visit with the folks, and this means a good bit of night time traveling. It has come to our attention that something is being neglected in the training of a considerable number of the drivers that are now occupying the highways of Baldwin at night. It must simply be carelessness, because no one thinking clearly would intentionally pass another vehicle on the road with his bright lights on full glare in the other driver's eyes. Yet we have noticed an increasing number of cars that are doing just this.

What all can happen when we forget to dim our lights in the face of an approaching automobile? The first retaliation that the other driver automatically thinks of is to brighten his own lights again, and so instead of having one blinded operator, we now have two. Reaction number two usually consists of hitting the brakes quickly, and this will cause a car traveling at a high speed to swerve; two cars swerving that close to one another has been the reason for a great many highway fatalities.

Supposing the driver approaching you somehow does forget to cut down his brights; this is certainly no excuse for you to do likewise, because he cannot help but notice when yours go down, and will in all probability follow suit.

We are reminded of the late young driver who bravely stated to his traveling companion: "Well, I won't dim mine till he dims his!" This classic remark is now filed under the heading of "famous last words."

CHECK THE CALENDAR

Fall begins today . . . That is according to the calendar, not the weather . . . Mr. George Washington Plunkett says, however, that it will be some time before hog killing time . . . One thing we like about the coming of Fall is oysters on the half shell . . . Looking at the pessimistic side, it won't be long before October and tax paying time . . . Every year we wonder where the money will come from to meet taxes but somehow or other November finds us with tax receipts in one pocket and a new bank note in the other . . . Now that summer vacations are over, you may be able to rest a little.

Looks like the Giants will face the Indians in the World Series . . . Just for the record, we'll say it'll be the Indians in six games . . . Sure shot football prediction: Auburn over Chattanooga Saturday . . . Long shot: Alabama over L.S.U. . . . A lady is a woman who makes a man act like a gentleman . . . Some people are prone to talk about how hard they work while other people are prone not to listen, mainly because they aren't interested in other's troubles.

Teachers who give children a lot of homework don't have much consideration for parents . . . If you think every person is in favor of progress and that progress is easy, just get something going for the benefit of the community and see how many people register complaints . . . If they can't find fault with anything else, they'll find fault with the way it's done . . . It's much easier to sit back and criticize those who are trying to do something than to get out and do something yourself . . . Fortunately all people aren't like this . . . Proper use of paint helps the looks of women and houses . . . Only about three months until Santa comes . . . Every person in this great county doesn't read this newspaper but many do and they find themselves greatly informed on factual doings and goings on . . . Try it please . . . All, time being.

March 17, 1955

STUDENTS EARNING WHILE LEARNING

The first Diversified Occupations class in the nation started about 20 years ago in Opelika, and is still going strong. Six years ago Baldwin County High School instituted the program, and it is growing, both in number of students and progress in the program. B.C.H.S. is the only school in the county that has this program, and its success should lead to others.

The man that started the program used a great deal of foresight. While knowing that D.O. would not completely take the place of the badly needed additional trade schools in the state, he realized that it would be a long time before the vocational education facilities met the need. Diversified Occupations now fills that gap.

It is an excellent training system, whereby the students are hired in actual positions outside of school, and pursue a course of study in class that corresponds with the type of job they hold. They are earning while learning.

J. D. Peterson and Gloria Hart, Baldwin County's Mr. and Miss D.O., accompanied by the program coordinator Adolphus Jones, are leaving today (Thursday) for the state convention in Tuscaloosa. *The Times* wishes them luck in the state contest, and sincerely hopes that the program continues to grow and thrive, making a better Baldwin County through better Baldwin citizens.

EDUCATION, NOT LEGISLATION, IS THE ANSWER

A group of civic-minded citizens in Baldwin County are trying to get a bill introduced into the legislature by Rep. L. W. Brannan that would prohibit the sale of certain objectionable comic books in the county. *The Times* does not agree with this proposition.

We will readily admit that some of the alleged "comic books" now on sale at the news stands are not suitable literature for anyone, and have no place in anybody's home. Moreover, we are delighted to see that enough people are sufficiently aroused to do something about the situation. We simply do not agree with the proposed method.

You cannot legislate morals. The quickest way to make a man want something is to tell him he cannot have it. We are an independent lot, and do not like to be told that we cannot do something. If the legal sale of these publications is prohibited, that would open the door for under-the-counter sales, and if that started, murder and crime would be mild compared to the subject matter.

There is another angle that we have not considered, and that is that the legislation would be a violation of the "freedom of the press" clause in our Bill of Rights. The way this proposed bill reads, any publication that contains incidents of crime, rape, murder, or suggestively lewd actions is to be banned. With this as a guide, practically any book, newspaper, or magazine published could fall under the ban.

Now let's face it, are we going to admit that we have no control over the way our children think? Are they so independent of the element of the family that their minds are made up by what appears in trashy literature? Is our own influence on our children so pitifully small that they can become delinquents and eventually criminals in spite of our teaching and training? If this is true, then we ought not to have children.

The logical answer to this question is not legislation, but education. This education can be provided in the home, and the churches and schools will gladly furnish all the help at their disposal. But let's not place the shame and disgrace on our county that would come if we admitted that a problem that is essentially one of the home, could not be handled there.

THINK YOU HAVE A FEVER?

Ah Spring . . . you needn't feel embarrassed, or start feeling your forehead to see if you're sick . . . we've had our air conditioners on this week, too . . . Romance seems to be about the best thing we can talk about these days, and it has reached international proportions . . . Question of the week is: "Will Princess Margaret marry Capt. Peter Townsend?" . . . We kind of secretly hope she does, and we think that is the general opinion in the U.S. . . . All the world loves a lover, the saying goes, and goes doubly on this side of the Atlantic, don't you think? . . . If this Salk Polio Vaccine works, what a wonderful thing it will have accomplished . . . we note where there is a good possibility of our county benefiting from it this Spring . . . we are keeping our fingers crossed.

Hope the employees and employers of the railroad and telephone companies can settle their differences before long . . . we never realize how reliant we are on a commodity until it suddenly is not available for a while . . . This Atomic Age . . . we exploded a couple more bombs recently, and if you saw them on television, you'll agree that they could certainly do a lot of damage . . . Old Mr. Plunkett remembers the good old days when the only place that you could find weapons that could destroy the world was in the minds of the boys that create comic strips . . . Saw a cartoon in the paper recently showing a hobo with two cups outstretched . . . one was labeled "Income" . . . the other said "Tax."

Have you become a member of the Red Cross yet this year? . . . right now is the time to do so if you haven't . . . Have you ever stopped to think how much of our county is planted in timber? . . . if you have, think also for a minute what would happen if we had a really bad forest fire raging throughout the county . . . we would then be calling on the Red Cross to come, and quick . . . They would be on hand in short order . . . they always are . . . and this newspaper is always on hand to keep you posted on what's going on here in the county . . . hope you are among the informed . . . bye now.

February 9, 1956

Baldwin County leader retires

(On Jan. 1, 1956, Cly T. Smith stepped down from his position as Post-master of Bay Minette, relinquishing the post to Aaron G. Weaver. Perhaps the highest acclaim that can come to a man for outstanding achievement in his career is to be praised by a member of his own occupation. We present here an article written by Harry J. Wilters, Postmaster of Robertsdale, expressing his feelings for the job that Smith has done, as published in the January issue of the *Bama Postmaster*. As we reprint Wilters' article, we would like to add that he is also expressing the opinion of *The Times*.)

Taken from the January issue of the *Bama Postmaster*.

"After 34 years in the postal service, Postmaster Cly T. Smith of Bay Minette, Ala., retired on the advice of his doctor.

"Cly had served as clerk, rural carrier, assistant postmaster, and postmaster at the Bay Minette office. This gave him a wide range of knowledge in postal regulations and we postmasters of Baldwin County looked upon Cly as dean of postmasters and when we got caught in the web of regulations and got so tangled up we did not know heads from tails, we always called on Cly to get us back on the beam, and he was always glad to help us. He will be greatly missed and the postal service is losing a most devoted worker.

"Cly has well earned his right to retirement and we postmasters of Baldwin County wish for him a complete recovery from his illness and a long and happy retirement. His devotion to his work and to our organization will long be a standard to which we should all try to attain."

SHOCKING TRUTH

In this month's issue of the *Kiwanis Magazine*, there is a lengthy article about the shocking lack of exercise our youth is getting these days . . . the author advocates compulsory athletics for all school children . . . we more or less hold with the theory of a college president who once said, "When

I feel the urge to exercise, I lie down on a couch until the urge passes" . . . could this possibly account for the spare tires around our midsection? . . . of course, you can go to extremes in both directions, and one is about as bad as the other . . . Plunkett tells of recently visiting a college campus and asking a student where the Science Building was . . . the student smiled and told him that he didn't know because he was there on an athletic scholarship.

Someone asked us not so long ago how we came by all the information that appeared in these columns . . . for want of a better answer, we said we simply dreamed up our stories . . . he said, "How you must dread going to bed" . . . Sidney Smith once said of Macauley, "He once talked too much; but now he has occasional flashes of silence that make his conversation perfectly delightful" . . . almanacs are wonderful gems of information . . . we picked one up this week to check a fact, and discovered that, believe it or not, despite a high level of education, the United States has the lowest proportion of book readers of any major English-speaking democracy . . . well, when was the last time you turned the TV off to read a book?

And speaking of almanacs, did you know that 95% of all American women have never eaten snails? . . .amazing, no? . . . whether or not you have ever dined on encased mollucsae, or read a good book lately, you can keep pretty well abreast of *The Times* by staying with this journal . . . that's all . . . hope you are among the informed . . . bye now.

February 23, 1956

FFA MEMBERS MOST VALUABLE RAW MATERIAL

From time to time we have occasion to mention trees and forest products, corn, potatoes, soybeans, and the countless other agricultural commodities that Baldwin County is famous for, but by far the greatest single raw material produced here is the children who will grow up to be our citizens of the future.

America must have an average of 130,000 new farmers each year to replace those who die, retire, or for any reason leave the farm. The new farmer of today must be a highly skilled and well-trained technician, as well as a good businessman.

The Future Farmers of America, which organization is being honored this week during National FFA Week, is providing the training necessary to furnish the farmers of tomorrow the know-how they will need to meet and master the problems connected with modern farming. You need only look at the farms of Baldwin County today to see that FFA training is paying healthy dividends.

The Times salutes the FFA boys, and the dedicated instructors that are doing such an excellent job of training them, B.C. Nix in Foley, T.V. Bishop in Robertsdale, Carl Grant, Jr., in Fairhope, and Byron H. Nall in Bay Minette.

HELP THE GUARD CAMPAIGN

On February 25 the National Guard of Bay Minette is to hold an intensive one-day recruiting campaign. Its purpose is increasing the strength of the National Guard to help take up the slack caused by reduction of our military forces. This makes sense on several counts. For one thing, it's good economics. A large and strong National Guard, composed of volunteer citizen-soldiers, is about the most in the way of defense we can get for our money. Guardsmen give their country much more in protection than they ever receive in dollars.

Now, at the request of Congress, and to meet a need for the particular kind of service which only the National Guard can offer, the Guard must increase its strength. Its coming campaign deserves our support.

JUST AROUND THE CORNER

This past weekend just could not make up its mind as to what sort of weather it wanted to have . . . sun shining brightly one minute, followed by a downpour that threatened to drown one and all the next . . . but at any rate, it gave a pretty good indication that summer is just around the corner . . . we were, however, considerably more fortunate than our neighbors in North Alabama, who suffered over a million dollars worth of damage and 15 known injured as the result of the erratic weather conditions . . . Plunkett said that it was a wonderful weekend for sitting in the house and noticing all of the leaks he is going to forget to fix when the sun shines again.

An editorial in Sunday's *Birmingham News* makes the following statement: "If only all the people of the world were well aware of our true aims and aspirations, how much less difficult our peace quest could be." . . . this statement is so true it actually hurts . . . Bennett Cerf, in last week's *This Week* magazine Sunday supplement, brought up the age-old story of how the fable of George Washington's cutting down the cherry tree just wasn't so . . . we had a history professor who got more pleasure out of debunking accepted historical facts than he did in giving us poor marks on our papers.

A good rule to remember in this critical election year is that you can only govern men by serving them in a democracy . . . this rule is with very few exceptions, if any . . . George Washington Plunkett came up with another of his uncalled-for definitions this week by saying that a confirmed bachelor is a man who has completely lost his nerve . . . if this office has not floated away by that time, we'll see you next week . . . that's all . . .

July 26, 1956

MISSIONARY TO JAPAN
HAS A SIMPLE REQUEST

Elsewhere on this editorial page we are printing a letter received in this office this week from Rev. Virgil McMillan, a Baptist Missionary to Japan from Baldwin County. The letter is full of interesting accounts of the daily life and work of an American family dedicated to demonstrating the working techniques of Christian theology in a foreign land.

Rev. McMillan has written to ask us for something, as well as to furnish a report on his activities. His request is two-fold, and we sincerely hope that the readers of this paper will take a few moments out to grant this request.

The Missionary has asked us for (1) our prayers for the success and the continuation of the work of his family and other Christian workers abroad, and (2) for letters from home.

Neither of these requests is unreasonable, and both will help Rev. McMillan considerably in his work. Our prayers will assure him that the purpose to which he has dedicated his life is one of the most worthwhile of all, and our letters will come as a great comfort to a family from our county so far away from home.

MONSTER OUT OF A MIDGET

Sensational headlines sell newspapers. Nobody will argue with that fact, us least of all. But another indisputable fact is that such headlines must convey accurate facts, and the desire for a strong and eye-catching lead does not give a newspaper columnist license to jump to conclusions.

On page one of this issue there is a story telling of an article written by a columnist for a large Alabama daily newspaper. This columnist had heard rumors and reports that the law enforcement officers in South Baldwin County had received orders not to patrol the area along Gulf Shores south of the Canal. He then made certain assumptions indicating that, if such rumors were true, Baldwin's Gulf area could become a new center of activity for gambling and other forms of vice.

This was a safe enough assumption. If there is no law in an area, then the area residents can become a law unto themselves. There is no argument there. Assuming that there are no law enforcement officers to prevent it, gambling, illegal beverage sales, and numerous other forms of corruption could flourish. However, we have established that there is no indication that law enforcement is lax in South Baldwin County.

The Baldwin County Solicitor, Kenneth Cooper, Monday told a *Times* reporter that the Sheriff and his staff have been extremely cooperative in keeping the county free of gaming devices. Since the countywide sweep in 1949, only one slot machine has been found in the county, and it was seized immediately.

According to Cooper, the entire rumor began as a result of an order from State Highway Patrol headquarters in Montgomery for the patrol to concentrate on the straight stretches between Foley and the Canal and the Orange Beach road. As Highway Patrol Director Smelley pointed out to him, the majority of cases of speeding and reckless driving occur on the straight road north of the Canal, rather than on the winding roads from the Canal to the beach areas.

We are proud of our county. We would be sorely disappointed if there were anything happening here that could link the name of Baldwin with the vice-ridden sections of Phenix City before the cleanup. To be fair and just, we do not think that any such situation exists.

But just in case the midget rumor which gave birth to the monster headline has given anyone any false ideas, we suggest that they stop and review the facts before attempting to set up gambling houses or any other dens of iniquity in our county. The Baldwin County law agencies are fast and efficient and will not put up with any foolishness along these lines.

SEASON NEARING END

Baseball season is nearing an end around here, and the government has announced that hydrogen bomb exploding season is over too for a while . . . we doubt if there's any connection, but its food for thought . . . the longer the McKeon trial goes on, the more convinced we are that Matthew McKeon is not nearly so much on trial as the whole Marine Corps philosophy of training men for combat . . . Harry Truman told a reporter this week that the only man he is against in the Democratic Convention is Harry Truman . . . Truman's indecisive attitude must be giving Harriman fits come sleeping time nights now . . .

A man who is a real booster and supporter of his own home town will do his trading at home because he realizes that the mail order houses never contribute one thin dime to the local charity campaigns . . . a man named

Emmons once said that we should never despair of a student if he has one clear idea . . . nowadays we almost think that's too much to ask for . . . the Irish playwright George Bernard Shaw once quipped that "Woman reduces us all to a common denominator" . . . to which Plunkett asks "How common can you get?"

Operatic tenors and Crosby-type baritones may come and go, but Elvis (The Pelvis) Presley seems to go on and on . . . frankly, the farther the better, for our two cents . . . a man without a conscience is like a newspaper without a reading audience . . . he has nothing to pat him on the back when he has done a job well, and has no reminder that he can do better when he slips . . . your letters to this journal keep us well informed as to whether or not we are best serving you . . . that's all . . .

January 10, 1957

Local minister welcomed to nation's capital

Like visiting royalty, a Bay Minette minister was welcomed to the nation's capital last week and, from all reports, really received the VIP treatment.

Rev. Gordon Earls, pastor of the Assembly of God Church here, finally gave in to the advice of his congregation and took a few days off last week following the Dedication Services of their newly erected church building. He chose Washington, D.C., for his brief retreat.

Rev. Earls was still glowing with enthusiasm when he stopped by to tell us of the welcome given him by George Grant, the Congressman from this District, who took him in hand, introduced him to all kinds of dignitaries, and hosted him and his family to a round of activities in the government center.

Perhaps the highlight of the entire trip came Saturday morning, when President Dwight D. Eisenhower addressed a joint session of Congress and the nation on television. For this event, Rev. Earls expressed, "I was closer to the President than Mamie!"

GOP Convention Chairman Joe Martin, Congressmen Scott of Tennessee, McCormack of Massachusetts, Bennett of Florida, and the House Chaplain were only a few of the well known hands that reached out to shake that of Rev. Earls.

The preacher told that he was very impressed with the U.S. Mint, where some $26 million are printed up each day. He said he had a funny feeling as the little carts rolled by him, each carrying $2 million.

He enjoyed witnessing the ceremony of the changing of the guard at the Tomb of the Unknown Soldier at Arlington, and toured the Smithsonian Institution and Lee's Home, among numerous other points of interest. But above all, he was appreciative of the hospitality and welcome shown him by Congressman Grant.

NEGOTIATION OF PEACE

The lady foreign minister of Israel said this week that her country was earnestly anticipating a direct negotiation of peace with Egypt . . .we suppose that's alright, but we don't want to be sitting in between the day Ben Gurion and Nasser come face to face . . . quite a few Yankees went back home after Saturday's Senior Bowl game in Mobile feeling that the whole thing was "rigged" . . . Why, the sneaky Rebels had even managed to hide the snow . . . the new year has brought the usual influx of tourists motoring through our county . . . we know they're tourists because we are certain that you never leave the sides of the roads littered and cluttered with trash, and that's how we can tell they've been here.

We've heard some talk about having a New Year's Day football game in Mobile every year with a Southeastern Conference team as host . . . it could be called The Azalea Bowl . . . the Jaycees, or some other alert and coming group, should latch onto this idea and make it go . . . we noticed Saturday that hockey has been added to the list of televised sports in this country . . . when they go to filming the championship matches each year from the International Chess Club, we're going to trade our set in for a set of Do-It-Yourself books or something.

Reports from Montgomery this week show that Alabama's National Guard strength now ranks in the top five in the nation . . . let's see Massachusetts get tough with us now over our state fish . . . in Proverbs we read that "In the lips of him that hath understanding, wisdom is found; but a rod is for the back of him that is void of understanding" . . . a well-placed foot can sometimes do almost as much good . . . in this county a man who possesses both wisdom and understanding is one who can be found any Thursday keeping abreast of what's going on right here by reading this journal . . . are we talking about you? . . . that's all . . .

January 31, 1957

BALDWIN RESIDENTS SUPPORT WORTHY CAUSES

Speaking with a slight prejudice, we believe that Baldwin County has always done just a little more than its share in contributing to the general welfare of its people and donating to reduce and relieve suffering all over the country and world.

This year three separate United Fund organizations are in operation, covering all of the county. These groups represent combined agencies in allotting funds for a number of very worthy causes. Harry D'Olive of Bay Minette is meeting with splendid cooperation in every Baldwin community as he pushes the 1957 March of Dimes toward a successful conclusion this week, and Judge J.S. McGough of Birmingham, state director of the American Cancer Society, stopped by *The Times* office last week to hand the county a pat on the back for the wonderful cooperation always given his organization here.

There is one organization in Bay Minette of which we are particularly proud, the Christian Charity League. This group goes about its business of helping those who need help in a quiet but efficient manner. Clothes are provided for children whose parents cannot afford them, and baskets of food for Christmas are furnished by this organization each year.

The Christian Charity League Monday named Lawrence L. Malone as its new president, taking the place of Perry S. Roberts, who had headed the group since its beginning. To Mr. Roberts, we want to offer our thanks for a job mighty well done, and we hope Mr. Malone is as successful as his predecessor. We think that the group chose wisely in selecting its new president.

AN EARLY SPRING

You might as well reach for your overcoats and galoshes, as we are predicting an early spring around these parts . . . Mr. Groundhog may disagree with us Saturday, but we've had others take issue with us before, so we won't get too concerned about that . . . we noticed where two children were killed when they were trapped in an abandoned ice box at their home in San Antonio, Texas, last week . . . how much warning does it take for some folks? . . . we wonder just what was accomplished in the Middle East recently—a skirmish took place, prisoners taken, U.N. stepped in, skirmish called off, canal blocked, now prisoners exchanged, canal still blocked, and both the Arabs and Israelis still distrust each other and the lid could still blow off at any moment—like we say, what's been accomplished?

A man was in the office this week talking about what the future may bring in the line of visual aids to education—said that someday each student's desk might possibly be equipped with a personal sized television screen as a training aid . . . we don't know how they'll do it, but we're betting on the kids to find a way to get Roy Rogers galloping through an arithmetic lesson . . . the Army must either be getting caught up on personnel, or they're having a shortage of spuds, as we see where Alabama is calling 100 fewer men in February's draft than they did in January . . . thinking of the Army makes us think of red tape and forms in triplicate . . . a wise buck sergeant once told us that the war could not have lasted another six months, as the Army would have run out of paper.

Our office is no different from anybody else's . . . our boss, like yours, is the type of fellow who comes in late when you're early, and who is early when you're late . . . can you ever remember a time when you were far away from here, and would have given anything to hear from somebody about what was going on in your home town? . . . if you have a boy, husband, or sweetheart off in the service, a subscription to this journal would answer a lot of his questions weekly . . . that's all . . .

March 7, 1957

Mobile River Soil Conservation District report

Baldwin County gave a mighty good account of itself in the annual report of the Mobile River Soil Conservation District, which was released this week by W.M. Hodgson, Sr., Baldwin County supervisor.

Besides completing a physical inventory of land capabilities in this county, the S.C.S. last year helped John Bauer of Summerdale increase his yield on soybeans from 28 to 41 bushels per acre by using a grass base rotation, encouraged several top paper producing companies to donate 250,000 pine seedlings to be distributed in the county, and helped promote the Farm-City Week in South Baldwin. This last was observed by holding essay contests in the schools, a proclamation by Mayor Max Griffin, and a fish fry that was open to the public.

Hodgson, as Baldwin supervisor, attended a national Supervisor's meeting in Boston, Mass., and this county played host to an inter-district confab down at Point Clear. All in all, we just can't see how the S.C.S. could manage without Baldwin County.

Speaking of the S.C.S., we were mighty glad to see Foley S.C.S. worker Cyril Bianco and the Missus in Bay Minette Sunday. They had come to visit North Baldwin S.C.S. worker Bill Friel, who is recuperating from a recent illness, and to attend services at Immanuel Episcopal Church, where the Diocesan Bishop, Rt. Rev. C.C.J. Carpenter of Birmingham, was holding confirmation.

GRASS IS GREENER

The grass is beginning to get real green around the courthouse square in our county, and Israel has agreed to pull out of the Gaza and Aqaba strips . . . actually there is no connection between the two—just the way our mind is running . . . talk about a vicious circle, we think we've got this situation whipped—or at least, we will have in a few years. . . . what we'll do is borrow a pile from the bank to pay off last year's income tax, then use the interest as a deduction next year on this year's tax, and in a few years we ought to about break even . . . or something . . . lots of folks must still be traveling through the county every week, because we know you aren't the ones cluttering the roads up with litter . . . are you?

If you don't believe that advertising in this newspaper is effective, just try running an ad here next week saying that you sell coffee at 50 cents a pound . . . the Arab nations are still making big talk over the Middle East, and big talk usually leads to big trouble . . . we hope we are big enough to keep the trouble restricted to talking . . . Alabama hats will be off next week to the high school bands as March 15 has been designated High School Band Day, with the U.S. Navy Band putting in an appearance in Montgomery . . . we used to play in a high school band, but gave it up . . . we figured we'd rather carry girls to football games than a horn.

Mardi Gras was quite a gala affair this year . . . we figure the policemen in Mobile will be the happiest of all when the parades can be televised in color, reducing the auto traffic by about one-third . . . sand lots ought to be dusted off pretty soon now, as the familiar cry of "Batter Up" will soon be heard all over the county . . . about the only place we know of where you can follow the weekly activities of the ball clubs of this county is this journal, so stay with us . . . that's all . . .

March 21, 1957

TIME TO GET TOUGH ON DRUNK DRIVING

Bay Minette Police Chief J.L. Barrow told *The Times* this week that law enforcement officers have been ordered to get tough and crack down on traffic violators. This statement came as a result of a traffic safety conference held recently in Montgomery.

Chief Barrow pointed out an interesting parallel that was discussed at the conference, and we agreed with him that it made little sense. He said that if a man went out, got stupid drunk, and shot another man dead, that was murder, and a maximum penalty was usually meted out. He said also that, in the past, if a man went out, got stupid drunk, and ran over someone with a car, it was generally considered accidental homicide, and a minimum sentence was the result. The Chief explained that the only difference between the two types of murder was the actual weapon used.

Last week the Grand Jury recommended to Judge Hubert M. Hall that stiffer penalties be given to traffic violators, especially second and third time offenders. Last week also, Felix Bigby, city clerk at Daphne, added a 30-day jail sentence to a $200 fine for driving while intoxicated to a man who had caused a collision on the highway near Fairhope.

For the past two years the traffic fatality toll in Baldwin County has been 35 dead and countless more injured. We cannot say how many of these accidents were caused by disregard of established laws and regulations, but if so much as one death has been the result of law-breaking, we agree that now is the time to get tough and do away with highway foolishness.

WORLD ATTENTION

It's getting harder every day for a man to make a name for himself . . . what with all the unperformable feats having been performed, and space travel being still a year or so off, about the only way a fellow could cause world attention now would be to swim the Atlantic, or something . . . unless we miss our guess, the Kansas City Athletics should make a big splash in baseball news this season, judging from the lineup of former Yankee stars they have with them this year . . . we would like to see Uncle Sam feed, clothe, and doctor a youngster for $600 in this day and time, the sum he allows off on the income tax . . . folks around here are welcoming the approaching signs of summer—so that they will have something different to gripe about besides cold weather.

We still can't help but be amused at the fellow who gleefully takes off for a big city to save a dollar or so at the big stores . . . the fact that he spends twice that amount going and coming would make it a funny situation if it weren't so true that it's pitiful . . . we think that dollars spent here at home usually find their way back to you in the long run . . . one has only to look at the expression on a child's face, who is walking for the first time after a long and crippling illness, to decide whether or not funds donated to the Crippled Children Easter Seal campaign are worth while.

Solomon said, "He also that is slothful in his work is brother to him that is a great waster." . . . two like that in the same family could lead to no end of trouble . . . if you are curious as to where all the cars were going and coming on our highways over the weekend, always read the society and community news columns of this paper to see who went a-visiting and where . . . we'll bet we are the only paper in existence that is really interested in what you do. . . . that's all . . .

March 6, 1958

Baldwin loses able citizen, M.H. 'Red' Wilkins

A senior citizen of Baldwin County, and one of its foremost public servants, passed into the annals of this county's history last Thursday, as Tax Collector M.H. "Red" Wilkins died in Pensacola.

Mr. Wilkins had spent the majority of his life as a servant of the people of Baldwin County, beginning his long and colorful career as a license inspector during the administration of Governor Bibb Graves.

Following this, he became Sheriff, and was then elected to the position of Baldwin County Tax Collector. He was serving his fourth term in this post when he passed away.

A public servant must be a hard-working individual in order to secure election to an office. He must then work even harder to maintain his position when next the all-too-often fickle minded public goes to the polls.

That "Red" Wilkins had managed the affairs of the office of Tax Collector with conscientious energy and praiseworthy efficiency becomes immediately obvious by the fact that he was reelected to the post, not once, but three times. During this lengthy period in office, Mr. Wilkins had become well acquainted with a large majority of the residents in this county, making him better able to apply a personal interest and give individual attention to the affairs of this office.

Baldwin County has lost an able and capable servant, one who has earned the acclaim of his hundreds of friends and thousands of citizens whom he served.

ROAD HOGS

Statistics show that life expectancy is getting longer and longer . . . This in spite of the road hog and the lickety-split drivers . . . The qualifying is over . . . Now the fun begins . . . We hope the candidates will still have their pleasant smiles after June 3rd . . . Advertising is still the best Spring tonic for business, but like medicine in a bottle, it won't work unless you use it . . . A lot of people tire of figures, but not if they are in modern bathing suits . . . Selfish people make money but they make few friends and never help make a community great . . . Mr. Plunkett says a good politician seems to have the ability to say two things at once without meaning either—but the weakness in this is that the people occasionally call the roll . . . Another way to live a long time is obey traffic regulations.

While some people seem to always be at the forks of a road, others are satisfied as long as they have a fork in their mouth . . . It's hard to believe that little more than two weeks ago we had snow in this county of sunshine . . . Honesty is the greatest asset a person can have, but it is more noticeable by its absence than by its presence . . . A friend is not always the man who tells you good things about yourself . . . It's amazing how many people know what is wrong with the world, yet do nothing about it . . . The same thing applies to this community—the people who criticize it and talk endlessly about its faults never seem to have time to help improve it.

We want to go fishing . . . Anybody want to join us . . . This warm weather is also causing a few old gobblers to start sounding off in the woods hereabouts . . . This is a reminder that gobbler season opens on March 20 . . . One of the best ways to help protect our wildlife is to be careful with fire in the woods . . . If you have loved ones in the service or living away from home, you can make them happy by sending them a weekly newsletter from home . . . this can be accomplished easily by sending them a year's subscription to this journal. All, time being.

April 2, 1959

'Cap'n Murph' McMillan

was a great man

Seldom does a man live who had so many friends as did Murphy M. McMillan. He had these friends because he deserved them. With an engaging personality and fine philosophy of life, he loved people.

"Cap'n Murph," as he was affectionately called, died in Stockton at the good old age of 82. As a member of one of Baldwin County's finest old families, he certainly lent dignity and prestige to his heritage. All agree he was one of the most, if not the most, liked man of his time in this area.

Those who had the pleasure and privilege of associating with him know it—to those who didn't, you can take our word for it—"Cap'n Murph" was a great man.

GET INTO THE ACT

Beards and bonnets have a significance in Baldwin County. These and many other signs mean practically every citizen is getting into the act of celebrating this, Alabama's largest county's 150th anniversary.

Baldwin is Alabama's third oldest county and among the richest in history and progress. Being exceeded in age only by Washington and Madison, she was made a county out of the Mississippi Territory, Dec. 21, 1809—10 years before Alabama became a state.

To recognize these and thousands of other interesting facts, a gigantic celebration will be held in all parts of the county May 1 thru May 9. Parades, pageants, picnics, queens, special days, kangaroo courts, displays and many other things are in the offing.

Never before in Baldwin's 150 years have so many citizens joined hands as willingly and enthusiastically. The cooperation is pleasing and amazing and another indication of why the county has and is making such phenomenal progress.

For such an undertaking, it has been necessary to get professional guidance. A company is being used who has been in this business for 56 years. For their services, they are paid a flat fee. But the hundreds on committees and individual workers are giving their time free because they are proud to be a part of the great County of Baldwin.

By your beards, your bonnets, and your talk, you too can get into the act.

"Ne Plus Ultra"—the very best—is the slogan for the Sesquicentennial celebration. Get into the act and let's tell everybody everywhere of Baldwin's greatness.

FEVERISH ACTIVITY

Warming weather and feverish activity through the great Baldwin County on the various Sesquicentennial activities . . . If everyone mentions the atrocious tie a man is wearing, the chances are that a black eye would create the same volume of comment and wonderment.

Many fail because of success while others succeed because of failure . . . Happy is he, according to Francis Quarles, the palace of whose affection is founded on virtue, walled with riches, glazed with beauty, and roofed with honour . . . World peace will come only when pacifists quit talking—they make too many people fighting mad . . . Better laugh today—your sense of humor may not be working tomorrow.

Have you noticed the youngster who receives a bicycle for school transportation usually rides with the friend who has an automobile for the same purpose . . . A friend is not always one who tells you good things about yourself . . . A successful man is one who can do no more in a pinch than people think he can . . . Teenagers are a wealthy group—it's estimated they spend about nine billion dollars a year—something to remember the next time allowances come up.

We can't help but think Southern motorists might miss the pleasant annual New England pastime of change from noisy snow tires to quiet normal treads . . . Most all communities have growing pains at intervals or either lie moribund . . . That Baldwin County is fortunate is evidenced by the large turnover in real estate transactions . . . Children would be more religious if parents were . . . Reading is a wonderful habit which too few people have bothered to acquire . . . And reading your *Baldwin Times* will keep you well informed and in turn more respected . . . Bye now.

August 6, 1959

S. M. THARP WAS A GREAT EDUCATOR AND MAN

The Mobile Press expressed it well and accurately in an editorial Monday when it said, "The name of S. M. Tharp, who died Friday in a Bay Minette hospital, will forever occupy a high place in the history of Alabama education. It can indeed be said that Baldwin County's present efficient school system is primarily the handiwork of Mr. Tharp, for he served as its superintendent for 35 years before his retirement in 1953."

Mr. Tharp was one of the most kindly yet courageous men it has ever been our privilege to know. He pioneered many new sound ideas in education, some of which met with considerable opposition but he always had the courage and intelligence to follow through. All of his ideas were backed by one basic principle—furtherance of education for the benefit of human beings.

His ability to see into the future caused him to purchase plenty of land where each school was located in the county. With Baldwin's rapid population growth, which makes additional class rooms and buildings necessary, our present fine school leaders don't have to worry about acquiring high priced, hard-to-get land. Mr. Tharp bought it when it was cheap and plentiful.

His fight for equal opportunities in education for Negroes is well known. He was the first county superintendent in Alabama to equalize pay for white and colored.

An indication of the esteem thousands held for him was in 1953 when he retired. A testimonial dinner was held for him and was attended by educational leaders who heaped praise upon him from throughout the South. His loyal teachers presented him with a new automobile in appreciation for his services to them, education and humanity.

Another proof of his love for people was the time and effort given by him to crippled children. He headed the drive for them in this county for years and consistently led the state in percentage of money raised for this great cause. Only God knows all of the many fine things he did. Certainly they are too numerous to mention here.

Again quoting *The Press*, "But the best evidence of the quality of his service are the thousands of successful men and women trained in the fine school system he worked so diligently to establish. Mr. Tharp set a pattern for living and public service that should serve as a guiding light and inspiration to those who knew him."

TIME IS PRECIOUS

When you begin remembering the "memory tunes" on the radio and television, that's a sure sign you're getting old . . . time passes fast, or hadn't you noticed it? . . . all the more reason, says Mr. Plunkett, why you shouldn't waste it. Most people have a sense of sound, a sense of touch, a sense of sight and a sense of smell, but some never develop a sense of time.

Freckles are coming back in style or so the headlines say . . . some dermatologist has taken the time to count more than 21,000 freckles on a newly discovered Swedish beauty . . . makes us wonder whether he was more interested in the freckles or the beauty . . . anyway it's interesting and a little relaxation from the commies' "cold war."

Some of our legislators are trying awfully hard to make it easier for our schools . . . which prompts friend Plunkett to allow that the schools' best friend are the state's newspapers, which is enough for some people to be against them . . . but this newspaper has always plugged for the schools and the legislators and the people . . . and we'll keep them all informed of what's going on in this county better than any other newspaper in the world . . . if you're not a subscriber, you're missing something . . . and what's more, we're missing your three-fifty . . .subscribe now . . . neither of us will regret it.

September 3, 1959

WILLIAM CRAIG BEEBE FATHER OF BALDWIN COMMISSION

In the death of William Craig Beebe, Baldwin County and Alabama lost one of their most prominent citizens. Long active in local and state politics, having served in the state legislature three terms, he was considered an authority on local and state government.

He had a passion for strong, efficient local government, and was the father of Baldwin's commission form of government. In the early '30s he had the vision to set up the government this county has been operating under since that time. He was one of the first in Alabama to advocate, and do something about, electing county commissioners in the county at-large instead of by districts. As attorney for the County Commission, he was, along with a few others, responsible for the fine, honest and financially strong government we have.

He was an interesting and brilliant conversationalist. He loved to serve in Montgomery but was by no means a politician in one sense of the word. Although he liked individuals, he was an introvert in crowds and with the public. Perhaps for this reason, he sometimes failed in his political campaigns. He often told this writer that he would like to be governor of Alabama "if he could go in the back door." Meaning he would not like to make the campaign and promises necessary to be elected in the usual way.

Billy Beebe was a man of many moods. At one time a financial failure, he died a financial success . . . which obviously he could have been much earlier in life if he had put his mind to it. But money never interested him much. He had a big heart and gave a lot of his belongings and himself to people he loved and to people he barely knew. His was an interesting life, and profitable to those near him and his fellowman.

BACK TO SCHOOL

As Baldwin's young'uns went back to school this week, one teacher reported this scribble over the hall drinking fountain: "Old Faceful!" . . . Our flat-topped friend just back from the barbershop, said Roy Davis told him about the barbers in an eastern town who struck for better pay—a razor else! . . . Bachelor Plunkett observes that if you marry in haste, you will have no leisure in which to repent.

Killing too much time often is a means of murdering opportunities . . . you'll never know how happy you can be until after you are married and then it's too late . . . two Baldwin County friends met at Gulf Shores last week and hadn't seen each other in a long time. Trying to fill in the time lapse, one asked the other, "Tell me, are you married yet?" "Oh no," was the reply. "I just look this way because I was kicked by a horse."

George Q. (for Quarterback) Plunkett says the Quarterback Club plan for raising funds for a new guest dressing room is tops—sort of double indemnity—for the Tiger fans . . . Good luck is a lazy man's estimate of a worker's success . . . doing nothing is the most tiresome job in the world because you can't stop and rest . . . a man who has nothing to brag about but his ancestors is like a potato—the best part of him is buried beneath the earth.

One of the best things to have up your sleeve is a funny bone . . . and one of the best things to have in your head is good thoughts . . . Sooner or later, a man, if he is wise, discovers that life is a mixture of good days and bad, victory and defeat, give and take . . . and one of the few bad things about Labor Day weekends is the high number of traffic accidents . . . this country journal likes to print the news, but not that kind . . .drive safely, don't be a statistic . . . a woman appreciates a man who always remembers her birthday and completely forgets her age—statistic . . . be reading us next week, please. Bye, now.

October 15, 1959

ORT H. ERTZINGER ALWAYS IN
WORTHWHILE ENDEAVORS

Though we can ill afford it, Bay Minette and this area have lost another fine citizen in the death Saturday of Ort Ertzinger.

He was a great character. Always active in things worthwhile, he retired several years ago from the daily business routine. Like so many of Baldwin's citizens, he came from "up North" when young. Broke in 1933, even though he was well into middle-age, he started again. By working 18 hours a day, he gradually lifted himself up the economic ladder and was a financial success long before he was 70.

Obviously his name was confusing to many. We affectionately called him "Ert Ortzinger." He had other habits that some thought peculiar, but most knew were great. Even in the depths of his economic depression and though he would get up at 3 a.m. to start work, which he often did, he always went fishing every Thursday. And on Sundays, he went to church. At death he had a record of 50 straight years of going to Sunday School without missing a Sunday.

In his younger days, he was a professional baseball player. And he played hard at everything he did. His was a great life. So perfect he even fulfilled the Biblical life quota of three score and ten.

WEBB AND STATE PARKS

Our state senator, Douglas S. Webb, of Atmore, is still waging his one-man war to get Alabama's state parks improved. He rightly thinks that Alabama has not taken advantage of her many recreational opportunities.

Webb long ago noticed other states were capitalizing on what natural sites they had for providing their people, and visitors, with recreational facilities. And that his native state, with more advantages, wasn't doing nearly enough, thereby failing to get its share of tourists and providing an incentive to industry. The young senator wants a big improvement program for Alabama's parks and other recreation areas which will attract the modern-day traveler. Believing it can be done with modest cost, he introduced a resolution in the legislature creating a committee to determine what this state has, what is needed and how to go about getting it.

The committee is at work. We can optimistically hope for good results. It has a determined chairman—Senator Douglas Webb.

BOTH TIDE, TIGER FANS HAD FUN

It's fun watching a winning football team, that is if it's your team . . . Fortunately both Alabama and Auburn fans had fun last Saturday . . . The Mobile City Commission has outlawed high heel shoes for women in downtown Mobile . . . For this they will probably be named most outrageous politicians of the year . . . Mr. Plunkett suggests they use all of the "fine" money to employ a few more policemen to improve the traffic situations at Mobile's college football games . . . Big decisions are easy to make, if you're making them for the other fellow . . . Paying cash for things is a wonderful habit—a habit we could never afford . . . This is National Apple Week . . . Let's all observe it by eating an apple.

Money either makes or breaks a man, it has been said—at least we know you are broke without it . . . A few unselfish leaders is an absolute must for any community to succeed and progress . . . Fortunately this county has quite a few . . . Have you ever met a person who thought he was overpaid and under-worked . . . Dun and Bradstreet says 95 percent of the business failures are from the ranks of non-advertisers . . . which proves that when business is good you ought to advertise and when it's bad, you've got to . . . flattery is much like perfume, it serves best if you merely smell it instead of swallowing it . . . grey hair is much more popular now than it was three or four decades ago, namely because we have so many more people to worry so many more worries.

A compliment a day may not make you rich, but it'll make a person better than if he was rich . . . This journal likes 'em too . . . and the best way you can compliment us is to keep your money coming in regularly to renew your subscription . . . Thanks and so long, for now.

Mumblings

through the

Nineteen-Sixties

❧

March 10, 1960

I. P. Mason had a courageous
career and life

The death of I.P. Mason last Friday night brought to an end a successful and courageous career. He was another of Stockton's many solid pillars who have entered into history.

Mr. Mason had to be good at many things to succeed as he wished to succeed. He was good and he did succeed. A successful schoolteacher and musician, perhaps his greatest achievement was the raising of his family of boys and girls. His wife and their mother died when the children were quite young. So he was a father, mother, schoolteacher, musician, cook, housekeeper, all wrapped up in one fine little package.

He was known far for his musical talents. Many people in these parts owe their organ playing ability to him. He was a good teacher. He loved people and liked to share the finer things of life with them.

STUDENTS AND SCIENCE

Judging from the science fair held in the city hall here over the weekend by our school students, the Russians had better watch out. These boys and girls will get ahead of them in everything.

They had over 250 exhibits. Emphasis on science education is getting results in our schools. Maybe one of these students will someday tell us how to get to the moon and back . . . or even more important give us a cure for cancer. Personally, we would be awfully proud of them if they solved the problem of the common cold, or dandruff.

The Times congratulates both teachers and students on an excellent science show.

DOING REAL WORK

Too many people are ready to carry the stool when the piano needs moving. The same is true in a community when there is real work to be done . . . A religion easy to hide is easy to lose . . . Cuba's Castro seems to take a delight in slapping at Uncle Sam . . . Mr. Plunkett, who has no doubts about the Communistic leanings of the Premier, predicts he will go the way most dictators go.

A man who has no hometown pride is one in whom the hometown doesn't take any pride either . . . Borrowers of cigarettes and books have one thing in common . . . Seldom does either bother to return them . . . Subscribers are to a newspaper what blood is to a human . . . take them away and the newspaper stops existing . . . now you know why we appreciate you so much . . . And it only takes three bucks a year now to get all the county news . . . Thanks and so long, time being.

March 17, 1960

SILVERHILL'S MAYOR IN OFFICE 28 YEARS

The Dean of the Baldwin County mayors is Emery Johnson of Silverhill. He has served in this capacity for 28 years. We don't know, but doubt if there is a mayor in Alabama with a longer record, or a better one.

We were glad to see where his community honored him and Mrs. Johnson at a big banquet recently. They are two of Baldwin's finest citizens.

Both came to Silverhill with their parents as pioneer families early in their lives. They are of Swedish descent and both consistently have contributed to the growth and betterment of their community, county and state.

The Times is happy to congratulate them for fine, successful and useful lives.

MARCH OF DIMES DRIVE SUCCESS

It is encouraging to see civic projects succeed. It means a lot of people have contributed time, energy and money to make this a better world. There is so much to be done and so few willing to do it. Those who are willing to work should be patted on the back. And we like to do it whenever possible.

This week the "Accolade Alley" belongs to Dale A. Raddcliffe who has successfully headed the March of Dimes campaign in Baldwin. This week he turned over a check for $4,292.84 to J.A. Wurst, treasurer of the county chapter of the National Foundation. The biggest amount raised in recent years in the drive. Twice as much as was raised in each of the last two years.

Congratulations Dale and to all your fine workers for doing a splendid job.

PREDICTING POLITICS

Weather and politics are warming up as May 3rd approaches . . . Pessimism among the candidates is conspicuously absent . . . in fact, if all the politicians were elected who say they're going to be, we'd have to double the county budget to pay the salaries . . . Politics and women are a lot alike . . . you can never accurately predict either . . . It is uncertainty, however, that makes life more interesting.

Only about a month until Easter . . . Our local stores are already showing their Easter outfits . . . Better buy early for best selections . . . Common sense is seeing things as they are and doing things as they should be done . . . If you have a good temper, keep it . . . If you have a bad temper, don't lose it . . . Springtime is almost upon us, we think . . . Which reminds us that spring is always a good time to clean up . . . The beauties of this pretty season should not be marred by trashy lots and streets . . . One thing is consistent these days . . . Our standard of living remains ahead of our standard of earnings . . . Perhaps a little more sweat of the brow and less wagging of the tongue would remedy this unfortunate circumstance.

What your conscience says about you is more important than what your neighbors say about you . . . Are you getting your share of the $49 million spent in this county each year . . . If not, we suggest you try the advertising columns of this journal which goes into the homes of over 3,000 of the finest families in the world . . . Most good people want to do better and expect to do better tomorrow . . . One way to improve your tomorrows is to keep up with what is going on today by reading this weekly newspaper.

May 5, 1960

Two Rhodes brothers
HAD FRUITFUL LIVES

About 45 years ago two brothers came to Baldwin County looking for a home. They found it and stayed for life. Theirs were fruitful lives, for themselves, their families, for their community and county.

They were L.T. Rhodes and V.V. Rhodes. Mr. L.T. was the first county agent of Baldwin and contributed much to the agricultural and civic betterment of the county. He died a few years ago. His younger brother, V.V., was a pioneer in the now flourishing dairy industry in the county. He had our first Grade A dairy. He was a good religious worker along with his other interests. Now he is dead.

It was the Rhodes brothers, and others like them, with vision and energy, who have built this great county.

CONGRATULATIONS "POP" HAMMOND

The grand opening of Baldwin's first shopping center will be held in Robertsdale this weekend when the Spaceway Shopping Center opens its doors to the public.

The building of this beautiful center is a result of the long-time dreaming and planning of one of this county's best and most popular businessmen. He is W.L. (Pop) Hammond.

Congratulations Pop . . . and good luck!

OUR HIGH SCHOOL BAND

The Baldwin County High School Band has brought honor to itself, Bay Minette and Baldwin County.

In a statewide contest at the University of Alabama our fine band was given a first division and superior rating. Also it was rated one of five top bands in Alabama in the BB class. This is the first time a BCHS band has ever won this high rating.

Ford Alford, who has directed the group for six years, and the 52 students in the band are to be congratulated on this fine honor. We're proud of you. Surely local citizens will show this pride tonight when they are in concert here.

May 26, 1960

Thanks, Mr. Beasley,
for fine super market

Today marks the opening of one of the most beautiful super markets in Alabama. It's Beasley's of Bay Minette. Wilson Beasley, who is a local-boy-makes-good citizen, is to be congratulated on his fine accomplishment. And *The Times* joins the citizens of this area in thanking you, Wilson, for having the faith in the future of Bay Minette to build this $200,000 retail grocery store here.

Towns grow and prosper for varied reasons, one of the most important being the type shopping center furnished the people. And in this connection, Bay Minette is making real progress. Several stores have completed expanding and modernizing and others are in the process.

Good citizens, plenty of industries, modern stores, good churches and schools, along with good government, will cause any town to grow and prosper.

PLEASE VOTE

Next Tuesday is election day again. Some important offices are to be filled and important issues are to be settled. Many elections are won or lost by people who do not vote. Enough do not avail themselves of the privilege of voting to have changed the election if they had.

Voting is a great privilege . . . and duty. So please vote Tuesday.

WE HAVE REASON FOR PRIDE

Baldwin County and Bay Minette are still growing at a rapid rate, according to preliminary census figures. Although neither has shown the percentage of increase the past decade as the previous 10 years, both are still growing with vigor. Figures haven't been received for the other county towns at this writing.

Baldwin grew from 40,997 in 1950 to 48,689 in 1960 for an 18.78 percent increase. For a predominantly rural area, she will probably show the biggest percentage increase of any county in Alabama. In 1950, we had shown the third largest increase in Alabama, being exceeded only by Mobile and Etowah.

Within the past 10 years, Bay Minette has jumped from 3,742 to 5,129, for an increase of 37.06 percent. This has been accomplished without the increase of city limits within the period. In 1950, this county seat town had more than doubled in size during the decade, to rank 9th in the state in percentage of growth. But part of the reason for this was the large area taken in by expanding the city limits. The 1,387 increase over 1950 means the biggest increase in natural growth ever shown.

Frankly, *The Times* had been too optimistic about the county's growth, expecting it to exceed 50,000. However, the growth is good and with hard work and the cooperation of all our fine citizens, the "soaring sixties" will see us do even better.

August 4, 1960

BUILDERS HARDWARE STORE REMODELED

One of Bay Minette's oldest business concerns, Builders Hardware & Supply Co., has been a consistent advertiser in *The Times* for the past 25 years. This institution has placed an advertisement with *The Times* every week for the past 1,300 issues.

When this publisher bought *The Times* 24 years ago (August 15, 1936), Builders Hardware was our biggest advertiser, running a five dollar ad each week. At that time, the late Mayor J.C. Burns and L. D. Owen, Sr., (who also became mayor) were partners in the business. Now the management has passed on to L. D. Owen, Jr., and his brother, Bobby.

This week a completely remodeled store will be presented to the public. Thus Builders Hardware becomes another of many fine stores in Bay Minette which have enlarged, been updated and beautified in recent months. All of which adds up to make this a better town and better trading center.

Congratulations go to the Owen family for their continued faith in the future of this area.

A REAL BIG STICK

Teddy Roosevelt said, "Speak softly, and carry a big stick."

Against the Communists, Uncle Sam has been speaking so softly that many felt that he didn't have the "big stick" to do otherwise.

Now that a Navy Polaris missile has been successfully shot from the atomic submarine, the George Washington, it is known that our Uncle has a real big stick. Mr. K. and his Russian gang surely will be wise enough to realize this new weapon is a devastating deterrent to their aggressive acts against a free world.

Speaking of the Polaris, *Time* magazine said: "The nuclear subs that are its launching platforms can roam the world's oceans at will, difficult to detect and destroy, ready to deliver their lethal birds on targets 1,200 miles away with an accuracy within a mile. One sub alone packs 16 missiles, and each shipload of missiles packs the explosive punch of all the bombs expended by both sides in World War II (including the A-bombs dropped on Hiroshima and Nagasaki).

Devastating is right! Thank goodness it's ours.

WE'LL BE IN STRONG HANDS

Before we get into the thick of the presidential campaign and start calling each other names, we should remind ourselves that both Democrats and Republicans have selected good teams.

The United States has been fortunate in having strong men at the head of our government in times of real trouble. The democratic system of electing presidents has worked well in the past. The free election processes for 1960 have gotten off to a good start. The conventions have nominated well, so well in fact that many voters will have a hard time deciding between the two sets of candidates.

We believe that the election of John Kennedy and Lyndon B. Johnson, or Richard M. Nixon and Henry Cabot Lodge, will give this country strong leaders upon whom we can face the troublesome times ahead with confidence and vigor.

August 25, 1960

FAIRHOPE GETS NEW THOMAS HOSPITAL

With the opening of the Thomas Hospital in Fairhope next week, Baldwin will have over 100 approved hospital beds. Only a few years back, we had none. Thanks to the Hill-Burton Act, sponsored by our own senior senator, Lister Hill, the aggressive leadership of local citizens, and the Baldwin County Commission, funds were made available to build ultra modern hospitals in Foley and Fairhope. Bay Minette has two privately owned institutions with over 50 available beds in the Mattie L. Rhodes Hospital and the Bay Minette Clinic.

This is encouraging progress and goes far in putting this county in the forefront with health facilities. As further needs arise, we have every reason to believe additional beds will be made available.

Under the Hill-Burton Act, most of the funds were furnished by the federal and state governments. But considerable money had to be raised locally. Although citizens in Foley and Fairhope did a good job, it is doubtful if the hospitals could have been built without the assistance of the County Commission.

About four years ago, the Commission, composed at that time of M.E. Bryant, R.J. Robertson, W.B. Cooper and Elmer Kinsey, gave $100,000 to

Foley and made a tentative appropriation of the same amount to Fairhope. Last year, Fairhope citizens raised their part of their hospital financing and called on the Commission for aid. The Commission, then composed of M.E. Bryant, John B. Hadley, David Barnhill and George Brown, voted to give them the $100,000.

This $200,000 cash for the health of Baldwin citizens was available because of the money the Commission was able to save from a local legislative act passed in 1951 giving the State Highway Department responsibility of building roads in the county.

As is the case with most progress, no one person can take the credit but results from the cooperation and work of many. Baldwin's fine people learned this important lesson long ago. Many benefits have resulted . . . among them our hospitals. To all those who helped, congratulations!

SWIMMING POOL IS DEDICATED

Last Sunday emphasized another important step in the development of Bay Minette as a better place in which to live. Our new swimming pool was dedicated.

This excellent recreational facility is an example of what good leadership and the cooperation of the people in a community can do. The $40,000 pool and bathhouse has been built entirely with private contributions. Naturally to do this, it took a lot of hard work and community spirit.

The Times is proud of the fine work done by the project chairman, Dr. Charles W. Gaston, and his many helpers.

December 21, 1961

ONE OF BALDWIN'S FINE SONS ABSENT
FROM THE COUNTY

This county has produced many fine citizens. Most still live here but we lose too many to outside opportunities. About six years ago, we lost a young man who had become one of Baldwin's outstanding business and civic leaders. His absence from the county scene is noted daily by his many friends and business associates.

George K. Page, son of Mr. and Mrs. G.K. Page, Bay Minette, started in the financial field at the Baldwin County Bank. After a few years, he became president of the Baldwin County Savings & Loan Association and helped start that firm on a phenomenal growth. He was state president of the Alabama Savings & Loan Association and achieved many other honors. He advanced so rapidly and attracted so much attention that bigger business opportunities were bound to come his way. Many did and finally he was lured off to Sarasota, Fla., by a big job and salary to match.

George is now executive vice president and managing officer of the First Federal Savings & Loan Association of that city. When he first joined the staff of First Federal, its resources were about $35 million. Now they are approaching $65 million.

Naturally his new associates are proud of him too. He has become a much sought after speaker, particularly in financial circles. We noted in one of Florida's leading daily newspapers recently where he was the principal speaker at a state meeting and the paper spent many paragraphs quoting his speech.

George still has many roots in Baldwin. He admits to missing the county and friends greatly. His parents, brother and sister still live in Bay Minette. His wife, the former Vivian Reed and sister to our Dr. Reed, is also a native. So maybe he'll come back but we're afraid the county can't offer a job big enough to hold him. In the meantime, congratulations and Merry Christmas to you . . . George and Vivian.

A SUCCESSFUL TEAM

We're glad President Kennedy's weekend trip to Latin America was a success . . . Uncle Sam needs a few diplomatic successes abroad and Jack and Jackie seem to be a successful team . . . even the Castroites couldn't work up any steam against them . . . they compromised by saying "Kennedy, No—Jackie, Si" . . . a lot of this country's citizens feel the same way. This younger generation is all right, in the main . . . certainly they're smarter at their age than the oldsters were at the same stage of life . . . you'll usually find those who criticize the younger group aren't so smart themselves . . . but that is almost always the case, it doesn't take a smart person to find fault with others.

This may not be the biggest newspaper on earth but it's more interested in you than any other . . . please show reciprocity. With the exception of several bowls, the football season is over . . . we're sorry because, sportively speaking, it's our favorite season of the year . . . we're guilty as accused by JFK, that as a sports spectator like most other Americans . . . spectating football from a living room easy chair or from the 50-yard line takes about the right amount of vigor for us.

Note in the news where a prominent Memphis preacher, Dr. Pollard, "wins church battle" . . . the congregation's members climaxed a bitter church feud by voting to retain their pastor . . . the vote was close and nobody but the devil won . . . anytime a preacher has to "battle" to stay with a congregation, he has already lost . . . being a good preacher of the gospel is a hard life and no intelligent person has ever claimed otherwise . . . important too! Last week's Rotary word of wisdom: "If Columbus had had an advisory board, his ships would still be at the docks." Try it . . . if you get into the habit, it's just as easy to say something good about a bad person as it is to say something bad about a good one. Thanks for reading and best wishes for a Merry Christmas.

December 28, 1961

Baldwin man promoted at University of Alabama

His many friends in his home county of Baldwin were proud to learn last week of the promotion of J. Jefferson Bennett at the University of Alabama to administrative vice president.

Jeff's promotion was announced by President Frank A. Rose, who stated, "Mr. Bennett will do an excellent job . . ." He has played an important part in the University's rapid expansion in the past 10 years and has been associated with the school in multiple capacities since 1941 when he graduated there with a B.S. degree. After spending four years in the Marines during World War II, he returned to the University and received his law degree in 1948.

He then practiced law in Fairhope where he had graduated from high school and where his father, Jas. H., was still school principal and his mother was a classroom teacher. In 1952, he returned to the University as assistant to the dean and associate professor of the law school. He has been with the University since and his success has been outstanding.

He is another example of a rising young man leaving Baldwin for greater opportunities and achieving them. We recall that considerable effort was made to keep Jeff from leaving the county at the time. He was offered an interim two-year appointment as circuit solicitor, which was quite enticing for a young lawyer, but he turned it down. Hearing his alma mater calling, he went, has stayed and has done well.

As with all people who leave, Jeff misses Baldwin and lets himself on occasion think of the far future when he can retire here. His parents now live in Bay Minette. Congratulations Jeff, and wife Chris, on your rapid rise and may we suggest that you have only started.

GREETING CARDS

Christmas is over again . . . but wasn't it fine? . . . hope it was for you . . . we liked it. There are many pleasant things about Christmas . . . one of the nicest customs is sending and receiving greetings cards . . . it gives you a chance to say "hi" in a pleasant way to old friends . . . we save ours and look at all of them on Christmas Day . . . fortunately this takes several hours, thus spreading out the pleasantness . . . to the quite a few who remembered us at 705 E. 5th this year, we say thanks. Those who do not appreciate the Christmas greetings idea must not receive many or send any.

We're glad Joe Kennedy, father of Jack, is getting along "fairly well" with his serious illness . . . he is a fabulous character, being one of the richest in the world . . . he deserves a lot of credit for raising a big outstanding family . . . of course many people do this but he accomplished the feat with the burden of also owning $400 million. Noting the death statistics, the Christmas spirit must have been in liquid form when it hit the highways. Most of us probably spend too much time worrying about what other people think about us . . . we wouldn't if we just knew how seldom they do . . . anyway, if your efforts are criticized, you must have done something worthwhile . . . Anger is a wind which blows out the light in the mind.

Many people are concerned about world affairs and the danger of war . . . the concern is understandable but world affairs aren't . . . they are so complicated we don't believe anyone, including our state department, knows what is going on . . . and we ordinary citizens really get confused when our kindly Uncle Sam hands out billions in foreign aid to enemies as well as friends . . . nations, like people, should spend all available time and money helping friends, then there would be no time left for kindness or hatred of our enemies. The year 1962 has had a good advance build up . . . it's bound to be good . . . so Happy New Year.

March 22, 1962

WE LOSE ONE GOOD MAN—GAIN ONE

Bay Minette lost a valuable public servant in the death of Rudolph Cromartie last week. "Rudy" had been city clerk for a number of years and before that was chief clerk in the Tax Assessor's office. As a result, he was well known and respected locally as well as throughout the county.

He had a reputation for his efficiency and diligence to duty. This was true with his work as well as with his hobbies. He was a great fisherman and hunter. He could catch fish when no one else could get a bite, it seemed. Rudy's vast knowledge of local municipal affairs was invaluable to his associates and the general public. He was recognized as one of Alabama's best city clerks. Rudolph will be sadly missed.

Fortunately, the City Fathers have selected a new clerk who has all the potential needed for making a good public employee. Clyde Steele takes over his important position under the handicap of having much to learn about city affairs. Bay Minette government, like most all cities small and large, has become big business. But Clyde will master the problems and with his genial personality and ability will do a good job. We congratulate all concerned in obtaining his services.

A LESSON FOR US

The Russians had an election last week and over 99 percent of the qualified voters went to the polls . . . we don't know why they bothered to have an election when it was already decided in advance but the fact so many went should be a lesson to those of us who live in a free democracy . . . we can vote anyway we want to but usually about 40 percent of the voters don't even bother . . . we don't believe in force but maybe we handle the poll tax the wrong way . . . perhaps we should have to pay a poll tax if we don't vote. Castro is headed the way of all crooks and bandits, down . . . but the communists are still in charge in Cuba . . . our state department may know what its doing but we always thought that if you found a rattle snake in you back yard, you were supposed to kill it.

Some politicians think the people are interested in the past . . . it's not what you have done for us but what you're going to do that interest most of us . . . as one sage has said: "Be sure to think of the future, for that's where you will spend the rest of your life." It's difficult to be wrong all of the time but some people do manage. For March, this month hasn't been very windy . . . not even for the politicians. Most people who think all politicians are dumb have never gained public office themselves.

Judging from the calls we have, we sometimes wonder if the State Employment Service is still active. Last month when Bobby was visiting in the Far East, we thought he might be the best Kennedy diplomat of all . . . of course that was before Jackie, the President's wife, went to India . . . one thing about the Kennedy clan, when they get into something, they work at it. Another thing we don't understand is what happens to time. 'Nuff, for now.

March 29, 1962

SOME MOTHERS-IN-LAW ARE FINE

Last Thursday one of Baldwin's fine natives died. She had lived a long life of 84 years in the county. She was Mrs. Ella Stewart Irwin. She was our mother-in-law.

In spite of the many stories to the contrary, 25 years of knowing ours convinced us that all the mother-in-law stories aren't correct. In fact, we now realize that mothers-in-law, if "Nanny" Irwin was a fair example, are more considerate of sons-in-law than vice-versa.

An interesting volume could be written about Nanny as would be the case with any mother, grandmother and great grandmother of 84. Most of her life was typical of all mothers. Some wasn't. She had a good sense of business. She had to have to raise six children with practically no assistance.

She married J.S. Irwin, who died at the age of 37, to which union there were three daughters and one son, with the son getting killed at the railroad crossing at Pine Street at the age of 13. She later married his brother, Wade, who already had a son and daughter. To this union, two children were born, with one dying as an infant, leaving only one daughter which is where we came into the picture. Then her second husband died at 35, leaving her with "your children, my children and our children" to raise. This she did, difficult as it was.

Most of us would settle for this kind of life, that is bringing up a big family and living to be 84.

AZALEAS MOST BEAUTIFUL

If you don't think we have had a beautiful Spring, you are too hard to please . . . every year we think the azaleas have been the most beautiful ever . . . this year they really were. Some of the voters may be concerned about the quality of some of the people running for office . . . but the candidates may just as well be concerned about the unconcern for good government of the voters. Politicians often refer to notes when making a speech . . . the voters take note of this and don't like it. The smartest politicians are the ones not running . . . The Irish potatoes like this cool sunny weather . . . folks too. It's not too difficult to get the idea that voters think there are only two offices to be filled this year . . . sheriff and governor.

Jackie Kennedy may not be the best ambassador of goodwill this country ever had . . . but she's the prettiest . . . since men still run most of the countries, this is important . . . if you happen not to like the Kennedy clan, you are very much in the minority at this particular moment. Fact is, it's going to take the Republicans the remaining two years before the next presidential election to find someone to accept the nomination . . . they may have to find another Alf Landon. Speaking of indecision, one smart man said: "It is a great evil, as well as a misfortune, to be unable to utter a prompt and decided "NO." . . . We plead guilty of the inability when deserving people come asking favors. Lazy minds are the worst enemy of people, nations and God . . . it was Pope who said, "Strength of mind is exercise, not rest."

A reader told us last week that this journal is one of the best weekly newspapers he had ever seen . . . we believed him . . . it may not be the best, but it is more interested in you than any other newspaper on earth. Our Mother told us that if we didn't enjoy our work, we wouldn't enjoy life . . . we enjoy life. Thanks again.

June 21, 1962

BRINGS HONOR TO BALDWIN COUNTY

When a citizen is honored with a high office, service, civic, political or otherwise, it also brings honor and recognition to the community and county in which he lives.

Harry J. Wilters, Jr., successful local attorney, has just been elected State Commander, Veterans of Foreign Wars, thus bringing credit to himself, his native county and his chosen community.

Harry is the third local citizen to be elected to this high office. Others were T.J. Mashburn, Jr., and L. D. Owen, Jr., both of whom did admirable jobs. We are confident that no other community, town or city could lay claim to having three sons hold the highest state office VFW has to offer. Congratulations Harry and best wishes for a successful administration.

COME ON DOWN VANITY FAIR

Thousands of people know the success story of Vanity Fair, the great manufacturer of clothing finery for ladies. In 1937, they placed their first Southern plant in Monroeville. Officials of the company have been so pleased with Alabama and the South they now have five plants operating in the southwestern part of the state. The company has operated so successfully under the management of M.O. Lee, president, and others that they now dominate nationally in their field.

Vanity Fair is now considering a sixth plant and there is strong reason to believe it will be located in Baldwin County. Probably Loxley, Robertsdale, Fairhope or Foley will be the lucky community. But wherever they decide to locate, the whole county will benefit greatly. Aside from the fine payroll, which will naturally increase the economy, Vanity Fair people are good citizens.

Bay Minette is not under consideration for the plant because of our proximity to Atmore where they are already located. We had hoped to get the plant that went to Atmore but failed because it was more nearly the right distance from Monroeville. Many women in this area work at the Escambia County location. Another reason we are not under consideration is because we already have an excellent, fast growing textile factory which means much to the local economy. A news story on the front page gives some indication of its size and continued progress.

It has long been our ambition to see Vanity Fair come to this county. We are delighted the hope may soon be realized.

LEGISLATORS ELECTED TO PASS LAWS

The Alabama Legislature is meeting in Montgomery but its members, according to reports, aren't making many friends back home . . . perhaps we shouldn't be too critical . . . it's easier for three federal judges to agree on something than it is for 141 lawmakers . . . but you can't get away from the fact the legislators were elected to pass laws and the people expect them to assume their duties. Those people who are saying Kennedy is trying to grab too much power are against him and those who are for him are saying he is a great leader. Obviously our prayers for peace in the world must become more fervent . . . border clashes, uprisings, threats everywhere . . . if all this keeps up the proverbial powder keg will explode someday.

Honesty is enough reward within itself . . . beware of those who try to tell you how honest they are . . . a person doesn't deserve credit for being honest . . . we're all supposed to be honest and intelligent people are . . .

statistics indicate over 95 percent of the people are honest . . . one thing is sure, if you aren't people will find it out, regardless of what you say. People keep saying that Cuba's Castro's time is fast running out . . . we hope so but the devil (not Castro, but the main one) has been around a long time and has little appearance of getting weaker. Sure, it has been hot . . . it usually is this time of year. We're on the side of the air conditioner salesmen . . . you buy heat in winter to keep comfortable, why not buy cooling in summer to keep comfortable? . . . right, and so is everything else expensive.

Phones and writing don't go together so well . . . phones are awfully handy but have you ever stopped to think how discourteous they can be at times? It seems that only our friends die and get sick . . . perhaps we just don't notice the others. Just as sure as progress continues there will be those who oppose it. 'Nuff, for now.

November 1, 1962

JOHN DOUGAL CROSBY LOVED QUIET
SIMPLE LIFE

Bay Minette and Baldwin County have just lost one of their finest characters in the death of J.D. Crosby.

Mr. Dougal seemed to be a permanent fixture in these parts. Certainly his character and philosophy of life are durable and permanent. A self-made man of much wealth, his tastes, mannerisms, and personality never betrayed his love of a quiet simple life.

In spite of his broad business activity, he always had time to talk, encourage and ask the advice of his fellowman. Although a frugal person in business and personal life, he quietly gave a lot to many and various worthy causes. A special delight of his was to help educate a deserving boy or girl without letting it be known.

John Dougal Crosby was a strong character. His word was his bond. His love and knowledge of timber was something to admire. He was respected by those who knew him. He was Mr. Honesty himself.

WAR CRISIS EASED

Sometimes we want to believe people and nations we don't trust . . . Uncle Sam is now in this position with the Cuban situation . . . Russian Premier Khrushchev has promised to dismantle the Soviet Missile bases in Cuba and to stop shipping offensive weapons there . . .since this is what President Kennedy demanded, it has eased the war crisis . . . naturally we have our fingers crossed since Khrushchev isn't noted for his truthfulness . . . since we all want to avoid an atomic war, and peace is so greatly desired, it is sometimes too easy to believe what we want to hear . . . our suggestion to Mr. Kennedy is to appear trusting for diplomatic purposes and to also keep his powder dry, very dry.

Southeastern Conference football teams must be the best in the nation . . . at least we have four teams in the top ten, Alabama, LSU, Mississippi and Auburn . . . no other conference has over two . . . we have noted several coaches criticizing the national football rating system . . . also note, the criticizing coaches don't have teams that rate rating . . .Which reminds us of the old story about people being down on what they ain't up on. One good thing has come out of the Cuban crisis so far, the world knows Castro is nothing but a puppet with a beard. People of Tuscaloosa, including the circuit solicitor, are organizing to see that law and order are maintained when the University is integrated . . . we always admired intelligent law-abiding citizens. Guess we all like to be flattered . . . had a call yesterday from a serious young businessman suggesting we could buy a certain company for $2 million . . . he should realize that some people aren't worth twice what they owe.

No one likes to be lectured . . . so just go and vote next Tuesday. We wish everybody was as nice as running candidates. Chalk up another plus for the Cuban crisis . . . reports are that church attendance jumped. 'Nuff, time being.

January 10, 1963

Hadleys honor loyalty of employees

During the holidays an incident happened in Bay Minette that was thought provoking.

John and Duck Hadley celebrated their 25th business anniversary by having a banquet for all of their present and former employees. They swept out the shop of their motor company, set up tables, prepared a lot of food and dined over 200.

They started in business here with a filling station, then went into the automobile business, and later added two more stations. During this period over 400 people worked with them at various times. Now they are scattered throughout the country; some coming 500 miles for the banquet.

The loyalty of Hadley employees has long been known. We have often heard people compliment their employee relations.

Obviously these employees have done their part to contribute to the economic and social betterment of this community. In seeking new industries and wanting expanding payrolls, we sometimes forget the importance of the workers of our retailers and other small businesses.

We all might take a cue from the Hadleys. Not necessarily in the form of a banquet. Just making a list of your former employees and writing them a note would be appreciated. Management can't be very successful in running a business without good employees who are loyal.

WE HAVE MOVED UPWARD INDUSTRIALLY

Alabamians have more money to spend than ever before and business in general reached an all-time peak during 1962.

Figures from the U.S. Department of Commerce prove the above statements to be true. The 238 banks have deposits totaling $2 ¼ billion or 11 percent over 1961. Savings are also way up. Baldwin has been an important part of this growth.

Reports just released by the State Planning and Industrial Development ment Board, headed for the past four years by Leland Jones, indicate that industrial development has been the highest of any four-year period in history for the state.

During Patterson's term, according to the figures, $663 million has been spent by new industrial plants and on expansion of existing factories. This has given the state 50,244 new jobs. If you take in all industrial expansion and include public utilities, transportation, warehousing and armed forces installations, the four-year figures will exceed $2 billion.

Since 1959 Baldwin County has had its finest years in industrial expansion. During this period 13 new plants have started operating in the county, or are under construction, most prominent of which are Hale Manufacturing Company, Foley, and Vanity Fair, Robertsdale. Numerically at least, only three other counties in Alabama did better, Jefferson, Etowah and Montgomery.

Baldwin also did well during the period in the expansion of existing plants. Fourteen expanded, including some of the new ones, such as Hale Manufacturing and Standard Furniture, Bay Slacks, Baldwin Pole and Piling, of Bay Minette. Only 10 counties had more plants to expand during the four years and no others in this section of the state.

No other county south of Montgomery, except Houston, grew more industrially than Baldwin since 1959. If, as is said, success begats success, we're on our way.

THE NEXT FOUR YEARS

Still have any unbroken New Year's resolutions? News of a statewide nature should be picking up as the new governor is going in and the legislature is meeting . . . a new broom sweeps clean but some people soon start complaining about the dust the sweeping causes . . . but we all can be good citizens by wishing and helping make the next four years one of good government in Alabama. Many people like the late Will Rogers like to poke fun at legislators and congressmen but most realize they are an important and necessary part of making this democracy run . . . and this democracy has run pretty well, don't forget.

Let one daily raise its subscription rates, or per copy cost and it is a news item that will make the front page of every daily newspaper in the country. For two years people have been predicting the downfall of Castro of Cuba before the end of the year . . . he may last this year out but we doubt it, and hope not. Well, we have seen many letters that are a real bargain for a five-cent postage stamp . . . and others that aren't worth an old two-center. All the figures say 1962 was a good business year, whether you are broke or not . . . people without jobs are just as hungry during good times as in bad . . . maybe more so if the theory that misery loves company is true.

Time flies . . . it's bill paying time again and when such a time follows Christmas, it's real bad. People in New York have been without a paper for 30 days because of a strike . . . just think how fortunate you are. "Unwanted Mobile" is an editorial subject in the *Tuscaloosa News* . . . which indicated that none of the remaining eight congressmen want Boykin's old district . . . just wait, whoever does get it will try to make the public think Mobile was always their first love. All smart people aren't rich and some rich people aren't very smart. 'Nuff for now.

January 31, 1963

FOLEY'S MAYOR CARSON HONORED

Every month the fine *Alabama Municipal Journal* selects a city official in the state and honors him. The current issue has chosen Henry W. Carson, Foley's energetic and able mayor.

Under the heading "Municipal Personality Sketch," by Jane Troy Hooker, a full page has been devoted to picture sketches and brief facts about Henry's life. "Self-possessed" is the word for him says the sketch and further states, "A logical person to head up civic enterprises, he is kept busy serving as head of drives such as the United Appeal, the blood bank, and similar services. His manner is quiet and friendly, and he is the kind of person who inspires trust in other people. Foley citizens believe in him wholeheartedly."

Among the many compliments paid Carson by Mrs. Hooker, was this, "He issues periodic bulletins to the people of Foley to bring them up-to-date on problems of city government and to point out possible violations of city ordinances." We have known of this policy of Henry's and admired him for it. Too many public officials don't think the people have a right to know what is happening.

We have long admired Henry Carson and are glad to see his qualities get statewide attention.

COST OF BUILDING

Note where Jackie Kennedy is building a seven-bedroom, five-bath home which she thinks might cost about $45,000 . . . obviously she hasn't done any building lately . . . looks like the President is taking work home with him and getting wife's help and advice on budget matters . . . maybe Caroline could do better. If you need further proof that men should be forced to retire at 70, just look at French President Charles de Gaulle . . . with his 72-year-old senility and ambition, he is causing more trouble among his Western allies than several younger men could . . . he is forgetting that it was American and British soldiers who freed his country from Hitler and then through the Marshall Plan Uncle Sam fed his people and rebuilt France . . . but he doesn't like what we have done for him lately.

Vultures and hummingbirds do not find the same things because they don't look for the same things . . . people with a buzzard outlook on life don't relish the aroma of flowers or enjoy a beautiful garden. Some folks don't enjoy success, the other fellow's success that is . . . jealousy is a big demon with big horns that loves little people. One way to keep people from jumping down your throat is to keep your mouth closed. Failure only comes when you fail to keep trying. The family economy would fair better if it would be as economical the first few days of the month as the last few. Maybe the reason more people don't smile when they give to good causes is because their consciences make them sad for being so stingy.

You can always find things to be thankful for . . . just think, Congress has been in session for a month and the country is still intact, although admittedly a bit shaky. If you don't agree with everything we say at least it proves you are thinking, even though you may not be smart. Politicians soon learn that people don't care how much they know, just how much they care ·. . . now this may not be the best family journal on earth (want to argue the point) but it cares for you more than any other. Could be, more later.

April 4, 1963

Dr. Michaelson heads national organization

This county has had several citizens outstanding enough in their field to head state groups but very few have achieved the honor of heading an important national organization.

So when Foley's Dr. Julius Michaelson was elected president-elect of the American Academy of General Practice at the academy annual meeting in Chicago Monday, he not only brought great distinction to himself but to his home area and state as well.

The American Academy of General Practice, composed of "family doctors," is the second largest medical association in the U.S. Only the American Medical Association is larger. Dr. Michaelson is the first Alabamian in history to hold this significant position.

A graduate of LSU medical school, he was a Phi Beta Kappa and received many other college honors. He has been active in varied civic affairs in Foley and is a past president of the Alabama Chapter of the American Academy.

We're proud to be a neighbor of such an outstanding citizen as Dr.

Michaelson and congratulate him on his important achievements.

FACING THE FACTS

The state planning and industrial development director, Leonard Beard, is getting off to a good start in his new position. He's getting results and impressing people. Having known him for a number of years, we aren't surprised.

In a speech before the Rotary Club in Birmingham recently, he made a lot of sense. The following statement is an example of his soundness: "If jobs are available, we keep Alabamians in Alabama and attract others as well. If jobs aren't available, our people will find them elsewhere. Success in creating job opportunities will assure the economic growth of our state."

To create these jobs, the former Sheffield mayor suggested "as a starter:" 1. Face the facts—both good and bad; 2. Correct our weaknesses, wherever possible; 3. Capitalize on our strength.

BIRMINGHAM ELECTS NEW MAYOR

Although the rest of the citizens of Alabama couldn't vote in Birmingham's municipal election Tuesday, they were vitally interested in its outcome. And most people are well pleased with the intelligence shown by the Magic City's electorate in overwhelmingly nominating former Lieutenant Governor Albert Boutwell to the post of mayor.

Boutwell is well qualified to give that city the type of aggressive and harmonious leadership that has been lacking. We predict Mayor Boutwell will lead the great city back into the ranks of one of the South's fastest growing metropolitan areas.

EDUCATION PROBLEMS

Alabamians are unanimous that we have education problems . . . all agree we need more money for schools and that the other fellow should be taxed to get it . . . the public education idea seems to be, "our children and your money."

We can't help but get agitated at those people and societies who continually sell Uncle Sam short . . . folk should no longer go around demanding that we "catch up" with Russia . . . if we did that, we'd have to sink eight of every nine ocean-going vessels, scrap 19 of every 20 cars and trucks, destroy 50 million TV sets and nine out of every 10 telephones, abandon three-fifths of our steel capacity, two-thirds of our petroleum, rip up 14 of every 15 miles of our paved highways, etc. . . . and we'd have to put 60 million of our people back on farms which they wouldn't own and give up most our freedoms . . . so if you still want to "catch up," go ahead, it'll be your funeral . . . we think 1963 is a perfect year for all Americans to stand up on their two feet and declare that this is the greatest nation on earth . . . start talking.

You've heard by now that *The Saturday Evening Post* will soon be changing hands and the new name will be The Bear-Butts Post. If you don't like the weather and the beautiful azaleas, you are hard to please . . . of course, realizing the farmers could use some rain. Writing comes easy when you have something to say. According to information gotten by Bob Ingram from the State Department of Revenue, Baldwin's property assessments are, excepting Elmore County, the lowest in Alabama . . . yet we don't know a single property owner in Baldwin who appreciates the fact or thinks his property is assessed too low . . . according to some complaints we hear, any thoughts on the matter are exactly opposite.

Those people who put newspaper front pages together know readers are more interested in football "scandal" than scandalous Castro . . . some regard scandal as a sort of evidence of their own goodness . . . a sage once said: "Believe that story false that ought not to be true." See you again, we hope.

June 13, 1963

MRS. ALICE J. DUCK BRINGS HONOR TO BALDWIN

The Times delights in taking note of our citizens who succeed in their professions to the extent they are honored by being named state president of their group or organization. No county has many, but Baldwin has had and is getting a fair share. We have mentioned others in the past.

Now we can add Mrs. Alice J. Duck to the list. Last week she was elected president of the Alabama Association of Circuit Court Clerks and Registers at the annual meeting in Montgomery. As we all know, she is the long-time and popular Circuit Court Clerk of Baldwin. She succeeded her late husband, R.S. Duck, Sr., to the job. Between them, they have served about 30 years.

"Miss Alice" is one of the few lady county officials in Alabama. She would be the first to deny that she is a politician, but actually she is the best. She attends more funerals, visits more sick people, and gets to more church functions, etc., than anyone we know. We have often said: "If we wanted any office in the court house and hoped to get elected, Mrs. Duck would be the last one we would pick on." Others who have tried it agree.

Mrs. Duck is to be congratulated on bringing this honor to her county and self.

"GIVE-EM-HELL-HARRY"

Senator Barry Goldwater, a very conservative gentleman who has an excellent chance of being the next GOP presidential nominee, said recently that he thinks Harry Truman will go down in history as one of our great presidents . . . this is what Jim Folsom has been saying for years . . . and we agree to the extent that he handled foreign affairs well and such things as Castro would have been nipped in the bud by "Give-em-hell-Harry."

If the theory that any kind of publicity is better than none, then Alabama should really prosper . . . we are in the news . . . a friend from Louisiana called and wanted to know why we let Governor Wallace push Bear Bryant off the front pages . . . we told him that Bear yielded to the Governor because he wanted a rest . . . chances are the great coach will come into the news again beginning next September . . . and it'll be bad news too, for Tide opponents.

People bent on revenge are hell bent. As someone said, malice drinks one half of its own poison. This week you don't have to look on a map to learn how to spell Tuscaloosa . . . one thing is sure, you couldn't give it back to the Indians right now . . . they would object. Wm. Pitt said, "Where law ends, tyranny begins." Wisdom makes fortunes . . . lose a fortune and it is called fate. Arthur Brisbane, the great newspaper columnist of a generation back, often said that what man can imagine man can do . . . he evidently was thinking such things as men are now doing in this space age. If you want to improve your game, play someone who can beat you.

Hottest in history, driest in history, coldest in history . . . what a dullard of history 1963 is making. The fact that June is usually a wet month in Baldwin doesn't water the fields now. We predict air conditioning is here to stay. We have people who would kill a good project to win a point. Hope we're all here next week.

August 22, 1963

THE GASTONS OF FAIRHOPE

Easily one of the most outstanding families in Baldwin County is the Gastons of Fairhope, E. B. Gaston and his descendants.

The late E. B. Gaston, in 1894, came from Des Moines to the Eastern Shore and established the Fairhope Single Tax Colony and *The Fairhope*

Courier. Since, *The Courier* has been one of Alabama's outstanding weekly newspapers. It was published continuously by the Gaston family until last week when it was delivered to its new owners.

There are many evidences that the paper's publishers have had the best interests of the Eastern Shore at heart. They have received many messages of congratulations during the past several days from wide sources. The chamber of commerce recognized the long service of the Gaston family to the Fairhope and Baldwin County area and told of "the vast debt the community owes the Gastons."

For years the daughter, Mrs. Frances Crawford, has been one of Alabama's favorite lady journalists. She edited the paper since 1937 and her brothers, Dr. C. A. Gaston, as associate editor, and Arthur F. Gaston, as business manager, gave her able assistance.

Another son, J. E. Gaston, Sr., has not been actively connected with *The Courier* but has made an outstanding record as a political statesman, business and civic leader and friend of man.

While the strong hands of the Gaston family will be missed at the helm of *The Courier*, *The Times* welcomes the new editor, Johnny Ferguson, and his associates, into the fold and wishes them well.

Lest you may not understand, we hasten to admit the Gastons have long been very high among our favorite people.

VOTERS MAY BE CONFUSED

Arizona's Governor Paul Fannin is doing everything he can to promote Senator Goldwater for president . . . he says of the senator, "he is neither a segregationist nor an integrationist, but a true American" . . . sounds sort of like accusing a preacher of being neither for sin nor against it . . . if this is an indication of the statements we're going to get out of next year's presidential campaign, the voters are apt to be more confused than usual.

American nuclear forces are "manifestly superior" to those of the Soviet, says our Secretary of Defense Robert S. McNamara . . . surprisingly enough, some Republicans objected to his making such a statement . . . if he's right, we hope he says it a million times and loud enough to let the whole world hear it.

Strange things happen, some caused by politicians . . . Gov. Ross Barnett tried to keep Negro James Meredith from graduating at Ole Miss . . . and all the time we thought Ross didn't want him at the University . . . schools have long graduated some "students" to get rid of them.

Times change, now fishermen spend more time lying about the fine lure, or bait, they use than they do about the big one that got away . . . we still use worms and you can't lie very much about them. School, teachers, education, books . . . these aren't smiling words to hundreds of kids in Baldwin this week . . . most think that Shakespeare's "In the good old summertime, in the good old summertime . . ." isn't the best time for book learning.

Now that the Butts–*Saturday Evening Post* battle has been decided, subject to a lot of appeals, and September is almost here, we can get down to the real issue . . . which is football. "A woman's lot is made for her by the love she accepts" . . . poor women. Like parachutes, minds only function when open . . . some never open, of course. We, like many folks, often get too busy to work, or so we think. Back again, perhaps.

August 29, 1963

Vail, Wilters, Barnhill and House

Twenty-seven years ago this month, we purchased *The Times* from R.B. (Bob) Vail.

He paid us a pleasant call last week. He and Mrs. Vail are now spending most of their time in San Antonio, Texas, where their older daughter, Mary, lives. They always like to come back to Baldwin to visit with friends and relatives. As he says, "Mary (Mrs. Vail) and I spent many wonderful years of our life in Bay Minette and we think this is the greatest area on earth."

Now back 27 years. Besides being *The Times* publisher, Mr. Bob was also postmaster. He had bought the paper in 1922 and sold it to us in August of 1936. He later resigned as postmaster and went to Washington as secretary to Congressman George Grant. He retired in Washington and later moved to Texas.

Also in '36 Harry Wilters, Sr., was postmaster of Robertsdale. In fact, he had been since '34 and remained so until a week ago Friday. Harry, too, was a popular postmaster. Unlike many people, when they become postmasters, or get a Civil Service job, who lose interest in community and civic affairs, Harry has maintained his position of leadership for the entire 29-plus years he struggled with the Postal Laws and Regulations.

He served under four presidents: Roosevelt, Truman, Eisenhower and Kennedy. He saw his office grow from third to almost first class and was postmaster in three different buildings. He was instrumental in securing the new post office building in Robertsdale. Wilters is a member of the Rotary Club, being a past president and director, a past master of Robertsdale Lodge No. 821, F. & A.M., and is now treasurer. Since 1924 he has held the office of secretary and treasurer of the Baldwin County Masonic Conference. From these, and other honors that could be mentioned, you see what we mean by saying he maintained a position of community leadership.

Bob Vail agreed with us that Harry Wilters has made Robertsdale a fine postmaster.

David Barnhill is the new Robertsdale postmaster. He resigned as a member of the Baldwin County Commission, District 3, and manager of the Silverhill Farmers Association, to take his new position.

Dave was elected to the county commission two times and it was generally conceded he could have continued being elected. This popularity was deserved because he was a dedicated public official and was always anxious to serve the people of Baldwin County. We predict he'll have the same popular success working for Uncle Sam.

We reminded Mr. Vail that next year his old *Baldwin Times* will begin her 75th year of publication. His natural reaction was, "time flies." He remembered that *The Times* is Baldwin's oldest continually operated business institution.

Times' personnel and management are already beginning to think about this important milepost of public service. Thus Jack House enters into the picture as our new news editor. For some information about his abilities, please refer to the front page. We have always desired to give the people of Baldwin the best possible newspaper. Although we know *The Times* is one of the best weeklies around, we are the first to admit that it can be improved.

Improvement is ever our goal. Many changes are going to be made before and during our 75th year of publication. Jack House is one of them. There is no better news editor in Alabama. Give him a few weeks and he'll prove it to you. Other big announcements will be made in the near future.

You see, when a fine gentleman like Bob Vail comes around, he causes an editor to do a lot of reminiscing, and planning.

September 5, 1963

SCHOOL PRINCIPALS HAVE BIG JOBS

Alabama high schools this year have had their greatest turnover of principals in the history of public education, Dr. John C. Blair, state superintendent of secondary education, has announced.

"Money is the big factor in this," he stated. He said 46 new high school principals were hired in the state this year to replace those who quit.

We have often stated that the hardest, and most important, job in any community is that of school principal. Take Bay Minette for example, Principal C.V. Daniels not only has 2100 boys and girls to keep pointed in the right direction, he also has their parents to try to please. How would you like to try it?

Fortunately Baldwin has been able to hold onto her principals. Fortunate because County Superintendent W. Candler McGowan has selected good ones, and because good replacements are hard to find.

We can make it easier for Mr. McGowan to hold onto ours by giving them complete cooperation and understanding. They deserve it.

MOBILE COLLEGE OPENS

Of significant educational interest in this area is the official opening this week of Mobile College.

This is Alabama's first senior college to be chartered in 57 years and Alabama Baptists' first college to be established in 120 years.

This first building will be dedicated at special services Friday evening at the college. Judson and Howard are two other state colleges operated by the Baptists.

Only freshmen will be enrolled the first year with one class being added each year until the college reaches four-year standing. Eventually they plan to have 16 buildings.

This is an important achievement for the cultural and educational betterment of this area and *The Times* congratulates the Baptist and others who have made this institution possible.

LABOR DAY

We have mixed emotions about Labor Day . . . we hate it because of the number of people who manage to get killed on the highways . . . but we like it because fall and football come soon thereafter. We hope the old law of supply and demand doesn't hold true this year so far as prices on pecans . . . Baldwin farmers should have one of the most bountiful crops in history . . . usually when yield is high, price is low . . . we hope they'll both be high this year, provided, of course, our friends continue to give us a few. Fall always brings color to the forests . . . this year it is also bringing color to Alabama schools.

There is natural resistance to change . . . This newspaper is making changes, some big ones are coming . . . not that we want to make them, fact is we don't want to . . . but we do want to continue eating . . . and in this fast moving day the wheel of providence constantly moves . . . the spoke that is up today will be down tomorrow . . . so life goes . . . Mama taught us not to be the first to try a new idea, but, if it's good, don't be the last to adopt it . . . we'll be the first in this area to do what we're going to do here at *The Times* in about 30 days but others have blazed the trail elsewhere.

Schools are essential to education . . . but going to school doesn't make you fully educated any more than going to a garage will make you an automobile. If you're honest you don't have to tell people, they'll find it out if you are but not as fast as if you aren't . . . fact is, telling of your honesty immediately arouses a suspicion. We admit to being unsure of what the Supreme Court meant when they ruled about reading the Bible and prayer in our schools . . . but we are positive about this: if there is plenty of both in the home and church it won't matter what the court meant. One way to find more than you are looking for is to be jealous. If you are looking for a liar, find the person who speaks often of himself. Perhaps if we knew when we had said enough, we wouldn't have talked at all. See you later, maybe.

December 26, 1963

JUDGE W. RAMSEY STUART

A heart attack took the life of Probate Judge W. Ramsey Stuart Friday morning. Thus Baldwin County lost one of its most successful political and business leaders of all time.

He started his political career early in life, having been elected county sheriff at the young age of 23. Back then a sheriff could not succeed himself but he was elected every other four years like clockwork. He was a popular and effective sheriff and as such was unbeatable.

In 1944 a vacancy occurred in the probate office because of the death of Judge G.W. Robertson. Governor Chauncey Sparks gave the appointment for the unexpired term to Sheriff Stuart. For four times, he was reelected by comfortable margins over all opposition.

Ramsey, as he was called by thousands of friends, not only had a knack of making political friends, he also had fine business ability. He was a perfectionist, wanted to see things done right and had the ability to organize to get things done.

The dean of south Alabama politicians, having successfully served the public for 40 years, he was one of the last of a fast fading group. He liked his friends and didn't waste too much time with those who weren't. He liked to do things for people but one of his greatest attributes was that his strong personality gave him the ability to get people to do things for him.

Judge Stuart was full of energy and liked to be doing things. He had strong opinions and usually didn't mind expressing them. He never learned how to play, always devoting his long days to his political duties, business enterprises, family and church affairs.

W. Ramsey Stuart played a big part in the growth and development of the county he loved, Baldwin. He knew every foot of this vast area.

This was his domain and he loved it.

His impact upon the life, both political and otherwise, of Baldwin and her people was great. History will long remember him and treat him kindly.

CHRISTMAS HAS CHANGED

Christmas, like other things, has changed . . . and like some other things, for the better . . . no more "good old times" for most people when it comes to the visit of Santa Claus . . . to the average American family, he brings 100 times as many goodies now as, say, 40 years back . . . then we sweet children gleefully hung up our long black stockings over the fireplace from the mantel . . . they had to be handy for the jolly fellow when he came down the chimney . . . it was hard for him to come down because he was fat, not because he was overloaded with toys and gifts . . . the apple, orange and three English walnuts he put in our stockings really didn't overload him . . . of course these items made Christmas very delightful, especially since our parents had let us spend 25 cents of our pig and cotton picking money for some two-inch firecrackers . . . one year our more extravagant brother slipped into a store at Steens, Miss., and squandered four bits on fire crackers, even buying one or two boxes of four and five-inch minsters . . . a stern lecture at home about throwing money away took some of the pleasure out of "shooting" them, but not much.

As we said, Christmas has changed . . . but if you want to be unpopular with the young boys and girls (and wife) you just try telling them about "Now, when I was a boy" . . . it goes over not at all.

Now it's almost impossible to buy something that will please, at least which you can afford . . . kids would hang Santa in effigy if he dared put fruit in a stocking and anything less than a dozen toys . . . as a wag said recently, it is easier to find a wife than it is to find her a present she will like. Of course, and unfortunately, there are still many families at home and abroad who need and appreciate anything they can get. Perhaps they have the best Christmas spirit, that of love, prayer and appreciation, peace and goodwill . . . regardless of what your status may be, our wish for you is a very, very Merry Christmas . . . full of joy and happiness.

January 30, 1964

ROBERT B. VAIL WRITES '30'

Few people influenced our life more than did Robert B. Vail, who died at the age of 72 last Saturday.

Mr. Bob, as we affectionately called him, was a man of great character and integrity.

Our personal experiences with him is sufficient proof. In July of 1936, our brother drove his kid brother of 20, who had a bright new journalism degree from the University of Missouri, to Bay Minette. We had heard the newspaper here was for sale. We found the publisher was also postmaster and owner of the Rex Theatre. That day he was postmastering.

The post office was then in the building next to Stacey's Drug, where Elmore's is now. We found the postmaster to be a fine looking man of about 45. He was in one end of the building at a desk talking to another personable man of about the same age, Judge G. W. Robertson. We awaited Mr. Vail in a nearby pool hall.

When the opportunity presented itself, we told the publisher-postmaster-theatre operator and gladioli grower that we had heard he wanted to sell his newspaper. He asked a few questions and answered something like this: "Yes, son, I have been interested. We haven't been giving the fine people of Bay Minette and Baldwin County the kind of newspaper they deserve. This is the greatest county on earth and the best people. However, I can't give you an answer today. There is talk of some group from Flomaton starting another paper here. If they do, it would not be fair for me to sell you *The Times*. In the event the paper isn't started, I'll let you hear from me."

That was that. We came by to look at the paper office which was a small block building to the rear of the lot where the present *Times* office is. After looking a few minutes, we decided it didn't matter whether we ever heard more from him or not. If we had been six months out of school instead of two, we would have hoped never to hear from him. In the meantime, we found out a little more about Baldwin. That was a good potato year. We liked what we heard about the county.

Within a few weeks we had a letter from Mr. Vail. He offered to sell us half interest in *The Times* for $3,750, with $1,500 down, and we could draw $25 per week for running it. We agreed and took over August 15, 1936. With one printer, Frank Taylor, making $12 per week, that gave us a payroll of $37. We never missed paying the printer but seldom paid the young co-publisher. We struggled until the following April.

Mr. Vail told us he was ready to sell us the other half. We didn't blame him. However, we were foolish enough to be delighted. The other half was the same price. We went out to his home on Old Daphne Road (which later burned) and closed the deal. He prepared the papers, neither of us thinking of using a lawyer. At the conclusion of the big transaction (for us it was) we asked him, "Now that it is over, why wouldn't you sell me all of *The Times* last August?"

His answer was a classic and proof enough about his character and integrity. "Jimmy," he says, "there were three reasons why I wouldn't let you have full interest in *The Times*. First, I wanted to make sure you would give the people a better paper than they had been getting for the past year or so. Secondly, I wanted to make sure you would be friendly to Lister Hill. (Hill was then congressman and had given Mr. Vail the postmastership, so essential to feeding his big family during the depression years . . . such loyalty was another Vail good point.) Third, I wanted to make sure you were a Democrat. I would never let *The Times* get into the hands of a Republican. You have satisfied me on all three points and I have made you full owner."

Mr. Bob was an excellent writer. He had a beautiful flow of words. However, when he set down to a typewriter he sometimes forgot his usual gentlemanly ways. He could really get rough with the written word. But he preferred and usually practiced praising people, especially his many friends like Lister Hill, Franklin D. Roosevelt and the Democratic Party. The Republicans never knew an ire like his, however.

In 1941, he made a big decision. He left his beloved Bay Minette and Baldwin County for Washington to become George Grant's secretary and assistant. His main consideration was his family. He had many to educate and Washington had schools of higher learning that Bay Minette didn't. But Bay Minette was always his home, even in death.

Few people remember it but Mr. Bob was a great lover of flowers. He was the first person to successfully raise field grown gladioli in Baldwin. He planted acres and shipped them everywhere. From this the great glad business began to flourish in the county.

Yes, in our book Mr. Bob was a man of great character, integrity, ability and was a true Southern gentleman. And his surviving widow, Mary Vail, helped him to be all these things, and more.

February 13, 1964

E.E. (MANNIE) DAVIS A GOOD
INDUSTRIALIST AND CITIZEN

Last week *The Times* made the important announcement that Bay Slacks, Inc., is to expand its pants factory here immediately. This marks the second big expansion for the plant since the present owner purchased it eight years ago.

As usual, there is an important man behind such success.

Comparatively few people locally know the owner of Bay Slacks. But those of us who do, know an excellent gentleman and a human dynamo of a businessman. As one close to him said, he has a little motor inside that keeps him running all the time.

This man is E.E. Davis. Although he makes his home in Okalona, Mississippi, he is one of the best citizens Bay Minette has ever had.

For the first time, as we recall, his picture was in *The Times* last week with a group of local citizens. The picture showed him handing over a check for $5,000 to start off the $175,000, "Project Progress for '64," drive. He has given many checks for local drives before but Mr. Davis is not a seeker of publicity and last week was the first time we were able to keep him still long enough for a picture.

Any community in America would be fortunate to have a citizen, even though absentee, such as E.E. (Mannie) Davis. Certainly Bay Minette is proud to claim him, and to thank him for furnishing employment to 500 local men and women.

BALDWIN HAS TWO STATE PRESIDENTS

We were delighted to see our neighbor and fellow journalist, E.M. (Sparky) Howell, the *Foley Onlooker* publisher, elevated to the presidency of the Alabama Press Association last week at its annual Winter meeting in Tuscaloosa.

It is a distinct honor to be president of your state organization, whatever your field of endeavor. This is especially true if you happen to end up at the head of the daily and weekly newspapers of Alabama.

By coincidence, Baldwin County also boasts the current president of the Alabama Broadcasters Association, Jim Stewart. He owns and operates Foley's radio station. This gives Baldwin County a monopoly on heads of the communications associations in the state for 1964.

Baldwin has had the state presidency of several organizations. However, we only recall two groups where the county has furnished three presidents of each at various times. Baldwin has had three State Department Commanders of the Veterans of Foreign Wars, in this order; L. D. Owen, Jr., Telfair J. Mashburn and Harry J. Wilters, Jr., all of Bay Minette. Now Sparky makes the third time a Baldwin newspaper has furnished top man in the Alabama Press Association. First was R.B. Vail, who died week before last, and next was his successor as publisher of *The Times*.

Sparky and Jim will serve well and we want to join their fellow Baldwin Countians in thanking them for bringing such honors to this county.

DEMOCRACY AT WORK

Birds are singing like Spring is almost here . . . but don't put your Winter clothes in moth balls for awhile . . . Winter is still boss. If you registered to vote and paid your poll tax, you are an important American . . . if you don't believe it, just listen to the candidates . . . having been one may contribute to the fact that we don't like to see candidates ridiculed, made light of, harassed, etc. . . . it takes candidates to make office holders and it takes public officials to make this democracy work . . . remember politics is fine because it is democracy at work . . . but it works better if you vote for good men.

You may not want to become excited about it just yet . . . William Shakespeare will be having a birthday in April, his 400th . . . no doubt about it, the Bard was quite a writer but, like most students, we didn't appreciate him while in school . . . one thing we learned from him, you can't judge people by their morals alone . . . we have discovered in life there are many people with a lot of ability and no morals . . . Hitler for example . . . we have also learned to like people best who have more morals and less ability . . . but contrary to the opinions of some, one can have both. We had a college teacher who thought William S. was a greater writer than Paul of the New Testament . . . we disagreed with him and almost failed the course . . . finally passed by admitting that Shakespeare didn't have as much help in his writing as did Paul. So many people, like us, are often talking when they should be listening.

You have often heard that if you want something done, get the busiest man in town . . . good advice, but just remember that it's possible for a person to get so busy and no busier . . . to put it another way, there can be a last straw . . . but seldom, because a real genius for hard work seems always to be able to do a little more . . . a person who has nothing to do only has time to do nothing . . like writing maybe? Thanks for staying with us.

May 7, 1964

UTILITIES BOARD MEMBERS
GOOD HELP AT BARGAIN PRICES

A good example of civic duty at its best is the hundreds of citizens throughout the state who serve free of charge on city water and sewer boards.

Locally it is the Bay Minette Utilities Board. This board has the responsibility of keeping the water and gas systems functioning properly and profitably. It has the added worry of the sewage system.

Members of the local board are Cly T. Smith, chairman, Harold Stuart and Wilson Beasley. All devote much time and thought to their duties. They receive many complaints, few pats on the back and no money for all their troubles.

Cly T., who is a retired postmaster, devotes practically all of his energies to his non-paying job.

Bay Minette, like so many other towns, is fortunate to have such able and dedicated people on the board. Besides the many daily problems, they must plan for the future of a fast growing community.

The gas system was built in 1941 at a cost of $50,000. It was the first one in Alabama to be municipality owned. After several months of operation, the system had 150 customers. Since then the gas customers have grown to over 1,700. It has paid for its own expansions, financed many other civic projects, is probably worth $1 million, with rates that have never been raised to the general public since 1941.

The water plant was bought in 1945 for $70,000 and had 500 customers. Customers now number 1,850, at least $193,000 in improvements have been made and the system is now undergoing its greatest expansion, with others planned in the immediate future.

The Times proudly tips her hat to Cly T., Harold and Wilson . . . the city fathers, who were intelligent enough to appoint them, and all others connected with the successful and progressive operations of our utilities.

OUR OWN COVER GIRL AND SON

Ladies whose pictures are carried on the front pages of magazines are called "cover girls."

This week we present our own "cover girl," Mrs. Bonnie White Baker, 150 South Summit Street, Fairhope.

Mrs. Baker is the mother of John Newton Baker, a native of Baldwin County, whose tribute, "Hi, Mom!," is printed as our Mother's Day feature this year.

Bonnie White Baker is a writer in her own right, having written numerous poems and other articles. She is author of the book, . . . *By Which Men Live*, with selected poems by Bonnie White Baker.

Since the death of her husband, the late B.B. Baker, who at one time was superintendent of the old Daphne Normal School, Mrs. Baker has resided at the Baker home in Fairhope.

Along with her writing, one of her main interests is flowers and shrubs, particularly her wisteria. In the photo on page one, she is standing by a wisteria vine that is more than 60 years old.

Among her other accomplishments, Mrs. Baker can be called the "mother" of the Daphne May Day Festival, which was held last Saturday. She recalls that she helped start the festival back in 1911. From that time until 1916, it was mainly a Daphne Normal School project, but in 1916 it was turned over to the Town of Daphne as a civic endeavor and it has gradually taken in all parts of the county.

Mrs. Baker is a young lady of 81 years. She is the mother of three children. In addition to John Newton Baker, she is the mother of Donnave Baker, of Fairhope, and B.B. Baker, Jr., of West Chester, Pennsylvania.

MORE ELECTIONS COMING UP

Election is over only for some candidates . . . you voters must remember that this is 1964, a real election year . . . now that the first Democratic primary is history, we have the second, or runoff, coming up June 2 . . . then city elections throughout the county will be facing voters in hot August . . . with one mayor and five councilmen to be selected in each of Baldwin's 10 municipalities . . . and if you haven't given out by then, you can get ready for the national roundup of voting in which a president and vice president will be named . . . for the first time in years, the Republicans will be trying to give the Democrats a real run for their money in November, with promised opponents for all state-wide Democratic nominees . . . in the same general election we voters will be given another shot at several state constitutional amendments . . . democracy is getting a real workout this leap year.

Everybody reads and heeds the national public opinion polls except Ex-president Harry Truman . . . he said they were wrong in 1948 and proved it . . . however, they have become a little more scientific and accurate since then . . . Sunday we read Mr. Gallup on what the rank-and-file Republicans are thinking of their presidential hopefuls . . . they opine, or so the poll says, that only 14 percent favor Senator Barry Goldwater for president . . . 37 percent want Lodge, Henry Cabot that is, and 28 percent like former vice-president and GOP presidential candidate, Richard Nixon, etc. . . . all of which surprised us a little but also increases our respect for the Republicans . . . it is encouraging to know that only 14 percent are fooled by Mr. Goldwater's generalities and light-lips-from-the-hips utterances . . . we now see bright hopes for the future of Uncle Sam's country even if President Lyndon Johnson doesn't win.

Thought on the future . . . this from a scientist; "Science and technology will advance more in the next 36 years than in all the millennia since man's creation," which is, friends, a lot of change. But you can't eliminate the past . . . our preacher gave this story for a thought Sunday .. . the little boy wanted to know why a wildcat is wild? . . . his teacher answered that probably it was because his parents were, 'Nuff, for now.

May 28, 1964

JIM STEWART—MORE HONORS FOR BALDWIN

Jim Stewart, the excellent radio man and owner of Foley's radio station WHEP, brought new state-wide honors to Baldwin over the weekend when he was installed as president of the Alabama Broadcasters Association. This is a fine honor for Jim and the county.

Baldwin has a monopoly of presidents for the communication field. E.M. (Sparky) Howell, *Onlooker* publisher, is the current president of the Alabama Press Association.

Jim is the first to be so elected in his field from Baldwin but two others, (the late R.B. Vail, and current *Times* publisher) have been president of the state press group.

Baldwin has a third person who is currently serving as president of a state organization, which is also a first for the county. Mrs. Alice J. Duck is president of the Alabama Association of Circuit Clerks and Registers. This is also a real honor and one seldom, if ever, achieved anywhere in the state by a lady.

The success of Bay Minette girls winning beauty contests county-wide, area-wide and state-wide is getting routine. We won't mention the fact that local girls served as queens of the Alabama Fresh Water Fishing Rodeo,

Daphne May Day, and other county affairs. But recently Miss Jeannie Stamps was one of the top five in the Alabama Junior Miss Contest in Birmingham. Last week our Miss Jeannie Reed reigned as Armed Forces Week Queen in Mobile. Miss Anne Thrasher was selected a member of the famed Dixie Darlings at Mississippi Southern. Miss Jan Kinniard is winning beauty honors from Birmingham Southern, etc.

Baldwin still holds the county record for State Commanders of VFW. Three have served: Judge L. D. (Dick) Owen, Telfair J. Mashburn and Harry J. Wilters, Jr. Mashburn also has been president of the Alabama Circuit Judges Association. Too, Taylor Wilkins has served as president of the Alabama Peace Officers and Sheriff's Association.

And the most distinguished honor of all is held by Dr. J. Michaelson of Foley, who is president of the American Academy of General Practitioners. So far as we can remember, this is the only person we have had to hold a nation-wide presidency.

Baldwin has one or more names in Who's Who of America, etc. Undoubtedly there are others who have received honors we should mention. Somewhere in the county a record of such accomplishments should be kept. One of the county libraries could well take this on as a worthy project.

All the above, and others, in honoring themselves have also brought credit to their community, county and area.

OPEN HOUSE AT BROOKLEY AIR FORCE BASE

Next Tuesday is election day . . . again . . . but last Saturday was the Mobile area Aerospace Fair and Open House at Brookley Air Force Base . . . all were invited and hundreds of Baldwin Countians went to see the many astounding sights to be seen at Brookley and witness the spectacular air show . . . being a pilot, we can understand some things about flying but the precision formation performance put on by the Blue Angels, U.S. Navy flight demonstration team, is difficult to believe even while looking at it . . . this was the second time we had seen the Blue Angels . . . the first time was at Las Vegas several months back . . . they did something at Vegas they didn't do Saturday, for which we were thankful because it is too nerve racking to watch it .. . of course you have to be a pilot to know how dangerous it is . . . at Vegas they took off and landed in formation . . . quite a trick if you can live to tell it.

Baldwin was well represented . . . and beautifully so with our own Jeannie Reed as reigning queen of the show. By the way, have you noticed lately how many beautiful girls Bay Minette has . . . almost every week another one is elected queen of something . . . perhaps Jack House will write an article about them and run all of their pictures at one time . . . if so, we'll print a few hundred extra copies as sales will boom.

Back to Brookley . . . at the show, they had the U.S. Navy Helicopter Team, "The Crickets," the U.S. Army Parachute Team, "Golden Knights" and other interesting shows . . . one of the parachute jumpers has jumped over 1,000 times . . . we naturally thought of the law of averages. As we watched and looked, we couldn't help but reflect on the hugeness of Brookley . . . officially it's the Mobile Air Material Area . . . and its economic importance to Baldwin County and this area . . . we don't know how many work there from Baldwin as they do not keep a list by counties, cities, etc., but they do keep a list of automobiles by counties that are registered on the field . . . Baldwin has over 500 . . . and you can judge from this we do have a lot of people working there . . .our estimate is about 1,500 of the almost 16,000 employed on this base . . . with a payroll of over $2 million each Friday, it is by far the biggest single economic factor in the Mobile area . . . it represents over 20 percent of the payrolls in Mobile and directly supports a family of at least 50,000 and indirectly many more.

Next year when you are invited to open house at Brookley, you will find it a day well spent if you will go. More after the election, perhaps.

June 11, 1964

HE WAS 'DOC' STACEY TO ALL

We all hate to lose friends. We lost a good one this week in the unexpected death of J.H. Stacey, Bay Minette flower lover and retired druggist.

"Doc" Stacey, as he was fondly called by the many who knew him, had long been a leading citizen of this area. He was active in growing and promoting camellias and was considered an expert on the hundreds of varieties and how to grow them. His yard grew them well, especially with the tender and knowledgeable care he and Mrs. Stacey gave the plants.

He was an active Rotarian and church member. Many considered "Doc" to be slightly on the frugal side. But we always found him generous and cooperative on matters that he understood and thought to be for the good of the community. He was always ready to do his part as a good citizen should. Too, he was good to his family.

When we served as mayor back in the early forties, he was one of the five councilmen. He was the first of the five to die. Although some of the others, E. Davidson, O.J. Manci, L. D. Owen, Sr., and E.N. Rodgers, are in failing health, they are all living. It might be a surprise to some, but "Doc" Stacey was one of the most progressive of the lot and was always ready to do what was necessary to see Bay Minette grow and prosper.

We could well use more of his kind.

LOSING IN AN ELECTION ISN'T EASY

"Well, you can't win 'em all," may be a good reply to give a defeated candidate but it will hardly make him happy . . . about the best advice we can give is to read Romans 8:28 and remember that time heals many things . . . but advising a losing candidate how to be a good loser, even if you have had experience at losing, as we have had, isn't easy . . . this is another case where experience isn't much help. Maybe some of us said bye-bye to Barry a little too soon . . . he won the Republican presidential primary in California and suddenly became a big man in the GOP order of things again . . . now it looks very much as though he'll be nominated for president and we can't say bye to him again until after the November election.

Some state politicians jumped for Governor Wallace's coat tail a little late . . . some that did jump and hung on for dear life didn't even deserve to be in the same league with him . . . however, in politics, as in the game of life, nothing succeeds like success and the good ole American public likes a good ole winner any time, any place.

Our preacher tried to urge his listeners Sunday not to worry so much about things here on earth . . . at least we don't devote all our worrying time to things here, we devote some of it to the hereafter . . . We don't like to see people worry too much either but we do prefer a person who concerns himself about things as contrasted to the devil-may-care fellow who doesn't give a hoot about anything, including paying up what he owes you . . . if some other folk would do a little worrying, we could get by with a lot less.

Line up city politicians . . . us voters are awaiting you. Naturally we aren't getting old but it doesn't take us as long to tire as it once did, just longer to rest up. Some people think you should have to meet a payroll before you are promoted to certain positions of importance . . . since we have almost 50 staring us in the face every Friday, we had about decided that the only thing it qualifies a person for is housed at Tuscaloosa, and it isn't the University. More later, maybe.

July 23, 1964

Grand Ole Man, E.E. Hale, retires

When we came to Baldwin in 1936, farmers were praising their county agent, E.E. Hale. It wasn't long until we understood why. He was a good county agent, citizen and gentleman.

But Hale came to Baldwin with a good record. He had graduated at Auburn with an excellent scholastic record, was elected to Phi Kappa Phi, the highest honor society and selected as Best All Round Junior in Agriculture. He then served as county agent in Marengo before being given the difficult job in Baldwin.

Baldwin has long been considered one of the most difficult county agent's positions in the South. This is because of the diversity of agriculture and people, as well as its bigness. However, during his tenure the county developed into the largest produce shipping county in the South. He worked day and night through community farm clubs and every other method of communication to help make farming here successful.

We went with him to farm meetings, chamber of commerce meetings, tagged along while he helped organize co-ops, the Baldwin County Electric Membership Cooperative, etc. He became our close friend and most trusted adviser. Then in 1944, while we were off flying in Uncle Sam's Air Corps, it happened. He had been offered a job as director of organization of the Alabama Farm Bureau. He moved to Montgomery. We hadn't imagined Baldwin without him. Many still can't.

His hard work and success continued and in 1947, he was selected as the first Executive Vice President of the newly organized Alabama Forest Products Association. He retired recently but not before he had helped to mold this state group into one of the most influential and successful forest associations in the country.

Much of Ernest Hale's success is due to his family. Just as popular in Baldwin, Montgomery and Alabama is his lovely, energetic and intelligent wife, Kathleen. Local people will remember their two sons as "Scooter" and "Brub." But now they have grown up into successful young men and go by their real names of Everett and Bradley. It's Dr. Everett and he is practicing in Tuscaloosa as a urosurgeon. Bradley is a tax attorney in Atlanta. Each has a son and a daughter, giving their parents four grandchildren in whom they are well pleased.

The current issue of the monthly magazine, *Alabama Forest Products*, features the Hale family and tells of their many achievements and honors.

It also gives one disappointing fact. They have retired to an 1800 acre cattle ranch near Uniontown, Alabama. It's sorta hard to imagine them not retiring down here. Oh well, that just means we'll have to drive farther to see them. The Black Belt acreage has three lakes stocked with bream and bass.

But there are two things we can't see, E.E. and Kathleen Hale retired or either holding a fishing pole.

GOLDWATER TAKES OVER GOP

Delegates have left the Republican convention in San Francisco to return home where they will continue their wars against the opposition . . . Goldwater was made the presidential nominee and some person from up East (down East to a Yankee) was given the vice presidential spot. Nothing is very certain in politics but these might be so considered . . . Goldwater has taken over the GOP party, or at least those who agree with him, and has told the others to join up or get out . . . Barry got two reasons for a smile within a week, first when he was nominated and second when George Wallace denominated himself.

If you think the Democrats and Johnson are quiet because they are scared to death, just wait until August and they start conventioning in Atlantic City . . . Republicans don't know anything about in-fighting compared to Democrats . . . and what can you expect when Democrats cover the water front all the way from the NAACP to George Wallace, which is, come to think of it, about the same distance as it is from the Birchers to Nelson Rockefeller.

Since another convention is coming up, a few definitions might help you understand them . . . having been to two makes us an authority . . . Delegate: a person eating a five-course, $10 dinner and complaining about the mess the opposition has gotten the country into. Caucus: a meeting called by the boss to give instructions . . . another thought, the word comes from the Greek word Kaukos—which means a drinking cup—at a convention, such a cup doesn't hold water. Rigged convention: one in which the other delegates control. Open Convention: you guessed it. Opposition: fools. The Press, TV and Radio: spies from the other party. Defeated candidate: the poor guy who smiles through tears and calls for unity. Nominating speech: flattery, pure but not very simple. Platform: something to fall out over, make up over and then forget. Alternate delegate: nothing.

Conclusion: 30 days ago, reading all the polls and everything, we wouldn't have been surprised if both parties had nominated LBJ . . . after listening to the GOP oratory in San Francisco, we aren't sure now that the Democrats will even nominate him. More enlightenment later, maybe.

August 6, 1964

PEOPLE WE CAN'T AFFORD TO LOSE

It has been said that tragedies often happen in threes. It could be such is the case of deaths of prominent people within a community. If so, Bay Minette has had its three.

Recently one of our most dearly loved and respected ladies died here. She was Mrs. Ned Noonan, Sr.

Mrs. Noonan had many excellent qualities which endeared people to her and her to people. She went about in her quiet way doing kind deeds, working to make people's lives more pleasant by thoughtful acts. For example, she gave us our first camellia after moving into our new home in 1938. We still have it and with it the thoughts of the kind person who gave it.

Then suddenly, Monday night of last week, Perry Prescott died. This was a shock to a host of friends throughout the state. Few had as many friends as Perry. He had friends because he was a friend. We know of no one that didn't like him.

Dying at the comparatively early age of 50, Perry had quite a record of accomplishments. But during the past few months he appeared to us to be doing better physically and otherwise than since he moved to Bay Minette a quarter century ago. He had been county tax collector, assistant director of the State Department of Conservation and assistant director of the Seafoods Division, past president of the Alabama Foxhunter Association, and his services were in demand everywhere as a judge for dog field trials, etc.

We know of no greater compliment we could pay him than say, Perry Prescott was just a plain likeable fellow.

Then last Wednesday came the untimely, but no sudden, death of one of Baldwin's outstanding citizens, Circuit Judge Hubert M. Hall.

Hubert, as he was called by most of his many friends, was popular in Baldwin as a person, as a politician and as a judge. He was re-nominated for a third term by an overwhelming majority in the Spring Democratic primaries.

Judge Hall had a wide reputation of being an able jurist. Able in the law, he was also sound in common sense and understanding. He was active in many organizations including American Legion, Elks, Masons, 40 et 8, Shrines, Cattlemen's Association, Chamber of Commerce, Kiwanis, etc., and held the highest offices in many of them. He had also been active in the Presbyterian Church and was a substantial contributor to the new building here.

His death leaves a big void.

DEMOCRATS TO CONVENE THIS MONTH

This is the month for the Democrats to convene in National Convention in Atlantic City . . . the turbulence the Republicans had in San Francisco will seem like mild breezes compared to the hurricane-like fights which will take place by the donkey emblem people . . . of course President Johnson, who has a habit of shooting his opposition before they leave the ground, eliminated some of the potential disturbance when he let it be known last week that Bobby Kennedy will not be the vice-presidential nominee . . . if he'll just push Senator Humphrey aside now, things might just end up being calmer than anyone imagined. The local political noises you hear may not be because of the city election, it's probably more akin to who's to be circuit judge, etc.

Sometimes we feel like the business executive who said 95 percent of the advice he got is no good, "but I have to listen to all of it to get the five percent that's worth having" . . . another reason why advice should be brief, constructive and seldom. It is said that the average American walks about 65,000 miles during his lifetime . . . can you imagine a person walking that far without getting run over several times by an automobile? The average person wears shoes two sizes larger than his father and mother did 50 years ago . . . the best we can tell, heads are the same size now as then, or should be. "One out of every three women in the country is bringing home a paycheck," says item . . . and three out of every three is spending one or more paychecks. Half of all U.S. women over the age of 25 haven't finished high school . . . which is proof that you don't have to be educated to catch a husband—just smart.

We were happy to learn that a study shows self-made millionaires rarely make their fortunes early in life . . . still hope. "Where law ends, tyranny begins," Wm. Pitt . . . no comment needed. Summer is fast fading into Autumn . . . and it seems that much of our crop hasn't even ripened, much less harvested. 'Nuff, for now.

August 27, 1964

L. D. OWEN, SR., GREAT FRIEND AND CHARACTER

Bay Minette, as we have had to mention all too often recently, is losing too many of her outstanding citizens.

No better example of this fact could be offered than the recent death of L. D. (Dick) Owen, Sr. He will be sadly missed in these parts.

Mr. Dick, as we affectionately called him, led a successful and interesting life in Baldwin County after he came here from Butler County. With the late J.C. (Jim) Burns, he operated a retail business in Bay Minette. Both prospered. Both served their town well and each served as mayor of Bay

Minette for several years.

Fact is, they almost succeeded each other as mayor. Largely at their suggestion and support, this writer was elected mayor to succeed Jim Burns in 1940, served until going into the Army Air Corps. Mr. Dick was mayor pro-tem, by virtue of the fact he led the ticket in the council race, and stepped up to the job of mayor, was reelected and thus served the most of two terms.

Mr. Dick was a strong character. He said what he thought when he thought it. He had a sense of humor and enjoyed life. His loyalty to his family, church and Bay Minette was never doubted. He was a good friend to have. He had many friends because he liked people and was himself friendly. We were fortunate to be among those who cherished his friendship.

THE USS ALABAMA IS COMING

Another rich chapter is being written in the illustrious history of the USS Battleship Alabama.

Citizens of Alabama are raising $1 million to bring it near the Tensaw River, between Baldwin and Mobile Counties, to enshrine her in the memorial park dedicated to the memory of the men and women of all the Armed Forces who served so gallantly in previous wars.

The mighty "A" is now being towed from Seattle, Washington, and as she neared the Panama Canal Saturday one of the tugs towing her "home" sunk, costing the life of one seaman.

Work has already begun dredging the channel to the park. If all goes well, and the funds are raised, people can begin viewing this historical ship sometime in early 1965.

The fund drive is succeeding. It will be a success. Over $700,000 is already in the bank.

Last Wednesday Governor Wallace called many leading citizens from over the state to Montgomery to give them an up-to-date report on the drive and urge the successful completion of it.

Many in Baldwin have already contributed. Many have not. Since we will benefit more than most counties from this great tourist attraction, it behooves all of us to help bring this venture to a speedy and successful completion.

DEMOCRATS IN ATLANTIC CITY

The Democrats are at it, and each other, in Atlantic City this week . . .
it's a great show . . . and though we citizens may be inclined to make light of
such political conventions, they are an important element in the democratic
way of life we enjoy in this fine country of yours and mine . . . such antics
as are carried on at these conventions indicate they aren't perfect (nothing
run by humans is), but nothing better has been suggested as a way for the
two principal parties to nominate a president and vice president . . . and
remember this, the president of the United States is the most powerful
and most important office on earth . . . so conventions are important, and
highly interesting.

President Johnson is a poor man compared to the late President Kennedy . . . but compared to most Americans, LBJ has done right well by
himself financially as well as politically . . . the same could be said of Senator Goldwater. In the upcoming presidential race, Goldwater will have to
be considered the poor man as he is only worth an estimated $1.7 million
. . . Johnson's auditors say he is worth $3.5 million which they admit is the
book value, not the value of his properties if sold . . . *Life* magazine, which
has been known to be off on facts, claims Johnson is worth $14 million . . .
in any event, our next president will be a wealthy man and shouldn't have
to put his fingers in the public till to feed his family . . . since money and
politics make such interesting subjects you can rest assured we'll all hear
much more about the wealth of the two candidates before November . . .
which is all right too.

Political polls are often accurate if they agree with the way you want
them to agree . . . very inaccurate otherwise. Keep this in mind about
scientific polls: they register the thinking of people at the time polled, not
necessarily on election day . . . but anyone is silly to ignore the polls when
they say Johnson is now ahead of Goldwater almost two to one . . . if you
must wager (a foolish thing to do in politics), take Goldwater in Alabama
and Johnson nationally. More later, maybe.

December 17, 1964

HENRY BRYARS . . . GOOD CITIZEN, RETIRES

Last week Henry Bryars, Stockton, resigned as a member of the Baldwin County Board of Education because of ill health.

He has been a leading Baldwin County citizen for almost three-quarters of a century and during the past several years was a valuable member of the education board. He has long been considered one of southwest Alabama's most successful businessmen, having particularly excelled in growing of timber and cattle.

Until ill health slowed him up, he was known to be one of the hardest working men around. We well remember a story told us by an automobile dealer not long after we had come to the county. The dealer knew Mr. Bryars hit the road running real early in the morning. To make sure he caught him before leaving his home just north of Stockton, the dealer arrived at 4 a.m., parked in the front yard to await him. After waiting awhile Mr. Bryars didn't come out. Finally the dealer knocked on the door and Mrs. Bryars told him that her husband had been up and gone since three o'clock.

We hated to see him resign from the education post but must admit to admiring him for so doing as he sincerely felt that his health prevented him from doing full justice to the important position. Unfortunately many people do not take such an honest and practical approach to public positions. They hang on and on long after their age and health permits them to serve well.

This area of the county has had several rugged, self-made men like Mr. Bryars. Sadly the breed is fast fading. But because of them, we have been given a great heritage.

BALDWIN NEEDS A LEGISLATOR

Rumors persist that Governor George Wallace is going to call a special session of the legislature in January. Presumably it will be for the purpose of furnishing free text books to all students up through the 12th grade and perhaps for another education bond issue for school buildings.

All of this is fine and sounds like real education progress.

But there is one small matter of interest to this county . . . and it could be of real importance in either a special or regular legislative session. Baldwin doesn't have a legislator.

Judge Telfair J. Mashburn resigned his legislative post to become circuit judge. His successor has not been elected.

May we humbly suggest to Governor Wallace that he call a special election quickly so we can be represented in the lower house in Montgomery. Please!

THOMAS W. MARTIN . . . MR. ALABAMA

"The last half of the 20th Century belongs to the South."

No man did more to see that this statement is coming true than the person who said it. He was Thomas W. Martin, chairman of the board and for years president of the Alabama Power Company.

Unfortunately this great man died last week. Fortunately he had lived to a ripe old age, and had spent the long years of his life building Alabama and the South.

Mr. Martin accomplished so many things and received so many honors it would be impossible to list them all here. He could well be called the man of the 20th Century for Alabama.

CHRISTMAS GREAT TIME OF YEAR

When Christmas comes it really comes . . . to youngsters it comes slowly but to oldsters it comes around in a hurry. But we think it's a great time of the year . . . fewer people seem to be mad at each other . . . and we like the lights and decorations too. We don't even mind the commercial part of Christmas that so many complain about . . . at least we're practical enough to know that if you did away with this phase of it the whole Holiday Season would diminish, at least so far as the celebration and happiness is concerned. Yes, we know it's supposed to celebrate the birth of our Saviour . . . and this thought of peace and goodwill we like too . . . but we like the idea of remembering the birth of Christ 365 days a year. The point is this . . . for whatever reason you celebrate Christmas, it's good, real good.

Murder is murder whether it is in the jungles of the Congo, the state of

Mississippi, or New York City . . . and it's murder whether it is black killing white or white killing black or killing each other . . . and when murder is committed, someone should pay the penalty for the crime.

You might consider giving this journal to a few of your friends for a Christmas present, please! We find our mind works better the more we work it. We don't mind work . . . in fact we like to work but we do wish so many other people didn't like to see us do so much of it . . . our boss has told us many times that we have never learned to say no to anyone except, of course, her . . . fact is we like to say yes, it's just more fun . . . but it does keep you real busy. Apparently a lot of people think our name is "George" of the "let George do it" variety . . . now we're not complaining, but we surely will when people stop calling on us for assistance in this, that and the other, etc.

"Mobile's Compost plant initiates squabbling," says headline in the *Birmingham News* . . . we sadly fear that Mobile and squabbling are getting to be synonymous in the minds of many people . . . and we well remember what one of the ingredients of compost was back on the farm . . . all of which just seems to fit in the above headline. Cuba and Castro are still down there but fewer and fewer people seem to care. Recruiting these days probably refers to football players, not soldiers for Uncle Sam. See you again before Christmas, maybe.

January 14, 1965

Two great attractions for area

Within the past two weeks two great projects have been completed and dedicated, following many months and even years of dreams and hard work . . . projects which are destined to attract more tourists to this area than anything that has happened since the Gulf was formed and Bellingrath Gardens opened.

Sunday before last the spectacularly beautiful Greek Orthodox Church was dedicated and opened to the public at the world famous Malbis Plantation. Envisioned by the great Jason Malbis years ago, the temple with its Grecian marble, original paintings and architectural splendor was completed at a cost of over $1 million and four years of labor.

As its reputation spreads over the land, we predict tourists will flock to see it by the hundreds. And nothing will make the members of the fine Greek community that Mr. Malbis built, with dreams and hard work, happier. They built it to share with the world.

Then last Saturday the Battleship Alabama was enshrined and dedicated. It will attract thousands.

Both add to the attractiveness of the area as a place to live and visit.

BAY MINETTE STILL ON THE GO!

Many who attended the annual meeting of the Bay Minette Chamber of Commerce last Thursday night expressed surprise at the many accomplishments of the organization during 1964.

Of course those who have worked closely with the chamber group were not surprised. They helped make the accomplishments possible. They also realize that there are still many problems to solve and that the opportunities for the future are great.

Bay Minette is a good town. It can be a better town if our citizens continue to work as a team. This county seat city is recognized as one of the two or three most progressive municipalities in Alabama.

This is a good reputation to have and a good foundation upon which to climb to even greater heights.

To the outgoing officers of the Chamber of Commerce, congratulations. To the new ones coming in, good luck!

AZALEAS BLOOMING TOO EARLY

The weather fooled mother nature and now the blooming azaleas feel rather foolish with the cold sneaking up right behind the warm spell. Things just aren't as good out of season . . . warm weather and tomatoes in winter, for example.

Finally football has gotten out of season and we just don't want to see any more games until next September. The Senior Bowl game with Joe Namath and Tucker Frederickson was real outstanding . . . and the game didn't last nearly as long as the traffic jams. The half-time show was sensational . . . in case you got your eyes off the Dixie Darlings and the other beauties, you may have noticed the outstanding designs, including the smoking Battleship Alabama . . . Bay Minette's Bootsie Noonan made them . . . good, eh?

Looks as if Russia and her new leaders, whoever they are, are trying to be friendly with Uncle Sam . . . we are willing to get along with other folk, particularly those with atomic bombs, but we do hope we'll keep a sharp eye open for double-crosses, stabs in the back, etc. . . . and maybe there's just a chance the communist Bear would like for us to be on her side in case she goes to war with her fellow-communists, namely the 600 million Chinamen. We have a sneaky feeling that people around here don't care too much whether Indonesia blasts Malaysia or the opposite.

It seems to us that the person who worries most about inflation is the one with hard cash in the bank . . . this may not be the way it should be but it is the way it is . . . we people with debts need a little inflation along to lighten the load. Dogs may be smart but not as smart as Little Orphan Annie's Sandy . . . of course he has been around for about 40 years and that's long enough for even a dumb dog to learn a little . . . yeah, we know about old dogs and new tricks.

"Stay alive in '65" is a sensible slogan . . . think we'll adopt it. You may be surprised to know who said, "I don't think we have any choice but to live with the Civil Rights Act of 1964." . . . it was Arkansas' Orval Faubus. Like Senator Huey Long said after being elected Senate whip, times have changed in the last 20 years . . . and if you're against change of any kind, you had better not hang around for another 20 years . . . things will happen whether we like them or not, and faster than ever. Back soon, perhaps.

January 28, 1965

A SALUTE TO OUR HIGHWAY WORKERS

For the second time in a matter of months, Baldwin County roads and bridges were badly damaged by floodwaters following heavy rains last Friday.

For the second time in a matter of months, most of the damage has been repaired and service has been restored to normal.

This is a credit to the excellent highway crewmen, state and county, who are called upon from time to time to do Herculean duty, often under most adverse conditions and at all kinds of hours of the day and night.

To Baldwin County Road Commissioner Harold Bryars, as well as all other county commissioners, Chairman John Hadley and Commissioners Dick Childress and Bill Cooper, and especially to all of the members of the State Highway Department and the county workers, we take off our hats.

Once again they have performed their duties most remarkably, and at comparatively little expense to the state and county.

LET'S ALL ACCEPT THE CHALLENGE

At a meeting in Montgomery last week, Gov. George C. Wallace challenged the State Legislature and the people of Alabama to take a major step forward in education.

He outlined a plan whereby school teachers would receive a 10 percent increase in pay, schools would receive a five percent increase for current expenses, and all pupils, grades one through 12, would be given free textbooks.

Included in the plan is money with which to finance the new junior college and trade school program, one of which is to be located in Bay Minette.

It was the most ambitious program ever proposed for education in Alabama and will cost approximately $32 million the first year and approximately $36 million the second year.

But all of this will be done without additional taxation. Surplus educational funds, it was pointed out, will enable the state to carry out this plan without increasing taxes.

State Superintendent of Education Austin R. Meadows calls it a "good, constructive program."

He asks everybody in the state to "get together and put over this Unified Program for Education." He says this program will "pay the greatest dividend we can ever receive."

Gov. Wallace is solidly behind the plan.

Superintendent of Education Meadows is behind the plan.

State Budget Officer James V. Jordan is all for it. Leading educators are 100 percent for it.

The Baldwin Times whole-heartedly endorses Gov. Wallace's plan.

Let's all accept the challenge and take this major step forward in education.

THERE ARE MANY GREAT MEN

If Winston Churchill isn't the man of the 20th Century, then who is? . . . We have many great men . . . Franklin D. Roosevelt might have made it if he had lived longer . . . the Communists no doubt would nominate Lenin . . . Gandhi of India must have been great . . . so was President Woodrow Wilson . . . and Henry Ford achieved greatness of another sort . . . too, the 20th Century isn't over, not by 35 years, and the greatest men may yet not have been heard of . . . don't laugh, but there will be some who will want to name Martin Luther King . . . and if some fool kills him the world may martyr him forever . . . right now we'll stick with Churchill.

The weather, like many people, is most inconsistent . . . take last week for instance . . . it started off warm, got below freezing, turned warm again and rained eight inches within a few hours, and Sunday it started the new week off getting cold again . . . small wonder weathermen can't always predict correctly . . . what is amazing is that they do as well as they do, which is pretty good.

Have you ever talked to a chain smoker who didn't think it was a bad habit? . . . guess we can't be too critical though, all of us have one or more bad habits . . . and some good ones . . . which reminds us of the old saying, "there is so much good in the worst of us and so much bad in the best of us that it behooves none of us to talk about the rest of us," or another one, "some go east, some go west, but you'll find an ass among the best."

ABC liquor stores have learned that "named brands" sell best . . . they became "named brands" because of advertising . . . which means, please, that advertising pays.

Since 50 percent of our population is under 25 years of age, it is easy to understand why a man of 50 can look around and see a changing world . . . so if you want to keep having friends, you had better keep on making new ones . . . friends, like life, pass on too. Give to something worthwhile and you keep something worthwhile. Selfishness may not be the greatest sin but it pushes laziness for the number one spot. Every boy should have a dog, unless the boy is a neighbor. It takes a lot of fixing around a house to make a home. This may be an "off" political year but this doesn't mean that politics will turn over and play dead. More later, perhaps.

April 8, 1965

Dr. John C. McLeod, family doctor

Few men have served a community so well as did Dr. J.C. McLeod during his 65 years of medical service in this area. We have read in the building of the West about the "pioneer" doctors, but none did more in the fine tradition of family doctors than did the fine old gentleman who died here last Thursday.

With little formal education, he started practicing medicine here before the turn of the century. He came here after only a few months in medical school to become the doctor for a lumber camp and mill. He stayed and did well in every sense of the word.

Many considered him rough and gruff. Perhaps he was, when he needed to be. But he was anything but most of the time. He was kind and considerate. He was always ready to serve and would come on being called when some other doctors wouldn't. He always had a story to tell to amuse his patients, often about Bay Minette characters of yesterday. Almost without fail his services amounted to much more than his bill, if he gave one at all.

Dr. McLeod actually began his education upon leaving school. He continually studied to keep up with the latest methods of healing the sick. For this reason he was considered by most to be an excellent physician. Many swore him to be the best.

He was many things other than a healer of men's physical ailments. He was also a Bible scholar and cared much about men's souls. A man of considerable frugality, he was also a man of good common judgment and made his small but numerous fees multiply by sound investments. He probably could have bought several banks on the fees he never tried to or didn't collect.

A book of rich experiences could be written about this great family physician. Bay Minette would never have been the fine place it is without Dr. McLeod's long service of healing people and it will never again be the same without him around.

WORLD POPULATION

Since people cause trouble, a reasonable explanation of why there is so much of same on the earth is just that—people . . . the world population is increasing by 180,000 per day, over a million a week and 65 million each year . . . the world will have twice as many people as today within 35 more years . . . and probably twice as many problems. Terrorists in Birmingham are trying to cut down the population figures with bombings . . . irate citizens have posted an $84,000 reward for information leading to the conviction of the bums who bomb . . . since every person is supposed to have his price, it seems that it is about time someone started talking, every decent citizen hopes.

There are 17,700 automobile junk yards in the U.S. that can be seen from the public highways . . . and there are 72 million autos on the public highways . . . ride around for a few hours any Sunday afternoon hereabouts, or most anywhere, and you will declare that you personally saw half that many junk yards and cars. "Knowledge essential to farmers," says headline . . . true, and the right kind of knowledge is right helpful to any person. We have been tending to lawns for a long time but still don't understand why fine fertilizers are finer for weeds than our grass. This is the time of year when the air conditioner is about to out maneuver the furnace. A "drop-out" is a dirty word which everyone knows refers to a student who doesn't have the good common sense to stay in school . . . and the business that doesn't advertise regularly will soon be a drop-out in the business world.

It was once written, "The things which must be must be for the best." . . . we hope this saying is for the best. Being partly honest is about as possible as being partly pregnant. If you work evil for another you also work evil for self. Hesiod, a Greek writer in 720 B.C., said, "Oft hath even a whole city reaped the evil fruit of a bad man." . . . Selma citizens can even name the man. If you don't think custom is strong, just try to change it. If you want to be happy, you must first think you are. Excellence is worth working for even if we never achieve it . . . unfortunately some wouldn't recognize excellence if it were staring them in the face cross-eyed. Too many of us want to become rich all at once. Prosperity makes friends, adversity tests them. Confession of one's faults is the next thing to being without them. If you want someone to hate you, first let them do you an injustice. Probably we'll be back next week.

June 3, 1965

Baldwin's cup runneth over

The Times has had considerable to say from time to time about the giant strides forward being made by Bay Minette and Baldwin County in educational, economic and other fields. For a change of pace, we would like to call your attention to the human element.

Early this month the Bay Minette Junior Chamber of Commerce went to the state convention and won many honors, including first for the best organization of its size in Alabama.

Last week W.M. Hodgson, Jr., president of the local Standard Furniture Manufacturing Co., Inc., was named the small businessman of the year for the state of Alabama. He was also selected as one of the top three in the Southeast.

Not long ago Bay Minette's own Ginny Henderson was named State Miss VIE (Vocational Industrial Education).

Foley's Jim Stewart and Sparky Howell recently stepped down, respectively, as president of the Alabama Broadcasters Association and the Alabama Press Association.

Dr. Julius Michaelson, also of Foley, is immediate past president of American Academy of General Practice.

The Times, which is the oldest business institution in Baldwin County, was the winner of the most awards at last year's annual better newspaper contests for the state.

Bay Minette's Key Club has won more state and national awards and contests than any other in the whole country. It has been selected the best in the state many times and the best in the United States several times.

Perhaps you'll forgive the parental pride which mentions the fact that this publisher's number two son won the Dean's Award for being the number one student in the graduating class at the University of Alabama Medical School last week.

We pay tribute to those responsible for the accomplishments above and beg forgiveness of others who may not have been mentioned.

THE STANLEYS OF GREENVILLE

The Times may be, and is, the oldest newspaper and business institution in Baldwin County but it is not the oldest newspaper in Alabama. Not by several.

One older is the fine *Greenville Advocate*. This week the *Publishers' Auxiliary*, the newspaperman's newspaper, selected the *Advocate's* editor, John Glenn Stanley, as its "Editor of the Week."

The Advocate is 100 years old and interestingly enough the weekly has only had two editors during this time. Both of them have been Stanleys. Glenn's father, James Bernley Stanley, served as editor for 70 consecutive years. He died in 1934, two months after Number one of Volume 70 had been reached. Since '34 Glenn has continuously made his family newspaper one of the best in the country.

We, like other editors, have our favorite newspapers. *The Greenville Advocate* has long been at or near the top of our list. Not only because it is such a good newspaper but because the Stanleys are such excellent people.

At newspaper conventions we like to listen to Glenn's wisdom and wit. The *Auxiliary* story revealed some of both, as follows: "There's no shortage of perils and pitfalls in the weekly newspaper business. On one occasion, a number of years ago, our Linotype operator combined the first line of one personal with the second line of another, thus proclaiming to the *Advocate's* public that an elderly local widower had spent the previous weekend with an elderly local widow. This item escaped the proofreader's eye and the paper was in the post office before the tragic error came to light. There was no rest for the weary staff that night. Overtime pay for reprinting four pages amounted to much less than a lost libel suit."

He doesn't like to print violence and sordid news. "We have discovered that a living may be made while remembering that 'The evil that men do lives after them, the good is oft interred with their bones,'" he explains.

"Newspapering, as a profession, is interesting, entertaining, challenging, exacting, hard work, and often rewarding," so says the sage of Greenville.

Long live the Stanleys and newspaper folk like them.

LT. GOV. JIM ALLEN LECTURES STATE SENATE

Last week Lt. Gov. Jim Allen lectured the Alabama Senate for their do-nothing delaying tactics . . . he suggested they face up to the issues facing Alabama such as reapportionment, etc. . . . of course they paid little attention to him but they might be surprised to know the public feels the same as Allen. Which reminds us that democracy is a poor form of government at best but hasten to say that at its worst it is better than any other kind of government found on this earth . . . and don't forget it. If you travel the back roads to see the country, you will find that thousands of others thought of it too . . . wherever you go there are cars, cars and more of 'em.

We sometimes forget what Memorial Day is for . . . then you further wonder when you read that over 500 are killed during the weekend holiday . . . maybe we need a memorial for Memorial Day. Rain, like good health, isn't appreciated until you don't have it. Congress has tried to change all the voting rules and regulations except one . . . voters' apathy . . . which is the main change that needs attention. We were like most people in their thoughts about the Sonny Liston-Cassius Clay boxing hoax . . . it lasted a minute and the loser, Liston, made $600,000 . . . frankly it doesn't concern us too much as we began losing interest in boxing when Jack Dempsey lost the heavyweight championship to Gene Tunney . . . which gives, besides our interest in boxing, or lack of it, some indication of our age.

A nut doesn't have to go to college to be one but judging from the anti-American activities and other antics of some of our students and college professors, education can make meat-heads nuttier. Work may not have hurt anyone but we know a lot of people who get considerable pleasure out of thinking it does. The reason most of us don't think life begins at 40 is because we think it will begin tomorrow, or the next day . . . we should know that life is today . . . and make the most of it. Being smart isn't so hard . . . if you don't believe it, just ask most any newspaperman. More later, maybe.

July 29, 1965

BALDWIN'S OLDEST BUSINESS VIGOROUS AT 75

This is *The Baldwin Times'* 75th year of publication. For such an old gal, she is kicking up her heels in high glee this week. Perhaps she has the right.

Everyone at *The Times* is humbled and appreciative at the fine showing made in the annual Alabama Better Newspaper Contest. It was announced Saturday in Decatur, at the annual Summer Convention of APA, that this county seat weekly had won six first place and four other awards in the better newspaper competition. Needless to say no other paper did as well and it was the best *The Times* has done in her three-quarters of a century.

Most of the credit for this showing must go to Jack House, *Times* editor. He is the one who worked late nights preparing the entries under the various contest categories. Also he is the one who weekly lays out the newspaper, does most of the writing and takes most of the pictures.

Jack would be the first to tell you however that publishing a good newspaper is a team effort. *The Times* has good printing equipment but people make the difference in a newspaper, like in everything else. Mechanically, *The Times* has never been so well staffed. The bright, crisp look the paper has doesn't just happen. Frank Windham, plant superintendent, and his men and women helpers take as much pride in the looks and contents of the weekly publication as the people on the business and editorial side.

Making up the paper also requires exceptional skill. *The Times* is blessed with the talents of Bufred Johnson and his assistants who deserve as much credit as anyone on the paper.

The front office personnel are dedicated and efficient. The assistant publisher does a good job of keeping the advertising and other business coming in. Our many fine community correspondents are loyal and good. In fact, we would hate to lose any of our 33 full-time employees or our many part-time helpers.

Above all, if Bay Minette wasn't a good town and Baldwin a good county, *The Times* could not have been so honored.

To all thanks! And please excuse us if we seem a bit addled with glee in our 75th anniversary year.

Wonder if any other town the size of Bay Minette can boast of the Nation's Best Key Club, the State's Best Weekly newspaper, the State's Best Jaycee organization and the Southeast's Best Small Businessman, all in the same year? . . . we doubt it . . . There should be some way of letting the world know how fortunate we are in Bay Minette to have all these things . . . why couldn't somebody, perhaps the Chamber of Commerce, erect a billboard sign on the outskirts of town calling all of this, and much more, to the attention of motorists? . . .

We also could brag about our industry, our recreational and educational facilities, etc. . . Come to think of it, that new motel Bay Minette is getting will do as much to promote Bay Minette as anything we know . . . Hotels are good about putting up signs letting you know how far it is to the next town, and if memory serves us right, there aren't too many signs now that tell you how far it is to Bay Minette . . . And while we're on the subject, wouldn't it be fine to have an observation platform at the Tensaw Ghost Fleet . . . They could take the old Maritime headquarters at Cliff's Landing and make it into a real tourist attraction . . . A lot of folks would like to see in person what *The Baldwin Times* showed in print last week, the 231 Victory ships now in mothballs in Baldwin County.

Almost anyone can tell you how to live your life . . . Dollars and sense lay the foundations for big fortunes . . . The best arguments are like fish hooks—they sink in easy, but are hard to dislodge . . . There are bigger things in life than money—bills! . . . The road to success is always under construction . . . A person who is always talking is bound to be right—now and then . . . Go as far as you can—and when you get there, you'll be able to see farther . . .

Inflation is a lot like overeating: it makes you feel so good, right up to the time when it's too late to correct it . . . Most of us are inclined to measure our achievements by what other people haven't done . . . A little voice within us used to be our conscience. Now it's a transistor radio . . .

An ounce of silence is worth a pound of explanation.

September 2, 1965

BALDWIN WELL REPRESENTED IN MONTGOMERY

Now that the regular session of the state legislature has come to a close, *The Times* would like to pay tribute to the county's two lawmakers, Senator L.W. Brannan and L. D. (Dick) Owen. They have ably and effectively represented Baldwin. Several bills have been passed by the two which should be of considerable benefit to the county. Of particular interest and importance to Bay Minette was the act to extend the city limits. With the rapid growth of the town industrially and otherwise, this move was essential. We feel confident that the few who disagreed with the move will soon see the wisdom of it.

Another measure of local importance was the passage of a constitutional amendment to be voted on by the state. If voted favorably, it will allow citizens in the first seven precincts, generally the area from Stapleton and Spanish Fort north, to tax themselves up to five mills for the purpose of building a 50-bed Hill-Burton hospital here. This will probably be voted on, both locally and statewide, within a few months.

For the third time, a constitutional amendment will be voted on statewide to place county officeholders on a salary. We suspect the third time will be the charm and the county will be taken off the fee system. Baldwin Citizens are overwhelmingly for the idea, having endorsed it both times when the state was voting against it.

Another bill Senator Brannan and Rep. Owen helped get through sets up the machine to have a feasibility study made of the possibility of building a toll bridge between Ft. Morgan and Dauphin Island. If this can be done, it would greatly boost the tourist and recreation business on our Gulf Coast.

They helped pass and passed other measures of importance to the county. They also distinguished themselves by helping kill bad legislation. Baldwin can be thankful for having good representation in Montgomery.

This great geographical subdivision of Alabama, Baldwin County, has many things other counties don't have . . . most of them good. However, the Alabama Legislature put an end to one of our "only county in Alabama" distinctions last week.

They legalized draft beer in Jefferson County.

Until now Baldwin has been the only county in the state that could serve draft beer, or beer on tap. It was an oddity that had caused considerable conversation and interest.

When Alabama adopted the local option Alabama Beverage Control Act in the '30s, Senator Robin Swift, who was then representing this county in the upper house, was successful in amending the act to provide that communities with a population whose forebears in the old country drank draft beer could legally do so in this state. Technically, this only included those areas in Baldwin and Cullman counties with predominant German population. Later, Cullman people dried up their county and that only left Elberta in Baldwin where draft beer could be served. During the Persons administration, the ABC board allowed it to be sold in any part of this county. The distinction remained for all these years until big Jefferson robbed us of it.

The hurricane season is approaching . . . things have been rather stormy for some time . . . Like in Los Angeles, parts of Alabama, Vietnam, just to name a few places. Uncle Sam wants peace . . . but, like in tango, it takes two . . . a fact some of the college long-haired group don't seem to realize. "Living Costs Rising in America," says headline . . . we know . . . after all we have to buy a few things. The state legislature has quit, gone home . . . for which we can all express thanks . . . now if we could just get the lawmakers out of Washington.

How Can Negro Gain Respect? is topic question . . . that one is easy . . . by just being respectable, like anyone else who has respect of himself and his neighbors. Estimates give China one billion population by 1980 . . . we hope they're all yellow, not red. You can almost smell it in the air as you sweat away the 90-degree heat . . . that is fall and football. If you are one of those who hasn't registered to vote, you are going to be in a small minority group . . . registering to vote isn't the half of it . . . you are supposed to vote when qualified . . . about 40 to 50 percent fail to do so each election . . . almost always there are enough people who fail to vote to change the results of an election.

"What maintains one vice would bring up two children," said Ben Franklin . . . vice may be expensive but we can speak with some authority on the cost of raising two children . . . and we suspect more fun resulted. Events continue to prove that when man is a brute, he is a brute of all brutes. Want to have good memory, have good attention. Admitted ignorance is the first step toward knowledge. Too much ego can be bad, but we never saw a hero without self-trust. Every person needs that invisible means of support—God. It's not the work that bothers us as much as the worrying about it. If we could do everything we're supposed to do or half what we'd like to do, the days would need to have 60 hours . . . but we pity more those who get bored in the 24. All, for now.

October 21, 1965

GRAND PERSON AND EDUCATOR DIES

Now and then a person makes his home in a community and his head sticks out above the crowd because of his ability, character and leadership. Such a person was Charles Fletcher Taylor of Robertsdale. He died last week after living 77 useful years. Professor Taylor, as he was called by his students and many friends, or C.F., by his fellow Rotarians, was a popular principal in Baldwin County schools for 40 years, four at Fairhope's School of Organic Education and 36 at Robertsdale. As we have often said, there is no more responsible, difficult or important job than being a school principal. He accepted the responsibility with graciousness and lived up to it with apparent ease.

He received many honors, most of which were in the field of education. He was a past president of the Alabama Education Association, of the Alabama High School Principals' Association and of the District Athletic Association. Although he held a doctorate degree in literature, we never heard anyone address him with that title. He was that kind of everyday fellow.

Professor Taylor will be long remembered in Robertsdale and Baldwin County for being an outstanding educator, civic leader, philosopher and friend of man.

FINALLY A GOVERNOR'S BEACH HOME

For years this newspaper and many citizens of this area have advocated and worked for a permanent summer home for Alabama's governor on our beautiful Gulf Coast. Such a clamor was accentuated in the early '30s when a home was built at Gulf Shores for the late Governor Bibb Graves. This home was given to him personally, but the attention and aid he gave to Alabama's Gulf Coast emphasized the fact that all governors should have such a home.

Though it took years to accomplish, the project was finished and dedicated last Thursday. Now the present governor and all future governors will have a beautiful home on the Gulf near Fort Morgan.

The completion of the home is another example of what cooperation and good leadership can accomplish. Many people contributed to the cost of the home. Although it is in Baldwin, many from Mobile helped with the project.

May the leaders of our state spend many restful and happy days in the Governor's Summer Home, return to Montgomery refreshed and relaxed, ready to serve Alabamians better and better.

MUMBLINGS . . . ABOUT LBJ AND MORE

Wasn't it amazing to learn how many friends President Johnson has around these parts . . . this is one conclusion you could draw from the fact so many wanted our president to have a speedy recovery from his operation . . . another thought is that people realize who is in the corner ready to take over in case something serious happens to LBJ . . . anyway we're glad he is getting along all right . . . think we would have some kind of gall trouble too if we had the responsibilities facing the president every day.

Thank you, thank you very much . . . we know this is a good family newspaper . . . with 30 years experience, you know when you put out a good issue and you know when you don't . . . we have also learned that the public knows, too . . . and doesn't hesitate to let you know, especially if you don't publish a good paper, or leave out something that should have been printed, or put in something that should have been left out, etc . . . interestingly enough, and this is advertising propaganda, the more advertising we have in an issue of the paper the more compliments we get . . . it never fails . . . which proves people like to read commercial news too.

A young doctor told us recently that his biggest problem in examining patients is deciding whether they are or are not sick . . . he says hundreds of people think they are physically ill when they aren't and these take up a lot of a doctor's time . . . in which case they must be mentally ill, or something. Fall has many things going for it . . . but we think most people who say it is their favorite time of the year have just forgotten six months past when it was beautiful Spring . . . don't you like things coming to life better than things dying?

All who say they are for progress aren't . . . fact is, there are a lot of monkey wrench carriers who seem ever ready to drop one into some smooth running engine . . . naturally such people don't live around these parts. It's the heart of the giver, not the gift that counts . . . and the manner in which the giver gives tells you a lot about the character of the giver. Judo is another art that proves brains and a little muscle is better than a lot of muscle and no brains. A mob is a monster with no heart and few brains. It's easy to convince a person of something he already believes. A big heart has kind eyes which sometimes see what the brain cannot. Some old sage said, "Bachelor's wives and old maid's children are always perfect." Many speakers aim at nothing and make a bull's eye. There is no tiredness as bad as too much rest. If nobody loves you, it is certainly your fault and the fault is probably because you don't love much either. 'Bye, for now.

October 28, 1965

CHARLES W. STRONG A GOOD CITIZEN

Bay Minette has gained many fine new citizens during the past few months, but we cannot afford to lose such a valuable person as Charles Strong. He died suddenly Sunday although he had been in ill health for a long time.

Mr. Strong came to Bay Minette a few years ago from Citronelle. He purchased the dry-goods business from A. Kahalley. He later purchased the building from the Kahalleys and a year or so ago did an extensive remodeling job, both inside and out. His department store prospered under his able handling and this week he had planned a grand opening to celebrate a big expansion program just completed.

His ability as a successful merchant was widely recognized. He was also a good citizen. He had long been an advocate of a Hill-Burton hospital for Bay Minette and area. He served as chairman of a special Chamber of Commerce committee to get a new hospital built here and when the official hospital board was appointed, he was made a member. Only last week he told us how delighted he was with the plans and said that everybody seemed enthusiastic.

It's strong people like Charles W. Strong that makes a community move forward and help create a better world.

HIGHWAY DEATHS TAKE NO HOLIDAY

The Times has many projects but none it devotes more time and space to than highway safety in Baldwin County. This newspaper has been honored often for its safety campaigns.

Despite the continued efforts on the part of *The Times*, State Troopers and many others, this county is going to break all previous records for highway deaths during 1965. Already with 34 deaths to our discredit, this year we have equaled the 1963 slaughter, which was the worst in history up to that time. And we have over two months to go.

What is the trouble? Is it because of our roads? Baldwin's roads are among the best in the state, but to date none of our interstate system is open to traffic. When I-10 and I-65 are complete, this will no doubt help the situation.

Highway patrolmen tell us that speed is our greatest killer. And many of our roads are narrow, curvy and hilly. This should inspire caution. Evidently it doesn't.

The Times, however, can take some comfort from its continuous campaign. Only 13 of the 34 killed were residents of Baldwin County. Seven came from Mobile, one from another county and 13 were from out of state. Our circulation outside of Baldwin is not great.

For the umpteenth time we say, please drive carefully!

MUMBLINGS—ON FOOTBALL AND OTHER THINGS

As football weekends go, the last one wasn't the best we ever enjoyed but it was considerably better than the previous one when nothing went right . . . this is similar to life however, very seldom does everything go exactly as you want it. Lady Bird's highway beautification passed congress along with a lot of congressmen feeling ugly about the situation . . . not everything is beautiful about beautification . . . naturally all of us are anxious to get the auto grave yards out of sight, unless you happen to own one . . . our thoughts on this, like many other government handouts—we didn't pass the laws—we will pay the bill—we should get our share of the money . . . so let's make Baldwin even more beautiful.

It could be that the jury system is suspect in Lowndes County, Alabama . . . and nothing could be worse under our system of government than to have our system of jurisprudence questioned and doubted. Last week wasn't all bad . . . congress and the Alabama legislature both adjourned. The fact that other people are ignorant too is small consolation. People who make a profit out of the profit system should be its greatest boosters, and usually are. Great knowledge brings great doubts.

Maybe we didn't have much to do with the part we have to play in life . . . but it is our responsibility to play the part well. If we spend all the time necessary to get even with all the people who we think have mistreated us, we would spend all our time . . . thus we would be doubly damaged. The Japanese say, "A man takes a drink, then the drink takes a drink and the next drink takes the man." . . . on the same subject, another sage said: "Whisky is a good thing in its place. There is nothing like it for preserving a man when he is dead. If you want to keep a dead man, put him in whiskey, if you want to kill a live man put whiskey in him."

Now that we aren't going to have succession in Alabama so far as the governor's office is concerned, it doesn't mean that we need to have secession from the union. Next year is a big political year in Alabama . . . in a little over 12 months, we'll know who the next governor is going to be . . . we learned who it wasn't going to be last week when the senate refused to let the people vote on a constitutional amendment to let the one we got succeed himself . . . one reason they wouldn't let the people vote is because the senators knew he would succeed himself . . . all of which comes under the heading of politics . . . and since politics is democracy at work, it simply means that democracy isn't all ways perfect . . . but it is always better than anything else, government-wise that is. You're silly if you don't think a villain or a crook is a hypocrite. Kindness is inexpensive and so valuable. Trouble with flu shots, they sometimes take . . . we know. We also know this is enough, for now.

December 2, 1965

IT TAKES HARD WORK TO BUILD A CITY

Edgar A. Guest was right when he said it takes a lot of living in a house to make a home and it is also right to say it takes a lot of planning, working, cooperating and some luck to make a good city.

Fortunately, many people are working to make Bay Minette such a city. Naturally some are working against it, but probably ignorantly rather than intentionally.

One phase of work needed in a modern town or city is planning. Most towns neglect this. Fortunately Bay Minette isn't. We have a City Planning Commission composed of: J.A. Wurst, chairman, J.B. Blackburn, C.A. Bodden, J.F. Dusenbury, Harry Still, Wilson Hayes, Sam C. Pruette, Johnny Stacey and a vacancy caused by the death of Charles Strong.

This group has met many times and is presently working with the Alabama State Planning and Industrial Development Board to get a master plan for future development of the city area. Just published is a booklet containing detailed information about the present land use, economy, population, etc., of Bay Minette.

Among other things, the study reveals that there is plenty of room to grow within the present city-wide area. Of a total of 9,061 acres in this area, only 1,839 are developed, leaving 7,221 for more homes, industries, etc.

The technical planner furnished by the state estimates the population of Bay Minette will be 7,200 by 1970. These figures are based on the old city limits. With the 25 percent added by the expansion, you come up with 9,000 by the end of the decade.

The people owe a debt of gratitude to those who are working hard at the present to provide for our orderly growth in the future.

MUMBLINGS

It finally got around to doing what we told you it would . . . the weather got damp and cold. Voting on constitutional amendments may be a nuisance but you might reflect on the idea that people in Russia don't have to vote on them . . . nor do they get to vote on anything . . . somebody just tells them what the constitution is, how it will be changed, etc., . . . that is, if they have a constitution. The football season is over with the exception of several bowl games . . . we like to see it come and we are about ready for it to go when it does . . . speaking of football, which we sometimes do, we never saw one team as kind to another as Auburn was to Alabama last Saturday . . . they gave up the ball nine times through the fumble and pass interception route. Seems like this is typical of some people, they give up the ball when they don't have to and shouldn't.

It's a real war in Vietnam now . . . it seems so far away until the casualty lists come in and then it can get real close to home. It's easy to argue against the war, but communism must be stopped somewhere and that may be the place. As we have often said, it is so easy to fault those people doing something. Wouldn't it be easy to write several volumes on ignorance . . . if we were just smart enough to know something about the subject. We may not print all the news that's fit to print . . . but we try hard not to print that which isn't fit to print . . . of course we print a lot that we wish hadn't happened, like deaths, etc. If you want to be for something popular, advocate good projects where no one will have to foot the bill. Wealth has its responsibilities, as Plato or someone said.   Progress is hard because so many people don't recognize it when they see it. Some go east and some go west but you'll find a fool among the best. It was a rabid segregationist that said people disintegrate when they die. Two women were talking who hadn't seen each other for 10 years . . . one said, "You have gotten so old I wouldn't have recognized you." To which the other replied, "I wouldn't have recognized you either except for the dress you have on." 'Nuff, for now.

December 23, 1965

TOM MATHEWS OF MALBIS

Malbis Plantation is a place of tradition, history, beauty and pride for Baldwin County citizens and many others throughout Alabama.

Many have contributed to the success of the Malbis story. Naturally none other compares with the man who started it all, the late Jason Malbis. But there have been several in the outstanding Greek family of Malbis.

One of the most popular, and certainly for years the best known in this area, was Tom Mathews. (He told us his Greek name, but he didn't expect us to remember it.) As all people must, he died Sunday.

Tom was salesman and goodwill ambassador for the Malbis Bakery for years. He visited throughout the county and area many times. Then several years ago he became manager of the famous Malbis Restaurant and it was here that he made friends from all walks of life from every section of the country. As we travel over the state about as many people inquire of Tom Mathews as any other Baldwin citizen. He could count many hundreds among his friends.

To lose a friend like Tom is sad. It is particularly so in this case as it strongly reminds you of the fact that many of the fine people at Malbis have died. And others are getting older.

EGGS AND BAY MINETTE

An industry that could turn out to be the beginning of an important economic move in the Bay Minette area got underway here this month with the opening of the Bay Minette Egg Co., Inc.

The plant is owned by E. J. Jones and George Shelley and they are pioneering in this type of egg production locally. The firm will process eggs, contract with farmers to produce the eggs, sell the eggs, furnish the feed, etc.

This type of thing has been done in other sections of the state and country with considerable success. The poultry and egg business, particularly broiler production, has become a mammoth business for farmers and others in the

South during recent years. In fact, the poultry industry exceeded that of any other farm product in total dollar volume last year, exceeding cotton for the first time in history.

There are many who think this area of Baldwin County is ideally suited for the chicken and egg business. We have many industrial workers living on small farms who could spend their spare time raising chickens. Marshall and Cullman county farmers have increased their income several fold by doing this.

The local plant, which is located about four miles from Bay Minette on the Pine Grove Road, will have 75,000 layers under contract within a few weeks and expects to have 100,000 by next summer. With 13 presently employed in the plant, plus feed and servicemen and the income of the farmers from the eggs, etc., the economic boost to the area is bound to be felt from the beginning. The growth potential is big.

The Times congratulates Mr. Jones and Mr. Shelley for their confidence in the area and their willingness to pioneer locally in their modern methods of egg production. We wish them success.

MUMBLINGS

As we have often told you it would . . . it has rained and turned cold. We have progressed in years enough to understand why older people have always objected to firecrackers . . . but we aren't old enough not to understand why the youngsters want to shoot them . . . so long as they don't hurt themselves, they don't bother us. Fifty-cent pieces are in short supply in these parts . . . dollars are the same during this Yuletide season. We can't understand why so many complain about the new silver less silver coins . . . they spend fast enough.

"A pill a day may make memory stay," is headline about new miracle drug . . . we thought you took pills to make you forget things, like headaches and pain. Restricting freedoms comes up all the time . . . like the congressman who wants to pass a law against Vietnam demonstrators . . . in this wonderful country of ours we have many freedoms, one of which permits people to make fools of themselves.

Don't you hate to see old men marrying girls 25 years younger . . . recently a Seattle man of 102 married a "child bride" of 77. Few ideas are original . . . where the wisdom comes in is the ability to steal only the good ones. It is said that football is a matter of inches . . . this being so, if Auburn had had another one a few times she wouldn't have lost to Ole Miss in the Liberty Bowl. Mobilian and University of Georgia football coach, Vince Dooley, has turned down the huge offer to coach at Oklahoma University . . . now Auburn fans can hope to bring him back home in about 10 years when Shug retires.

Bear Bryant has come up with another one to go with "Winning isn't everything but it beats anything that comes in second." . . . he has put this on the bulletin board for his boys to contemplate: "Always begin somewhere. You can't be a champion on what you intend to do." . . . we hope the Crimson Tide starts and finishes the job of defeating Nebraska in the Orange Bowl. True, Christmas does bring good cheer to most . . . and we hope you are among those who are happy and cheerful this Holiday Season.

January 6, 1966

JAMES A. CARNEY OF BALDWIN WAS FINE CITIZEN

One of Baldwin's fine old citizens died Friday after a lengthy illness. He was James A Carney, Sr., 89, of Daphne.

Jim Carney was a member of a prominent Baldwin County family. His family at one time owned and operated big Carney Mill Company of northeast Baldwin and Atmore. He had many responsible jobs during a long life.

An interesting character, he was sharp with his tongue and crisp with his thinking. You never had to wonder how he stood on a subject. If he didn't like you, he didn't leave you guessing about it. As the old saying goes, he said what he thought and thought what he said. He was caustic and honest with it.

The likes of Jim Carney don't come around often and he will be missed. We liked him.

PERSONAL, IF YOU PLEASE

Good newspaper editors are hard to find. That this newspaper has had the best for over two years can hardly be doubted. But Jack House quit editing *The Times* as of last week.

We were acquainted with him before but really got to knowing Jack during two campaigns for governor, 1954 and 1958. He handled the publicity for the Bay Minette candidate both times. He did an excellent job.

It was about January of 1954 when he came to see us in Bay Minette. He had been offered the job of handling the publicity, etc., for James E. Folsom. He flattered us however by wanting to work with our campaign. We soon came to terms but not before he had given Big Jim a powerful slogan, "Y'all Come." Jack didn't support a winner but he helped elect one.

Between the two campaigns, he had a number of jobs, one of which was booking and managing the famous Harlem Globe Trotters basketball team. He can keep you listening for hours telling about experiences with them. But he had all his private business in hand by the time the second campaign came around and was ready to go. He, like some others, knew he had a winner. At least it wasn't his fault that he didn't. He again did a bang up job.

After June of '58 we were forced to part company again. For three years he was the successful editor of The Sun papers in Birmingham. We ran into him at the summer convention of the Alabama Press Association at Dauphin Island in '62. Among other things, the conversation came around to coming to Baldwin County. He wanted the Fairhope paper which was for sale at the time. That didn't work out. He had become so sold on the idea of coming to Baldwin he finally accepted the suggestion of working for *The Times*. You readers know the rest of the story.

Jack isn't leaving Bay Minette and Baldwin County. For a spell he is going back to the basketball business. He and his wife, Dot, are going to maintain their home here and *The Times* is going to retain him as associate editor. From time to time he will have contributions for you readers and will continue to advise us on how to improve.

As a newswriter, picture taker and editor, Jack is an artist. He can smell a feature or a news story a mile off, so to speak. The most amazing thing about him is his ability to turn out work. He literally works day and night at lightening speed. No other man living could fill a 22 to 28 page paper with live news, pictures and features single-handed as he has done. Now you know why he quit. Jack is older than he use to be and there is a limit to what even he can do.

Although no one can entirely replace Jack, we were fortunate in obtaining the services of one dandy young newspaper man in the name of Steve Mitchell. We know he's good because Jack helped to train him and says he is good. Of course Steve has a lot to learn about this area and county. Unlike Jack, he has never been here before. But give him a few weeks and we think you'll like him.

February 17, 1966

RYAN DEGRAFFENRIED'S DEATH WAS A POLITICAL TRAGEDY

The untimely death last week in an airplane accident of gubernatorial candidate Ryan deGraffenried is one of the political and human tragedies difficult to understand.

Ryan was the runner-up to Gov. George Wallace in the governor's race four years ago. He was considered by many to be the strongest contender in the coming Democratic primaries and few doubted that he was among the top two. Few had ever worked harder to become governor.

Taking his first defeat in good humor, he continued to campaign day and night until the tragedy snapped out his life last week. He had made at least 600 speeches all over the state during the past four years. Few realize the drudgery, hardship and privation suffered by candidates and families who seek high political office. To have it cost your life too is indeed tragic.

deGraffenried is dead at 40 but "DeGraf" will long be remembered as a great Alabamian. In politics he stood for honesty and progress. In church, civic and legislative matters, he was outstanding. With such a reputation and a good family, he leaves a greater heritage than most. If he had been allowed to live out his three score and ten he undoubtedly would have achieved real greatness.

BALDWIN COUNTY BANK LOOKS GREAT

A city or area cannot make progress without aggressive and sound financial institutions. In this instance, as in many others, Baldwin is richly blessed.

During the past year the county's six banks and one savings and loan reached total assets of almost $60 million. This is an increase of over 30 times during the past 25 years.

Within the past several months all of these institutions have enlarged, remodeled or built new buildings. Having faith in the area which they serve, all have taken steps to keep up with the demands of modern banking.

Although one of the last to do so in the county, none has done a more outstanding job of providing new and remodeled facilities than the Baldwin County Bank of Bay Minette. It is the town's oldest bank and one of the oldest in the area.

We don't like to use superlatives but you can't describe the looks of the bank's enlarged and remodeled quarters without so doing. We feel it is nothing but the truth to say that the bank's home office is one of the most beautiful in this section, if not in the entire Southeast. Certainly this is true if you stay in cities under 25,000 population.

The remodeling of the bank's "Arcade" building has added much to the looks of the city. The structure is imposing and gains the attention and admiration of passers through as well as local citizens.

This week the local state bank is having open house to show its new face. The expenditure of the quarter-million dollars necessary to bring the new look about is another strong indication of the faith the officers and directors have in the future of this town and area.

For this faith and the desire to continue to have a vital part in the growth and progress of the area, *The Times* is happy to join with hundreds of others in congratulating the Baldwin County Bank's officers, E. Davidson, Jim Wurst, J.B. Blackburn, the directors, and others responsible.

SEEKING HAPPINESS

Happiness is a great thing but no two people will agree exactly on what it is . . . sort of like beauty . . . but if you don't have happiness you continue to seek it . . . not so with beauty, if you missed it the first time you might as well forget about it. Peking accuses the Russian reds of joining imperialistic United States, India and Japan to encircle China . . . why not? . . . Russia, Japan and India know they have nothing to fear from Uncle Sam unless they tamper with him unduly . . . all the world should know how dangerous the half-billion staring Chinks are . . . and since politics make strange bedfellows, you can reasonable assume wars do too.

The only thing worse than a loudmouth man is a loudmouth woman. Not everything we get through the mails is worth reading . . . but we get lots that is . . . of this we are sure, we must learn to read faster or learn to live with less knowledge and curiosity . . . the latter might be hard to do so we had better work on the other end.

A dead lie, like a dead wasp, still stings sometimes . . . but if unborn, neither can hurt you. Some people aren't smart enough to take advantage of luck if it stares them in the face . . . so there is little reason to stand around awaiting it . . . someone said, "Luck is a very good word if you put a P before it." Honesty is fine, particularly when applied to self. Words may not make a man but it has killed millions.

Attention parents: There is no better legacy you can leave than a well educated family . . . importance of education cannot be overemphasized and there is no one who should stress its importance into young minds than parents . . . sad is the boy or girl who goes looking for a job during these times and has to say "no, I didn't finish school" . . . education has many values . . . it first teaches one to walk alone . . . and not of the least significance is its value in money, dollars if you please . . . recent information indicates that a four year college education is worth about $176,000 in additional earnings during a person's lifetime . . . this means that to the average individual, 36 months in college, which can be done in three calendar years, will pay almost $5,000 per month for every month a student goes to college . . . parents don't you love your children enough to get this point across? . . . dropout students may be caused by droopy parents. 'Nuff lecture, time being.

March 10, 1966

ONE GOOD MAN FOLLOWS ANOTHER

We have often said the hardest and one of the most important jobs in Bay Minette, or in most any town for that matter, is that of high school principal.

Filling this difficult post here the past 22 years has been C.V. Daniels. He has done the job well, certainly better than most could. To fully appreciate the task of performing the duties of school principal, you must first think what his responsibilities are.

Here at Baldwin County High School, Mr. Daniels had in charge about 2,400 boys and girls from the ages of six to 18 or over from the time they leave home in the morning until they return home at night. Many came from as far away as 30 miles. About half of this number have to be fed lunch. All have to be scheduled in classes with competent teachers, kept profitable occupied and disciplined.

Add to this the important job of finding good teachers and keeping them busy and happy. We suspect this many students have at least 3,000 parents, mothers and fathers, who like to be kept happy about the way their little darlings are being taught and treated. To top all this, the school's business is everybody's business. Many think it is right down to the very details, particularly when it comes to athletics and such.

Last week we were delighted to see Mr. Daniels rewarded for his years of service by getting a promotion. Into his shoes has stepped Wallace R. (Pinky) Williams, who has been assistant principal for a long enough time to know what it is all about. Both have received deserved promotions. The 2,400 students, 3,000 parents, and everybody seem to be glad they were made.

THE POLL TAX IS GONE

Finally three federal judges have thrown out the poll tax as a prerequisite to voting in Alabama.

There has been much argument about it, of course, but it is generally conceded the tax was imposed in the Alabama Constitution of 1901 for the purpose of discouraging a wide electorate.

There will be few tears shed because the tax is no more. Most Alabamians realized long ago that it had long since quit serving any useful purpose, if it ever did. This is another case where a state refused to do what should have been done and left it up to the federal government for eventual correction.

If paying the dollar and a half has kept you from voting, you can now go and register by simply signing you name, answering one or two simple questions and be qualified, legally, to vote. Certainly this is a bargain every good American and Alabamian should take.

BAY MINETTE HONORS

From the *Alabama Municipal Journal*: "We are indeed grateful to publisher Jimmy Faulkner and his outstanding '*Baldwin Times*' for reproducing our *Journal* Personality Sketch of Mayor Sam Pruette. In commending Mayor Sam as our Mayor of the Month, Editor Faulkner called our attention to the many honors which Bay Minette has received during the past year—their Key Club was judged the best in the nation—their Junior Chamber of Commerce was selected best in Alabama—the '*Baldwin Times*' was again proclaimed Number One in the State—W.M. Hodgson, Jr., was chosen the outstanding businessman of the Southeast by the Small Business Administration—a Bay Minette medical student at the University was honored number one in the senior class—and two Bay Minette citizens were named in 'Who's Who in the South and Southeast.' Under Mayor Sam's leadership and with Publisher Faulkner's spirited journalism, there is no wonder that Bay Minette collects the honors."

POLITICIANS OFF TO THE RACES

Quit fussing . . . the weather is always cold, rainy, windy and unusual in March . . . this month is one of our least favorites of the 12 . . . besides the weather, it was the month in which we were born. Politicians are now off to the races and we won't know which ones get in under the wire until next November . . . which is a long time to put up with politicking . . . and by the time all is over, most of us, and the politicians, too, will be ready to murder the person who says that this state needs a strong two-party system.

Oh joy, just six more months to football time. Last week a friend scolded us for all time doing so much for so many, etc., . . . we suspect it would be all right if we had had time to do what he wanted. We have told ourselves over and over that we aren't an employment agency . . . but some people are hard to convince. We have just finished several hours labor writing an article for a magazine about Baldwin . . . free to be sure, but it's our county as much as anybody's . . . and no man hath greater love, etc. . . . and it is our intent to keep it that way . . . but we do hope you like it if you see it and read it.

If a friend leaves you when you are down . . . you had one less friend than you thought in the beginning. Nothing is simpler than the truth because it's . . . well, it's simply so. Don't be a litterbugging bug. Some of us don't seem to know the difference between an open mind and a vacant one. Many a leading man became so because there was a leading lady who pushed him. If you want to lose control of your car just teach your teenager to drive. A nickel goes farther today because you have to carry it around so long before you can find something cheap enough to buy with it. It has been said that a man is like a tack . . . he must be pointed in the right direction, driven hard, and then he will go as far as his head will let him.

Venus can't support life, or so the scientists say . . . it's getting harder and

harder on Earth. "Too many people undervalue themselves," says speaker
. . . true, but they're easier to live with than the other kind, of which there
are also too many. The tongue may not be but three inches long . . . but
the way some wave in the breeze they could easily be three feet. Egotism is
the young man in love who thinks nothing is good enough for her except
himself. Just because we don't always get up early is no indication that our
phone doesn't. The other night at 2 a.m. when an intruder of our sleep called
long distance, he apologized for calling so late, to which we said, "that's all
right, I had to get up and answer the phone anyway" . . . to which he said,
"- well I'm glad I didn't get you out of bed" . . . believe it or not, this has
happened many times. 'Nuff, for now.

March 24, 1966

Welcome IP Container Division

Last week, Friday and Saturday, will be long remembered as great days
in the annals of Bay Minette and Baldwin County history. International
Paper Company's Container Division dedicated their fine corrugated plant
here.

International Paper for years has been a friend and neighbor of Baldwin
County. Her huge paper mill in Mobile employs many of our people and
our pulpwood goes into the plant by the thousands and thousands of cords
each year. Too, I-P owns a sizeable chunk of Baldwin County, some 11 or
12 percent of the finest pine timberland in the world. Knowing what good
citizens I-P people are by experience makes it all the more pleasant to have
one of her 22 Container Division plants here.

The dedication of the plant went off well and praise by those who attended
was loud and still continues. At the last moment, one of the speakers had a

freak accident and, being hospitalized, couldn't show up. But the substitute did such a good job that the original was hardly missed.

For national location purposes, the local factory is referred to as the Mobile plant. We don't mind, since we know better. Since it is better than we could do, we'll let you read what one of the company's brochures has to say about the "Mobile" plant.

"Paperboard used in Container Division plants is manufactured at I-P mills at Georgetown, South Carolina; Panama City, Florida; Springhill and Bastrop, Louisiana. It is shipped to the plants in huge rolls where it is made into corrugated sheets and shipping containers. Rigid quality controls are maintained over production every step of the way from the preparation of the pulp used to make the paperboard until the end product is in the customers' hands.

"Located on a 24-acre tract just south of the Bay Minette business district on Highway 31, this ultra-modern 112,000 square foot plant is geared to serve the rapidly expanding agricultural markets of Alabama, portions of Mississippi, Georgia, Florida and Louisiana.

"The heart of every Container Division plant is its mammoth corrugator, a machine which combines the flat board liners with fluted corrugating medium. The Mobile plant's corrugator can manufacture a virtually endless sheet of corrugated board up to 87 inches wide. One day's production produces a three-foot wide sheet of corrugated long enough to stretch from the front door of our plant here to the Mobile Municipal Airport. . . . Modern facilities are maintained for employee safety and comfort, including locker rooms, washrooms, employee parking lots and a lunch room."

Bay Minette is proud to welcome I-P's Container Division plant to the family of fine industries already here. Real proud!

TWO VETERAN LEGISLATORS

For the first time Baldwin County will have two representatives in the Alabama Legislature. This results from reapportioning.

Also, it seems fairly certain that the county will have two veteran legislators represent her in Montgomery for the next four years. Both are unopposed in the Democratic primaries and hence assured of nomination.

They will probably have Republican opposition in the November general election but. . . The senior member, in age and in length of service, will be L. W. Brannan of Foley. He is presently serving as state senator of Baldwin and Escambia counties and prior to this served four terms in the house. This is, we believe, longer than any person has ever served the county in this capacity.

The junior member will be L. D. Owen of Bay Minette. He got valuable experience in the recent session of the legislature, having been elected in a special election last year to fill the unexpired term of Telfair J. Mashburn, now circuit judge. His anxiety to serve a full term will, with his experience, make him even more valuable to the county.

Experience is a great thing in legislative halls. Because of this and their abilities otherwise, it is doubted if any of the 67 counties will be better represented in the lower house than Baldwin during the next administration.

MORE INCOME TAXES

Who said there is a more beautiful time of the year than Spring? . . . wasn't us . . . we think it is . . . if you don't believe it, just wait a few more days until everything is putting out, including the fabulous azaleas. More income taxes are on the way to help pay for the war in Vietnam . . . something else to gripe about . . . we hate to pay them but every time we do we hope to make so much money next year that we'll have to pay more taxes than ever . . . one thing is sure, if you don't make it you don't have to pay it . . . besides, you pay it to Uncle Sam, who is the bestest with the mostest on earth . . . if you don't think so, you should move.

Benjamin Franklin invented bifocals . . . in some of his many words of wisdom he should have advised clumsy 50-year-olds who wear them for the first time not to walk so fast until they get accustomed to them lest they fall flat on their face. Hindsight is wonderful.

"Where does Bryant's Tide go from here?" sports writer asks . . . it's an old saying that when you're on top there isn't but one way to go . . . of course you can stay on top and make the top more rugged for your opponents to reach . . . we trust Bryant's boys will do just that.

The reason we write so late at night is because we can't seem to get organized during the day . . . perhaps we try to do too much, as the boss of the house has reminded us 'nigh on to 30 years . . . a friend recently told us that we take on too much responsibility . . . we agree . . . who wants to relieve us of some? . . . Please!

Liberty cannot be established without morality . . . and morality assumes faith and responsibility. "A laugh is worth a hundred groans in any market." Be careful what name you apply to a person because it has been said that nicknames stick to people, and the most ridiculous are the most adhesive. If you speak of yourself too often, you will find it harder and harder to tell the truth. More later, maybe.

April 14, 1966

SUNDAY WAS A PROUD DAY FOR BALDWIN

The weather and other conditions were perfect for the dedication of the State Junior College here last Sunday. Over 3,000 came and were pleased with the school, the program and everything involved.

In spite of a fever, Governor George C. Wallace came and gave an interesting dedicatory address, explaining how the junior college program originated in the state and its meaning to the future generations in Alabama. The Governor knew that the show must go on and did not let his illness deter him from making a good speech. He returned to Montgomery Sunday afternoon and immediately went to bed where he stayed with 'flu Monday and Tuesday. Those who knew his condition were all the more appreciative of his coming to what was one of Baldwin's most important days in history.

Congratulations go to Dr. L.N. Sibert (who also was confined early this week with the 'flu), his efficient staff and all others who helped plan and execute the dedication exercises.

THE HOSPITAL RALLY

Perhaps we should have more town meetings. In years gone by they were quite often called to thrash out community problems.

The hospital rally last Friday was well attended by 400 to 500 citizens interested in the future health conditions of this area. An orderly and lengthy discussion of the problems confronting us in getting a new hospital, and keeping the old ones open until the new one does, was held.

As is usual in such matters, there was considerable misunderstanding. It would be in error to say that all problems were solved by the meeting, but certainly those in attendance left with a much better understanding. Too, they voted unanimously that they want a hospital and are willing to pay for same. The town is much more unified on the subject, and a hospital, of which we can all be proud, is bound to come.

EASTER WEATHER NICE

The Easter cool snap was snappy . . . and nice. We think the same thing every year: the azaleas have never been prettier, but didn't the blooms last longer last year? If you want to realize how fast a week passes, just watch a weekly TV show or write this every seven days. This we surmise after years of experience: if you spent all your time working solely for self, you would make fewer people mad, make much more money, have fewer friends, die and go below, and live a life of misery while on this Earth . . . but surely there is a happy medium.

An old wise preacher often said that when it came to the Bible it was awfully hard to underestimate the ignorance of an audience, some couldn't even find 1st or 2nd Samson. Best thing to give to your enemy is forgiveness . . . which he may not appreciate. The traffic sign "Keep Right" is a good short sermon. Unless we have within us some of that which is above us, we'll end up in that which is below us. Some figures aren't worth noting but it strikes us as interesting the fact that there are 15,000 shopping centers in this country which do 35 percent of the retail business . . . and the fact that they spend $1.1 billion a year in advertising is real interesting.

As we said, all political races are different but some more so than others
. . . take this year's governor's race for example . . . there are 10 candidates
but it seems only one is running for first place and the others are running
for second place . . . guess the gentlemen know that it's polite to let a lady
go first . . . two candidates have admitted to us, in a bragging sort of way,
that they are second . . . we ask one why he wanted to run second and he
said he had rather be second than fourth . . . which is, of course, right . . .
but we can vouch for the fact that second isn't nearly good enough. After
the May 3rd primary we have the May 31st runoff, then the general election in November . . . we can work that voting privilege to death this year.
See you soon, we trust.

May 5, 1966

JAMES E. GASTON, A GREAT CITIZEN

James E. Gaston, Sr., was just plain Jim to his thousands of friends.

He died last week in the town and county he loved, Fairhope and Baldwin, where he had been a resident for over 70 years.

Jim Gaston served his people and county for 16 years as county commissioner. During this period he was recognized as one of the best county
government officials in Alabama. In fact, he was often referred to as "the
best county commissioner in Alabama." He was particularly interested in
the roads of the county and was able to live to see the fruits of his early
work enable Baldwin to have the most paved farm-to-market roads of any
county in the state.

He was a successful businessman, having been an automobile dealer in
Fairhope for a number of years. Jim was active in various civic projects and
was a leader in many facets of Fairhope's growth and progress.

It's difficult to write an editorial of this nature about a personal friend and a person we admired and appreciated greatly. He was a man of high integrity. His honesty was never questioned. He was outspoken in his views but never to the point of being impolite or overbearing. His sincere interest in everybody and everything pertaining to Baldwin County and Fairhope was nothing short of astounding. Few, if any, ever loved his fellow man more than Jim Gaston.

If we had to select just three words to describe his character and the type of man he was they would have to be; frank, honest and sincere. In the area and level he served. James E. (Jim) Gaston, Sr., was a great man.

A CLEAN TOWN IS A GOOD TOWN

When a city like Bay Minette has growing pains, it is hard to keep all facets of growth and progress moving on an even keel. Cleanliness is one of these problems.

Bay Minette has often been referred to as a clean, beautiful little city. We like to think this is true, and it probably is in comparison to some others. However, much improvement can be made.

One of the problems for many years has been vacant lots with their high weeds, trash, etc. Some business houses are negligent about keeping their premises clean. Some people forgetfully throw paper, cans and other unsightly items on our streets.

Bay Minette has wide streets, beautiful homes with attractive lawns. Our citizens, in the main, have considerable civic pride. These are the necessary ingredients for a beautiful city.

As with most things, however, people need to be encouraged to do what they should do at times. In this connection, the Chamber of Commerce is starting a clean-up campaign for the entire city.

This is fine and it is hoped that all governmental, civic groups and individuals will cooperate.

SEE ROMANS 8:28

Democracy is great . . . you can vote as you please . . . fuss at whom you please . . . and you can not be pleased at any of it if you like and still not get shot . . . you may deserve to be, however. Now that the first of the three big voting dates for 1966 is over we can quieten down for a day or two, we hope. You unfortunate people who lost Tuesday may be fortunate . . . who can tell? . . . anyway, we commend Romans 8:28 for your consideration and consolation. To you who won, you need not feel so cocky . . . the voters might have been voting against your opposition and not for you . . . we have always heard that voters are inclined that way . . . that is, to vote against something rather than for something. As we began, democracy is great.

Personal income was the highest in 1965 of any year in history . . . Alabama's increased seven percent over 1964 to $1,910 which is still only 70 percent of the national average . . . Alabama was in seventh place among the Southeastern states in per capita income last year with $6.6 billion . . . Florida was first with $14 billion . . . all of which means: 1. Times are good. 2. Alabama is still behind.

A well-kept yard is . . . well kept . . . which means a considerable application over a long period of time of elbow grease. Being civil doesn't cost much but it buys much. If a politician goes to church for political reasons, it won't get him to heaven, nor will it get him many votes. A child says memory is the thing he forgets with . . . and as you get older your forgettery will have less and less memory. A Louisiana judge told us last week that he likes his friends and gives justice to his enemies. You may find it unwise to pray that your enemies understand you . . . you had better pray that you understand them. "Bachelor's wives and old maid's children are always perfect." Work won't hurt you but the dread of it will. All, for now.

May 26, 1966

FRANK BREITLING DESERVES HIGH HONOR

It is good to see proper honor given people. This is especially true when the duties and services the person has performed may not be of the earth shaking variety, but still important in a quiet ordinary sort of way. School teaching is a good example.

The Times doesn't often comment on such people who live outside Baldwin but the case of Frank W. Breitling, retiring principal of Mobile County High School in Grand Bay, deserves special attention. Besides he has two sisters, Mrs. W.C. Beebe and Mrs. W.M. Hodgson, Sr., and many friends living here.

There is no more difficult and important job than being a high school principal. The fact that Frank Breitling was one for 30 years, all at Grand Bay, is evidence of his success and popularity. He was given credit for all of this last Sunday afternoon in a special program in his own school auditorium. Being a friend, we too can enjoy the luxury of being proud of him.

HIGHER EDUCATION CHANGING IN SOUTH ALABAMA

Gov. George Wallace dedicated over a million dollars worth of new buildings at the University of South Alabama Sunday.

This fact is even more interesting and significant when you stop to realize that two years ago the nearest state supported school campus for higher education to the Baldwin-Mobile area was Troy State or Livingston State, each over 100 miles away.

Now we have the University of South Alabama growing rapidly in her second year, and junior colleges growing in their first year at Bay Minette, Mobile, Monroeville and Brewton.

All of this has come within the past 24 months, which happens to be during the Wallace administration. A positive program the Republicans are bound to envy, but can't duplicate.

BRYANT'S BOYS

A week's rest rushes by . . . we suspect, however, two weeks or more would get sort of draggy. SEC coaches think Alabama, Bryant's boys that is, will be No. 1 in the conference again this year . . . we do too, so for all practical purposes that makes it unanimous . . . being No. 1 in the nation three times out of the last five years has a tendency to make fans expect a lot, and hard to please.

Sayings, remembered and heard, pro and con: A stitch in time saves nine—better late than never. Early to bed and early to rise, makes a man happy, healthy, wealthy and wise—haste makes waste. Do unto others as you would have them do unto you—DO others. A dollar saved is a dollar made—nothing risked, nothing gained.

You can and should vote again next Tuesday . . . please do and you'll be pleased you did . . . you may not like who was elected but you'll know you did your part to see that he wasn't. LBJ says he had rather have worries over inflation than worries over unemployment . . . us too. Some newspapers have too much advertising . . . not this one, we doubt if there is that much advertising . . . one thing is sure and certain, the merchants and business-men who want your trade don't mind asking you for it in the columns of this, your favorite (we hope), family journal.

Uncle Sam's tax take was 16 percent more this April than last . . . with Vietnam, etc., we don't know of anybody who needs it much worse . . . and he's such a fine fellow, too . . . just hope we have to pay him more this year than ever before, at the same rates, or less, of course. Well now, how would you like to be president with Vietnam, inflation, congressmen, senators, Vietniks, beatniks, race problems, DeGaulle, etc.? . . . Maybe you could do better? . . . No, and us either . . . we all might help some by being less critical, especially about those things we don't know much about anyway . . . let's try it for a few days. 'Bye, time being.

September 1, 1966

WELCOME HOME G. MAC HUMPHRIES

If we had to name the most faithful, dedicated, loyal and intelligent public servant in Baldwin County, right at the top of the list would be G.

Mac Humphries.

Mac, as he is affectionately called by thousands, became clerk of the Baldwin County Commission in 1937. Shortly thereafter he was given the additional post of County Treasurer. He has held both jobs since.

He has served under many commissioners during this period, some good, some not so good, but he has been loyal to all. Not one ever thought of letting him go, the only fear or thought has been that he might quit for something more lucrative. In his humble and unassuming manner, he has helped guide the destinies of Baldwin County's government.

To say he is frugal with the people's money is to put it mildly. However, he has the intelligence to know that people pay taxes to be spent and he doesn't mind seeing it spent for the right things. For him, "right things" covers anything that will help build the county and help the people.

When he came with the County Commission, the county owed over $500,000. Mac has helped pay this debt and at the same time seen the greatest growth and development in history and a substantial cash surplus build up in the county treasure. He isn't one to take credit and is quick to let any and all know that he has four bosses to whom he gives credit for everything done. Of course he has been accused of hiding money from them to get debts paid and to keep them from over spending. We wouldn't know if there is any truth in this or not, but we have known commissioners (present ones excluded) who couldn't tell you anywhere near how much money the county had on hand. We can also assure you that you will get an evasive answer on the subject if you ask the county treasurer. In fairness, he publishes the county's financial statement twice a year.

Sadness fell over the county courthouse, Bay Minette and Baldwin recently when Mac became seriously ill. He was taken to Mobile where he remained in the hospital until this week. As his friend and as a friend of Baldwin County, we're thankful that he is recuperating. He will have to remain at home for a much needed rest for several more weeks but after that we can all rejoice to see him resume his important duties. Yes Mac, welcome home!

ASA ROUNTREE RETIRES

For 30 years Alabama has had only one director of the Department of Aeronautics, Asa Rountree. In fact, he is the only one the department has ever had. He started it in 1936.

He is retiring. During his service, the Alabama airport system grew from 32 airfields to more than 175. Through his direction and untiring efforts, Alabama has one of the best airport systems of any state. Of these, Baldwin has benefited with four, Bay Minette, Fairhope, Fort Morgan and Foley.

He has been the friend of small towns. He thought all that wanted airfields should have them. With his retiring will go an era. We daresay few small town airports will be built in Alabama in the future. The Alabama legislature is changing from rural to urban.

The big city boys will tell you in a hurry the money should be spent on their big airports. But all segments of Alabama will miss Asa Rountree and his enthusiasm for aviation.

FALL APPROACHING OR HURRICANE FAITH?

The tinge you feel in the air may be hurricane Faith or Fall approaching, or both. Jim Folsom always said, "you can't take politics out of politics" . . . you can't take it out of the year 1966 in Alabama . . . we have already had more than the law allows but we have another big campaign coming up for November . . . in this the Democrats will tell you how bad the Republicans are and vice versa . . . neither party is as bad as the other says it is, nor is either as good as it proclaims itself to be . . . and, as we have said, "we like politics because politics is democracy at work . . . and we like democracy."

Things we wouldn't know if we didn't read: This country has 141,980 registered civil aircraft, of which the airlines only own 3.2 percent. There are 9,185 civil airports and airlines only serve 556 of these . . . but airlines carry about twice as many passengers per year as all general aviation aircraft, 80 million to 40 million last year.

As you know, Alabama has two great football powers, Auburn and the other one . . . Ralph (Shug) Jordan has coached at Auburn since 1951 . . . and of his great teams, all have had one thing in common, a strong fullback . . . remember the winning seasons with Tucker Frederickson, Ed Dyas,

Billy Atkins and Joe Childress? . . . this year Shug has what may be one of his greatest fullbacks, 200-pound Tom Bryan . . . last year he started as quarterback but was switched late to fullback where he hit pay dirt . . . in the last four games he ran for 427 yards in 66 carries, or an average of 6.5 per . . . this year he is a senior with more experience and a better offensive line in front of him.

The other team is coached by Paul (Bear) Bryant and he has an opportunity to do something that hasn't ever been done before, win three national championships in a row . . . the Tide has two consecutive wins under its belt . . . and this is something only four other teams have done in history, Minnesota, Army, Notre Dame and Oklahoma . . . the Bear has won three out of the last five years and if he can't win three in a row, it probably won't ever be done . . . we Alabamians have much to be thankful for and much for which to be hopeful.

We don't know how we got on the subject of football but it surely is easy for us to do, mumblings or no. Why do wives think old easy chairs get horrible looking just when they get curvy and comfortable? Heard in Sunday School: little fellow to teacher's scolding for not knowing who the greatest character that ever lived, "I knew Christ was the greatest but never knew he was a character." We have noticed one characteristic of pleasure boats, most drift right by church. All, time being.

October 6, 1966

STANDARD FURNITURE EXPANDS AGAIN

For the sixth time in as many years the Standard Furniture Manufacturing Co., Inc., Bay Minette, announces another expansion this week. This one will be the biggest development since the plant was burned to the ground and rebuilt in 1960.

This is good news for this fine local home owned and homegrown industry as well as for this industrial expansion minded Bay Minette area.

What seemed like chaos when the plant burned, and for several weeks thereafter, has turned into a Cinderella's dream of progress, growth and expansion. Upon the ashes and despair is growing an industrial complex covering over three acres of buildings, employing 350, sales of over $5 million annually and serving most of the 48 states with fine economical grade bedroom furniture.

Local citizens had a part to play in this great story, but probably not as important as the owners would have you believe. Following the fire, Bay Minette Mills, Inc., a local non-profit industrial development corporation, helped obtain a $250,000 Small Business Administration loan. This was done in record-breaking time of 17 days.

Senator John Sparkman, who has been the inventor and leading light of SBA, beams with delight when he sees his idea put to profitable use by Standard Furniture and other companies in similar circumstances over the nation.

After much of the original loan was repaid, with the tight credit situation, and the company needing to expand again, the natural thing has been done. The proprietors went back to the SBA. Again in rapid order the money was forthcoming.

Of course credit for the success of the company goes to the Hodgson family, W.M., Sr., W.M., Jr., and Robert. These three make a good team. Robert runs the plant with efficient help and has become an expert at manufacturing and all its complex problems. Mack, Jr., is the front man and concerns himself with sales and promotion. The father, Mack, Sr., stands back and watches for the most part, usually with understandable pride. But he is there with sound business judgment when needed.

Again, *The Times* joins with hundreds of other admirers in congratulating the Hodgsons and all those at Standard Furniture on their continued growth. May the progress and success continue.

"BE COURTEOUS"

The nights were bound to get nice and cool . . . and they have . . . when it's Fall we think it is the best time of the year . . . but we feel even more so about Spring . . . but we object to both though in that they come and go so fast, here of late.

The Apostle Peter commands Christians to "Be courteous." (1 Peter 3:8) . . . maybe if you aren't courteous you aren't a Christian . . . there are so many ways to be discourteous . . . mainly it means not treating someone else like you would like to be treated . . . like with most everything, we can all improve on being courteous and thoughtful of others.

A Boston school adopted a set of rules for teenagers which were read to the students once a week . . . some of them: "Don't let you parents down; they brought you up." . . . "Stop and think before you drink." . . . "Ditch dirty thoughts fast, or they'll ditch you." . . . "Show-off driving is juvenile; do not act your age." . . . "Don't go steady unless you are ready." . . . no doubt you parents can add some others just as good or better . . . might as well give them some more to ignore.

Bear's good. To all of you who have been kind enough to say thanks or that you like the sign on top of *The Times* building, we say thanks . . . don't worry, if the local Tigers are still the best in their class when the season is over, we'll find room on the sign for them . . . we may have to build onto it since we prefer not to take anything off.

Bay Minette has eight industries employing 50 or more people . . . how is that for diversification in a town of 8,000? . . . who can show us one better? . . . hope we can right here before too long . . . rest assured it is being worked at even if tight money is a great deterrent. Hey you! . . . do you love and brag on your community like a good citizen should? All, time being.

October 20, 1966

Two great ladies—educators

Such things are never easily understood but the fact that two of Baldwin's outstanding ladies, both long associated with education in this county, died Saturday is doubly difficult.

The two ladies worked together for years at the Baldwin County Board of Education under the late Superintendent S. M. Tharp. Miss Lilla Simmons was his assistant and right hand in county education matters for a long, long time. Mrs. Marguerite P. Hayes was county supervisor of education, also for a long time. Both had retired.

Miss Lilla had lived at Montrose since her retirement and remained active in many causes until illness intervened some time ago. She will be missed by many who appreciated her devotion to education and other things of importance to this county.

Mrs. Hayes was one of this county's finest personalities. She was recognized statewide for her educational leadership and ability. In addition to teaching, she held many responsible positions in the field of education. Education leaders from far and wide sought her advice and counsel.

She had a keen intellectual wit. She built a cottage at Josephine which she named, "Bored of Education." We have often told parents what she once told our boys' mother. She asked if she should take one of our sons out of school to go on an important trip. Mrs. Hayes' prompt reply, "Never let school interfere with your child's education."

Maybe Mrs. Hayes did finally get "bored of education" as she died suddenly Saturday. But we doubt if that fine lady ever got bored with anything, unless it was mediocrity.

WELCOME TO BALDWIN, LURLEEN AND GEORGE

Governor George Wallace and the first lady of Alabama, Lurleen, who happens to be the Democratic nominee for the office her husband now holds, are getting big welcomes throughout the entire state. No county should or will welcome them more appreciatively and overwhelmingly than Baldwin.

The Times has often pointed out the many things George has done for Baldwin and her people during his term in office. We won't detail them again now because of the lack of space. Roads, industry, education, and practically every phase of our economic, political and social life—he has helped with all while in office. Suffice it to say that no other governor has been so consistently considerate of our needs.

And Lurleen promises four more years of the same. This should suit everyone in these parts.

So welcome, Lurleen and George, to your second home—Baldwin County.

FASTEN YOUR SEAT BELTS

In a recent survey it was found that 40 percent of the persons who died in automobile accidents would have lived if they had been wearing simple seat belts.

Shoulder harnesses and belts would have saved 20 percent more.

These were the results found by two University of Michigan scientists in what has been termed "the most intensive first-hand study of traffic deaths since the car was born." It involved an analysis of 139 fatal accidents.

They stated further, "We have had only one case of a survivor who owes his life to not wearing a seat belt. We have had at least 71 who owe their deaths to not wearing them."

A hint to the sufficient should be sufficient.

GO TO THE BALDWIN COUNTY FAIR

The county Fair is the best ever. Much work and effort has been done to make it a great success.

The county is indebted to J.D. (Josh) Sellars and his helpers.

Don't take our word—go see for yourself.

"BEAR" CAN WALK ON WATER

Even so, the cool snap was a long time in coming . . . this is late October you know. If we wrote an editorial on every subject we should, we wouldn't have enough room left in this family journal to run any advertising . . . without advertising there wouldn't be any paper in the first place. We are sock up in the middle of the football season . . . half past and half to come . . . two of our favorite teams are doing all right, having won'em all to date . . . the other is still fumbling around, mud or no mud . . . there should be no further arguments about it, the Bear can walk on water . . . he even had his team doing it the last few minutes of the Tennessee game, else he wouldn't have won.

Political name calling and truth stretching arguments are getting louder and louder . . . and will get more so for the next three weeks . . . from here on in, believe little you see and nothing you hear. Heard two people talking, in all seriousness, one said to the other, "the way to make money in the stock market is to buy low and sell high" . . . now that we have this valuable information we may try it, when we get some spare money.

Do you have a good cause you are working for? . . . if so, remember it takes longer to live for it than to die for it. If we husbands could only have half the fun our wives think we have when we're out! Saying no to temptation is the right thing to do . . . but Mr. Plunkett says that by so doing you may rob tomorrow's memories. After viewing two or three television shows the other night, we finally cut the thing off with the firm conviction that the real hero in most such shows is the viewer. Had you rather be discovered, or found out?

Somewhere we read or heard something like this: . . . If you want your father to take care of you—that's Paternalism . . . if you want Uncle Sam to take care of you—that's Socialism . . . if you want your comrades to take care of you—that's Communism . . . if you want to take care of yourself—that's Americanism. Don't insist that a thing is impossible just because you haven't done it . . . Something you should teach your child: positive thinking creates an attractive personality . . . negative thinking produces the opposite effect which repels people rather than attract them. So many things worth thinking about . . . but that's enough, for now.

December 1, 1966

A.K. EASLEY WILL BE LONG REMEMBERED

We have always admired people with the intelligence, push and ability to start from the bottom and work to the top. One such person was A.K. Easley, who died here last week.

Mr. Easley, 70, lived a rich and fruitful life. He came to Bay Minette from Monroe County when he was about 50 years old as an employee of another company. Not long thereafter, he decided to go into the pole business for himself. With very little money but with a lot of drive and good common sense, he jumped in and became well known in this area. When he died he was president of the successful enterprise, Baldwin Pole and Piling Co.

Most of his friends, and he had many, called him "A.K." He was outspoken in his views but was tolerant and thoughtful of other people. He was religious and did much to build a new Methodist church here.

He not only left a thriving industrial business but a heritage of two sons and a son-in-law to carry on the enterprise. Although he will be missed, memory of him and his accomplishments will linger long.

ALABAMA'S SENATOR HILL

The state's senior statesman and United States Senator, Lister Hill, has received so many honors for his service to humanity in the field of health that he finally had to get a filing system to list all of them.

Now he has another. This latest honor is of particular interest to citizens of the Bay Minette area, this time because it has to do with the 20th anniversary of the signing of the famous Hill-Burton Act, of which he was co-author and sponsor.

We are in receipt of a beautiful booklet prepared by The American Dental Association in connection with a dinner it had planned to honor Senator Hill on the anniversary of his hospital act which has been responsible for building thousands of hospitals throughout the United States.

August 13 was the exact date of the signing of Hill-Burton in 1946. The dinner had to be postponed and the recognition was rescheduled to coincide with the annual meeting of The American Dental Association in Dallas on November 14.

The book is beautifully printed and full of pictures, history and facts of Alabama's great Senator. It is a fine tribute to a man who richly deserves it.

The document begins, " 'We stand today at the threshold of a Golden Age of Medicine.' The words are those of Lister Hill. They are appropriate words for him to speak for he is eminently one of the men who has led the nation and the world to that 'threshold.' No man has done more than he to shape the health future of America, to give it promise and hope."

Because of his foresight, next year there will be available to the Bay Minette area $834,400 in Hill-Burton funds to build a 50-bed hospital here. All we have to do is furnish the other one-third. If we lived in New York or one of the richer states, we would have to pay a much higher percentage of the cost. It was also through his wisdom and ability that he put into the bill a provision that poor states would get a higher percentage of Hill-Burton funds.

Over 200 such hospitals have been built in Alabama alone with the funds made available by Hill's act. In fact, so many have been built that a representative from the Alabama Department of Public Health last week made the public statement here that no town in the state needs a new hospital as badly as Bay Minette. When we get it built we can join with the American Dental Association and the dozens of other important groups in America who have tipped their hats in recognition to "Mr. Health, U.S.A.," Senator Lister Hill.

THANKSGIVING WEEKEND

No one has prettier weather than we do around here at times . . . but it changes. We, like so many other people, stuffed ourselves too much with stuffed turkey over the long Thanksgiving weekend . . . it makes you feel stuffy, but oh so nice . . . of course not everyone was overstuffed . . . we still have those among us who don't get all they want or need to eat . . .

and millions in the world are hungry . . . opinions of silk suiters notwithstanding.

The South has risen again this year . . . the civil rights crisis moved northward during the year and has done much to lift this heretofore strange and unique shadow from the South and made it a national problem . . . we have suffered from it alone long enough . . . the agonies have been spread nation-wide and it could be that the era of finger-pointing toward the South is coming to an end . . . and we have made progress elsewhere in education, industry, farming, etc. . . . and where there are problems there is plenty of opportunity . . . the South, in this sense, still has lots and lots of opportunities.

We admit to prejudiced eyes on the subject but this is the way we look at this football championship deal . . . Alabama was No. 1 last year and the year before . . . like in boxing you stay champion until someone whips you . . . no one has whipped Alabama, in fact it is the only major football team in the nation that is undefeated and untied . . . all of these wins have been in the Southeast which even *Time* magazine admits plays the best and toughest football in the nation . . . while writing this we have convinced ourselves we aren't prejudiced even . . . but right as rain.

We may have more Indian chiefs than Indians in these parts . . . or so it seems by the noise . . . money is making many Indian feathers rise . . . but $4 million won't give 40,000 of them but about $100 each, which is hardly enough to scalp anybody about . . . but even though they deserve more, we hope even this small amount will be paid out soon.

The Viet Cong wants a Christmas truce and promises to be good Communists for a few days if Uncle Sam will toe the mark, etc. . . . . All Communists are many things bad and lying is one of them . . . this country is willing to have a permanent truce if the Communists will just get out of South Vietnam and quit trying to conquer the world.

A good laugh would crack the face of some people we know. Show us a stingy, greedy person and we'll show you a person who seldom laughs, because he is seldom happy. Little Johnny thinks all the good vitamins could just as well have been put in candy and cake rather than vegetables and pills. The trouble with enemies is you can't always select the ones you want. "The liberal soul shall get fat."—Proverbs. Most of us couldn't stand justice, especially from God. All, time being.

December 22, 1966

H.I. WEST, J. ARTHUR CORTE
WIDELY KNOWN

H.I. WEST

Bay Minette has lost another fine citizen. H.I. West died here last week.

He was one of the most versatile beings intellectually we have ever known. Still he wasn't a person you would think of as brilliant. He just had a lot of hobbies and knew much about all of them.

He was fundamentally a man of the soil and thought Baldwin County's the best to be found anywhere. He taught vocational agriculture at one time. When he finished college his studying about soils, crops, plants and farming really got underway.

We delighted, as did many, in seeing him and saying "Hi! H.I.," and then listening to him tell about one of his recent travels, some of his fine roses which he grew so expertly, or some other story laden with facts about the superiority of farming in Baldwin County. He was one of the county's greatest farm boosters.

He was a good writer and reporter. He wrote some fine farm articles for *The Times*, was also an expert photographer and delighted in showing the many colored slides he made throughout the U.S.

Mr. West always appeared easy going and making a living seemed to come easy. His many hobbies and long line of civic interests proved his energy, ability and love for people. He was four times president of the Bay

Minette Chamber of Commerce.

You may wonder how a person could accomplish all of these things without being brilliant. H.I. West was brilliant, he just didn't appear to be on first acquaintance.

J. ARTHUR CORTE

There is no name greater than Corte in Baldwin County. It was made so by the late A.A. Corte, his six sons and one daughter.

As much, if not more, than any other family, they have helped develop Baldwin into one of the greatest agricultural counties in the United States.

Of the six sons, the oldest and possibly the most widely known, was J. Arthur Corte. He was friendly, likeable and had a lot of good common sense.

He died last week and this county suffered a real loss.

A REAL COUNTY ASSET

One of Bay Minette's newest industrial plants, Kaiser Aluminum & Chemical Corporation, has been a wonderful asset to this area since its opening in 1964. In addition to its fine payroll, the company has brought in many excellent people who have become local citizens and assumed their civic responsibilities.

One good example has been the plant manager since its opening. Richard E. Null has been a live wire and a great worker for Kaiser and the area.

Although we are delighted to see him get a deserved promotion, it is with great regret that local people give him up to assume his new position at Bristol, R.I. Although he has been here a shorter time, the same could be said about the plant's administrative manager, Frank Panzarella, who is also leaving for Bristol.

Their replacements will also be excellent people and citizens, according to Kaiser tradition, but it will take some doing locally to get use to the idea that Dick Null is no longer here. He is a go-getter. And it is naturally selfish for us to want him here go-getting for Bay Minette.

Regardless, we sincerely wish Dick and Frank the best of everything in their new assignments but that their hearts will always have a yearning to return here.

CHRISTMAS TIME

People are never more generous than around Christmas time . . . if you are an average person, you are more concerned over whether or not you have forgotten anyone you should give a gift to and if the ones you have bought will make the receiver happy or not . . . you are probably a child or more selfish than most if you are more concerned about what you are going to get than what you are giving . . . all of which is to say, wouldn't it be wonderful if we all could be like that all year . . . the happiest people are.

Here's a happy thought for Christmas, or anytime . . . not long ago it was estimated that the actual worth of one's body was about 98 cents . . . under the light of new processes, uses of compounds and chemicals, and inflation, it is now said that each human body is worth $800 . . . aren't we important?

Mickey Mouse, Pluto, Donald Duck and the many other characters of Walt Disney's imagination and art are sad little creatures, along with millions of humans in the world, because their master is dead . . . it is probably true that Walt entertained more people during his lifetime than any dozen other people that ever lived . . . and because of his creative genius as shown in his comic cartoons, full length movies, TV shows, Disneyland, etc., his show will go on for many, many years . . . he was the greatest.

Headline says we may receive live TV from mars by laser beams . . . That's fine because the programs we are receiving from earth are pretty dead, with the exception of sports . . . a lot of people are joking about poor TV programs but the more intelligent ones are dead serious about the poor quality . . . actually we think Gunsmoke is as good as it was 10 years ago . . . it was the best then and still is . . . which isn't saying much for the rest . . . in fairness to TV, it could be that the people are just getting harder to please . . . Negro Congressman Adam Clayton Powell of Harlem is probably the most notorious law-breaker in the land . . . he has defied the courts for months . . . he was sued for libel and lost in a $164,000 judgment . . . he has continually refused to pay . . . he has used much of your money to take junkets everywhere . . . he also has his fourth or fifth estranged wife on his congressional payroll at $20,800 annually and deposits the check in his own account . . . he also preaches when he can slip into Harlem on Sunday without getting arrested . . . he's a disgrace to honesty, integrity and patriotic Americanism . . . congressmen are talking about unseating him . . . a good idea . . . if an Alabama congressman had acted half as disgracefully, he would long since have been booted out . . . like they did Senator Bilbo of Mississippi.

Amid it all we wish for you and yours a very happy and merry Christmas.

February 9, 1967

J. ALBERT HILL RECEIVES HIGH HONOR

We think one of the finest honors that can be bestowed upon an individual who lives within the geographical confines of a city is to be honored as its "Man of the Year." Albert Hill, pastor of the First Baptist Church, Bay Minette, has been honored, and deservedly so.

Albert Hill is not only a popular preacher within his own church but is popular with all who know him throughout this area, even though he is comparatively a newcomer in our midst. He takes a civic interest in many things, although he always makes it very clear that he puts his church and spiritual interest before anything else. He is president of the Bay Minette Rotary Club and devotes considerable time to the success to this fine organization. Incidentally, he was president of the Rotary Club at Wetumpka where he lived before moving to Bay Minette. This is just an indication of his willingness to serve his fellowman.

Mr. Hill was selected as "Man of the Year" for Bay Minette for 1966 because of his able leadership in the passage of a two-mill property tax to make it possible for us to get a 55-bed hospital built in this area within the near future. He was chairman of the citizens committee for passage of the tax and worked effectively and hard to achieve success. His fellow citizens are proud of his accomplishments and we gladly join in his praise for being a fine citizen.

WELCOME TO BAY MINETTE, KAISER FRIENDS

Bay Minette and Baldwin County are the proud possessors of one of the many plants of Kaiser Aluminum and Chemical Company. This week we are also the proud hosts to their nationwide sales organization. We welcome all of them to this great county.

Beginning Sunday, the sales organization of this fine international company started gathering at the Grand Hotel on beautiful Mobile Bay for a week's sales briefing and get-together. Friday, the some 150-odd representatives of Kaiser will travel to Bay Minette to inspect Kaiser's local plant. They will spend several hours here looking over this modern up-to-date facility. We hope they will be as proud of it as we here in Bay Minette are.

Kaiser people make good citizens. At least this is true locally and we feel sure it is true throughout their vast organization. Anyway, welcome to all of you. We hope you like this area of the United States as well as we like you.

May 25, 1967

W.G. McKIBBON INFLUENTIAL BUSINESSMAN

Recently when W.G. McKibbon died, Baldwin lost one of its most successful and influential businessmen.

He came to Baldwin in 1935 from Dallas County. He was an inspector with the State Health Department and made some $200 a month. It was through this connection with the Health Department he met Mr. John Fugard, who at that time was operating the Silverhill Dairy. The two became friends and later were associated in the organization of Woodhaven Dairy, a milk distribution plant at Robertsdale. Its success has been widely proclaimed.

During his administration, Governor Gordon Persons appointed McKibbon as a member of the Alabama Milk Control Board. He held many other positions of honor, being director of the Mobile Area Chamber of Commerce, etc. He was one of the county's best golfers and enjoyed the association of friends while playing the game. He had the natural touch of a successful businessman and seemed to know when to get into a business and how to organize and operate it successfully.

Following his death, his oldest son, W.G. (Billy) McKibbon, Jr., was selected by the stockholders of the company to be Executive Vice President of Woodhaven Dairy. Other members of his family are taking over his multiplicity of business enterprises which he successfully started and operated.

Thus the name McKibbon is destined to continue as one of success and service for years to come in this area. We hope all of his descendants achieve the same degree of success attained by W.G. McKibbon, Sr.

BALDWIN CONTINUES TO GROW

This county has been one of the four fastest growing in population in Alabama since 1940.

In the 1940-50 decade, Baldwin was the third fastest growing county in Alabama, being exceeded only by Mobile and Etowah Counties.

In the 1950-60 decade, we ranked fourth.

According to recent estimates by the State Health Department's Bureau of Vital Statistics, Baldwin still ranks near the top in percentage of growth between 1960-67.

In 1960, Baldwin was the 15th largest populated county in Alabama with 49,088 people.

In 1967, we had jumped to be the 12th largest with an estimated 54,900.

During this seven-year period, we climbed ahead of Houston, Lee and Walker Counties. Baldwin has shown an 11 percent climb in this period. The state has averaged nine percent.

Of course the reason for all this is the fact that Baldwin County has so much to offer happy home seekers.

MUMBLINGS—THE WORLD WE LIVE IN

We have written a lot about our recent American Study Mission tour to Southeast Asia and Vietnam . . . it was an amazing trip for this country editor . . . to all of you who have been kind enough to mention that you enjoyed the articles, we do humbly thank you . . . naturally while on this trip we did much thinking about the world in which we live . . . we have gathered some figures of our own and recently we read where another man had done some thinking and we think the combined facts might be of interest to you.

The writer attempted to illustrate the kind of world we live in by reducing proportionately all of the people of the world into a theoretical town of 1,000 people . . . naturally no such town exists:

There would be 60 Americans . . . the other 940 persons would represent the other nations of the world . . . the 60 Americans would have a full half of the income of the entire town.

One-third, or 330 persons, would be classified as "Christian" in the widest use of the term . . . there would be 80 Communists in the town with 370 or more persons under their domination . . . there would be 303 white people in the town, and 697 non-whites.

One-half of the 1,000 people would never have heard of Jesus Christ or what he taught . . . over one-half would presently be learning about Carl Marx, Lenin, and the philosophy of Communism.

The 60 Americans would have an average life expectancy of 70 years, and each American would own 15 times as many possessions as the other 940 citizens . . . the 940 would have a life expectancy of less than 40 years and most of them would go to bed hungry every night . . . the American families would be spending an average of $850 per year for military defense, but less than $4.00 per year to share their religion with other people of the community . . . and less than that to tell the rest what a wonderful thing the free enterprise system is.

How would you like to live in such a town? . . . we can be grateful that the presentation is hypothetical and that we do not live in such a town . . . but we do live in such a world!!!

Wherever you travel, wherever you go, you will immediately learn that we Americans live in the greatest country on earth . . . and we should all become more and more appreciative of the fact. More later, maybe.

June 1, 1967

IT TOOK A LADY TO DO IT, MRS. INA MAE BECKER

Baldwin citizens are liberal and cooperative people. Most all drives for worthy causes succeed in this great county. One of the most worthy annual drives of them all is the Cancer Crusade. But it has never gone over the top. That is, not until this year.

For the first time in the history of the county crusade, Baldwin has exceeded her quota. And it took a lady as county chairman to get the job done. In the past, some of the county's finest and most successful businessmen and others have been Crusade Chairmen—but no one had ever met the goal.

Mrs. Ina Mae Becker, chief clerk in the Tax Assessor's office, has done it. As county chairman of the annual drive, she has collections of over $5,500 with some important communities yet to report.

With a high quota of $4,400, we would say that this is a successful record. It not only speaks well for Mrs. Becker, but for the liberality of the entire county.

This money will be used to fight cancer wherever it raises its ugly head. Much of it will be used for cancer research with the hope that a discovery will be forthcoming soon for cure of this dreaded disease.

The Cancer Crusade is not only for the purpose of raising money, but for the education as well. It has been learned long ago that if people will have a regular examination and discover cancer early enough, their chances of recovery are excellent.

Congratulations are due Ina Mae and her hundreds of well-organized workers.

GOOD LEGISLATIVE SUGGESTION

County Coroner Jim Hathcock has come up with a suggestion that if put into effect, could make his office more efficient and in a position to render faster service to the citizens of Baldwin.

He wants to appoint three deputy coroners for Baldwin County. He says his interest is in streamlining the functions of his office in order to provide better service. He said if two calls come at the same time, or in the event of a case being at an extreme distance from his office in Fairhope, it takes him too long to reach the scene of an accident.

He feels the coroner should reach the scene of an accident and make his report as soon as possible so a victim's body will not have to lie on the roadside for a long period of time. Mr. Hathcock said he will pay such deputy coroners from what he receives for the office, thus, it would not be an additional expense to the county.

Jim Hathcock has asked Baldwin's representatives, L.W. Brannan and L. D. (Dick) Owen, to give consideration to getting a law passed that will enable him to do this. It seems like a good idea to *The Times*. It could not hurt anything and obviously, it could make for faster service, which is important at times.

TWO OUTSTANDING PUBLISHERS DIE

Two of Alabama's outstanding newspaper publishers have died in recent weeks. The first to die was Glenn Stanley, long-time publisher of *The Green-ville Advocate*. He died while we were out of the country and of course we were saddened upon our return to learn of his death. Mr. Stanley was truly the sage of Greenville, Alabama.

Saturday, another fine Alabama publisher died. He was Bonnie Hand, who at only 54 years old had been publisher of *The LaFayette Sun* for 28 years.

Bonnie was a dedicated newspaperman, citizen, and all-around good person. He was a past president of the Alabama Press Association and perhaps no man in this generation had contributed as much to the association as he had. He had been chairman for a long time of the Legislative Committee of APA and did a fine job in this capacity.

A man of dedication and sincerity, he had a host of friends among newspaper men and in other fields throughout the state. He started in the newspaper publishing business in LaFayette as a partner of the late H.H. Golson of Wetumpka. We were also a partner of Mr. Golson with *The Atmore Advance* about the same time Bonnie started his venture. Bonnie was a successful businessman.

We offer our sympathies to the wonderful wife, Pearl, and their two fine children, Mike and Bronwyn. The state has lost a good man and a good publisher.

MUMBLINGS ON A GOOD COLUMNIST AND OTHERS

The Times is fortunate in having several good columnists . . . we hope you read all of them . . . "Second Thoughts" by Martin Johnson is worth reading every week . . . we were particularly impressed with what he had to say week before last . . . he talked about one of our favorite gripes, and that is people griping so much about government and our public officials.

Martin said, "I write as an American who dearly loves his country, and is saddened to see her being weakened from within. For that exactly is what is happening, my fellow Americans, and often by people who would be horrified if you accused them of that" . . . like us, he is worried by the constant stream of criticism, carping and downright vilification of government and government officials . . . of course public officials, like other human beings, are not perfect, neither are they worse than other human beings in general

. . . it doesn't seem likely that the people we elect to office, according to Martin, are a bunch of "clowns, crooks, and con men" . . . we often think that one of the greatest faults is the fault of fault-finding . . . let's look for the good things in life . . . certainly you can find plenty of them in our government officials and in this great country.

One of our favorite local people died last week . . . she was Miss Clara Jernigan Hall . . . one of the well-known three Hall sisters (so called because they were seen together so often) that lived in Bay Minette and contributed so much to the community for such a long time . . . Miss Clara was active in many affairs . . . she was a leading Democrat for many years, and in church and other civic activities . . . she was a well-educated person and we always enjoyed discussing different ideas with her . . . being well-read, she always had excellent thinking on many subjects . . . of the three Hall sisters, Miss Neil, Miss Louise, and Miss Clara, only Miss Louise is left and she is in bad health . . . history passes on.

You have heard many of George Wallace's critics state that he never takes a stand on things . . . he certainly took a stand last week on every conceivable subject . . . *The Birmingham News* asked him questions and the questions and answers took up four complete pages of Sunday before last's edition . . . if you want to know how George Wallace feels on any subject, obtain this issue of *The News*. See you later, we hope.

July 6, 1967

JOHN HADLEY BRINGS HONOR TO BALDWIN

John Hadley, the longtime chairman of the Baldwin County Commission, brought honor to himself and Baldwin County last week when he was elected President of the Alabama County Commissioners and Probate

Judges Association in Birmingham.

There is perhaps no stronger political organization in the entire state than this association. For a person to achieve the high honor of being president of this strong and worthwhile group is a credit to his ability and sense of service to his people.

This, of course, will keep John out of Baldwin a considerable part of the coming year. But we feel confident the voters and citizens of the county will be willing to lend him part-time toward the well being and development of the rest of the state. In the meantime, we join with the rest of his constituents in wishing him well and congratulating him on this fine honor.

GOVERNOR LURLEEN WALLACE

Last week when Governor Lurleen Wallace announced the fact that she had a recurrence of cancer, a pall of sorrow covered the entire state. This brave and courageous little lady has captured the love and admiration of practically every citizen in Alabama and of millions throughout the entire world.

Tuesday, she left for Houston, Texas, to undergo further tests and possible surgery at the M.D. Anderson Hospital. The hopes and prayers of all the citizens of this great state will be with her in her time of anxiety and trial.

Friday has been set aside by a resolution passed unanimously in the State Legislature as a statewide Day of Prayer for Governor Lurleen Wallace. Of course millions have already been praying for her. But we think the idea of everybody doing it on the same day may be effective. We certainly hope so.

A recent poll indicated that Governor Lurleen is one of the six most admired women in the entire world. She certainly deserves this honor and recognition. Of course many people in Alabama find it difficult to understand why they did not rate her first.

YOU CAN'T WIN THEM ALL—AND WE DON'T

Bay Minette has had its fair share of good luck in attracting new industries during the past few years. In fact, many leaders throughout the state jokingly kid us that we get everyone that comes within our reach. Unfortunately, this is a sad joke. We have lost many more than we have gotten.

Proof of this is a headline in the *Birmingham Post-Herald* last Friday, which says, "Cordova gets $13 million plant." The story states that the stud mill and particle board plant will provide 675 new jobs and that it will be in operation within 18 months. Bay Minette figured with these fine people for over a year before they decided to look at the situation in Walker County. The headline tells the unhappy story for Baldwin County and happy story for Cordova and Walker County.

Some five or six years ago, we lost a $50 million plant that we felt confident of obtaining because they had already gotten options on several acres of land. But they finally decided to go to Tennessee. We could tell you of many other instances of such sad endings of our industrial pursuits.

However, we are happy for Walker County. These fine people have worked hard and long for this good industry. Incidentally, the reason it did not locate in Baldwin County, was the fact that the competition for our timber is too great and thus slightly higher priced than in some other sections of the state. This being the case, we are delighted to see them go to Walker County.

So, we lose some and get some. But we can assure you that no other community the size of Bay Minette works harder to get new industries than we do. And fortunately a lot of people cooperate.

August 31, 1967

FORT HATCHETT CHANDLER

Even in death Hatchett Chandler caused a ruckus.

This widely known and controversial figure, who spent 30 years of his life bringing Fort Morgan into the limelight, died last week at the age of

87. His longtime dream of restoring Fort Morgan and bringing about its rightful recognition as the site of one of the oldest (he claimed the oldest) white man's settlements in the new world was largely accomplished.

He traveled thousands of miles, wrote millions of words and spoke continuously about the old Fort. To him, it was a thing of perfection.

He wrote and said so much about the park, it sometimes became difficult to know which was history and which was legend. He intimated that rumor became legend and legend became history, so far as Fort Morgan was concerned. He admitted that a little folklore made history more interesting.

Be that as it may, he did Baldwin County, the State of Alabama and Fort Morgan a great service during his 30 years of controversial serving the old Fort. He fought for what he believed was right, doggedly and without wavering. Less stubborn men would have given up the fight long before he did. In fact, he never did give up until he became too weak to talk.

In 1961, he wrote: "When I came here 20 years ago, this place lay in total darkness. It lay in weeds, mosquitoes, neglect and oblivion, as the mean stepchild of eight other parks . . ." When first arriving at the Fort, he slept in the open while he cleared the Fort of underbrush, snakes and other rubbish. A few years later, the legislature built him a house in which to live. He was allowed to work on after retirement at $141 per month.

He was a thorn in the side of all of those people for whom he worked. He was often very critical of the state conservation directors, under whose authority the Fort lies. He often became outspoken against them. He referred to them as "holy apes." He could and did use words sharply against his enemies. Above the door of the conservation director's office, Chandler said; "We can see the inscription 'For mediocrity only. No talent allowed.'"

It was natural for such a person to have enemies. This goes with progressive minded people. But he also had many friends. And we predict, as history records his life, he will have more and more. Many more than his enemies could have dreamed of.

He once said that he had won at least one victory over his adversaries in the conservation department. But he almost lost his one. He extracted permission from the then Governor John Patterson, Attorney General Gallion and the Baldwin County Health Department to be buried within the grounds at Fort Morgan. But after his death last Wednesday, efforts were begun to keep him from being buried on what was to him holy ground.

The Fort Morgan Historical Association drafted a resolution stating that it was not practical to bury him there. Immediately, Hatchett's friends went to bat and it is a happy ending to a fine, even though controversial career, that he was buried Tuesday afternoon on the ground that he did so much to preserve and commemorate.

Through all of his 87 years of life, Hatchett Chandler stood like a fort against his enemies and for his friends. Hatchett Chandler has become a legend as well as history. May God rest his soul.

ANGI GROOMS, OTHERS VISIT VIETNAM

This is week 35 in the year of our Lord, 1967 . . . 17 more to go and to do what you must . . . it also means that it is just 16 more weeks 'til Christmas . . . doesn't time fly?

Angi Grooms, a Birmingham beauty and Miss Alabama, is one of five in a Miss America troop traveling in South Vietnam building the moral of our boys over there . . . speaking of our GI's, she said: "They don't like being over here, they want to go home. But they feel that they are here to do their job, and we haven't seen any who are not enthusiastic about doing it well, as long as they are here." . . . upon our return from over there, we often made a similar statement, but naturally, not as prettily or as effectively as does Miss Grooms.

We are often amazed about how many people who do not read the funny papers . . . however, most people do . . . so that makes us average . . . average means that there are just as many people better than you as those on the other end . . . we can hardly wait each week to find out what Buz Sawyer is doing in *The Baldwin Times* . . . if you have been keeping up with him, you will know that he may have found his long lost wife.

This will be another long weekend . . . Labor Day is Monday and many will vacation for the last time this year . . . others for the last time during this life as hundreds will be killed in automobiles . . . be careful and you won't be one of them. Be cheerful children, in one more week, plus nine months, school will be out again. If you think doctors are plentiful, you probably haven't tried to see one. Like most newspaper people, we can truthfully say we do not make the news . . . but, like most people, we must admit we would like to in some cases. See you again soon, we hope.

September 28, 1967

MUMBLINGS—ABOUT JOSH

Thursday night, September 21, was Robertsdale night in the history of this great Baldwin County . . . and more specifically, it was J.D. (Josh) Sellars night at the "Hub City" . . . reason for it all was to dedicate the fine high school football stadium there and to name it in honor of that city's Mayor, Josh Sellars.

It was an elaborate affair, with a huge crowd, and the Robertsdale Golden Bears won their football game in fine fashion and in keeping with the other successes of the night . . . indicative of the crowd present was the fact that the ladies sold over 1,000 fish plates . . . they cooked 925 flounders and 50 lbs. of mullet; nothing was left . . . the Touchdown Club made over $900 raffling off a shotgun . . . through it all, we were privileged to be present . . . if it had been 1,000 miles away, we would have been present, as Josh knows . . . he's traveled some (and then some more) for us.

It was a great night . . . Robertsdale and Josh deserved such a night . . . the whole community had spent long, hard, discouraging hours getting ready by building one of the finest small city football stadiums we have ever seen . . . it is easily the biggest and finest in Baldwin . . . forgetting Ladd, in Mobile, it is probably the best in Southwest Alabama.

It was right and fitting that it be named after Josh . . . on this there can be little doubt . . . he is one of Alabama's finest, oldest (in point of service) mayors . . . he is the town's fulltime Mayor, for which he gets little salary . . .

he is more adequately paid by being manager of the city's utilities, including electricity, water, gas, and sewage . . . it isn't often you can elect a person to do a specific and technical job . . . but Robertsdale voters have and they are so proud of him, they were anxious to honor him in some way other than just voting and re-electing him over and over again . . . of course, they'll keep electing him, too . . . they know a good thing when they see it.

Actually, we may be prejudiced, but we don't know of a better all around mayor anywhere than Josh Sellars . . . we could mumble on and on about his good qualities . . . but we'll save the rest until he retires from mayoring, 20 years or so hence.

FALL AND FOOTBALL

The Fall of the year and the football season both began in Alabama last week. We, like so many others, didn't like everything that happened. However, we can have a sympathetic feeling for the "Bear" and understand what he meant when he said, "Winning isn't everything, but it is better than anything that comes in second."

Auburn made a good start by trimming little Chattanooga in fine fashion. Alabama's Crimson Tide, slated to be number 1 or 2 in the nation, unfortunately, had a set-back when independent and unrated Florida State tied them 37-37.

Those of us who listened to the game on radio, or saw it, felt that Alabama was lucky to come out with a tie.

However, this may also be fortunate. It should make Alabama players realize that there are a lot of other good football teams. We still have confidence they will end up the season being number1 in the nation, or at least close to it. In fact, we wouldn't be surprised if both of our big state teams are good enough to be invited to a bowl game, come New Years. We certainly hope so.

THE UNITED NATIONS

We, like so many other people, sometimes wonder what good the United Nations is doing. We are particularly concerned when the United States foots such a large portion of the cost in running the UN and find so many other nations using it merely for a propaganda tool, all too often against the United States.

However, we always come back to this thought; if we do away with the United Nations, how can we replace it? There must be some worldwide institution with the avowed purpose of seeking peace in this war-torn world. Until something better comes along, let's stick to the United Nations. All, for now.

October 19, 1967

JIMMY GRIMES OF LOXLEY
HAD MANY FRIENDS

We have been to most places in Alabama and in many of them we would run into friends of Jimmy Grimes, that produce man from "what's the name of the town down in your county?"

Yes, James C. Grimes had a host of friends everywhere. All were saddened at learning of his death Saturday, October 7, at the age of 69.

Jimmy, as he was called by all, had a knack of making friends. This was because he was friendly and liked people. Many people who claimed him as a friend, may not have ever seen him but once. But they remembered him with kindness.

He moved to Baldwin from Monroe County at an early age. Right after World War I, he went into the produce business in Loxley. In fact, Jimmy Grimes was one of the pioneers in cash markets for potatoes and other fresh produce in this great county.

Along with the Cortes and Bertollas, he helped develop a market system that did as much as any one thing to make this one of the most successful agricultural counties in the Southeast. He also experimented with different kinds of crops, trying new markets, etc.

We don't know anyone who didn't like Jimmy Grimes. He never took advantage of people and always more than kept his end of a bargain. He gave away thousands and thousands of dollars. His word was his bond.

He wasn't a joiner of clubs, groups, etc., but he helped them all. He had a big heart. He'll never be replaced.

FORT MORGAN'S HATCHETT CHANDLER

Friends of the late, colorful, Hatchett Chandler, the person who did much to make Fort Morgan a great tourist attraction, are indebted to Roland Cooper, state senator of Wilcox, a native of Baldwin County, and other senators and legislators who passed a resolution commending the historian.

The Times is in receipt of a certified copy of the resolution memorializing Hatchett Chandler from Senator Cooper, who wrote and sponsored it. Cooper said, "Mr. Chandler's efforts and work toward restoration of Fort Morgan will certainly be remembered by all people who were fortunate enough to know him or to visit Fort Morgan. May the enclosed resolution be a memory of his great work."

The resolution can be found elsewhere in this issue. *The Times* wishes to commend and thank Senator Cooper and others who were thoughtful enough to pass this resolution in memory of Hatchett Chandler.

A FINE GOVERNMENTAL HELPER

The Federal Government has many bureaus, commissions, and departments which have the avowed purpose of helping the citizens of the United States. Some do, some don't. One of the best such programs is the Small Business Administration, which furnishes financial assistance by lending money to small businesses throughout the nation.

Next Thursday, citizens of Baldwin will have an opportunity of learning in more detail what the SBA can do to help solve their own financial problems. Representative William L. Dickinson and Paul Brunson, SBA Regional Director, will be at the city hall in Bay Minette at 10 a.m. to help disburse this information to those present.

The philosophy behind the SBA program is simple enough—self help.

The idea, basically, is to help communities and individuals help themselves. Of course many individuals in this county have borrowed money from the SBA.

The Standard Furniture Manufacturing Company, of Bay Minette, has taken advantage of their "502" program to expand to the point where it is now the largest employer of males of any industry in the county. The owners of this fine company are quick to say that SBA has been a great benefit to them.

Maybe the SBA is the answer to your financial problem.

MUMBLINGS—BUSINESS GREAT IN BALDWIN

With Guevara down, we only have Castro to go. Business in Baldwin is better than in the rest of Alabama . . . retail sales increased 17.9% in July of 1967 . . . statewide, it was down 6.9% . . . however, July, 1967, was down 1.0% over July, 1966, in the county . . . statewide, it was down 2.6% . . . it's nice to be better off than others, but it is best to be better off, period.

A man's reputation is made up of what he is—what he lives, thinks, says, does, loves, and writes—and what he is will far outweigh what is said about him. No extra charge for this bit of wisdom.

Football gets better . . . always does as your favorite teams keep winning . . . however, football is changing . . . it may offer a clue to some things happening in this country . . . remember when many gridiron games were won by one touchdown like 6-0, 7-6, 3-0, etc.? . . . but look at the scores this year . . . Alabama scored 37 points to tie Florida State with 37 . . . Auburn beat strong Clemson 43-21, etc. . . . in 1957 when Auburn was national champs, she won several games by one point, three points, or one touchdown . . . apparently the offense of the teams has outstripped the defenses, or something . . . whatever it is, the coaches also wish they knew the answer, certainly we don't . . . maybe the same thing is happening in all walks of life in America . . . at least our defenses are down on many things . . . note the street riots and other items we could mention. See you later, we hope.

November 2, 1967

DOCTOR PERCY A. BRYANT

One of the most prominent family names in this section of Baldwin County is Bryant. Last week one of the outstanding members of the family died. He was Dr. Percy A. Bryant of this city.

After finishing his medical education, Dr. Percy, as he was affectionately called, practiced medicine in Washington, D.C. After the war, he came back home and set up practice in Bay Minette.

Dr. Bryant had many good qualities as a human being. He had a fine personality, which helped him in his bedside manner with people of all ages. Our children, if they had to see a doctor, wanted to go to Dr. Percy.

In spite of his busy career as a doctor, he always found time to assist in civic activities. He was unusual in this respect. Some professional people do not have, or do not take, time to assist their communities in civic affairs.

This was not the case with Dr. Percy. He was always available for aid and advice and, at least as far as we knew, never turned down a worthy cause with financial or other assistance. He was active in many community affairs.

Unfortunately, Bay Minette was not in any position to lose any of its fine doctors. This was particularly so with Dr. Percy A. Bryant, who was dean of the local medical profession and had such a wide influence for good with many people and in so many fields.

THE BEST FAIR YET

Those who were fortunate enough to attend the annual Baldwin County Fair in Robertsdale are unanimous in their opinion that it was the best one that has ever been held.

The citizens of Robertsdale in particular, with Mayor J.D. (Josh) Sellars in charge, deserve a lot of credit for the success of the fair over the years. The Baldwin County Fair has done what other county and community fairs have failed in during the past few years. Most fairs have gone out of existence.

The Baldwin fair has continued to grow and get better and better. This is a fine thing and all of those who are responsible deserve the commendation and thanks of the other county citizens.

OUR LOCAL STATE JUNIOR COLLEGE

Many fine things have happened to Bay Minette and Baldwin County during the past few years. Nothing, perhaps, has been more important than locating the State Junior College here.

It has already made a good name for itself. It has furnished at least a part of a college education to hundreds of boys and girls. Its future is assured and will play an even greater part during the coming decade in giving the high school graduates in this area an opportunity to obtain a higher degree of learning.

One of the most significant things to happen to the college in its brief history was the announcement last week that the school will get dormitories and a cafeteria. New junior colleges in Alabama, which were conceived by former Governor George Wallace, are commuter colleges. All have buses and students get free rides to and from school.

After two years of local effort, the State Board of Education approved the dormitories. They did this partially on an experimental basis and partially because Baldwin County needed them worse than some other areas.

One of Baldwin County's assets is the fact it is a resort section. Students have been coming to the school from other sections of the state already. With dormitories, more will come. Too, they and the gymnasium will make for a better collegiate atmosphere. College spirit is important, too.

BOMBING NORTH VIETNAM

How can anyone be so ridiculous as to say and think that bombing North Vietnam isn't hurting the Communists and helping the United States? . . . the trouble is we have too many people in this country who don't want the Communists hurt . . . in other wars they were called traitors.

Our former Governor, George Wallace, has been in the West for the past few days and was received enthusiastically . . . he made the tour to boost his presidential aspirations . . . he got standing ovations in San Francisco,

Seattle, Washington, and other cities . . . according to newspaper reports, he is going over big in many places . . . he is making an all out effort to get on the ballot in California as a third party presidential candidate . . . it'll be a big job as it will take 66,059 names on a petition to get him on the ticket . . . if George manages the difficult task in huge California, he'll be a major candidate next year . . . there is a distinct feeling of dissatisfaction and unrest among many elements in this country . . . Wallace can take advantage of this to garner votes for himself . . . if a few riots come off before the election, they will be a big boost to his candidacy . . . those who have counted him as a minor factor in the election may have to guess again.

"Hog Island Hippies Wed," says headline . . . why? Last week our preacher gave us the following sage advice: pray as if only God can help you and then work as if He can't do anything. The old saying is that it's a great life if you don't weaken . . . up until now we have never seen anyone who didn't weaken on occasion . . . regardless, it is a great life, all in all, if you work to make it so. See you soon, we hope.

January 11, 1968

Two prominent citizens leave us

R.J. (JACK) ROBERTSON

Baldwin County has lost another leading citizen, and us a good friend.

R.J. (Jack) Robertson died after a long period of suffering last week at the comparative young age of 47. Other than living out his normal three score and ten years, he lived a full life as his accomplishments prove.

Jack was the second son of a great mother and father, the late Judge

G.W. and Mrs. Pearl Robertson. He was to politics born, so to speak, as there were few peers to his father.

Jack served two terms as chairman of the county commission. He did not choose to seek re-election and retired from politics. During his terms he helped pioneer the present road program in Baldwin County, which is conceded to be the best in the entire state.

He was comparatively a quiet person. But he loved people, liked to serve them, and his character, word and honor were always above reproach. In addition to his other accomplishments, he has left a good heritage in his wife, Mary Frances, and three fine young boys, Jack, Jr., Cleveland and Jim.

C. AGNEW THOMPSON

C. Agnew Thompson was the Rock of Gibraltar type—sturdy, solid, honest and dependable. His death early Sunday morning came as a shock to many.

Mr. Thompson was one of the pioneers of this area and contributed much to its growth and development during his 75 years. Perhaps not as well known personally as some other citizens, as he was of a retiring nature usually and preferred to stay in the background. However, you always knew where he stood and could count on him when the going got rough.

Perhaps he was best known for his business ability, having succeeded in real estate and other investment ventures. He was a director of the Baldwin County Bank and helped bring it back from its closing days in the early thirties to one of the strongest financial institutions in the county.

He had a large family and treated them well. Mrs. Thompson was always a strong helper for him.

MUMBLINGS—WEATHER, FOOTBALL AND MORE

Since cold weather we must have, January is as good a time as any for it . . . and we've had it. Football is about over for this season . . . we hope the Southeastern Conference does something to get back in the upper league . . . Coach Shug Jordan has been proven right in his fight to correct the conference rule of limiting recruiting to 40 scholarships each year . . . this won't cut the mustard when independents and others give as high as 80 scholarships . . . when our boys lose four of five bowl games it is time to take action . . . we are accustomed to winning four, five or six.

Too many of our friends are dying . . . the old saying is that if you attend more funerals than weddings, you are getting old . . . we must be getting ancient . . . several of our good local friends have died recently and within the past two weeks three of our statewide friends died . . . all former State Senators, they were J. Miller Bonner of Camden, Handy Ellis of Columbiana, and Clarence Inzer of Gadsden . . . the last two were also Lieutenant Governors of Alabama at one time . . . we had been associated with these gentlemen in various capacities, having served in the Senate with the great Senator Bonner . . . he was a strong courageous person . . . we supported Handy Ellis for Governor in 1946 and in '48 were one of the 26 delegates to the Democratic National Convention in Philadelphia . . . Senator Bonner and Mr. Ellis were among the 26 and were also two of the 13 who walked out . . . we never had the respect for Mr. Ellis after that we once had . . . not because he walked out but the arrogant method he used accomplishing his purpose . . . Mr. Inzer was one of the finest men the state ever produced . . . he came down while Lieutenant Governor and went fishing with us up in the swamps . . . great men like these come and go but the world does and must go on.

Most everyone in this country is eager for peace in Vietnam . . . because of this, we may be grasping at straws hoping for peace feelers from the Communists of North Vietnam . . . all the rage so far has been for peace talks . . . we forget that in the case of Korea, the war continued two years after peace talks began . . . and they haven't yet signed a peace treaty . . . Communists are liars of the first order . . . any agreement they make isn't worth the paper it is written on unless it is backed up by arms and ammunition . . . what we are trying to say is the only way to win the peace in Vietnam is to overwhelm the enemy militarily . . . actually this is true in any war.

It is horrible for us to accidentally bomb a Russian ship . . . but it is all right for them to supply our enemies with guns and ammunition . . . presumably we are to sit back, say nothing and do less. How is this for a slogan, "Do something, and make it do." See you later, we hope.

May 23, 1968

J.H. 'Judge' White honored again

We were delighted to see this community pay tribute to John "Judge" White again.

He has done a great job with his Key Club boys here over the past 17 or 18 years. Because of his untiring work, the Bay Minette Key Club has won more state and national honors than any other club in the world.

For four years running, it was judged the outstanding club in the nation. This is quite a record. But the finest thing of all is the fact that "Judge" White gave his hundreds of Key Club boys something they would never have received had it not been for his attention and hard work.

It is easier to understand his great value to the teenagers of this community if you have been a parent of one of his Key Clubbers. We were, two times. He instilled the boys with qualities they never would have gotten without his help.

It would be interesting to have a record of all the boys who have come under his influence since 1951, when he began the great work. We'll wager that 99% of them have been successes in their chosen fields.

"Judge" White has been honored many times for his achievements. He'll be honored many more times, too, we hope.

OUR JAYCEES BRING HOME THE HONORS

We have come to expect it of them, but we realize that their award winning is the fruit of long hours of planning and work on a year-around schedule of very worthwhile projects.

We refer, of course, to the Bay Minette Jaycees who have just returned from their State Convention in Birmingham this past weekend with their hands full of awards. These young men are due great credit for having received top honors as the outstanding Jaycee organization in the State in Division II for the last five out of six years.

Saturday night the Bay Minette Jaycees received the Geissenbier Memorial Award, the highest in the State; five first place category awards, one second place award, and three third place awards.

MRS. ALLEN BEATS JIM ALLEN

It seems that women nearly always win in Alabama politics.

While former Lt. Gov. Jim Allen polled 34,200 votes more than his nearest opponent, Armistead Selden, his wife, Maryon, outpolled his nearest opponent's wife by 40,000 votes.

Mrs. Allen and Mrs. Selden were running for presidential electors on the slate of former Governor George Wallace. Both won, but Mrs. Jim Allen won better.

The two husbands in the case are still battling it our for the Senate post, however.

For Selden to win, he will have to poll almost twice as many of the 127,853 votes cast for the four other candidates who were eliminated.

This is a difficult task, particularly since it is generally assumed that the total vote cast on the June 4 runoff will probably be 10 to 30% below the vote May 7. Making the task even more difficult is the probability that Negroes will not turn out next time.

CLAUDE KIRK RIGHT ON THIS ONE

Florida's Claude Kirk, Jr., has been running over the country criticizing former Governor George Wallace as a presidential candidate.

Kirk is an Alabamian. Many Alabamians have been critical of him for being critical of our George.

Florida's Governor has gained friends here by criticizing other states for not lowering their flag to half-mast when beloved Governor Lurleen Wallace died. Kirk immediately had flags lowered in Florida.

In fact, officials in Virginia called upon Governor Kirk to apologize to their Governor for his criticism for not lowering the flag. If you know Kirk, you will also know that he is not one who quickly apologizes. He made this reasonable statement, "Florida lowered the flag and if the rest of them are impolite, I can't help that."

Many people in Alabama and the rest of the United States were incensed that Washington did not make proper proclamations for all the country to lower the flag to half-mast when Governor Lurleen died. She was designated as one of the ten outstanding women of the world. Anger was heightened when it was realized that such courtesies were extended for the funeral in Atlanta.

This is just another case of what the Washington crowd, as Jim Allen would say, thinks of Alabama.

MUMBLINGS—YOU'LL NEVER OUT-GIVE GOD

With the wonderful two-inch rain we had over the weekend, it was tempting to forget the fact that we have had the least moisture in this area for over a hundred years . . . of course it takes more than two inches to make a wet spell.

We don't know why some people aren't interested in other people . . . too interested in themselves, we suspect . . . which is a selfish and short sighted policy . . . to help others is to love them . . . you may out-give people but you'll never out-give God. Most people spend their vacation too far away from their budget.

We're sorry that France is having so much social unrest and labor trouble . . . we can't say the same for Charles deGaulle . . . he's been asking for trouble a long time . . . we think it is fitting that his own people are giving it to him since he has tried to give the United States and other countries some of what he is now getting.

We are not a pessimist and never want to be accused of being one . . . however, we must admit to being somewhat on the doubtful side about some of our prospective presidential candidates . . . with Governor Rockefeller endorsing the poor people's march on Washington Sunday as a "new imaginative way of creating a lobby" for the poor . . . he said "the poor people have not had a lobby because they haven't been able to afford it." . . . this billionaire doesn't seem to know the difference between a catastrophe and verbal pressure . . . anyone with any conscience has a feeling for poor people and desires to help them . . . anyone with any sense knows that you cannot use force in this country and get by with it for long . . . at least, we hope not.

We hope you cannot buy the president's job . . . Senator Robert Kennedy is trying to do so with his father's half billion dollars of wealth . . . Bobby is poor, however, compared to Governor Rockefeller . . . his family is worth over one billion dollars, or so we understand . . . with Rockefeller spending money right and left and encouraging chaos with the poor people's march in Washington . . . Bobby spending money right and left, advocating the Viet Cong help run South Vietnam . . . and other such un-American radical statements, we may all have a tendency to wonder whether wealth should have the power it sometimes does. See you again soon, we hope.

November 7, 1968

THROUGH STORM AND RAIN, BAY MINETTE IS OUR CITY

Sunday night, about 7 o'clock, the worst tornado ever to hit this county seat city of Baldwin County brought devastation to the extent of about five million dollars in its swath across town from West to East.

Local residents cannot remember Bay Minette ever having another severe storm.

To those residents and others who lost personal property, we extend our sympathy. We also extend our thanks to God that no one was seriously hurt.

We have often heard that if you want to appreciate Bay Minette, have trouble and see how your neighbors flock to your aid. This was proven again many, many times while people were digging out from the damage of the storm. Our neighboring cities were great in sending help of all kinds. To them, we are also grateful.

The tornado was bad. Bay Minette will overcome it. Citizens of this good community will have something to talk about for the next several generations as we look back to the terrible tornado of 1968.

MUMBLINGS IV

This has been a great Presidential race . . . it was great for America and especially great for Alabama . . . we are writing this Monday night and for all practical purposes, the campaign is at end, but the results are unknown . . . we do know this, that George Wallace has served his country well . . . too, he has been worth untold millions of dollars in favorable publicity to Alabama . . . only three or four years ago, one was hesitant to drive up North or out West with an Alabama tag on his automobile for fear of being insulted or physically harmed . . . this is no longer true, people are delighted to see you.

Many Alabamians have spent much time, money, thoughts and energy helping George in this great campaign . . . Baldwin Countians, as previously mentioned, have contributed as much as any other county in Alabama, and more than any other according to population, no doubt . . . this writer has spent much time during the last three months campaigning throughout the United States . . . although this was a sacrifice in some ways, it was a great experience in many others . . . we are glad we had the opportunity of serving him and his cause . . . we did it for several reasons, not the least of which was the fact we strongly felt that George Wallace and his opinions deserved a forum in this country . . . too, we knew the campaign was not only good for America, but good for Alabama.

For the last five weeks, we were in California serving as national campaign chairman for that State . . . it was one of the most divided states because of friction, lawsuits and other things in the Wallace camp . . . campaigning in California, with its 20 million people, is like being in charge of five or six Southeastern states . . . we met many wonderful people, made speeches and learned a lot about what makes politics in this country move . . . we had 108 campaign headquarters, almost 10,000 workers, who were able to distribute literature into over three million homes before election day . . . with money to buy the necessary mass media advertising in radio, television and newspapers, the vote in California would have been better.

Sheriff Taylor Wilkins did a good job getting the divided factions in San Diego working together . . . Matt Metcalfe of Spanish Fort spent the last two weeks with us in California and was successful in raising considerable money.

Judge Telfair J. Mashburn spent over three weeks in Orange County, with a population of two million people . . . when he arrived there, the county was divided and had no organization to mention . . . the organization there was fighting among themselves and not getting any results . . . Judge Mashburn pitched in and worked 16 hours a day and by election day had the county well organized with literally thousands of people working for George Wallace . . . at this writing, we suspect it will be one of the strongest counties in California for the Wallace-LeMay ticket . . . last Saturday the campaign had a 150-car Wallace caravan going over that huge county . . . several incidents occurred, not the least of which was the fact that Judge Mashburn got smashed in the back of the head with a raw egg . . . he was in an open automobile and they went through the wrong section of town where hippies and other beatnicks were too prevalent . . . he arranged for a dinner and rally for General LeMay Monday night of this week . . . he was one of the last Alabamians to leave California, catching a plane early Tuesday morning for home to vote.

Shades of the past: early part of last week, we spent our time visiting headquarters in the San Francisco Bay area . . . on arriving back in our Los Angeles headquarters, we were notified that we were to go to Portland, Oregon, the same night to appear on a 12-hour radio marathon the following day . . . we spoke on the Portland radio station for 12 hours, from 11 o'clock in the morning until 11 o'clock that night . . . it was a talkathon affair in which we answered questions called in by the radio audience . . . several kooks called in questions and made ugly statements, but before the day was over the six telephones were all ringing in favor of George Wallace and complimenting us for coming to Oregon and letting them know more about this man from Alabama . . . 12 hours is a long time, as we knew from previous experience, to be on a question and answer program continuously.

Saturday night we had another interesting experience by appearing on a television program "How do you vote?" . . . it was on Channel 5 in Hollywood, a station owned by Gene Autry . . . 60 girls were at telephones and people were to call in their preferences for the presidency . . . from the opening Wallace was getting about 20 percent of the votes . . . Clint Walker, television star who you will remember as Cheyenne, spoke for Richard Nixon . . . we talked to him and he said Wallace was a good man, his only interest was America, but he certainly did not want Humphrey . . . following his was Gene Barry (Bat Masterson) who spoke for Mr. Humphrey . . . we then spoke for George Wallace . . . we were pleased that after this his total jumped to 24% and ended at about this figure . . . also speaking for Republicans was Maureen Reagan, daughter of Governor Ronald Reagan . . . we told her that she was very unfair competition . . . she is a beautiful young lady and gracious.

We returned home Sunday night just after the tornado hit Bay Minette. We voted Tuesday and are proud of the way we voted . . . hope you are. See you again soon, we hope.

January 2, 1969

Bay Minette's Arthur W. Clements dies

Arthur Clements was a prizefighter, songwriter, politician, talker, critic, and businessman. To put it plainly, he was quite a character. Unfortunately, he died last week.

Arthur also was a humorist. He ran for political office many times and even though never getting many votes, he could always joke about it. One time he ran for county office and got less than 100 votes. Later he ran for the same office and got twice as many. He jokingly stated that if he doubled every time he wouldn't have to run many more times before being elected.

His last unsuccessful race was his recent campaign for mayor of Bay Minette. Percentage wise, he did better than ever, but he still lost. About two weeks ago he came to tell us that he would never again seek political office. We sort of wondered if he really meant it. Obviously he did.

Recently we were in Baton Rouge and a taxi driver heard us say we were from Bay Minette and inquired if we knew "Fatty" Clements, who used to be a boxer. We couldn't think of such a person but finally decided he must mean Arthur. He did. On our return home, we asked Arthur about the "Fatty" title. He told us about his boxing career and the fact he used to be considerably heavier around the middle.

Arthur was a friend of Louisiana's Jimmie Davis, a great singer and songwriter. Governor Davis told us several times he wanted to take one of Arthur's songs and make it into a big hit. He thought he could do it as Arthur had some good ideas about words and music.

Arthur liked to do nothing better than talk. He was always anxious to "blow the dust out of a microphone," as he put it. He always meant what he said and said what he meant. You never wondered about how he stood on an issue.

Arthur Clements had many good qualities. He visited us often and we enjoyed his remarks and thoughts on things.

CLEAN UP, BAY MINETTE

If there were just one New Year's resolution for the people of Bay Minette to make, it would be for us to make this the cleanest city humanly possible.

Many people ride through town and compliment it for being a clean little city. Comparatively, it may be, but we still have a way to go.

If you want to realize how many things need cleaning up here, just ride a person around you are trying to sell on moving his family or a plant here.

Truly, we have many things to offer people who want to make this their home. But we can make it a better place. Cleaning up more is one of them.

OUT OF THIS WORLD TO THE MOON

Apollo 8 and its three interplanetary pioneers blazed back to earth in glory last Friday to become the first human beings to literally "be out of this world" as they circled the moon 10 times. They traveled 500,000 miles in their success in unlocking man's door to the universe.

The commander of the team, Frank Borman, said the moon "is not made of green cheese at all" but it's "made out of American cheese."

This is literally true because the United States has now surpassed Russia in her efforts in space. This country has often been criticized because some thought Russia was ahead of us in space exploration. The success of Apollo 8 proved otherwise.

There are so many fantastic things about the successful trip, it is impossible to contemplate or imagine all of them. For one thing, think of seeing a television program and hearing live voices over 200,000 miles away. It is fantastic.

This country has poured billions of dollars in our space efforts. Success of Apollo 8 makes the tax sting seem more tolerable. Now man will never be content until he knows all there is to know about the universe.

MUMBLINGS—LOOKING AHEAD

A lot can be said for 1968, but much can be said in its disfavor too . . . we think 1969 can be better . . . 1968 has been a year of protests by many people in this country as well as the rest of the world . . . we hope 1969 will be a year of obedience, patriotism and respect for authority . . . we have had enough of this "aginner" business to do everyone a lifetime.

It may be true that New Year's resolutions are made to be broken . . . but why not make several good ones and if you break a few of them, you still have some left to the good . . . our trouble is we can think of too many good ones we should make . . . think we'll just narrow it down to two or three and try to keep them all.

The Apollo 8 story in which the astronauts went over 500,000 miles to circle the moon 10 times is easily the greatest story of 1968 . . . it is absolutely incredible . . . other important stories were freeing of the 82 Pueblo crewmen who were illegally captured and imprisoned by the North Koreans, the Vietnam war and the presidential campaign, including Wallace's great third party movement . . . of course, there were many other important events and happenings during the year, but the moon trip will be recorded in history books forever and ever . . . some of the other stories may be also, but they will only take up a bit of space.

The astronauts did such a perfect job and made everything seem so easy, that next time their wives will probably want to go to the moon with them. Lots of people complain about the high cost of living, but most of us think it is worth the price. Plenty of sleep helps prevent old age, especially while driving. If you can think of anything to say that is better than being quiet, speak up. Watch out folks, the Alabama Legislature will be in session for several months this year.

Don't be mad at us Alabama fans, we can't help it now because we graduated with a Bachelor of Journalism degree at the University of Missouri . . . how did we know back then that they were going to beat the stuffings out of us in the Gator Bowl in 1968 . . . seriously, while at Missouri, we pulled hard for the Tiger football team to win, but they never did win any important games . . . then last Saturday in Jacksonville, Fla., we were pulling for them to lose and they won like nobody's business . . . it rained right up to game time, then the sun came out and it was beautiful . . . of course everybody gave credit to the Bear for stopping the rain . . . but even he couldn't do anything with the Missouri cyclone. Happy New Year! . . . See you again soon, we hope.

January 30, 1969

THE WILKINS BROTHERS

Back in 1936 when this writer first came to Baldwin County, the sheriff was M.H. (Red) Wilkins . . . then a sheriff could not succeed himself so as his term expired, he ran for the office of tax collector . . . many thought he was going up against impossible odds, however, he won and continued to serve in this position until he died a few years ago . . . Mr. Wilkins was one of the smoothest and most popular public officials this county ever produced . . . he was humble and accommodating . . . he was a powerful ally . . . at the age of 23, we ran for mayor and he was one of our most effective supporters . . . we believe every time we ever ran for office he helped us, a fact we have always appreciated.

Many of Mr. Wilkins' attributes rubbed off on his two sons, Taylor and Marion . . . they both observed him, learned from him and as time went on added intelligence and techniques of their own . . . the older of the two, Taylor, (by some four or five years) is the better known in Baldwin County.

Taylor Wilkins has served as Baldwin County Sheriff longer than any other person in history . . . and most think he has done a good job . . . we like to think we helped start him on his political way . . . it was during the early part of World War II and the then County Agent, E.E. Hale, was looking for a farm labor recruiter . . . he came to *The Times* office and asked for suggestions . . . without hesitation, we mentioned young Taylor Wilkins . . . after a little persuasion, this was agreed to and Taylor became active all over the county, getting to know nearly all of the farmers and many other people . . . he then volunteered for service and served several months before being discharged with frost bitten feet . . . after the war, he decided to run for sheriff and although he had a tough tussle, he was elected and has been winning since.

In fact, the first three times Taylor ran for sheriff, he had narrow squeaks . . . but as time went on, he grew with the job and became more and more popular . . . the last time he had opposition, he ran away with the votes . . . he didn't even have an opponent in 1966 and is now considered invincible in the position.

Taylor is one of the best known sheriffs in Alabama and probably is the best known rural county sheriff . . . he has served as president of the Alabama Sheriff's Association for four or five terms and is well respected among his fellow law officers everywhere . . . He is quiet, effective, and hard working . . . he seldom, if ever, gets entirely away from his job ... the sheriff's phone extends to his home and he is actually on duty 24 hours a day . . . if there is a harder job in Baldwin County than that of being sheriff of this big, diversified, geographical subdivision, we don't know what it is.

Taylor is a typical politician in that he loves his friends . . . fortunately, his friends by far exceed those on the other side of the fence . . . as President of the Alabama Sheriff's Association, he was largely instrumental in establishing the Boys Ranch near Selma . . . this ranch is a place for underprivileged boys, who are given every opportunity to grow up into fine young men.

During the recent presidential campaign, Taylor came out to California and assisted in San Diego, an area of some two million votes . . . it was completely disorganized and disgruntled so far as the Wallace campaign was concerned . . . Taylor spent several days there and accomplished much in welding the organization into an effective unit.

It might be said that Marion is a college educated copy of his father and brother . . . He finished high school here and later graduated from Auburn with a degree in civil engineering . . . for the past several years he has been county engineer for Conecuh County . . . he was effective and popular in that county and was considered one of the finest county engineers in Alabama . . . in fact, his reputation was such that he was given serious consideration for the post of State Highway Director by Governor Albert Brewer . . . however, another Evergreen citizen, Robert Kendall, was made Highway Director . . . Kendall insisted that he would not accept the job unless Marion became the assistant highway director . . . he accepted the post and will do an effective job for all Alabama citizens.

Marion is quiet, dignified and has a pleasant personality . . . he is smart and has the respect of those people who work with him . . . we have already

heard many compliments about him in his new position in Montgomery
. . . many people will remember that he married Mildred Mayo, one of the
two beautiful daughters of Mrs. Sally Mayo of Bay Minette.

Marion is the second Baldwin Countian to serve as assistant highway
director . . . the first was E.N. Rodgers, who at the time of his selection
by Governor Chauncey Sparks, was county engineer for Baldwin . . . he
later served as Highway Director under Governor Sparks and the second
time under Governor Wallace . . . we have little doubt but Marion also will
some day serve as State Highway Director, if he chooses so to do . . . he has
been offered many other positions and just before accepting the job with
the state, was urged to accept a job in Montgomery that would have paid
more money than he is now making . . . but Marion likes highway work
as this is his life.

So it goes with Baldwin's Wilkins brothers . . . like their father before
them, each has two sons and we predict they, too, will make records for
themselves . . . but there'll be plenty of time later to talk about that. See
you again soon, we hope.

February 13, 1969

FRED C. GRIFFIN OF LOXLEY
OUTSTANDING CITIZEN

Few people succeed in life like Fred C. Griffin, Sr., of Loxley did. He
was successful in many ways.

He lived his biblical three score and ten years fully, in every respect. His
death Friday, after a long illness, ended the career of one of Baldwin's most
outstanding citizens.

There are many ways of judging a man's success in life. Fred measured up in most of them. He was successful financially. He started from scratch and by intelligent, hard work all of his life, accumulated much. He was recognized far and wide as a good, honest businessman. However, business achievements didn't just fall in his lap. He worked hard at it. His usual working day began long before sunup and he stayed late.

He was also good at making friends. He liked people and they responded by liking him. Full evidence of this was the hundreds who attended his funeral Sunday.

He loved his country, but was critical of what he considered unbusiness-like and un-American aspects of the way the federal government is run. He took an active interest in politics and usually was willing to speak his opinion on civic and political matters. He was liberal in his giving for the causes for which he believed. He contributed much to the success and growth of his community, county, and state.

Fred Griffin was a man among men. He was a fighter for what he believed. He was a good man to know and have as a friend. We know, first hand!

MUMBLINGS . . . W.M. (MACK) HODGSON

We always like to see a person get his just desserts . . . this is particu-larly true when the reward is an honor deserved . . . last Wednesday night at the stupendous Regency Hyatt House Hotel in Atlanta, we saw justice in spades.

It was at the 23rd annual convention of the National Association of Soil and Water Conservation Districts, commonly called NACD . . . the recipient of the national award was W.M. (Mack) Hodgson, Sr., farmer, businessman, civic and church leader, and an all-round good citizen of Bay Minette . . . the award, before 2,000 people, was made because of outstanding service to soil conservation and the Soil Conservation Districts for a number of years . . . he was one of the founders of the NACD and was one of three people honored at the banquet Wednesday night . . . the other two were from Michigan and Minnesota.

Not many here are acquainted with Mack Hodgson's service to soil con-servation, locally and throughout the United States . . . his service has been extensive . . . it has lasted over a period of 30 years, during which time he has been national director of the Association for two years, state president of the Association of Soil Conservation Districts for two years, on the state committee for 16 years, and has been on the local Soil Conservation District Committee for 25 years.

He received two beautiful plaques . . . Gov. Albert Brewer also sent a telegram which was read to the audience . . . one plaque stated, in part:

"For his enduring belief in Soil and Water Conservation Districts as effective instruments of farmers, ranchers and other landowners in meeting their responsibilities as citizens of a democracy and as stewards of the American supply of soil and water resources . . ."

Few people ever receive a national award of any kind . . . this was a signal honor well deserved and we think it couldn't have been given to a finer person . . . following the presentation by the national president of NACD, Mr. Hodgson made a brief statement, which turned out to be the best speech of the night.

Several people were there from Baldwin including his two sons, Mack, Jr., and Bob, Mac Aylin (Mr. Aylin got his car stolen out of the parking lot, but recovered it due to the alert Highway Patrolmen the next day) and this writer . . . we stayed in the Regency Hotel which is one of the wonders of the world . . . if you ever go to Atlanta, go in the lobby and gawk at it like we did . . . there is an article about it in the current issue of the *National Geographic*, which is worth reading. See you again soon, we hope.

February 20, 1969

The G. W. Robertson family

Alabama Cattleman's Association, the nation's largest state Cattleman's Association, held its 26th annual meeting in Montgomery yesterday . . .

among other things, the news report of the meeting said "Officers of the 10,500-member cattleman's association are: president, G.W. (Billy) Robertson, Gallion, Alabama" . . . of course we knew this fact but it started us thinking.

Billy Robertson is a junior . . . the senior G.W. "Billy" Robertson was Tax Assessor and Probate Judge of Baldwin for a number of years and was one of the most able and popular political leaders this county ever produced . . . it was about 25 years ago, in 1944 or '45 as we recall, that he died, as a comparatively young man . . . we were in the Army Air Corps at the time, stationed in Pampa, Texas . . . his death saddened and changed our life.

Judge Robertson had been our friend and advisor almost from the first day we arrived here, August 15, 1936 . . . he was one of the first people we met as he was in the post office talking to R.B. Vail the first time we ever saw Bay Minette . . . we talked to Mr. Vail about purchasing *The Baldwin Times* . . . the next time we met Judge Robertson was a short time later in New Orleans with Mr. Vail where we had gone to buy a Linotype machine.

Although he had two sons of his own, he seemed to have time for us and almost everyone else who cared to seek his advice and friendship . . . Judge "Billy" had made up his mind and had talked us into the idea of running for Congress upon returning from the wars . . . with his death, we lost interest or at least lost nerve, without his assistance . . . no one will ever know, but in all probability, we could have won, particularly with his help, as practically all war veterans who ran for office in 1946 were elected . . . this was one of the reasons "Big Jim" Folsom went in as Governor . . . old heads were turned out and new ones were put in . . . it was the mood of the election.

We started out to talk about the "Billy" Robertson family . . . not long after the war, Billy, Jr., and his younger brother, R.J. (Jack), took over their father's cattle and farming business . . . they had extensive holdings in Hale County and Billy, Jr., moved up there . . . he has been a successful cattleman, and was named "Alabama Cattleman of the Year" recently . . . the fact that he is well liked and respected indicates he is a "chip off the old block," having that friendly air and personality about him that made his father such a popular person . . . as you know, it is quite an honor to be president of the

Alabama Cattleman's Association.

Jack was also successful . . . he was elected to the Baldwin County Commission and became chairman in his early thirties . . . he served two terms and then decided to give his full time to his farm operations . . . several months ago he died, also at a young age.

Other members of the family are girls, all living . . . Hazel married Ed Pepperman and they live in Montgomery . . . Winifred married Charles Byrne of Bay Minette and they live in Foley . . . the youngest, Jean, married W.M. Hodgson, Jr., president of Standard Furniture Manufacturing Company, and they live here.

One thing about getting old is you remember many interesting things, some pleasant, some not . . . one reason our life has been so interesting is because we have had the privilege of knowing so many fine individuals and families . . . the "Billy" Robertson family of Baldwin County being one of them.

THE VALUE OF OUR FORESTS IS INCREASING

A special section in *The Baldwin Times* this week features the forest industry and its value to Baldwin County, our State and Nation.

The section tells a fascinating story in pictures, stories and advertising about the industry which is a major part of the economy of Southwest Alabama and of Baldwin County.

District Forester Knox Davis tells us that the industry represents or generates over $30 million of business in Baldwin County, over $300 million in the five-county District Eight, and some $750 million in the state as a whole.

The forest industry in Alabama has grown until it is now second only to steel in the economy of the State.

It is with pride that we point out that 80 percent of the total forest land in the State is in District Eight which includes Baldwin, Mobile, Clarke, Washington, and Choctaw counties. In District Eight, and the whole state for that matter, Baldwin has the largest forest acreage of any county.

From all appearances, forestry will continue to grow and will become the leading industry in Alabama. We are delighted Baldwin County will be right in the middle of this prosperity from wood.

We further note, from stories in the section on forestry, that some major breakthroughs are occurring in the forestry industry with respect to developing superior pine trees which will mature in half the present growing cycle. This, combined with the mechanization of harvesting operations, means a great future for forestry, and in turn for Baldwin County. See you again soon, we hope.

April 17, 1969

ANNE D. GILMER, A GRAND LADY

Bay Minette was saddened last week at the death of Mrs. Anne D. Gilmer. For years she had been one of the city's outstanding citizens. She was 90.

Mrs. Gilmer had many accomplishments, but one of the greatest services she rendered Bay Minette was the founding of the Hampton D. Ewing Library. She took motherly pride and interest in the local library. She was responsible for the contribution of the land, on which the library was built by the Bay Minette Land Company.

Mrs. Gilmer moved to Bay Minette with her husband, T.W. Gilmer, in 1908 when he became manager of the Bay Minette Land Company. Upon his death some 30 odd years ago, Mrs. Gilmer assumed the responsibility and kept it until her death. She was active until a few months ago.

Anne D. Gilmer was well educated and had a lot of common sense. She was a wonderful conversationalist and we always enjoyed talking and listening to her.

She was a practical person, too. Only a few years ago she fell and broke her hip. Realizing her age, she knew the doctor would be discouraged about her hip healing. So she did what any lady is privileged to do, reduced her age. Her hip healed.

In honor of this great lady, and to serve this good community and area, *The Times* suggests it is time for Bay Minette to build a new and bigger library. Naturally, it should be called the Anne D. Gilmer Library.

MUMBLINGS, PERSONAL IF YOU PLEASE

Family reunions are interesting events . . . it is always good to see relatives on such occasions, realizing that if you saw them too often, they might not like you too well . . . last Sunday we traveled 240 miles to Vernon, Lamar County, in the Northwestern section of the State, to attend the biggest Faulkner reunion we recall . . . it was a special occasion.

In the early part of last century, Isaac Dickerson Faulkner came to Alabama from Virginia . . . he had four sons . . . three went to Arkansas and one, Burrell Lanier Faulkner, stayed in Alabama and became the first Probate Judge of Lamar County . . . Judge Burrell Faulkner was born in 1827 and died 70 years later in 1897 . . . he was our great grandfather and must have been quite a character . . . at least he was a successful politician and family man.

It was he who started leaving the "U" out of Faulkner, stating that it did not change the pronunciation and saved one letter which was important as he had to write it many times as probate judge . . . now, practically all Lamar County Falkners spell it without the "U" . . . our mother started putting it back and we find the name is more easily pronounced with it in . . . however, our mother's and father's tombstones have it spelled Falkner.

Great Grandpa Falkner had ten children, the oldest of which was Wiley Polk, who was our grandfather . . . he married Alabama Jane Hayes and they had six children . . . three boys and three girls . . . the oldest son was Henry L., our father . . . he was the first to die, having been fatally burned in 1928, in a gasoline lamp explosion . . . three of Grandpa's children are still living.

Of Judge Falkner's ten children, only one is still living, Uncle Burrell Stanton . . . and he was the reason we had a special reunion Sunday . . . we were all celebrating his 100th birthday . . . he was present and quite obviously enjoying himself in front of several hundred relatives and visitors . . .

Senator James B. Allen eulogized his life and presented him with a personal letter from President Nixon.

At one time Uncle Burrell taught school, but said he had to quit because he couldn't make a living, and started farming . . . he has spent his entire life near where he was born, on Yellow Creek in Lamar County . . . he is amazingly spry and in good health for his age, having never been to the hospital but once in his life and that for only a short period . . . he has his original teeth.

Upon being presented, he was asked if he wanted to say something . . . he came to the microphone and in a clear, distinct voice stated, "I have never made but one public speech in my life . . . it was under a big oak tree on the side of a hill. That tree is now dead and I do not want to destroy any more timber." . . . he then sat down and said nothing more . . . he did say privately that he expected to be present next year at the family reunion . . . someone asked him why he was so sure he would be present since he was so old . . . he said, "I have checked the vital statistics and found that very few people die between the ages 100 and 101." . . . he always had a keen sense of humor and apparently has always enjoyed life . . . he stated his secret to longevity is the fact that he never smoked, never chewed, worked hard, ran around after the prettiest girls he could find and never drank much.

Papa's brother, Rufus Edward Falkner, is still living and we also use his birthday every year as an excuse for the Polk Falkner family to get together . . . Uncle Ed is 83 and was able to take in the entire family reunion Sunday . . . of the Polk Falkner family, there are only three men with the Falkner name in the third generation . . . one has never married and perhaps won't and so it was left up to our brother and ourselves to carry on the family name . . . our brother had two daughters and thus left it up to us . . . we have two sons and they apparently are doing their part to carry on the family name . . . between them, they have five children and between them they are going to have three, and perhaps four, more next month . . . apparently there will continue to be Faulkner reunions for years to come . . . we hope all of them will be present at our 100th birthday. See you again soon, we hope.

April 24, 1969

BAY MINETTE'S JOHN A. GARRETT
MOVES UP

Of all the good things you can say about Bay Minette's Clarence Garrett, not the least is the fact that he and his wife raised a fine family of several boys and girls.

Last week one of his sons was named by Republican President Richard Nixon to take over the reins of the Alabama office of the Farmers Home Administration. He is John A. Garrett, who has lived in Snowdoun community near Montgomery for a number of years.

John A. Garrett is a frank and enthusiastic person. He has accumulated a wonderful record in many fields of endeavor. As he stated, he "put on shoes" to go to Auburn University where he graduated as a civil engineer. He has successfully operated a 577-acre livestock farm and at the same time, has taken an active part in civic and governmental affairs.

John visits Bay Minette and Baldwin County often and takes pride in his hometown and county. And his home people take pride in him.

We are delighted that he has received the appointment and because of his native ability, honesty, integrity and educational background, he will do a splendid job in this important position.

LOCAL ANTI-POVERTY PROGRAM PRAISED

Many people, some of whom do not know what is going on, are prone to criticize any program to help the poor. Part of the criticism may be deserved, but much is not.

We were delighted to learn that the Little River Community Action Program, with headquarters at Daphne, has impressed a House Committee staff in Washington as being one of the most successful of its kind in the country.

Recently, Robert E. McCord, Chief Clerk of the Education and Labor

Committee, has suggested to Representative Carl Perkins (D-Ky), Committee chairman, that a weekend field trip to Daphne might be helpful in winning support for Perkins' effort to keep Anti-Poverty programs going.

Chairman Perkins is holding hearings designed to build up his arguments for extending the Office of Economic Opportunity another five years—instead of one year suggested by President Nixon.

To bolster Perkins' case, his staff sent out questionnaires to directors of anti-poverty programs in various parts of the country. The reply from Daphne, according to McCord, was exceptionally impressive.

"Not only were there good answers on the questionnaires," McCord said, "but the Daphne people sent along a number of testimonial letters showing that their program has the endorsement of many leaders in the area. There were letters from several mayors, some members of the Alabama Senate and House of Representatives, quite a few county and local elected officials.

"That kind of backing is rare, particularly in the deep South."

We are confident the Little River Program is not perfect, but we are glad that it is far above average.

THE BEST ARMY EVER

As everyone says, "the azaleas were the most beautiful ever . . . while they lasted." Over the past weekend, it was light sweater weather . . . and before that, it was heavy raincoat weather . . . much of our weather has been beautiful, too . . . whatever type we have, there isn't any local organized effort to do anything about it.

We are apt to get the idea that most of our young people are hippies and such . . . fortunately, this isn't true . . . several months ago while visiting Vietnam, we learned that our boys in the armed services are among the best fighters the world has ever produced . . . confirming this, an old soldier told Alabama's Congressman Bill Nichols, while he was visiting the armed service camps, that "this is the best army, man to man, this country ever had. Don't let anybody tell you otherwise."

Alabama urbanite senators and representatives want more of the tax cut for their own bailiwicks . . . if they have the votes, they'll get them . . . in the past the rural area had the votes and they got most of the pie . . . this is what can be called democracy . . . and another name is power politics . . . whatever you call it, right doesn't always prevail, even in a democracy.

The dastardly act of the North Koreans in shooting down one of our unarmed reconnaissance planes costing 31 American lives, has let President Nixon know what it is like to be president of these United States . . . he has discovered suddenly that it is harder to be president than it is to criticize a president, as he was so good at doing when LBJ was president . . . Nixon was critical when LBJ didn't retaliate against "the fourth rate nation" when they captured one of our spy ships . . . now Nixon isn't saying much and is doing less, which under the circumstances may be the best thing to do . . . however, if we are going to be a world power, we are going to have to quit letting everybody kick us around . . . See you again soon, we hope.

July 3, 1969

Mumblings about Norman Van Wezel, M.D.

"Doctors are not supposed to get sick—but I did!" This is what Dr. Norman Van Wezel, Foley doctor, wrote hundreds of his patients last week . . . he further stated, "I have now developed a heart condition, which the doctors feel will prohibit my return to the practice of medicine."

Naturally, this was a big shock to Dr. Van Wezel, as well as his many patients and friends . . . after 34 years of practice, it must be difficult for a doctor to give up his personal relationships with his patients . . . this is a blow to the medical profession in Baldwin County.

Dr. Van Wezel moved to Foley from Montgomery several years ago because he wanted to take life a little easier . . . he never expected his practice to reach the levels it did . . . no other doctor in this county had patients from a wider section of the United States than did he . . . we were in his waiting room one day when a lady, also waiting, had come down from Indiana to see him.

Dr. Van Wezel is a well-known and respected physician for many reasons . . . first of all, he is the acme of efficiency and dedication . . . he had a loyal, efficient group of nurses and other people helping him serve many patients each day from a wide area of this country . . . he is not only well-known for his ability as a physician, but has an humble, quiet type personality that is fetching . . . his modern, up-to-date clinic on the Foley-Magnolia Springs highway was a place of pleasant, courteous efficiency.

We first went to visit him on a professional call about 1951, with severe hay fever problems . . . after giving thorough tests, he has controlled our hay fever ever since . . . he is also a qualified FAA doctor . . . because of this, we went to him annually for a physical examination which is necessary to fly an airplane and get a pilot's license.

Although always very busy, he had time to chat with us a few minutes on each visit . . . he gave us advice on many subjects, which was always sound . . . he always was complimentary and, as we thought, flattering . . . now, we, like hundreds of other patients, will have to find a new doctor in the categories he served . . . unfortunately, there are no other doctors in Baldwin who do exactly the same things Dr. Van Wezel did.

Dr. Van Wezel was an active Rotarian and has traveled throughout the world . . . he has a lovely family with two daughters . . . naturally, we join thousands of other people in regretting the fact that he is giving up his very fine medical practice . . . but more important, we hope his heart condition is not too serious and that he will be around a long, long time . . . good luck, Dr. Van Wezel, you have served well!

HOW HIGH SHOULD A BRIDGE BE?

The bureaucrats in Washington are giving this area a hard time.

After considerable study and many hearings, including one here in Bay Minette, a decision was made by local interests and the State Highway Department that the height of the bridge across the Mobile River on I-65 should be 125 feet above the river. It was also agreed to have about 65 feet across Middle and Tensaw Rivers. Several months ago all felt confidently that Washington would approve the high level bridges.

But the Bureau of Public Roads says no. In fact, they are planning a bridge of 52 feet in height above the Mobile River which is less than half the height sought by the industrial development people and others in this area.

It would be absolutely ridiculous to build a bridge only 52 feet high on the Mobile River. This would simply mean that ocean going vessels could never go up the river any farther than the bridge.

Eventually, the Tombigbee-Tennessee River canal will be dug, and then big vessels can go much farther up the river than is now possible. Obviously, a low level bridge would stymie the industrial development along the river.

Fortunately, the United States Coast Guard has the final authority on such matters. We predict the Coast Guard will side with the Alabama State Highway Department, the local chambers of commerce and others against the federal bureaucrats in Washington. We hope so. See you again soon, we hope.

July 10, 1969

Mumblings about G. Mac Humphries

Occasionally something happens that is just exactly right . . . such an event was last Tuesday when the Baldwin County Commission and other friends gave G. Mac Humphries a surprise reception and honor for 41 years of service to Baldwin County.

Mac Humphries started off working in the county courthouse during the time when his father was Probate Judge . . . during this time, he went to Auburn University and had other interesting experiences . . . as a young man, Mac was a good singer, musician and Bo Brummel, according to reports . . . he sang with the famous Jan Garber orchestra . . . he also served with the state as an auditor . . . he left the auditing business about 1937 and returned to Baldwin County as clerk of the County Commission . . . later, he became county treasurer and has held both of these positions for many years.

Amazingly, when Mac was employed by the County Commission, there was some criticism, because they gave him a starting salary of some $200 a month . . . there were some people in the county who thought this was a rather exorbitant salary . . .if it was, Mac Humphries has made his salary many, many times over in his efficiency and frugality with county funds.

Mac Humphries is truly "Mr. County Government" in Baldwin . . . not merely because of his seniority at the courthouse, but because of his efficiency, ability and astute knowledge of county government . . . he dearly loves Baldwin County and her governmental affairs . . . he has devoted the best years of his life to it, quite successfully . . . he has served through a score or so of county commissioners and has always been loyal to each, because, as he says, they are his bosses.

He has kept a firm hold on the finances of the county for all of these years and as a result Baldwin is probably in the best financial condition of any county in Alabama . . . the county is not only debt free, but has more paved roads than any other county in the state . . . this was a long way from being the case when he became clerk in 1937 . . . in fact, the county owed over $500,000 at that time.

In 1951, Mac made a suggestion to the then senator and representative in the state legislature concerning the transfer of Baldwin County roads over to the state for maintenance and building . . . his one suggestion has meant some $3 million in additional revenue to Baldwin without costing our citizens one extra cent in taxes.

Mac Humphries is many things good . . . he perhaps typifies the gracious southern gentleman better than any other person we know . . . he is always the gentleman and is considerate of other people, their opinions and all . . . this is not to say he does not have strong convictions because he certainly does . . . perhaps no one knows it better than this writer . . . he thinks we think he is a mite conservative . . . we think he thinks we are a mite the other way . . . actually we agree most of the time on things economic, social and political . . . he is a genuine conservative, but is for progress, especially if it is in Baldwin County and if it doesn't take much money out of the county treasury.

It is always said that no man is indispensable . . . if any man is indispensable in our county government, it is Mac Humphries . . . it will be a great loss when he has to end his years of competent service as treasurer and clerk . . . our four present County Commissioners fully agree and get nervous indigestion when even thinking that they may have to replace him some day . . . this has been the thought of every county commissioner who has served with him . . . they think this way because they know his value.

FRED NALL BUYS JACKSON NEWSPAPER

Another who has passed this way at *The Baldwin Times* is taking over as publisher of a weekly newspaper. He is Fred Nall.

Fred has bought the *South Alabamian* of Jackson from Bill Stewart of *The Monroe Journal.* He has been Bill's right hand for nine or ten years.

Fred worked at *The Times* for many months following the war as shop foreman and in various other capacities. He left here to go to Jackson where he edited the paper for a time and then went to Monroeville. Now, he is returning to Jackson.

Fred is one of the few men left in this country who can do well anything around a weekly newspaper. He is a fine printer, pressman, editor, writer, salesman, and what have you.

His many friends here wish Fred and Thelma Nall the greatest of success in their new venture. They richly deserve it. See you again soon, we hope.

July 31, 1969

BALDWIN'S FRANK F. EARLE
IMPORTANT LEADER

Few, if any, people ever headed so many organizations and held the positions of leadership as did the late Frank F. Earle of Blacksher.

For a period covering more than a half century, Mr. Earle devoted long hours in helping numerous and varied organizations in Baldwin County and Alabama by assuming personal interest and direct leadership in them. In fact, he participated in so many activities of a public nature, it would be difficult to identify him exclusively with any particular one.

Unfortunately, this man of action died last week.

Although he was by profession a farmer and timberman, he devoted most of his time to the general welfare of the county. He loved Baldwin County, her traditions and history and wherever he went he delighted in telling others about her greatness.

Whichever civic, religious or educational activity Mr. Earle participated in, he was immediately put into a position of leadership. For years he was director of the Alabama Farm Bureau. Also on a statewide basis, he was president of the Alabama Farmers Marketing and Exchange from 1932 until 1938. He also served for years as a member of the Board of Trustees of Birmingham Southern College.

In the county, he served for 27 years as president of the Baldwin County Farm Bureau. He served for 40 years as a member of the Baldwin County Board of Education and half of that time as its president. He was also president of Bay Minette Production Credit Association. He headed the Baldwin County Electric Membership Co-op from its beginning until resigning in 1968.

Locally, Mr. Earle helped organize the First National Bank and served as its president from 1954 until 1964. Then, he served as chairman of the board until 1968.

Frank Earle wore out many automobiles traveling from Blacksher to the rest of the county to do whatever he could to be of assistance to his fellow-man. Many wondered why he did not move to Bay Minette so he would be closer to the people he served. However, he loved the soil on which he lived and never would have consented living anywhere else.

Always polite and a southern gentleman, he was pleasant to talk and listen to.

He delighted in discussing the history of the county, particularly the area in which he lived, and could do so at length and in detail. His name will long be remembered as an important leader of this area.

GOOD NEWS FROM KAISER

The best news heard in a long time around here was received from Kaiser Aluminum and Chemical Corporation this week to the effect they are going to double the capacity of their local plant.

Perhaps it's more exciting to announce a new industry. However, the most encouraging news that can be had is expansion of our existing industries. This means another local success story.

Bay Minette has been fortunate over the years in acquiring excellent industries. One of the finest is Kaiser. They are good citizens from every standpoint and mean much to the economic stability and growth of the Bay Minette area.

Thanks, people of Kaiser Aluminum for having continued faith and confidence in us. We hope you will continue to expand and meet with ever-increasing success.

Few companies in the nation are as aggressive and growth minded as Kaiser. It is a real pleasure and honor to have them in Bay Minette and we join with all our citizens in expressing delight and thanks over the fact they are expanding again here.

ASTRONAUTS LAND ON THE MOON

Rest assured the rain will stop some day . . . at least, it always has. It is natural that many people in this country and throughout the world do not believe the astronauts really landed and walked on the moon . . . we find it hard to believe because we cannot fathom how it was possible to do such a thing . . . people are always suspicious of those things they do not understand . . . in such instances, faith must take the place of wisdom and understanding.

O' joy, football season will soon be here. The frowns you see on children's faces these days are caused by their realization school will soon start. Many farmers in this area have just about had it . . . too dry, too wet, too much disease, low prices, small demand, no labor . . . you name it and they've had it.

Definitions: Diamond—stepping stone to success for a woman; Detour—the roughest distance between two points; Drunk—when a person feels sophisticated and can't pronounce it; Egotist—a man who tells you those things about himself which you intended to tell him about yourself. See you again soon, we hope.

September 25, 1969

G. Mac Humphries leaves great void

In July, G. Mac Humphries was given a surprise reception in honor for his 41 years of service to Baldwin County. Following this, an article was written in *The Times* paying tribute to his ability and his many years of fine service.

The article deplored the time when he would have to be replaced as county treasurer and clerk of the Baldwin County Commission. Unfortunately, that time is now. Mac Humphries died last week and left a great void in the hearts of many people as well as in the operations of our county government.

As stated, "Mac Humphries is truly 'Mr. County Government' in Baldwin." He had worked in the county courthouse for over 40 years. But he was "Mr. County Government" not merely because of his seniority at the courthouse, but because of his efficiency, ability and astute knowledge of county government.

We are happy that he was honored by his associates in July. It is better to give flowers to the living, particularly those who deserve it like Mac Humphries did.

It is in order to repeat some of the things already said: "Mac Humphries is many things good . . . he perhaps typifies the gracious southern gentleman better than any other person we know . . . he is always the gentleman and is considerate of other people, their opinions and all . . . this is not to say he does not have strong convictions because he certainly does . . . he is a genuine conservative, but is for progress, especially if it is in Baldwin County and if it doesn't take much money out of the county treasury.

"It is always said that no man is indispensable . . . if any man is indispensable in our county government, it is Mac Humphries . . . it will be a great loss when he has to end his years of competent service as treasurer and clerk . . ."

Mac Humphries' death is not only a great loss to county government, but a personal loss to his many friends, one of which we were proud to be. As stated, Mac Humphries was many things good.

FOOTBALL AND FALL ARE HERE

We won't say that the Fall of the year is the best season of all, but we will say that football adds much to it.

This week football got off to a real start throughout the nation. In fact, the great American sport is celebrating its 100th anniversary this season.

Nothing could have happened that would have made the beginning of the season more pleasant for most people in Alabama and particularly those of us who love football in Baldwin County. Our county teams won, as well as Auburn and Alabama.

Although Bay Minette, Foley and the University of Alabama won the squeakers, the other teams won easily, particularly Auburn. In fact, Auburn trimmed Wake Forest 57 to 0 and gave indications that they may be another power this year. We hope so.

The overall opening of the season went so great that we didn't cry too much when Joe Namath and his New York Jets got slapped down Sunday by the Denver Broncs. We favor Joe and his Jets, however.

Most anyway you look at it, Fall is a great season. It is so even if October does bring on city, county and state taxpaying time. The whiff you feel in the air brings on dreams of hunting, football, warm fires and many other things pleasant.

Mumblings

through the

Nineteen-Seventies

❧

February 12, 1970

Welcome to Baldwin, Mayor Mims

If, as they say, home is where your hat is, it is many places for Mobile's Public Works Commissioner Lambert C. Mims, because he travels far, making speeches and telling people everywhere about his philosophy of life and the greatness of this area.

A native of Uriah, in Monroe County, Lambert now counts his home, of course, in Mobile. At 35, he was the youngest man ever elected to the Mobile City Commission and at 38 was the youngest man to ever serve as Mayor of the city. In accordance with the Mobile system of rotating the Mayorship, he will again serve as Mayor beginning in June, 1972.

Baldwin County also likes to claim Lambert Mims. He spent many years working in this county and his wife is the former Reecie Phillips of Little River. Percentage wise, he probably knows as many Baldwin Countians as

Mobilians. This gives us a reasonable claim to him.

This outstanding young man of politics, religion and business has many personal attributes. Although it has been our privilege to know him for a number of years, we learn to admire him more and more.

Perhaps his greatest personal attribute is honesty and straight forwardness. He is not one to beat around the bush and, although humble and polite, he does not hesitate to let you know where he stands on a subject. Unlike some politicians, he readily admits he is subject to mistakes, but this by no means proves he is not self-reliant and confident. He works hard and enjoys serving people.

He is the author of a book recently published, *For Christ and Country.* Perhaps these four words explain his main concerns in life.

In his book, Lambert frankly tells of his problems in early life. He relates how he sank to the depths with whiskey and sin but finally overcame them with the help of the Lord. No doubt this experience, his success as a political leader and his speaking ability are the reasons why he is in great demand as a speaker at many important occasions all over the country.

Bay Minette is fortunate in that he will speak here twice this weekend. He will talk to a youth rally at the City Hall on Saturday night and again Sunday morning at the First Baptist Church. Since Baldwin is partly his home, we can say, "Welcome home, Lambert Mims."

We don't profess to know whether this man of courage and ability has further political ambitions. If so, we wish him luck and predict that whatever he tries to achieve his main purpose will be to serve "Christ and Country."

OUR FINE STATE JUNIOR COLLEGE

Last week, we dedicated our wonderful new hospital. About five years ago, we did the same thing for our excellent state junior college. Both are fine institutions, of which everyone can be proud.

This Friday, citizens in this area will again have an opportunity to show how much they appreciate their local junior college. It will be homecoming for the institution and two new buildings will be officially named and dedicated.

Perhaps no other achievement has meant so much to Bay Minette and area as has our college. Under the able leadership of Dr. Lathem N. Sibert, and members of his fine faculty, the school has exceeded all expectations in quality and students served. Although education is its prime function, it does mean much economically to the area.

One way to show your appreciation is go out and participate in the homecoming festivities Friday, beginning at 10 a.m. You'll be glad you did.

WONDERS OF THE UNIVERSE

Don't look now, but Spring will soon be here. An old saying is that problems make opportunities . . . no wonder this world is so full of opportunities.

When a person walks up and tells you how fine you are looking, the first inclination is to be appreciative . . . a little more thought and you can easily wonder if the person is surprised, disappointed or happy.

It's amazing how many things we doesn't understand . . . we don't even understand how the telephone works, much less radio, television, computers, etc. . . . they are bound to be kidding us about someone going to the moon and returning . . . now, astronomers have come up with something even more confusing . . . they have recently discovered new objects in space which they call quasars . . . they say the most remote are 10 billion light years away . . . since light travels at 186,000 miles per second, a light year works out to about six trillion miles . . . you may figure how far these quasars are from the earth, it's much beyond our limited imagination . . . they also claim the objects may be a million times bigger than the sun . . . remember the sun is many times bigger than the earth . . . confused too?

Government licensing of newspaper, radio and television reporters has been suggested by a member of the President's panel on violence, stating it would help weed out "totally inept" individuals . . . many newspapermen claim this would be a threat to freedom of speech . . . we hardly think so but it would be a threat to freeloaders who call themselves reporters . . . doctors and many other professions have to be licensed before they are permitted to practice their skills on people . . . maybe it is not too farfetched to have professional people issue licenses to men and women who want to be reporters . . . after all, we newspapermen think this is an important profession and there is little doubt that we could improve.

We like to quote the old sages . . . one of our favorites is America's own Benjamin Franklin, who lived from 1706 to 1790 . . . he had the ability to put wisdom in concise words . . . remember some of them?: "be in general virtuous, and you will be happy" . . . "there never was a good war, or a bad peace" . . . "some are weather-wise, some are otherwise" . . . "necessity never made a good bargain" . . . "three may keep a secret, if two of them are dead" . . . "dost thou love life?, then do not squander time, for that's the stuff life is made of" . . . "we must indeed hang together or, most assuredly, we shall all hang separately." See you again soon, we hope.

June 18, 1970

DR. BAYLESS EDWARD BILES
HAD HOST OF FRIENDS

This area lost another good citizen last week in the death of Dr. Bayless Biles, local veterinarian.

Few local citizens had more friends than this hardworking man of many interests. He devoted his time and energy unselfishly to benefiting others, particularly young people who were interested in sports and athletics.

He would go anywhere day or night to take care of his sick patients. Most patients aren't anxious to go see their doctor, but we often felt that our dogs looked forward to paying Dr. Biles a visit.

His sudden and untimely death is tragic. He leaves a fine family and a host of friends. A Bayless Edward Biles scholarship fund is being established in his honor to benefit some deserving Baldwin County youth who has excelled scholastically and in the field of sports. We trust people will give generously to this perpetual fund which will be a lasting tribute to a man who devoted so much of his time and energy to the cause of bodybuilding sports and recreational activities.

FRESH VEGETABLES ARE GREAT

Rain or shine, wet or dry, this is a great time of the year . . . rains several days ago made the vegetables in this area grow and they are delicious . . . food-wise at least, this is an ideal season when you have fresh peas, tomatoes, peaches, squash, etc . . . at the dinner table you just wish you had capacity to eat more and more of the delicious food . . . too bad everybody in the world can't enjoy it as we lucky people do here.

Voting is over for awhile but politics just won't die down . . . people refuse to get the recent governor's race off their mind . . . some still remain bitter about the campaign . . . this is unfortunate . . . in America, politics can be rough and tough but the name of the game is to forget and forgive after election day . . . this is a good idea and all ill feelings should be put aside and men of goodwill will wish the winner success, because he will need it to serve all the people effectively . . . the winner needs the good wishes and the help of those who voted for him as well as those who voted against him . . . if you happen to be one of the fussy, bitter ones, please think of these things.

Alabama's per capita personal income reached a record level of $2,567.00 in 1969, an increase of $206.00 over 1968 . . . this is a 9 percent increase and is above the national average of 8.7 percent . . . all of this would be encouraging but there are 11 states plus the District of Columbia with per capita incomes of $4,000 and over, almost double that of the people in Alabama . . . there are only two states below Alabama, Arkansas and Mississippi . . . Arkansas people have a per capita income of $2,520.00 and Mississippi $2,192.00 . . . the national average is $3,680.00 . . . Alabama has been gaining on the national average but still has a long way to go . . . which simply means that all of us have a lot of working together to pull ourselves up from the bottom . . . we are making progress . . . for example, in 1948 per capita income in the Southeast was about 30 percent below the national average, in 1969 it was only about 20 percent less.

Sunday was Flag Day . . . we were proud to see many beautiful flags in front of homes, this made the homes beautiful, too . . . every day isn't Flag Day but it could very well be . . . any day is a good day to display "Ole Glory," both where you live and where you work. You've heard the old expression that a person has so much money that he doesn't know what to do with it . . . actually most people who have a lot of money know exactly what to do with it, or else they wouldn't have it. If we all minded our own business, we wouldn't have much to talk about over coffee. One advantage of taking the middle stand is that you have company on both sides of you. George Washington Plunkett said, use you head—it is little things that count.

It is nice to be important but more important to be nice. No one is so bad he isn't good for something—he may be used as a horrible example. There are many advantages of being an American, one of which is the words "I CAN." A lose tongue can get you into tight places. Tact is the ability to close your mouth before someone else wants to do it for you. See you again soon, we hope.

September 3, 1970

EUGENE OVERSTREET, A FINE AMERICAN BOY

It was thrilling to see a full color picture of Eugene Overstreet on the front page of the magazine section of the *Montgomery Advertiser-Journal* Sunday.

He is a Bay Minette boy who recently returned from Vietnam. He is at the Montgomery Veterans Hospital getting an artificial leg fitted where he can learn how to use it. Eugene worked with *The Times* last year, was drafted into the Army and was sent to Vietnam almost immediately.

He was severely wounded, losing his right leg below his knee. For several weeks, it was nip and tuck as to whether Eugene would make it or not. His grit and faith won out.

The Times force is looking forward to having him back on the job in the near future. One of the finest things about Eugene is his attitude. You might think that he would be insolent and downcast. Of course, he does get discouraged at times, but his faith in this country and himself is something that all young men could use as an example. There is no bitterness in this fine young man.

ERNEST M. 'SPARKY' HOWELL

Ernest M. "Sparky" Howell, publisher of *The Onlooker* of Foley since 1949, contributed much to his community and his fellowman during his 62 years of life.

He passed away suddenly Monday morning leaving a void in Foley and over the State for his hundreds of friends, and for his family, which will not soon be filled.

He was one of the most popular newspapermen in the State among those in the profession.

Over the years, he carried a lion's share of civic duties and performed them well. Among his honors and achievements, he attended Auburn University, served at one time as a City Councilman for Foley, served as president of the Alabama Press Association, was a president of Foley Optimist Club, was a past Master of Foley Lodge 766 F & AM, was a member of Sigma Delta Chi, a professional journalism society, and was a member of First United Methodist Church of Foley where he sang in the Chancel Choir for nearly 40 years.

"Sparky," as he was affectionately known by all, had the rare ability to always greet you with a twinkle in his eye, a smile on his face, and a note of mirth in his voice. You never talked with him without feeling better as you went on your way.

He had a sympathetic ear for all and a calm, reasoned approach to their problems.

We consider it one of our greatest privileges to have known and have been associated with "Sparky" Howell.

PATRIOTISM AND VOTING

We're just not going to discuss the rain this week . . . it does no good . . . it just keeps on raining. Too, it won't be very long until there'll be some frosty mornings and autumn will be here to the pleasure of most people.

A lot of people wonder why 18-year-olds are so anxious to vote . . . 47 million people did not vote in the presidential election in 1968 . . . almost always there are enough people who do not vote to change the election . . . maybe youngsters can show the oldsters a thing or two about patriotism and the responsibility and privilege of voting every chance we get.

One friend says that recently he has taken so many tranquilizers that he's nice to people he ought not be speaking to. The same brilliant friend says, "Who recalls when the town square was a place, not a person?"

We love doctors, just wish there were more of them to love. A lot of people complain about how expensive good health is . . . good health is not expensive, what really costs is when you have bad health and try to make it good again . . . many people are always telling us to take better care of ourselves . . . these are timely admonitions which are much appreciated and for those who may have a slight wonderment about the proposition should know we try to be real careful . . . after all, it doesn't hurt anyone to work hard.

Among the finest Americans are our policemen and other law enforcement officers . . . in the big cities, radical Communists are killing them right and left . . . Chicago alone has lost 12 by enemy fire this year . . . yet, they keep on trying to maintain law and order . . . maybe someday the American people will know how really valuable they are and support them all the way . . . hope so.

Women must be dangerous, at least most men increase their life insurance when they marry one. A lot of people think about "getting ahead" . . . which isn't a bad idea, provided it is a new head. See you again soon, we hope.

November 12, 1970

ALFRED M. NEUMANN WISHED A SPEEDY RECOVERY

Before 1955 perhaps one of the most widely known, respected and popular bankers in Baldwin County was Alfred M. Neumann, president of the then State Bank of Elberta.

The bank, under his progressive leadership, was recognized as one of the most successful rural banks in this part of the country.

For many years, Alfred was the guiding light and leader in the fine agricultural community of Elberta. His local customers were his friends and followed his advice in his civic and business matters In fact, people went to him for their banking needs from all parts of Baldwin and from outside the county.

He was a leader in all community affairs. For years, he was even active in a fine glee club composed of singers from his area of the county. Naturally, he sang bass.

Unfortunately in 1955, because of ill health, he had to retire from the banking business. Since then, he has been in semi-retirement and living in a restful home on Perdido Bay. He has maintained considerable business activity with his farm, timberlands and waterfront property in that area with his son, Miles.

His health in the past several months has deteriorated further and only recently he has had two serious operations.

Until his recent serious illness, he maintained activity in many things, particularly bowling. He has always enjoyed life. Throughout his years, he has kept abreast of local and national news and has been an interesting conversationalist on most any subject.

His many friends throughout the county wish for him a speedy recovery.

MUMBLINGS—ELECTIONS OVER FOR AWHILE

Now is a good time for all elected people to come to the aid of their county, state and nation . . . isn't it wonderful not to have to be talking about an election coming up? . . . now everyone can spend the next few months discussing the results of voting in 1970 . . . then, human nature being what it is, the voters will forget how tired they were of politics this year and start talking about possible candidates for 1972 . . . let's not knock it, Russian citizens don't have the privilege of worrying about elections.

If Alabama had made one more touchdown against LSU, it would have been a near perfect football weekend . . . we really wanted to see Alabama make another touchdown to keep them from losing to LSU 14 to 9 . . . we wanted them to win because we always want to see them win and, in this case more importantly, because if they had defeated LSU, it probably would have made Auburn Southeastern Conference champions . . . as it is, LSU will be the champion since they will more than likely beat Mississippi as the Rebels have lost their outstanding quarterback, Manning . . . if Alabama had won, LSU and Auburn would have had one loss each, and so would Mississippi if LSU beats them . . . but since Auburn will play more SEC Conference games than any other team, that would automatically give them the championship, assuming they win their other two games . . . Southeastern champions or not, in the eyes of most people, Auburn's great football team is the champion of the Southeast and will no doubt have the privilege of selecting any bowl they choose.

Both Democrats and Republicans are claiming victories in the voting last week . . . it seems neither party won very much . . . fortunately, we think, the Republicans did defeat two unworthy senatorial candidates in Gore of Tennessee, a Democrat, and in Goodell of New York, a Republican . . . we can't recall who beat them, but whoever they are they are bound to be better Americans than the two defeated men. It is also difficult to tell what issues were the most important during the campaign . . . Republicans tried to win on George Wallace's theme of law and order . . . it was effective to a degree, too . . . most Americans are for law and order and against the burning of school campuses, etc., but they are more interested in bread and butter issues when the economy is dragging like it has been recently . . . the Democrats campaigned on economy and kept the Republicans from running away with the campaign . . . people are for law and order and things of this nature as long as they can afford it, but with a depression in the offering, they don't feel like they can afford the fringe benefits and are more interested in having food in the pantry than anything else.

The man who lives for himself is ruined before he starts because of the bad company he keeps. One man put it wisely when he said, "An ungrateful man is like a hog eating acorns under the trees, yet never looking up to see where they came from." Unfortunately, most things that are too good to be true just aren't. We have never regretted nearly so much things we didn't say as some things we have said. Everyone has a chance to buy happiness . . . most people just aren't willing to pay the price. If you can't do what you like, you might try liking what you do. See you again soon, we hope.

November 19, 1970

BCHS GRIDSTERS WIN STATE HONORS

For the second year in a row, a Baldwin County football team has wound up in the state playoffs.

Last year, it was the fine Robertsdale team who made it to the finals in playoffs in Class 3-A. This year, the Baldwin County High School at Bay Minette has won sixth place and a place in the playoffs in Class 4-A competition.

Class 4-A teams are the bigger schools in the state. Friday night, Bay Minette will travel to Legion Field in Birmingham to play their first game with West End of that city.

When the local gridsters beat West End, they will then play the winner of the Minor vs Cobb Avenue game with the game site to be Ladd Stadium in Mobile. This will be fine.

Under Coach Lyle Underwood and his fine assistants, Lowell James, Joe Hendrickson, and Herbert Ellis, Bay Minette has had two excellent football years. Last year they went undefeated, but were not rated in the top four and therefore did not win a spot in the state playoffs. This year, they had almost a perfect season, losing one game by two points to the strong Murphy players, who also won a place in the state playoffs.

Bay Minette was rated as high as fourth place last week, but dropped to sixth following the games over the weekend. The teams are selected on a point system and unless you play a team of your same classification, it does not increase your rating to win. Therefore, when Bay Minette trounced Atmore to the tune of 50 to 6, it did not help since Atmore is a 3-A team.

People in this area are real proud of the football players, town and coaches. It is excellent therapy for a town to have a winning football team. Local people have always backed their team, win or lose, but it is much easier to be enthusiastic about a winning team, naturally.

The Times hopes many people will follow the local boys to their game in Birmingham Friday night and give them the encouragement they deserve.

May the best team win, provided it is BCHS, which we think it will be.

DEMANDS FOR VOCATIONAL EDUCATION

More people are going to high schools and colleges than ever before. More people are interested in education in the United States than in history. This is fine.

Another facet of education that is getting more attention from the public is vocational education. Never before has the demand for vocational training been so great as it is today.

Last Thursday night, T.L. Faulkner, State Director, Alabama Vocational Education, made an interesting speech at the local junior college to area vocational people.

Among other things, he made the following observations: (1) Our businesses, professions, and industries must be manned more fully with trained people in order that we maintain full production; (2) More of our people must be made productive taxpaying citizens to support increasing cost of government and be able to consume the goods and services from increased production.

He further stated, "The thinking public is not going to tolerate much longer the existence of a large army of out-of-school unemployed youths who are not employable because they have no skills and knowledge useful to the employers."

People must be taught to earn a living. They must have a profession. One area of vocational education that is growing is such training in our high schools. The fact is, vocational education should be available to all high school students.

Here are some of the reasons: Less than half of our children finish high school. One in 12 first graders finish college. One in six high school graduates finish college. Ninety percent of jobs do not require college degrees. The jobs do require training and skill. And jobs today are more specialized than ever.

Above are some of the reasons people are going to demand more than ever that vocational education be expanded at every lever.

MUMBLINGS

It finally got really cold . . . it always does some time during the year. This is a great season of the year, particularly if you like hunting and football . . . we like them both but, as we become older, it is much easier to sit at home and watch football on television or listen on the radio, than to get out and freeze on a deer stand, etc.

Anything can happen in football, and usually does . . . what about Auburn, for example? . . . Mississippi State beats Georgia and Florida beats Georgia . . . Auburn beats Mississippi State 56 to 0 and Florida 63 to about 12 . . . and then Georgia comes along and really wallops Auburn . . . football is just like life, you relax and get stomped no matter how successful you have been in the past.

If you are successful in getting even with somebody, that puts you down on his level. It is important to pick your friends—but not to pieces. Gossip does not travel very fast alone—someone must pass it along for it to grow and prosper. Two things will get you in trouble—blowing up yourself and blowing down others. The best way we know of to make a long story short—just don't tell it.

People are down on things they are not up on . . . another way of putting it is that people are suspicious and against those things they do not understand. Silence isn't always golden, it is sometimes just plain old yellow. See you again soon, we hope.

January 14, 1971

GULLEDGE MAKES WALLACE CABINET

For the first time in 25 years, a Baldwin County citizen has been named to a cabinet position in state government.

In the Sparks Administration, during World War II, Ed N. Rodgers, Baldwin County Highway engineer and resident of Bay Minette, was named State Highway Director. Last Saturday, Governor George Wallace announced the selection of 38-year-old Robert I. Gulledge of Robertsdale as State Superintendent of Banks.

Another Baldwin native, Marion Wilkins, is present State Highway Director. However, he was a resident of Evergreen and County Highway engineer of Conecuh County for several years before moving to Montgomery.

In making the appointment, Governor Wallace said, "I am delighted to have this fine young man associated with my administration. His honesty, integrity and character are above reproach, and I am confident he will serve the people of Alabama in a fine manner."

Baldwin is honored to have a native son and citizen as a member of the State Cabinet. Robert Gulledge, the youngest bank president of any of

Baldwin's six banks, has an outstanding record as a businessman and civic leader. He will serve the new administration and the people of Alabama in a fine way in the important position.

The Times congratulates him and wishes him success in his new venture.

MUMBLINGS ABOUT FOOTBALL

Perhaps you have noted this mumbler is fond of the spectator sport of football . . . but we're up to here on the subject at this time . . . there is to be a Super Bowl next week and we are not too interested in who wins it . . . of course, we can't help but remind ourselves that Leroy Jordan of this neighborhood is playing for the Dallas Cowboys and, naturally, that gets our interest up again . . . speaking of football, which we are about to quit doing until next fall, we had an experience at the Senior Bowl that we never thought would happen . . . that is seeing a football game in which the halftime ceremonies were more enjoyable than the game itself . . . the game wasn't much to behold, of course, if the Southerners had won, it would have been considerably better, but not much . . . but the halftime was something . . . of course the Dixie Darlings of the University of Southern Mississippi can make any halftime show, but in addition to this, they had a circus performance by students of Florida State University which was quite entertaining . . . the Senior Bowl means a lot to this area and is much more than just a football game, fortunately.

If you feel ill at ease this week, it might be because the legislature is in session in Montgomery . . . but you have little reason to worry, they can't pass any laws . . . they can only organize themselves for action later on. People who expect a governor or any other officeholder to get elected by politics and then quit being a politician when elected are sort of silly . . . politics is democracy at work . . . however, we know of no reason politics shouldn't be played clean and above board at all times.

Old Ben Franklin was showing his smartness when he said, "Three may keep a secret, if two of them are dead." We've been told that one trouble with being rich is that you end up having to live with other rich people. You have often heard the expression, if you want something done, get a busy man to do it . . . perhaps you have heard of the British economist and writer, Parkinson . . . the Parkinson theory on this is, "work expands so as to fill the time available for its completion . . . the thing to be done swells in importance and complexity in a direct ratio with the time to be spent." Another famous Parkinson theory is, "expenditures rise to meet income . . . individual expenditure not only rises to meet income but tends to surpass it . . . what is true of individuals is also true to government." We, like most people, don't believe Parkinson's theory, but do practice it. See you again soon, we hope.

January 21, 1971

THANK YOU, MRS. ALICE J. DUCK

Tribute was paid to a fine lady last Friday when the Baldwin County Bar Association, public officials and many other friends honored Mrs. Alice J. Duck as she retires from the office of Circuit Clerk and Register, which she has held for the last 30 years.

Mrs. Duck is an humble, kindly soul with friends by the legend. She obtained these friends by being a friend herself.

There have been few political figures in this county as popular as Mrs. Duck. She has worked at it hard. She loves people and likes contacting them. She has been a most persistent funeral attender and visitor of the sick.

While serving, she has received many honors, among them being State President of the Circuit Clerk's Association.

The Times is glad to congratulate this excellent lady for her years of successful service to her fellowman. We wish her continued happiness in her retirement and venture to say she will not retire from her many every day good deeds.

BALDWIN COUNTY HISTORY

Mrs. Kay Nuzum is to be congratulated for her excellent *History of Baldwin County* which is now available to the public.

The 176-page hardbound volume is the most complete history of the county ever written.

Mrs. Nuzum has spent many long hours in study and research to compile the interesting information included in the historical volume of this great county. She has covered many subjects and has done it factually as well as interestingly.

The volume has many names of Baldwin County citizens, past and present. And in its 20 chapters, many highly interesting subjects are covered, such as the Massacre of Fort Mims.

The history was printed and published by *The Times*. It is a book that everyone who loves this great county, its past, present and future, will want to have on his book shelf.

MUMBLINGS OF GOOD NEWS

Now football is over . . . which is good . . . but a few weeks from now it'll be nice for September to arrive with a new football season. At least part of the time you should have liked the weather during the past several days . . . have had all kinds, from hot to cold and from sunny to rainy.

There is lots of good news if you just look for it . . . the trouble with most people, they look for the bad news, or so it seems . . . one good item is the fact that FHA and VA insured mortgage interest for houses has decrease from 81/2 percent to 71/2 percent . . . on a $20,000 mortgage, over a 30-year period, this means a saving on payments from $153.79 per month down to $146.76 or about $7.00 per month . . . this means people who need a home can get more house for less money.

Here is some interesting news . . . the percentage of black pupils attending integrated schools rose from 18.4 percent to 38.1 percent in the last two years in the South . . . this is more than double . . . during the same period, the integration in the North increased by only one-tenth of one percent . . . this merely means that the South is still enduring the double standard . . . the North still likes to talk about the South's failures, or slow progress, while they look the other way at their own faults . . . reconstruction is still around.

Happenings by the long hairs and others on our campuses reminds of the sage who said something like this, "Nonsense and noise will oft prevail, when honor and affection fail." The person who said that a newspaper should be the maximum of information and the minimum of comment was right. See you again soon, we hope.

January 28, 1971

CONGRATULATIONS—OWEN, BENTON AND KINSEY

Baldwin County's two representatives and one senator have done well in committee assignments in the state legislature.

Senator L. D. Owen has been named chairman of the important Conservation Committee. He has also been named a member of the powerful Finance and Taxation Committee, as well as three or four others. It appears no other freshman senator has done as well in committee assignments. This speaks well for his ability and the confidence his fellow legislators have in him.

Thomas Benton has been named to membership of the important Agriculture Committee in the House. He has also been named Vice Chairman of the House Conservation Committee. These two committees are vital and Benton is in an enviable position to serve his constituents well.

House member Dan Kinsey has been placed on the powerful House Rules Committee. He also will have membership on the Insurance Committee. As a member of the Rules Committee, he will have a strong hand in deciding what legislation will come up for voting. He, too, is in an excellent position to serve this county.

MUMBLINGS—WEATHER, FARMING, CENSUS, ETC.

As has been mentioned before, if you don't like the weather, hang around, it will change . . . during the past week, we have had Summer weather in January . . . but don't think Winter is over.

In this southernmost Alabama county, plowing and planting time is already here . . . this used to be a great potato county, and it still is an important one . . . but the potato is no longer king, mister soybean has taken over . . . but it's potato planting time now, not soybean planting time.

The final census count gave Baldwin almost 60,000 people . . . that compares to 13,000 in 1900 . . . in all probability, this fast growing county hasn't seen anything yet . . . wait until the twin tunnels and the I-10 bridge are completed under Mobile River and across Mobile Bay and you'll see the Mobilians flooding to this side where living conditions are great . . . there'll be at least 75,000 people living here by 1980 and the 100,000 mark will probably be reached by '85 or '90 . . . we hope they continue to be like the fine folks that we already have.

The Kennedy family of Massachusetts is one of this country's great clans . . . 10 years ago, President John Kennedy was murdered . . . not long thereafter, his brother, Bobby, was also assassinated . . . previously, the oldest son, Joe, lost his life in World War II while flying over Europe . . . the youngest of the brothers, Senator Ted, is also an attractive Kennedy, but doesn't seem to have as much on the ball as did his brothers . . . of course, he was elected senator when he was 30 years of age and was recently reelected with 62 percent of the Massachusetts vote . . . however, he got his come-uppance last week in the Senate . . . Senator Robert Byrd of West Virginia defeated Teddy as Democratic whip . . . this can only be interpreted as a severe setback to young Kennedy's presidential ambitions . . . this suits us and most other Southerners.

This mumbler has quoted Ben Franklin at lot, but this one hasn't been written here before; "if a man empties his purse into his head, no man can take it away from him.

An investment in knowledge always pays the best interest." In a democracy, the government is no better than the public opinion, which supports it. Hate will de-energize you and losing your temper will poison your body and soul. History is somewhat dependent upon who writes it. The person who is hurt most by an insult is the one who tries to avenge it. Leisure makes a beautiful cloak but it will not stand constant wear. See you again soon, we hope.

February 18, 1971

MUMBLINGS ABOUT FINE OLD STOCKTON

Few small communities in America, if any, have the tradition of wealth, strength and character, fine families, etc., that Stockton does . . . those who live in Stockton never cease to talk about her and those who were born there and moved away also talk unceasingly of the village and return at every opportunity.

But things haven't been too good for the fine old community, which lies nine miles northwest of Bay Minette on the Tensaw River . . . last year her two schools were closed and students commute to Bay Minette.

Real tragedy has hit the community within the last few days . . . last week, it was announced that Bacon-McMillan Veneer Manufacturing Company, Inc., is going to close within the next few weeks . . . this great old company, which has been in existence for 61 years, was the economic mainstay of the area and was the main reason why the village continued to have so many fine and wonderful people.

Bacon-McMillan made it economically possible for the people to remain and continue enjoying the beautiful surroundings in Stockton . . . some great people have been connected with the company . . . started by the late Captain John McMillan, it continued to grow and prosper and reached its zenith under its modern management . . . now, sadly, the mill is closing and the 150-odd people who depended on the plant's manufacture of veneer and plywood for a livelihood, will have to look elsewhere.

The company started as Bacon-Underwood Veneer Company in 1909 . . . for many years, it was the first or second largest industry in the entire county . . . for a long time, Newport Industries of Bay Minette and Bacon-McMillan of Stockton were the only two industries of consequence in Baldwin . . . Newport was not started until 1913, so Bacon-McMillan was the oldest continually run industry in the county . . . the tragedy of the mill's closing will probably not be full understood until months to come.

To compound the sadness and tragedy in the community, the president and general manager of Bacon-McMillan, Norman M. McInnis, Jr., died Sunday morning . . . of course, no death is timely, but it seems Norman's was most untimely . . . if there is anything good to be said, however, it may be that he did not have to see the closing of his beloved veneer company.

Bacon-McMillan was always run by a strong hand . . . during the first half of its existence, the founder, John McMillan, was the guiding light and steady hand that kept the company growing and prospering . . . following him was Norman McInnis, who also ran the company with a strong hand, and for about the same length of time . . . also active in the operation of the company has been the McMillans, Hasties, Gauses, Lonnie Jones and many others.

Originally a veneer company, under Norman's aggressive guidance and management, the company expanded into the manufacture of plywood in 1941 . . . the family and company also held a huge tract of fine hardwood timberland . . . this was sold a few years back but Bacon-McMillan continued to operate with timber purchased locally and shipped in from South America.

This writer saw Norman last Sunday at a funeral and commented about how well he looked . . . he had his fatal heart attack within a few hours after that . . . late last week it had been determined that this column would be written about Bacon-McMillan and Norman McInnis . . . however, little did we realize that he would never be able to read it . . . we regret this.

This mumbler has never stood in awe of many people . . . Norman McInnis was one of these few . . . we always admired his get-up and go and ability to get things done . . . it was not until several months ago it finally dawned upon us why we did stand in awe of him . . . we realized that he reminded us of our father . . . they were a lot alike in looks, size, temperament, ability to work long hours and love it, a concern for their fellow man, intolerant of lazy, incompetent people, an abundant amount of good, common horse sense that was able to do and get things done in a methodical, efficient manner . . . it had been our intent to tell him about the comparison some day, but never really felt the opportunity was right . . . his death proved that opportunity should be made and not awaited sometimes.

Norman McInnis, Jr., like many other fine people who have died in Stockton, cannot be replaced . . . fortunately there are many good ones left . . . on these and, perhaps with help from the outside, Bacon-McMillan, or at least a factory somewhat like it, can be replaced . . . it will take at least 61 years for it to have the tradition of success and grandeur of a Bacon-McMillan, but hopefully another company can be persuaded to come into the community to take up the economic slack.

Regardless of these tragedies, the spirit and tradition of Stockton will go on forever . . . Stockton has too much history, character and pride to be knocked out by one factory closing.

ONE QUARTER CENTURY OF FURNITURE MAKING

Last week, Bay Minette's fine Standard Furniture Manufacturing Company celebrated its 25th year of operation.

It was in 1946 that the company started in a small building with little capital and know-how. But the people that started it had determination and after experiencing failures and set backs, a formula was finally hit upon to cause the company to grow and expand to be Baldwin's largest manufacturing plant and employer of men.

The successful formula was the W.M. Hodgson family.

W.M. Hodgson, Sr., was the longtime president and guiding hand of the bedroom furniture making plant. His two sons, Mac, Jr., and Bob, have taken over and gotten together one of the finest furniture management teams in the entire country. The company's success proves this.

Shipping up to 3,000 bedroom suites weekly to every state in the union and employing over 400 people, the Hodgsons have rendered this community and county a great service. We wish them many more years of success. See you again soon, we hope.

March 4, 1971

MUMBLINGS ABOUT ROBERTSDALE, THE 'HUB CITY'

From 1921 to 1971 is a long time, 50 years in fact, and that is exactly how old the town of Robertsdale is . . . Sunday afternoon, hundreds of people from all over Baldwin County went to the coliseum in Robertsdale and helped that fine group of citizens celebrate the fiftieth anniversary of the "Hub City" . . . the ladies served birthday cake, soft drinks and coffee to the many guests, but the best thing served to the crowd was a few short talks by some of the older citizens who reminisced and told of some of the history of the town.

Harry Wilters, Sr., who was mayor from 1932 to 1934, and city councilman before that time, 1926 to 1932, was the first to speak and the title of his talk was "I remember when . . ." Harry himself came to a place where Robertsdale now is in 1907 . . . besides being mayor and city councilman, he was also city treasurer, superintendent of the water works and postmaster.

The master of ceremonies was Mayor J.D. (Josh) Sellars . . . Josh has been mayor of the Baldwin town longer than anyone else . . . in fact, he is in his sixth term, having first been elected in 1948 . . . he prides himself of the fact that during his time he has never missed a council meeting . . . Josh told an interesting fact about the early establishment of Robertsdale . . . Mr. Oscar Johnson owned the land in 1900 where Robertsdale now is . . . he said he would give it a site on the railroad for a depot, provided they would name it Silverhill . . . naturally, the people agreed to do this . . . actually, Silverhill is some four miles to the west of where the depot was and as Josh humorously told it, people back then could buy a ticket to Silverhill, but they couldn't get to Silverhill because the railroad didn't go to Silverhill . . . however, you could buy a ticket to Silverhill and get to Robertsdale . . . but Robertsdale was not on the map and there was no way to buy a ticket to Robertsdale . . . this wasn't very satisfactory and later the name was changed to Robertsdale after a Dr. Roberts.

The town has had eight mayors and 46 councilmen. The first mayor was W.A. Hammond, the father of W.L. (Pop) Hammond, who was later a member of the town council, as well as his son, Walter W. (Scrugg) Hammond . . . the second mayor was George A. Strong, in 1922 . . . he took office in October and moved in November to teach school in Foley, so he only served as mayor a few weeks . . . Mr. Strong now lives in Montgomery near his son, Dr. Quentin Strong . . . then, other mayors in succession were F.A. Mulack, R.G. Pearson, L. Glendinning, all deceased, H.J. Wilters, Dr. Amos Garrett and Josh . . . present councilmen are Michael W. Baldwin, whose father, M.W. Baldwin, was also councilman at one time, Walter W. Hammond, whose father, W.L. (Pop) Hammond was also councilman, Calvin Kendrick, Jr., John K. Lassitter and James Palmer . . . city clerk is Miss Amelia Johnson, who has held the job since 1949, and the assistant clerk is Mrs. Mamie White.

Pop Hammond, who is one of Baldwin's most popular personalities, made an interesting talk telling about some of the past events in the progressive town . . . since his father was the town's first mayor, the Hammond family has been a tradition in the town for many years . . . in fact, his father opened the store and, as Pop said, there's been a Hammond store here for many years and since he has a son and grandson interested in the business, he predicted there would be a Hammond store in Robertsdale for at least another 65 years.

Robertsdale has many attributes . . . the citizens like to claim that it is the hub of Baldwin County, and it is population-wise, at least . . . geographically, the honor belongs in the vicinity of Stapleton . . . Robertsdale also has the largest industry, Vanity Fair, according to number of people, both men and women, employed, in the county . . . it also has a fine school system, which will be improved to the extent that by this fall, they will have an area vocational school serving the entire south end of the county in vocational training.

The town government is also in strong financial condition and has practically every street paved and the sewage, water, gas and electric systems are in excellent condition, financially and physically . . . the town also has one of the best livestock auction yards in this area as well as the county's largest financial institution, the Baldwin County Savings and Loan Association . . . it is also the home of Baldwin's REA . . . but as Harry Wilters said, the town's greatest asset is its fine, progressive people . . . it is a pleasure to salute all of them. See you again soon, we hope.

August 5, 1971

CONGRATULATIONS—STEVE, JOHN, BILL, FRED, FORD

Southwest Alabama did outstandingly well in the Alabama Press Association Newspaper Contest for weekly newspapers as announced last week.

Baldwin did better than any county.

The Onlooker, Foley, was selected as the Number One newspaper in general excellence in the bigger weekly newspaper category, or those above 3,000 circulation. *The Baldwin Times* was selected second best in this category.

In typography and layout, *The Times* was first and the *Onlooker* was second. Both papers also won other honors. Of course, *The Times* and *Onlooker* are sister newspapers which made the honors even more significant.

There are four awards given in each category of small and large weeklies, honorable mention, third place, second place, and first. Thus eight awards were given for the two categories in general excellence and, of these, five awards went to editors and publishers who now work for *The Times* publisher, or did in the past.

Bill Stewart's fine *Monroe Journal* was selected as third best in the bigger weeklies in Alabama. As has been said here before, Bill is probably the best all around weekly newspaper editor and publisher in Alabama. He is a hard worker and is a perfectionist in whatever he does. And he certainly puts out an excellent newspaper. Recently the *Journal* was honored as being the third best weekly newspaper in general excellence in the entire nation. This is one of the highest honors ever won by an Alabama newspaper.

Fred Nall's *South Alabamian* of Jackson was selected as the top small weekly newspaper. Fred lived in Bay Minette for a number of years and worked at *The Times*. Fred is an excellent person and a fine newspaperman. Congratulations, Fred, on your honor and for the fine job you are doing for the people of Clarke County.

Ford Cook's *Fairhope Courier* was also honored by being given honorable mention for general excellence in the smaller category. Ford worked at *The Times* several years ago, in fact, he started his newspapering career here. *The Courier* has traditionally been a fine newspaper and we are proud Ford is getting recognition for the work he is doing.

Steve Mitchell has been the editor of *The Times* for five years and has won more newspaper awards than any other editor in Alabama during this period. Steve is a hard worker and likes to put out a newspaper of fine quality and of real service to the people.

Since being with *The Times*, he has won first or second place in general excellence several times as well as many other awards, state and national. Steve will be the first to tell you that much of the credit goes to others who contribute to *The Times* and is particularly complimentary to the people in the back shop who work hard for perfection.

John Cameron has been at the *Onlooker* only three years but has won many awards during this time. Three years ago his *Onlooker* was selected the first in general excellence, as it was this year.

Last year, the *Onlooker* was not eligible as you cannot win first place two years in a row. But John was honored by the United States Steel Company as Journalist of the Year in 1970. John has a fine staff of people helping him put out the excellent weekly. Congratulations John, and the others who work with you at the Onlooker.

Newspaperwise, as well as in many other categories, Baldwin County is doing all right.

MUMBLINGS

Let 'er rain . . . it really has, and for many days . . . it has often been said one of the advantages of this great area is the fact that the average rainfall is higher than in other places . . . for example, Baldwin gets over 60 inches a year as compared to about 45 inches in the rest of Alabama . . . this makes the corn grow, and grass too . . . but you can get too much even of a good thing and that is what has happened during the past several days . . . however, if we have a choice, too much rain is better than too much drought.

This is August and next month is September and football gets underway big . . . and that's another good thing about Fall. When you think of schools, you think of a lot of things but you also have to think of money . . . in 1960 Alabama spent $217 per pupil per year for education in elementary and secondary schools . . . this was low, but Tennessee, South Carolina, and Mississippi were in about the same position . . . however, in 1968 all other states started spending more than did Alabama on educating their boys and girls even though Alabama's per student expenses rose to $489 in the 1970-71 budget year . . . this, as you might guess, makes us 50th among the states, which is the bottom in case you have forgotten.

Doctors know that it is not what you eat that causes ulcers but what eats you. A lot of people have radios but they had rather broadcast than tune in. You can't have happiness if you don't share it with people. Speaking of happiness, one philosopher said, "Happiness can be thought, sought, taught, and caught, but not bought." See you again soon, we hope.

August 12, 1971

W.R. COOPER OF BALDWIN A FARM LEADER

Baldwin has lost another fine citizen in W.R. Cooper of Rosinton. He died last week at the age of 86.

He has been a leading citizen and farmer in the County for many years. As a farm leader, he was well-known throughout the State.

Mr. Cooper served as a member of the Agricultural Stabilization and Conservation County Committee for many years. He started serving when the agency was called the Triple-A, as we recall.

He was also active in Farm Bureau work and other organizations whose aims are to benefit the lot of farmers.

Mr. Cooper was an energetic, aggressive, and optimistic man. We have often said there wasn't a lazy bone in his body, nor his children either.

Among his accomplishments, he was a successful father. Surviving him are three sons and two daughters. This world could use a lot more W.R. Coopers.

NONAGENARIANS, GARRETT AND BEDSOLE

Being ninety years old is something unusual as not many people make it. But last Sunday two distinguished gentlemen of this area were honored on their ninetieth birthdays, Clarence Garrett in Bay Minette and J.L. Bedsole in Mobile.

As his age would indicate, Mr. Garrett has been in Bay Minette for a long time. He was born in Monroe County and his other living brother, Rufus Garrett of Uriah, was honored for his eightieth birthday at the same time at the Bay Minette City Auditorium.

Actually, Mr. Clarence will be 91 years old this month. He has been active in politics and civic affairs and is well-known in Alabama.

He is the successful father of eight children and now has 17 grandchildren and 5 great-grandchildren.

Clarence Garrett has been a good citizen and *The Times* is happy to salute him and his brother Rufus for their many good deeds and wish for them a long and successful future.

One of South Alabama's great citizens was honored at Mobile College Sunday by having the new library there dedicated and named for him. J.L. Bedsole has been "Mr. Mobile" for a number of years in the opinion of many people.

A successful businessman, he has been a great philanthropist for a number of years and is always interested in the betterment of things in the Mobile area.

Born in Clarke County, he started his dry goods business in Thomasville, which since has spread out to be a big chain of successful stores.

He has been successful in various enterprises too numerous to mention. He gave $400,000 to the library at Mobile College and has also given liberally to many other causes, including the Bay Minette Infirmary here.

Mr. Bedsole is truly a great citizen and *The Times* is happy to congratulate him on such a full and wonderful life of service to people, God, and country.

It is great to pay tribute to good men while they are still alive. To reach ninety and still be going strong is a tribute in itself, much less the contributions these two ninety-year-olds have made.

BLAKELEY NEEDS RESTORING

Congratulations are in order to the Baldwin County Commission for their interest and determination in seeing that the old city of Blakeley is restored for posterity.

The County Commission members have been talking of this great possibility for many months and seem determined to get the ball rolling on it.

According to Commission Chairman John Hadley, they are working now in an effort to get 120 acres of land which encompass the old city site on Mobile Bay.

As most people know, Blakeley is no more, but one time was a thriving city situated about four and a half miles north of Spanish Fort and about two miles west of Alabama Highway 225.

The city was established by Josiah Blakeley in 1814. The town continued to prosper until 1826 and 1828 when residents were hit by epidemics of yellow fever. At one time, Blakeley was bigger than Mobile and considered by some to reach the population as high as 8,000 people. It had a daily newspaper.

Another historical site that needs restoring is Fort Mims, where the largest massacre in North American history took place.

Baldwin is rich in history and advantage can be taken of this fact to attract thousands of tourists if these two sites are restored.

MUMBLINGS

Last week we were talking about the rain . . . the conversation can continue about the same subject because there has been plenty of rain to talk about . . . as stated last week, however, it is still better to have too much rain than too much drought.

Read an interesting article last week about the high cost of hospitalization and medical care . . . after several pages of facts and alarming figures about the high cost of good health, the writer concluded that the best thing to do is to stay in good health and not need a doctor or a hospital . . . a more logical conclusion would be difficult to find, no doubt . . . and so far as this writer is concerned, we are 100 percent in favor of the whole idea of staying in good health . . . hope everyone else can do the same, so here's good health to all of you.

"Nixon Aide Says Busing A 'Non-Issue' For Wallace," says headline . . . wanna bet? . . . there has not been a more nonsensical statement made by anyone here of late . . . instead of being a non-issue, it will be a vital issue in the next Presidential election . . . if there's anything that 95 percent of the people are agreed upon, it's against busing the school children across town to get proper racial distribution . . . too, President Nixon has verbally come out against it but his Supreme Court, including two of whom he appointed, has voted unanimously for busing . . . this is one issue Mr. Nixon can't escape.

Many people think of the church and a hospital in the same light . . . they really don't want to go to either but are glad they're there if they ever have to go. A person may have brains but he gets paid for using them. Oftentimes a little squirt imagines himself to be a great fountain of wisdom. When times become trying, it's no time to quit trying. See you again soon, we hope.

September 9, 1971

MUMBLINGS ABOUT FRIENDS, DEPARTED

It is an old saying that when you go to more funerals than weddings, you are getting old . . . during the past few weeks, this mumbler has really aged because there have been far too many funerals to attend.

Friends are great and they are not easy to come by . . . when you lose a personal friend, one who has been a booster of yours through thick and thin, it is a great loss . . . some people go through life without having over two or three friends . . . we have been far more fortunate but are losing them far too fast.

During the past few weeks we have lost several . . . a few weeks ago, an outstanding local citizen, George T. Byrne, died after a long illness . . . George had been an outstanding and popular citizen in this town for many years . . . he was a great person and enjoyed doing things for his community and friends . . . fortunately, he left a fine heritage of sons and daughters.

Also recently, W.R. Cooper died in Rosinton . . . although we editorialized about him at the time, because of his prominence, his name is mentioned again as he was always such a good friend.

Then, only a few days ago, Gene Wooley died in Fairhope . . . a native of Bay Minette, he lived for a while in Birmingham and then several years ago moved to Fairhope where he continued to be a successful contractor and friend of God and man . . . it was our good fortune to serve on a board of directors with him, and we got to appreciate his business ability as well as his true friendship and greatness.

Then, within the last few days, it seemed as if the roof fell in so far as losing longtime, valued friends . . . Friday, we attended the funeral of a first cousin, Vance Johnson, Millport, Ala. . . . although it was our privilege to have 84 first cousins at one time, they have now narrowed down to about 60 . . . even though it is a privilege to have so many close relatives, you never want to lose any of them . . . Vance was an outstanding citizen in his county and community and was always a good friend and booster . . . needless to say, he was one of our favorite cousins.

No sooner had we returned to Bay Minette than we received a sad phone call informing us of the death of a longtime personal friend, Alfred M. Neumann, of Elberta and Perdido Beach . . . recently, we had an article about Al's fine qualities and what he had meant to the Elberta area and the county as a whole as a successful banker and leader until his retirement from active business about 17 years ago . . . our household had spent Labor Day weekends with the Neumanns at Perdido Beach for 17 or 18 years . . . it was always something to look forward to and enjoy . . . this year, we attended his funeral on Labor Day as he was buried Monday morning in Elberta.

We had hardly returned home from Al's sad funeral when a call came from our great and good friend, A.G. Allegri, Jr., telling us that our mutual friend, Mac Lowell had just died . . . not many people had the opportunity of really knowing Mac Lowell, but those who did knew him to be a genuine, fine person who enjoyed doing things for his friends . . . Mac lived in Loxley and ran a motel on Highway 90, between there and Malbis . . . he was successful in business and was certainly successful in having a host of friends whose loyalty he enjoyed, but most of all to whom he enjoyed being loyal . . . it was a privilege to be included among his friends.

Sometimes you wonder at the rate friends die if you're not going to run out . . . fortunately, if you continue to be friendly this will not happen as you will make new ones . . . although it is a pleasure to make new friends, it is our sincere prayer that we won't lose any old ones by death or any other manner soon . . . it is too heartbreaking. See you again soon, we hope.

December 23, 1971

SHERMAN LEMLER, A GREAT BALDWIN
CITIZEN, RETIRES

For the past 40 years, one of Baldwin's most outstanding and civic-minded citizens has been Sherman Lemler of Foley.

Last week he retired from his post as general manager of Riviera Utilities. He had been connected with the public utility for 40 years, having come here from Minnesota in 1931.

When he joined the utility, it was serving only 700 customers. During his management, the facility expanded and is currently serving over 12,000.

When this writer came to Baldwin in 1936, Sherman Lemler was already a prominent county citizen and active in many worthwhile causes. He was president of the old Baldwin County Chamber of Commerce, which was instrumental in promoting many county-wide causes.

We join hundreds of others in commending Sherman Lemler for having a successful business career and for helping develop the county into the fine geographical subdivision it is.

Men like him can and do great things for the businesses for which they work and for the community in which they live. Although he is retiring, being the man he is, he will continue to serve others as he has in the past. Congratulations and best of luck, Sherman.

PRESERVE OUR HISTORY

The Baldwin County Commission took a step forward recently when they named George A. Brown, Bon Secour, as Development Coordinator for Baldwin County.

His more specific and urgent duties will be to develop and preserve the historical sites and landmarks that are so plentiful here in Baldwin County.

The Commission could not have selected a more capable person to achieve this important assignment. George has been a history buff and student of Baldwin County's varied and interesting history for a number of years. He probably knows as much about it as any other living person.

If Brown, with the continued cooperation of the County Commission, can just promote and develop one of the many historical landmarks, he will have done this county a great service. The tourists attracted would pay his expenses many times over, besides other benefits.

As the title indicates, George will be expected to lend a helping hand in other areas of development in the county, such as tourism, industrial development, etc. If he will just lend all of his efforts in promoting our fine historical heritage, he can achieve great wonders for the future of Baldwin. Congratulations to all concerned for this important move and best of luck for success.

MUMBLINGS—CHRISTMAS BRINGS GOOD CHEER

Hot or cold, wet or dry, there is nothing monotonous about the weather . . . always changing, it continues to be an interesting subject . . . of course the changes are not the only thing that make the weather such an interesting subject, the most interesting thing about the weather is that it effects everybody and it is something everybody likes to talk about, good, bad or indifferent.

Christmas comes but once a year, but when it comes, it brings good cheer, or words to that effect, according to the old saying . . . it is the desire of this writer and everyone at this newspaper office that this be true so far as you and yours are concerned . . . even though it doesn't come around but once a year, it does roll around real often, and the older you become, the more often it comes, or so it seems . . . but so far as it bringing good cheer to everybody is a moot question . . . there isn't any doubt but what it does cheer up most people and gives everyone a chance to sit down, relax, receive presents, see old friends, think about the Master and His dear Son and pray for peace upon this earth and goodwill among all men . . . even though the prayer may be forlorn and impossible, it is certainly imperative that all human beings pray for peace upon this good earth . . . if we don't pray for it, there is no chance of it ever happening.

If everybody in the world believed in Christ like Americans, there certainly would be a greater chance of achieving peace in this generation . . . unfortunately the Communists, who have no religion, and many others who have religions other than Christianity, do not pray for peace as much as Uncle Sam and his children . . . may peace be with you and may all of your loved ones enjoy good health and be with you for this holiday season.

Although it is still over a week off, it is not too early to start thinking about some New Year's resolutions . . . a good suggestion is not to make many but make a few important ones and keep them . . . if we resolve to do something, that is the same thing as taking an oath that it will be done . . . the Bible teaches us that all oaths are to be kept, so remember this before you step off into too many resolves.

With all the bowl games coming up, everyone has a few more days of good college football . . . then, the Senior Bowl in Mobile, the pro-bowls and it will all be over again until Fall of next year . . . it's sort of sad to see it go, but many wives and others will be glad to become acquainted with their husbands who monopolized the TV sets for too many weekends during the past several months . . . so nothing is so bad that it doesn't blow someone a little good.

Merry Christmas, all of you! See you again soon, we hope.

February 3, 1972

Welcome to Baldwin, Jack Edwards

For the first time ever, Baldwin is in the First Congressional District of Alabama. We are now in the same district with Mobile instead of Montgomery.

Due to the redistricting forced on the Alabama Legislature by the losing of a congressman in the last census, Baldwin and Escambia will no longer be in the Second Congressional District, but will be in the First with Mobile, Monroe, Wilcox, Clarke, Washington and Escambia.

This suits us.

Although the old Second District was an excellent one, most will agree that the seven southwest Alabama counties have more in common with one another than with the old setup. We'll see how it works.

During 1964, the Goldwater landslide carried five Republican Congressmen into office. Since then, one has been defeated, another chose to run for another office and was defeated. Three are left.

One of these is Congressman Jack Edwards of the First District, who lives in Mobile, and the others are Bill Dickinson of Montgomery, who still is, legally, Baldwin's congressman. The other is Congressman Buchanan of Birmingham.

This newspaper's loyalty to the Democratic Party has long been known. However, this writer has often said that of Alabama's Republican congressmen, Jack Edwards is the best.

We have observed Jack since he has been in office and had the pleasure of knowing him previously. He is a fine, hard working, dedicated gentleman.

He has conducted himself well in Washington and is ever alert to the needs of his constituents and is a loyal American with a Southern accent.

There aren't many Democrats and no Republicans at all who tower over him.

MUMBLINGS ABOUT MEETINGS AND BANQUETS

Phooey on the weather . . . it's been so bad we're not even going to discuss the subject.

This is the time of the year for annual Chamber of Commerce meetings and football banquets . . . Baldwin County is no exception and they've had some good ones during the past several days . . . Foley area Chamber of Commerce had an excellent banquet at the Holiday Inn on Gulf Shores Saturday night and reported an excellent year of accomplishments . . . week before last, Bay Minette had its annual C of C meeting and many proclaimed it as one of the best the organization had ever had . . . of course, they had the added advantage of just having announced a fine, new industry for the area by the name of Den-Tal-Ez . . . also making the meeting more enjoyable was the excellent, humorous talk by Bob Abernathy of Tennessee . . . such organizations should have learned a long time ago a group of people don't get together to hear a long, serious talk . . . they prefer to be entertained as well as enlightened . . . Bay Minette certainly achieved this goal with the Tennesseean.

Saturday night, the local Quarterback Club sponsored their annual football banquet for the Baldwin County High School boys and they also did an excellent job . . . 400 or 500 people turned out to see many awards handed out and for the opportunity of seeing and hearing Heisman Trophy winner Pat Sullivan, and also Southeastern Conference Lineman Tommy Yearout, both of Auburn . . . helping this annual affair be a success was the fine record the team had last year, the best in history . . . you will recall, with a great deal of pride, that the Baldwin High Tigers went to the semi-finals in the State 4-A playoff, which is the highest any team has ever gone south of Montgomery.

Coach Lyle Underwood made an excellent talk thanking everybody for making the season a fine one . . . quite obviously. Bay Minette has a fine coaching staff led by Underwood . . . they have the confidence of the players, school officials and the townspeople . . . of course all winning coaches enjoy that same confidence . . . when they'll really need us is when they have a losing season, which we all hope they never will.

One of the highlights of the program was the obvious indication that the future of local football is encouraging . . . from the looks of several of the boys who will play again next year and from the record of the junior high team, which went 10-0 for the season, good things can be expected next year . . . Coach Pridgen of the Junior High boys hit a home run when he told the audience that Bay Minette Junior team had a sort of Sullivan to Beasley combination of its own . . . quarterback Al Wasdin threw 32 touchdown passes, 14 of them to end Charles Norman . . . for the benefit of the coaches, perhaps it is better to poor mouth a little . . . the team did lose some mighty fine players who will be awfully hard to replace . . . but we're eternal optimists, like most football enthusiasts.

The following by an unknown writer has just been read . . . it is entitled "Slow Me Down, Lord" . . . "ease the pounding of my heart by the quieting of my mind . . . steady my hurried pace with a vision of the eternal reach of time . . . give me, amid the confusion of the day, the calmness of the everlasting hills . . . break the tensions of my nerves and muscles with the soothing music of the singing streams that live in my memory . . . help me to know the magical, restoring power of sleep . . . teach me the art of taking minute vacations, of slowing down to look at a flower, to chat with a friend, to pat a dog, to read a few lines from a good book . . . slow me down, Lord, and inspire me to send my roots deep in the soil of life's enduring values that I may grow toward the stars of my greater destiny."

Perhaps the above was written for us, or you . . . anyway, if the shoe fits, wear it. See you again soon, we hope.

March 23, 1972

THE GASTONS OF FAIRHOPE

One of Baldwin's great families is the famous Gaston clan who came to the Eastern Shore in 1894 and established a family tradition of helping to build Fairhope and Baldwin County.

In February, the last of the E.B. Gaston descendants retired. He is Dr. C.A. Gaston, who had been secretary of the Fairhope Single Tax Corporation since 1936.

In 1894, Mr. And Mrs. E.B. Gaston came from Iowa, established the Fairhope Single Tax Colony and edited *The Fairhope Courier*, which was established even before coming to Fairhope, in 1891 as we recall.

The oldest of the five children was J.E. "Jim" Gaston, who was an automobile dealer in Fairhope for a number of years and also served as county commissioner for several terms. Many people proclaimed him as the best county commissioner in Alabama. He was a successful businessman, politician and civic leader.

Dr. Gaston, a brother, A.F. "Spider" Gaston, and Mrs. Frances Gaston Crawford all worked on *The Courier* at one time or another until about 10 years ago when the paper was sold. Mrs. Leah Gaston McGill also lived in Fairhope.

All except Mrs. McGill and Jim are still living, and Jim's widow and one son, Jim Gaston, Jr., still live in Fairhope.

It has been this writer's privilege to know all of them. We only knew Mr. E.B. Gaston for a short time but he was a great man by reputation and achievement.

Not only because of the founding of Fairhope and the establishment of the Single Tax Colony, the Gastons have been one of that city's most prominent families for other reasons.

Hopefully, those who are still living and in retirement will enjoy their long deserved rest. They will continue to work for and boost the Eastern Shore and Baldwin County, which they love so dearly.

MUMBLINGS ABOUT LAND OF THE FREE

We resent people who criticize the weather in this area . . . it is supposed to be good, bad, and indifferent . . . at least it is always changing and who can deny that this is at least an interesting situation?

And just think, the political season has just started for the year 1972 . . . there is still a lot of talking, arguing and debating to go on before you hear the last of the politicians this year . . . and this is wonderful . . . Russians and people in other Communist countries do not have the privilege of hearing the melodious (?) voices of statesmen seeking high office . . . here in this great land of the free and the home of the brave, people have an opportunity of selecting people who they prefer to rule them . . . in dictatorship countries, the dictator says who shall rule and ruin you . . . politics is great since it is democracy at work and everybody, at least most everybody, in Uncle Sam's country likes democracy . . . if you don't, move on, there are other countries where you will be more welcome.

Scientists say that the human voice is always unique . . . in other words, each person has a voice that is different from every other person's . . . there is another distinction, too, some voices have a bigger main spring than others and keep running longer. Last week a railroad boxcar full of U.S. mail was found on a Birmingham side track which had been lost for two years . . . Jim Martin and Bert Nettles, Republican candidates for the U.S. Senate, against the former postmaster general, will have something like this to say, no doubt, "Now let's see, Red Blount took over the post office department about three years ago, did he not?"

Farmers have always been important but they are now more important than ever . . . 50 years ago, one farmer fed himself and one other family, now one farmer must feed 50 other families . . . to put it another way, 50 years ago, 84 percent of the people were born on a farm, now only about 5 or 6 percent are.

Mr. Plunkett tells us there are a lot of good four letter words, such as; work, Lord, soap, free, work, wash, love and work. The Treasury Department reports that 55 of America's 1,203 millionaires in the 1969 tax year paid no taxes . . . times are so tough, it looks like it's even difficult for a millionaire to make enough profit to pay taxes. You'll find it's hard to get anywhere doing either one, that is, running up hill or running down people. Those people who think there are such things as little white lies are color blind. Apparently it is easier to run with the devil than walk with God. Someone has said, "sympathy is your pain and my heart." See you again soon, we hope.

March 30, 1972

JANIE SHORES FOR SUPREME COURT

One of Alabama's most brilliant lawyers is seeking a position on the Alabama Supreme Court to succeed Associate Justice Robert T. Simpson, Jr., who is not running for reelection. The attorney is a former resident and high school graduate of Baldwin County.

For the first time in history, the brilliant attorney seeking this high office is not a man. She is very much a lady. She is Janie Shores.

Few lawyers of her age have obtained the honors and experience she has. If elected, and most people predict she will be, she will be the first lady to serve on the Alabama Supreme Court and the first one to seek the office.

Mrs. Shores is the daughter of John Wesley and Willie Scott Ledlow of Loxley. She has a brother living in Bay Minette and another sister living in Loxley. She moved to Baldwin with her parents from Georgiana at the age of seven. She attended school in Loxley and graduated from Robertsdale High School.

After graduating from high school, she worked for the late Vincent F. Kilborn, Jr., as a legal secretary in Mobile.

Janie attended Judson College before enrolling at the University of Alabama. She entered law school without completing the requirements for an undergraduate degree, which was possible at that time. She graduated number one in her class, completing her studies in August, 1959.

After graduation, she opened a law office in Selma and later moved to Birmingham.

In addition to finishing number one in her class academically, she was president of Phi Delta, a woman's legal fraternity. She and C.M.A. Rogers, III, of Mobile, were the winners of the Law Day Moot Court Competition. She also was elected to Farah Order of Jurisprudence, the scholastic honorary for law students at the University. She was also an editor of the Alabama Law Review, which is the professional semi-annual journal.

In Birmingham, she went to work for Liberty National Life Insurance Company in the Legal Department. She began serving as Justice Simpson's law clerk in 1959, while practicing law in Selma. She is still law clerk for Judge Simpson.

It has been known among the legal profession for a long time that Mrs. Shores' legal opinions, handed down through Judge Simpson, have been masterpieces.

At the present, she is a full professor at Cumberland School of Law, Samford University. As a teacher, she has taught many important subjects and has a great following among young lawyers throughout the state who admire her legal abilities. She has authored a number of articles which have appeared in professional journals, and is the co-author of a textbook used by lawyers studying at Cumberland.

She has many other legal honors thus proving her superior capacity to be the first lady to sit on Alabama's Supreme Court.

She is married to Jim Shores, also a prominent and successful lawyer of Birmingham. They own a cottage at Montrose and spend considerable time in Baldwin. They have one daughter, age eight.

In addition to her legal abilities, she has sound common sense, which further proclaims her fitness for election to this important position.

Janie Shores would tender justice with common sense, great legal knowledge and human understanding. She is strong on law and order and her election would add dignity and beauty to the court.

MUMBLINGS—SPRING AND SPORTS

Spring has sprung and is doing beautifully to date . . . as stated here before, there have been years when the azaleas were more profuse and beautiful at one time but this year they have been beautiful, even though less profuse, over a longer period of time than for some years . . . undoubtedly this was because of the various unseasonable weather, particularly warm, from time to time early in the season . . . but have you ever seen dogwoods so beautiful?

UCLA has won its sixth national basketball championship . . . in order to do so though, they had to beat a Southern team, Florida State, in the finals and then they only won on their home court by five points or a score of 81 to 76 . . . if we had had the play-off down South, it would have been a different story, no doubt . . . the South has come into its own in many categories, maybe it will do the same thing in basketball someday . . . basketball is a great spectator sport but does not compare with football in popularity and gate receipts . . . but it is a real fine game and it takes a lot of stamina and ability to play the game like it should be played.

Talking of sports, an interesting article was in the Alabama daily newspapers recently . . . it said Alabama's Coach Bear Bryant was investing in a dog racetrack in Mobile . . . whether it's true or not, we do not know, but doubt it . . . it had been assumed the Bear was as good a public relations man as a football coach . . . he certainly is smart enough to have taken a lesson from one of his former greats, Joe Namath . . . you recall Joe had to sell his nightclub in New York because gamblers ate there . . . no doubt gamblers will appear at the dog racing track when it opens to Mobile . . . and what's sauce for the player should be sauce for the coach, and it is, so far as the public is concerned.

Must be a lot of people don't read these mumblings . . . perhaps not enough has been said about throwing trash on the highways and littering up the countryside . . . certainly it doesn't seem to have improved much although you can talk to many people and they admit they have stopped throwing anything out their car window, even cigarette butts . . . so maybe progress is being made but we still have a long way to go . . . keep talking it up and some law enforcement officer will make an arrest and a judge will fine him $500, which will attract plenty of attention and will be a great deterrent factor in causing people to do what they ought to do anyway.

It's not smart to trust your wife's judgment—after all, look at whom she married. If a woman arranges a match for her daughter, she will probably continue refereeing it after it happens. One of America's greatest, Abraham Lincoln, once said, "He has a right to criticize who has a heart to help." You should spend your time getting even with those folks who have helped you.

Too many people think the world can't go ON unless they tell people OFF. See you again soon, we hope.

June 1, 1972

LINDA BYRNE STATE JAYCEETTES'
PRESIDENT

Thank you Mrs. Linda Byrne for bringing a fine honor to Bay Minette and Baldwin County, as well as to yourself.

And congratulations for being the first state president of the Alabama Jayceettes ever elected to that important office south of Clanton.

With this prestigious honor given to you by your fellow Alabama Jayceettes, you now can join the roll of other important people in Baldwin who have in times past been elected state president of various organizations.

Linda, your friends in Bay Minette, Baldwin County and this area, are real proud of you for bringing this good honor this way, and thus giving you the distinction you rightly deserve for the many worthwhile endeavors you have successfully undertaken.

We trust your term as president of this important organization will be successful.

CONGRATULATIONS AND SYMPATHY

Congratulations go to the citizens of Bay Minette for the successful cleanup campaign conducted Saturday.

Many groups of young boys and girls, and grow-ups, too, pitched in to make Bay Minette look spic and span. One could ride through the town Saturday afternoon and be real proud of its cleanliness.

But not everyone cooperated.

Sunday morning 13 cans were seen along one block in a residential section in the eastern part of Bay Minette. It was cleaned of trash Saturday.

Admittedly, this block is a haven for litterbugs but it is discouraging when so much energy, publicity and pride has gone into cleaning up the town. The fact that at least some did not get the message is discouraging.

This simply means that keeping a place clean is an everyday affair. Of course, it would be no problem at all if the litterbugs would cease and desist.

MUMBLINGS—ABOUT REA

Probably not over 25 percent of the present population of Baldwin County were born or lived here at the time . . . but this writer well remembers back in 1937 when the good news came from Washington, through Congressman Lister Hill and Senator John H. Bankhead, that a loan of $200,000 had been made by the Rural Electrification Administration to the Baldwin county REA . . . this was a great day for our rural people . . . this money was used to build some 211 miles of rural electric lines to serve about 200 consumers . . . the first Board of Trustees members were Frank Earle, P.A. Bryant, Alton Hankins, Frank Hoffman, and Tom Steele, Jr. . . . the first General Manager, or Project Superintendent as they were then called, was Carl L. Schlich, Jr., and the other two employees were A.C. Bryant and Herbert Crandall . . . after these 35 years, about everything has changed . . . John Chason was, with his partner Charlie Hybart, the attorney . . . he is still attorney but his firm is now Chason, Stone and Chason.

Baldwin's REA has changed with the upward trend of things . . . it is now called the Baldwin Electric Membership Corporation and the $200,000 investment has increased to $8,472,000 . . . the number of employees has increased to 76 and the 211 miles of transmission is now about 1500 miles . . . the number of consumers has changed from 200 to 11,000 . . . Baldwin's EMC is now big business.

Last year it had total revenues of $1,843,000 and the payroll alone was $671,000 . . . conservative estimates by the officials of EMC are that by 1977, plant investment will be $11.6 million with 15,000 customers . . . giving credence to this growth is the fact that 844 new customers were added last year . . . some people estimate that the county will increase in population by 10,000 within the next two or three years.

Much of this growth is in and around Gulf Shores where EMC serves the entire area which is growing by leaps and bounds . . . this beautiful Alabama Gulf Coast section, which is called Pleasure Island, is finally coming into its own and is fast being recognized as one of the fastest growing tourist meccas in the country . . . officials of EMC are trying to stay ahead of this rapid growth . . . so far, they have done an excellent job.

In an attempt to stay up with this progressive, fast growing county, Baldwin EMC will move into a fine new building near Summerdale within the next few days . . . this is a fitting time for this important move to be made because it ends years of moderate to rapid growth, and is just before a growth period that will exceed any in the history of the county.

The present General Manager is the popular Don R. Sutherland . . . he has gathered around him a fine group of loyal and dedicated workers . . . other officers and trustees of the cooperative are: George W. Engel, president; J.O. Sims, vice president; Jim Swoboda, secretary-treasurer; and other trustees are Thomas L. Steele, John H. Schenk, John Weatherford, and Raymond McMillan.

The Times congratulates the fine group of people who are running this great co-op and wishes them continued success in their efforts to serve the rural residents of this great county.

MUMBLINGS INTO THE TWENTY-FIRST CENTURY

∾

September 17, 1992

DR. WILLIAM COX, JR., A SUCCESSFUL
PUBLISHER

Sometimes the world doesn't seem very big.

Recently, a friend called from Washington to tell me of an experience his wife had . . . he was Gary Cooper, retired Major General, who became the first African-American General in the history of the United States Marine Reserves and is presently Assistant Secretary of the Air Force in charge of personnel, etc. . . . although brought up in Mobile, he has a home in Daphne.

He said his wife was seeking some information and went to the national headquarters of a successful magazine publisher, and in talking with him, she learned he was from Alabama and reminded him that her husband was also from Alabama . . . asking him where he was from, he said, "Bay

Minette."

She asked him if he knew Jimmy Faulkner . . . his reply, "Do I? I used to work for him and he has always been my idol and is the reason I am in the publishing business."

However, General Cooper could not remember his name and since numerous people have worked for me at *The Baldwin Times* and other county newspapers, I could not imagine who it was. That night, I was talking to Bootsie Noonan of Bay Minette and told him the story . . . he said, "Oh, that's Bill Cox and he's visiting his mother in Bay Minette right now." He called Bill's mother and the next day, he dropped by my office for a chat . . . it was good to see him and hear his story.

His mother is Mrs. Artensie Cox and his father, who is deceased, was Jesse Cox of Bay Minette.

He has two brothers, Walter and Jesse, and one sister, Linda . . . he is also a cousin of James Cox, the successful director of the Bay Minette Middle School, which has won national honors.

He is Dr. William Cox, Jr., now . . . after graduating from Douglasville High School, he earned his Bachelors Degree from Alabama A&M University . . . and his educational credentials include a Doctorate in Higher Education Administration from George Washington University, a Masters Degree in Counseling Psychology, and a second Masters in Public Administration, both from Ball State University.

He is President and Co-founder of Cox, Matthews, and Associates, Inc., a Fairfax, Virginia, based firm specializing in publishing, satellite television production, training, education, and consulting.

Dr. Cox is also president and managing editor of the eight-year-old company's bi-monthly national news magazine, *Black Issues in Higher Education,* which is received by virtually every college and university in the United States.

He was kind enough to put me on his mailing list and I must say, it is a very fine publication, full of news about black colleges and, best of all, is full of advertising which indicates its tremendous success.

His company also owns a second national publication, *Community College Week,* which is targeted for community, technical, and junior college professionals . . . I also receive this publication and it seems to be getting off to a good start.

His company has earned a reputation for producing the best videoconferences in the U.S.A. that focus on issues relating to black and other minority participation in higher education.

The company's "Beyond the Dream: a Celebration of Black History" series is the only live television program in America that serves as the national kickoff for Black History Month.

Among his extensive administrative and organizational experiences, Dr. Cox has developed and administrated higher education programs for the U.S. Army and Air Force.

During his involvement with the military, he taught courses on the electronic guidance systems of sophisticated missiles at Red Stone Arsenal, Alabama, and his corporate experience included a stint with General Electronics where, among other assignments, he performed design work on the Apollo spacecraft ground support system.

He has received many professional appointments, among which he is a former member of the advisory board at Harvard University's Graduate School of Education, Management of Life Long Education Program.

In spite of his impressive success story, he is still humble and was kind enough to write me upon his return to Fairfax, Virginia, a kind letter in which he stated, "As a result of my visit with you, I have become more inspired to continue to make my publications the best that they can possibly be."

He certainly deserves a lot of credit and is another good example of many Baldwin County citizens who have moved on and made a tremendous success. See you again soon, I hope.

September 27, 1997

JOHN SNOOK AND GULF TELEPHONE COMPANY

Where would you go to find the following?

A profitably owned company worth in excess of $200 million, with revenues of over $30 million a year, a payroll of about $12 million per year, 350 employees, and spends $10 to $12 million a year on expansion, repairs and updating equipment.

A company in the process of spending $155 million to serve nine southeastern states, largely owned by its employees, whose chairman of the board and chief executive officer is a lovely lady, one of three top taxpayers in the county where it resides, has 45,000 customers and is and has been expanding at the rate of 10 to 12 percent per year since 1934.

And soon to be under construction will be a new badly needed administration and office building . . . costing some $3 million.

And whose CEO and Chairman is called by her first name by almost everybody, including her beloved and devoted employees.

The business is Gulf Telephone Company, headquartered in Foley and serving all of South and Southeast Baldwin County.

When this writer arrived here in 1936, Gulf had fewer than 300 customers . . . in fact, only 224 during the depression year of 1933, but had grown to 274 by 1934.

The lady in question is Marjorie Younce Snook, the widow of the late beloved, brilliant and unique, John McClure Snook, whose father, Ward H. Snook, started Gulf Telephone in 1929.

Even though Gulf charges one of the lowest rates of any company in the U.S. for private phone services, it has grown and prospered through the years, but with many obstacles to overcome.

In spite of this low cost, Gulf has been very aggressive in community affairs, contributing much money and many services to the area it serves

. . . it is also one of the three largest taxpayers in Baldwin, possibly exceeded only by CSX Railroad and Alabama Power Company, and has paid millions in taxes over the years.

In some previous years, the company has paid as much as $1 million in Christmas bonuses to its loyal employees.

Although 39th in size of hundreds of telephone companies in the U.S., it continues to grow because of the prosperity and progress of its trade area . . . and the continued modernization by aggressive management.

Gulf serves customers east of Fish River, north of the Gulf to Stapleton, and east to Perdido River, with an exception of a small area in Belfountain, which is served by a Florida company . . . and which Gulf wants to buy.

Gulf has not always been as successful and prosperous as it is today.

In the early days, everybody that did not know anything about the subject was critical of Gulf because of its comparative poor service . . . in fairness, it must be taken into consideration that the Snooks were in a huge scattered area of residents and often had to go miles to serve one or two customers . . . all of this was very expensive and made it difficult for the company to expand and modernize the equipment, even though it did so as rapidly as finances, mostly borrowed, would allow.

The Eastern Shore and the Bay Minette area are served by the Bell System and for many years, these two areas considered themselves rather lucky that their servicing company was not Gulf . . . this is no longer true, because in many respects, Gulf is as good or better than the Bell System . . . besides, they are locally owned.

Obviously, this is a big and interesting subject and I hope to tell you more about the company and the new service they are going to render, beginning in October, and more especially about Marjorie and John Snook . . . but mostly about Mrs. Snook and her family.

See you again soon, I hope.

March 7, 2002

BALDWIN IS HOME TO MANY
WELL-TRAVELED

Referring to this column, people constantly ask, "Where are you going next?"

Readers are a writer's best friends. Many tell me they read my column every week. This is highly appreciated.

Several asked me to write more about politics while others seem to prefer economics or other things. I concluded several years ago that more people prefer personal travel. Of course, I could be prejudiced because such comments give me an excuse to travel, which I like.

Several months ago it was written here about the number of countries visited to date. The figure at that time was 91 countries and that is still the correct number.

It was suggested that those people in the county, or elsewhere, write and tell me how many countries they have visited. Fortunately, several replied, but it appears that I rank second according to these calls and letters.

All of them will not be mentioned here but here are three of the most widely traveled.

Wayne Lampshire, of Foley, has been in 72 countries, lived in Bolivia for four years and Columbia for eight years. He has had a job with an international company which required his services throughout the world. He says he has an eight-year-old daughter who has lived in 49 states and been in 13 countries.

Paul Frederick of Fairhope has been in 61 countries.

Perry Zarr, whose husband, Bob Zarr, previous owner of Foster Ford in Bay Minette for a number of years, called and said she has remembered visiting in 31 countries, but Bob has been to over 100. He was a pilot during the war and before retiring, traveled all over the world and thus saw many places.

My goal of reaching 100 will not be sufficient to be a record in this county. Perhaps Bob can give an exact number and that will give me something to shoot at. Of course, he is not through traveling either.

As to where I am going next? My traveling partner, Matt Metcalfe, has traveled a million miles or so more than I have, but has been in fewer countries. He is arranging a trip for us to Central America, which excluding Mexico, has seven countries, only three of which I have visited. They are Belize, Guatemala and Panama.

Ones not visited are Nicaragua, Honduras, El Salvador and Costa Rica.

All of these countries are comparatively small and poor. However, they have a rich history and offer travelers some interesting sites even though they are not appealing to many people.

One of the most visited of the small countries is Costa Rica. Several from this county have visited there and some do business with them and live there much of the time. In area, it is about 40 percent the size of Alabama, 20,000 square miles and population of over two million.

Anyway, hopefully we will be able to visit three or four of these additional countries in the near future and, if so, naturally it will be my pleasure to tell you something about them.

March 21, 2002

CALLAHAN'S CAREER MARKED BY GREAT ACHIEVEMENTS

Tragedy hit Baldwin County, this area of Alabama, the whole state and nation, when Congressman Sonny Callahan decided to retire.

Having served this First Congressional District for 18 years, he attained an influence and power in Washington that few have equaled.

He not only had the seniority but personality, intelligence and political understanding to yield great influence for his constituents in this area, as well as the entire country.

Although a Republican, Sonny managed to have the confidence and respect of both parties in Washington. He has been known to say he didn't care which political party they belonged to as long as they could be of help to him in gaining his objectives, which were many and important.

He was a member of the powerful and prestigious Appropriation Committee in the U.S. House of Representatives where he was able to use his abilities to benefit his congressional district. He made no bones about the fact that it was his desire to bring all the money and help to this area that he possibly could. And he was quite successful.

The number of projects he has aided in Baldwin County are numerous and will be recorded in history as time goes on.

He has served so well, some monument should be named in his honor. Perhaps this could be the new I-10 bridge across Mobile Bay. This huge project will benefit millions of travelers and commuters when completed.

He well deserves this honor, not only because of his effective service, but for the simple fact that he got the money in Washington to pay for the study and engineering and start the construction.

His first money, $15 million, was for the purpose of correcting the dangerous west end of the Wallace Tunnel. It was learned the cost expense of this project was so high and would not improve the traffic and state highway engineers, mainly led by Ronnie Perioux, District Engineer of this area, concluded a new bridge would better serve the public. Later, Sonny got $10 million more through the Alabama Highway Department to continue this idea, which is expected to come to fruition within the next few years.

This beautiful new bridge will be the icon of Mobile and Baldwin Counties when completed.

Unless you understand how things work in Washington, it is difficult to estimate the importance of having a congressman on the Appropriation Committee. Unfortunately, it may be a long time before this district has another. You have to be high on the political ladder to achieve such an honor.

Fortunately, Alabama has two other congressmen on this important committee, Bud Cramer, a conservative Democrat from Huntsville, and Republican Robert Aderholt from the Jasper area.

Although Sonny's decision not to run for reelection came as a shock and disappointment, we must readjust our thinking and be thankful that a number of people have already announced their intentions of seeking his job.

Congressman Jack Edwards, who served with distinction in Washington for 20 years, endorsed Sonny to succeed him and this was helpful to his being elected.

In like manner, Sonny has strongly endorsed his longtime right-hand man and administrative assistant, Jo Bonner.

Jo has worked closely with the congressman for 18 years and knows his way around in Washington and has many friends there, as well as in this district.

At this writing, six other good men have announced their intentions of being a candidate and by the time you read this, no doubt others will have also made such wishes known.

Hopefully, all of them will be discussed in this column sooner or later. I congratulate each one for his desire to serve in such a high position and just wish all of them could be elected, but that is impossible.

Voters in this congressional district, which includes Baldwin County, have very intelligent people and will select a good man, who in time, will have the seniority that Sonny has enjoyed.

Two Baldwin publishers inducted into Hall of Fame

Baldwin County was well represented last Saturday in the Auburn University Media Day.

Each year, two Alabama editors and/or publishers are selected to the Alabama Press Association Hall of Honor. Those selected must have been dead for five years before they can be considered.

The two selected this year were both from Baldwin, Ernest M. "Sparky" Howell, who was owner and publisher of *The Foley Onlooker*, and E.R. "Bob" Morrissette, who was editor and manager of *The Baldwin Times*.

The only other person ever selected from Baldwin for this honor was Robert B. Vail, who was owner and publisher of *The Baldwin Times* from the mid-twenties until 1936. He was an outstanding newspaperman and had great ability for writing pungent, sharp editorials.

Sparky Howell was editor and publisher of *The Foley Onlooker* from 1949 until he sold it to my son and me in 1968. He remained there and managed it until his death in 1970.

Howell was a popular editor and person during his active life. He was aggressive and a great booster of this county, particularly the Foley/South Baldwin area.

He was well respected among newspaper people throughout the state and served as president of the Alabama Press Association in the years 1964-1965.

He never expected a member of his staff to do anything that he could not or would not do and worked at every aspect of the country newspaper, including running the linotype, making up ads, writing, selling, running the press, etc.

After serving in the Army during World War II, Bob Morrissette graduated from the Journalism Department of the University of Alabama before cutting his teeth as a news reporter at *The Monroe Journal*, Monroeville, and later *The Daily Mountain Eagle* in Jasper in 1948. He then came to Baldwin County as editor and manager of *The Baldwin Times*, where he served from 1948 to 1959.

In '59, with this writer and another former *Times* editor, Phil Sokol, he bought *The Atmore Advance*.

I later sold them my interest in *The Advance* at the original cost and after Sokol died, he purchased Sokol's interest from his widow and became sole owner.

He threw himself into the civic life of Bay Minette and Atmore and became known favorably as a popular person and editor. After selling *The Advance* in 1979, he became U.S. Senator Howell Heflin's executive assistant in southwest Alabama where he served until his death in 1996. In 1976, he received the distinguished Journalism Award from his alma mater and in 1978, he served as president of the Alabama Press Association.

Another outstanding editor, Bill Stewart, and I bought *The Monroe Journal* in the late 1940s . . . Stewart eventually purchased my interest and became sole owner and won outstanding national and state journalism awards. He also became president of the Alabama Press Association and five years following his death, he also was selected into the Alabama Press Association Hall of Honor.

Other outstanding publishers were Mike and Linda Breedlove, who ran *The Fairhope Courier* for my son and me until we sold our papers in 1974.

Jimmy Jr. and I had purchased the *Southwest Alabamian* and later we sold our interest to them. They have been editors of the fine newspaper since.

Interestingly, both Mike and Linda have served as president of the Alabama Press Association. They continue to do a good job for their community.

April 3, 2003

Bronner invests State's money wisely

Who is David George Bronner?

He is a very important American citizen and fortunately, he lives in Alabama.

The 58-year-old Bronner was born in Iowa and received his bachelor's and master's degrees from Minnesota State University, then later got his law degree and PhD in Business Administration at the University of Alabama.

He taught in various graduate schools of education and business, was Assistant Dean of the University of Alabama Law School, and for a time served as Dean of Jones School of Law in Montgomery.

But where his real importance came was in 1973 when he was invited to accept the CEO position with the Retirement Systems of Alabama. It is his responsibility to invest the funds that have been saved to pay the retirement of teachers, state employees and others.

When he began, the fund had $500 million, but now, under his guidance has increased to $25 billion, making the RSA the largest financial organization in Alabama.

Dr. Bronner's expertise in the field of finance and investment is recognized throughout America, and has been featured in business periodicals, including *International Investor*, the *Money Manager*, the *Wall Street Journal*, *Business Week*, *Forbes Magazine*, and now, in this column in the Gulf Coast Weekly Newspapers.

He is always thinking of ways to increase the economy of Alabama by use of the investments in his responsibility.

Perhaps the most widely known are the several Robert Trent Jones Golf Courses scattered over the entire state. First class courses, as is everything Bronner builds, they may not be profitable as individual golf courses, but they have been worth fortunes to Alabama. With the controlling interest of over 200 newspapers in the United States, he regularly has them advertise the assets in Alabama, particularly the golf courses. This has brought thousands to the state to look us over and to play the courses.

One rumor, and we like to think it is so, is the fact that one of these fine courses in Greenville, Alabama, was at least partially responsible for the billion dollar Hyundai automobile plant being built in that area. Japanese and Koreans are crazy about golf.

In Baldwin, the RSA funds have been used to improve the great Grand Hotel, with the expenditure of millions of dollars to make it truly one of the outstanding resorts in the world.

He has constructed several fine buildings in Montgomery, where their state offices are housed. Of importance locally, is the fact that he has agreed to invest over $100 million in the restoration of the great Battle House Hotel in Mobile, and at the same time, build a 34-story office building adjoining. No doubt this will be the icon of Mobile—at least until the I-10 Bridge is built.

Can you imagine the enormous responsibility of keeping $25 billion profitably invested? Let me tell you a story: a few years back we needed $2.5 million to match Federal funds to construct the William Green Veterans Retirement Home in Bay Minette. I went to Montgomery to talk to him, and when the $2.5 million was mentioned, he laughed, stating, "Jimmy, how on earth can I invest $25 billion by lending such small amounts at a time?"

However, he smiled and said, "Tell the city if they want to borrow the money, to write me a letter, they can have it immediately, and they can pay it back in 30 days, 30 months, or 30 years. But, one thing they must do is pay 8.75% interest."

Dr. Bronner has made many wise investments including one of the largest office buildings in New York, which he bought for pennies, and remodeled it to the point it is now—the place to be in New York.

Now he is in the process of purchasing 37% of United Airlines for over $300 million. This is the largest airline in the United States and considered by many to be a risky business, as the airline industry is not thriving at this time. But, watch it, he will probably make a billion or so dollars out of the investment over a period of a few years. To put it bluntly, he is smart.

He is a very interesting person with whom to participate in a conversation. Fortunately, you don't have to talk much, he does most of it. He has strong feelings about Alabama, and even though he is not a native, he has become a southern gentleman, and truly loves this great state. No one individual has done more to promote and build it than Dr. David Bronner.

May 29, 2003

RAY LOPER LEAVES GREAT LEGACY

Some people pass through life and leave a great legacy at their death . . . others just pass through. One of the former was Ray E. Loper, a resident of Bay Minette and Tuscaloosa, who died in Tuscaloosa seven days before his 99th birthday.

Many newcomers to Baldwin did not know him, but for the 30-plus years that he was a resident, he became well known, renowned, as a brilliant businessman, benefactor, and friend to many.

Among his many honors were an Honorary Doctor's Degree from the University of Alabama and Faulkner University. He was Bay Minette Citizen of the Year, was inducted into the Alabama Business Hall of Fame, and received many other honors.

He never told me, but I was told by many others, that he referred to me as his best friend in Baldwin County. I was honored to be his friend, which was recognized by his family, by naming me an honorary pallbearer at his funeral in Tuscaloosa.

As most shrewd businessmen are, he was also known as a hard trader. His wisdom in this was proven over and over again with the fact that he made millions and millions of dollars for his companies.

Ray was born in Mississippi, and started working for James Graham

Brown when he was 18, and because of his hard, energetic work and wisdom, he was elevated rapidly in this huge organization.

How he arrived in Bay Minette, in itself, is an interesting story.

In 1954, Brown's businesses were in Fayette, Alabama, where timber was fast disappearing, so it was decided to move the operation to southern Mississippi.

My brother, Dr. T.L. Faulkner, was a vocational education teacher in Fayette, and Paul Corwin, who at one time was the editor of *The Baldwin Times*, bought the newspaper in Fayette. Both became friends of Ray.

One day Paul called and told me the Brown Foundation was going to move, and I asked him, if he would, to get Ray to visit us here in Bay Minette, which he did.

He and his wife and two friends from Birmingham came here, and J.B. Blackburn and I took them freshwater fishing near Stockton. He liked fishing with a cane pole and worms, and was good at it.

Looking over our assets, he decided that Brown's companies would be wise to move here. One of his first land purchases was 8,000 acres from Henry Bryars of Stockton for $32 an acre. Other timber land buyers thought the price was too high and that Loper was foolish.

To this, he and his company eventually owned 40,000 acres in Monroe, Escambia, Mobile, and Baldwin Counties. A few years after he purchased them, he refused to sell any for less than $2,000 an acre. Now the Brown Foundation owns fewer than 5,000 acres in this area, as it has been sold and given away.

After moving to Baldwin, he started the Ray E. Loper Lumber Company in Bay Minette, which later employed over 300 people. After closing the mill, he concentrated on the real estate properties and philanthropy.

Mr. Brown died in 1969, and Ray was named president and CEO of the James Graham Brown Foundation. Also, he was selected to lead the Brown operating companies, which included lumber mills, wood treating plants, the Mobile and Gulf Railroad, and real estate holdings, oil wells, three hotels, and stock in Churchill Downs Racetrack in Louisville, Kentucky.

Right after Brown's death, I was coming from Washington, and Ray got on the plane with me in Atlanta. He was kind enough to let me read Mr.

Brown's will, leaving everything to the James Graham Brown Foundation. Among other things, the will stated the majority of the money should be given away in Kentucky. Beginning at that time, I argued with Ray that 49% of the, then, $60 plus million foundation money was a lot. Although he was chairman of the foundation and controlled all the businesses, most of the money over the years has been given in Kentucky.

Alabama has been given considerable money, including gifts to the City of Bay Minette, North Baldwin Hospital, Bay Minette Airport, a private school in Robertsdale, and other gifts throughout the area.

Although the foundation had to give away millions, through his management, the assets have grown now in the neighborhood of $200 million.

Ray is survived by one son, Graham Brown Loper, who resides in Mobile, and continues to serve on the Board of the Brown Foundation, and is well known in this area. He is a wise and energetic friend. He also is survived by his widow, Mary Frances Loper, who will continue to live in Tuscaloosa.

There are many successful stories that can be told about Ray's business adventures. Several of them involved me, but I'll reveal to you, just one. I was advised of 3,000 acres that could be bought for $3 an acre between Frisco City and Uriah in Monroe County. I had the sense, but not the cents, to make the purchase, but his company did and about three years ago, sold the acreage for about $16 million.

It is sad to lose a friend like Ray Loper, since they do not come along very often.

November 27, 2003

Visiting Bay Minette native Mary Ellen Cooper

It was not a surprise, but you can imagine what a pleasure it was to visit with a native of Bay Minette. Mary Ellen Cooper Chatwin was raised a couple of blocks from our home on East Fifth Street in Bay Minette. She is a brilliant, pleasant, kindly, attractive lady of middle age. She is one of five children of Kenneth and Anne Cooper, who most of you who have lived in Baldwin for the last 15 to 20 years knew. Kenneth was an Army officer, a district attorney and a successful attorney until his death. He grew up in Rosinton with two sisters, Dorothy Cooper Martin and Georgia Cooper McMillan, and two brothers, Roland and Carl. All are deceased now, except Dorothy.

Mary Ellen Chatwin is the mother of four grown children, one of whom she adopted from Brazil, who live in various parts of the world. Even with all the responsibility of the international job she holds, she is also raising her 10-year-old granddaughter. Both visited in Bay Minette a few months back and we fed them at the Stage Coach Café in Stockton. The young lady, Leyla, is obviously intelligent, well-mannered, and can speak three or four languages.

Mary Ellen has lived in various European countries since the 1970s, including Switzerland and, now, Georgia.

She does not work for the United States government, but she has a very important job with a U.S. agency, which is headquartered in Washington. She has the responsibility to help develop social policy in underdeveloped countries with private donations.

She is obviously held with high respect in Georgia, whereas recently there was a several page article in one of Georgia's newspapers about her job and what she does for the country, with a big picture of her at her desk.

As you can imagine, she is an interesting person to listen to, but you kind of have to keep asking questions to get her to talk about her various activities, which obviously are important in Georgia.

In a recent speech and interview, as recorded by *The Georgian Times*, she stated that with a slow transition from Communism, there is a great need for social reform and social programs in Georgia.

She continued by saying that many international donors were interested in assisting with funding for college-level training programs in social work at Tbilisi State University.

She goes out in the country visiting communities trying to train leaders to help develop social education and other important programs.

Mary Ellen is held with high-esteem in Georgia, and having worked there for 10 years, she has a clear understanding of their wants, needs and possibilities. Obviously, the country needs a lot of things, including a higher economic level of living.

Salaries are very low in Georgia, with doctors only making $500 a month, and teachers only $10. (Some teachers have to practice prostitution in order to make a living.)

However, she obviously does much better, and an indication of her kind heart and interest in helping people is that she pays the tuition for two or three students to attend the university.

Mary Ellen has two sisters, Carol Anne Brown and Susan Schuelke, and two brothers, Kenneth, Jr., and Riley, all brought up in Bay Minette, and now living throughout the world.

Her aunt, Dorothy Martin, stays in touch with her over the Internet and Mary Ellen delights in visiting home, and is expected back here in the near future.

It would be an interesting gathering if some civic or other worthwhile organization could persuade her to tell of her important work in Georgia.

Jimmy Faulkner, seated, with many of his coffee club friends who gathered to honor him on his 88th birthday in 2004. From left, Ralph Thompson, Bernie Steele, Claude Eubanks, Melvin Fleming, Bob White, Walter Smith, Jerry Perkins, Berlin Sims, Phil Pridgen, Tommy Langham, Bruno Strack, Jim Garner, the late Virgil Rhodes, and John Blackmon. (Photo by John C. Lewis of The Gallery)

April 22, 2004

ALAN WHITE—A LOCAL SUCCESS STORY

Over the years, one of the pleasures of writing this column has been telling about people who have started at the bottom and made it to the top.

There have been hundreds of such successes in Baldwin County, most unrecorded in newspapers and otherwise. Since it is impossible to report all of them, I will select one now and tell you the interesting successful story.

Alan White is a Baldwin County native, born in Stapleton, and he still lives there with his wife and three children. He finished high school in Bay Minette and attended the county's community college. For several years, he worked for *The Baldwin Times* and the Gulf Coast Newspapers, and in the process "got ink on his hands." Liking the outdoors, he started the successful *Gulf Coast Outdoors* magazine.

This is a monthly publication of some 80 to 100 pages printed and read by 40,000 people in what Alan refers to as the "Gulf Plains area." This area includes Northwest Florida, South Alabama, and Southern Mississippi.

Almost exactly in the center of the county, east and west and north and south, he has just moved into his new red building on Highway 31 South just north of Stapleton. Here he purchased three acres and plans to expand his 3,600 square foot building as needed for his business, as well as for the other businesses to whom he may rent space.

He began his adventures several years ago, investing $40,000 in Outdoors, Inc., which has an annual average income of about $1 million. White's staff consists of eight full-time and six part-time employees.

He is contemplating starting one or two other publications as soon as they seem practical and when he has the staff and other financial stabilities he desires.

In the meantime, he has stepped into a new business venture connected with the outdoors and the thousands of people who are interested in such a life. He is now a representative of Dixie Outfitters and girls' apparel for convenient stores, sporting goods stores, country and western stores and similar outlets in Alabama, Georgia, Florida, Mississippi, Louisiana, and plans to take these apparel lines to others across the southeast. In the roadside building, he also plans to put in other products connected with the outdoors and similar interests.

He is supposed to have all of these plans underway by July of this year, and after this his company plans to spread its aggressive approach to distributing throughout the nation.

"We are very excited with the growth we have had so far. The magazine has opened many doors for us over the last six years and being selected by companies such as Haas Outdoors and Mossy Oak is a credit to the folks who work here," Alan said.

Thanks, Alan, for proving once again that in this great country of America, people like yourself are working hard and using sound judgment to have such accomplishments.

***

No one realizes better than I, that every ball hit makes some people happy and some unhappy.

My recent article about expanding the 17 mile Highway 27 from Highway 90 South to Highway 98 caused thousands to be happy, and a few to be unhappy. Some people along the proposed route that the five-lane highway will take are concerned, understandably so, about the possibility of right-of-way taking too much of their property.

Since this is a state highway, the Alabama Department of Transportation will select the right-of-way, not the Baldwin County Commission.

Concerned about the amount of right-of-way to be taken, the state is making it a five lane road instead of a four lane, because the five lanes take less right-of-way. If you think about it, you will realize that five lanes will join each other, whereas four lanes will have to have considerable space between the lanes.

I can well remember, as many of you can, back when a new road was announced, practically everybody was happy. Not so anymore, because super-highways increase traffic, making more noise and taking more property to expand. Most people call this progress, some don't.

***

For years, people have been suggesting to me that I publish a book containing many of these columns. I have always objected, feeling that it would not be of great interest. However, several months ago, I was persuaded and in a few days, there will be an announcement where such a book has been completed in a limited edition and will be available to those who might want it.

April 29, 2004

MARY FRANCES STEWART WILL BE MISSED

Mary Frances Stewart was killed in a tragic highway accident at 6:45 a.m., Saturday, April 17th, just east of Elberta, Alabama.

As people learned the news, tears were shed and people were left in disbelief and shock. The death of no other person in Baldwin at this time would have been as devastating.

If you had run into her at almost any time in this county, you would see the face of this smiling, popular, energetic lady. She was in the midst of a campaign for reelection to the County Commission to serve a second term. She was first elected four years ago when she ran against and defeated five men without a run-off. Most everyone believed she was heading for another victory.

It has been my privilege to know her as a friend for a number of years. She worked for Loyal American Life Insurance Company, a company founded by me, and then taught high school in Mobile and Foley before retiring.

She really became interested in politics when the recent Governor Fob

James was running for election, being his county campaign manager. Proof that she was a good one was the fact that Baldwin was the only county in Southwest Alabama that he carried.

Then, she was persuaded by her many friends to run for County Commissioner. Her district included the Foley-Magnolia Springs-Elberta area.

Being wise, she started her service on the commission watching and observing and quietly until she could catch onto things. But, she grew into the position and became an intelligent and effective member.

Growing in ability, knowledge, and acquaintances, she had become well-known and respected in Montgomery. She was a human dynamo, full of energy, adaptability, a great attitude and hardly ever met a stranger—if so, she became acquainted before leaving his or her presence. As a matter of fact, she was dearly loved by thousands and thousands throughout this county and state.

The popular former presidential candidate, Bob Dole, called her on the phone to wish her success on her campaign. He also sent her an autographed picture, plus a book.

She was one of the leaders in persuading the Alabama Highway Department to five-lane Highway 27 from Highway 90 in Malbis South to U.S. 98. She had become an influential friend of Highway Director Joe McInnes. The Governor is supposed to be here soon to announce and dedicate this much needed highway improvement. It is sad that she will not be present to enjoy the occasion.

The statement that she was one of the leaders in obtaining the money for this is true, but she had a lot of help. Therein lay another one of her attributes, in that she was able to garner support around her to get good things done. One of the last things she told me recently was that she was thankful that she had so much energy so that she could work for so many different worthwhile things.

Recently, I had the privilege of going with her to talk to the Highway Director and his right-hand man over lunch and it was interesting to note her ability to persuade and to charm these two gentlemen. She was never caught short on verbiage, but could talk on and on and never hesitate to make her position clear.

It was suggested by me that they name Highways 27 or 83 the "Mary Frances Stewart Highway." Hopefully, this will be done, but only time will tell. Anyway, each will not be completed for many months.

A graveside service was held because no building was large enough for the crowd.

Of course, our sorrow goes to her family, but also a great loss is being felt by practically every citizen in this great county.

The heritage left by this honest, intelligent, smiling lady will be remembered a long time in political, religious and social circles.

Thank you, Mary Frances, for being with us and leading us for years. You will be missed greatly.

February 10, 2005

PETITE LADY MAKING BIG IMPACT ON BALDWIN COUNTY

Everybody calls her "Seven." Born in northern China, her real name is Wang Caiwen.

Twelve years ago she came to Bay Minette, and was introduced to me by her Chinese name, which sounded like "Seven." Thus, that's what she has been called since. A popular, small, intelligent, 30ish looking Chinese lady (but actually is 52, and doesn't look it) has been well received and loved here among hundreds of people.

The Bay Minette Industrial Development Board persuaded the Chinese to put an assembly plant here in Bay Minette and she came over with several men who established the electronic company. Sales were good but because, at that time, it was difficult to get parts for the complicated machinery, it was not successful. While here, she joined a Leadership Class of the University of South Alabama and Baldwin County United. Also, she volunteered at the Bay Minette Public Library.

Seven went back to China at the end of six years but returned to Bay Minette the following summer and was employed by Standard Furniture Company in the Merchandising Department. She has been with them since, becoming an important person in their operations. Standard is a hugely successful furniture company employing 1,300 people in Bay Minette and Frisco City. They buy much of their furniture from various countries including China, Vietnam, Malaysia, etc. It is easily understood why she is important because she speaks about 14 different languages, including 10 dialects of Chinese.

Along with a group of other Standard people, she goes back to China three or four times a year to work with factories there. She can naturally converse with them in person as she does by telephone. While there, she has the opportunity to visit her family, a husband, one son, two sisters and her parents.

Actually, Ms. Wang is very personable, outgoing and pleasant. She achieved one of her main goals recently when she became an American citizen. To give you an idea of her intelligence and determination, she went to Atlanta where she took a two-hour examination by Uncle Sam's people to become a U.S. citizen. The lady in charge said she answered everything perfectly, meaning 100%, and because of this she did not have to take a written test that is given to most applicants. She was immediately sworn in as an American.

Probably not one person in 50 could pass the exam, because they ask such questions as "Which amendment gave black males the privilege of voting?" Answer: 16th. Or "Which amendment made all women eligible to vote?" Answer: 19th.

"What was the Boston Tea Party all about and when did the Revolutionary War start?" Answer: 1787 and taxation without representation. "Who was the main enemy of Uncle Sam in WWI?" Answer: Germany. "WWII?" Answer: Germany, Italy, and Japan.

Now, as an American citizen, she can get her husband and son over here.

When she was 16 years old and was in the ninth grade, there was a "Cultural Revolution" in China. Her father was arrested for political reasons and served three years in prison. At this time, Seven was ordered to quit school and was sent to a farm for six years to be "re-educated," which meant hard labor. She worked in rice fields and was hungry all the time.

While on the farm, she taught herself with high school textbooks sent to her by friends. After the "Cultural Revolution," she passed the National College Entrance examination, studied at Nanking University and later at Shandong University. She received a master's degree in Comparative Literature. While in her post-graduate study, she published seven books, most of them literary critics. One was 600 pages and the others were about 300 pages each. Obviously, she is a good writer in Chinese and is anxious to write more about her life in English. In 1991, she was awarded Hansuyin Literature Translation Prize by China Translators Association and British writers.

After gaining her citizenship, Seven stated, "After living here for more than 10 years, I feel like this is my own country and love it for its generous and gracious people, its beautiful landscape, its freedom and opportunities. Last week, I passed the test in the Immigration office and was sworn in. When the national anthem, "The Star Spangled Banner," was played, I felt a lump in my throat and tears running down my cheeks. I am so proud to be an American."

Seven is the third Chinese girl we have been able to bring to Bay Minette. About 20 years ago, two sisters, Wang Yin and Wang Yi, came over, lived in our home and we helped them get educated. They too were smart, each making either Cum Laude or Magna Cum Laude.

Now both girls have adopted American names and the younger is called Yvonne and the older Ingrid. They live in Houston, Texas. One is a lawyer and the other an accountant. The younger one is married, has two children and lives in a beautiful new home in a fine section of Houston and obviously, has come a long way since coming to Bay Minette.

We enjoyed having them in our home and they came over with nothing, just the typical Chinese clothing that is still prevalent in China.

February 24, 2005

WOMEN TO MAKE BIG IMPACT
ON STATEWIDE POLITICS

"The hand that rocks the cradle rules the world," someone has said. It has also been said that women control 51% of the vote, 80% of the wealth and have enhancements that attract men.

Of course women have always played an important part in political affairs, even before the 19th Amendment of the American Constitution allowing them the privilege of voting.

The above was mentioned because of the possibilities of two ladies making a big splash in state and city politics within the next several months.

These two are selected due to the fact that both have made races statewide and are well known.

The first lady is Lucy Baxley, present Lt. Governor of Alabama and former State Treasurer. She has made three statewide races and is preparing to make the fourth, perhaps the most important of all. She's going to seek to be Alabama's second elected lady governor. Lurleen Wallace was the first.

The other lady, Ann Bedsole of Mobile, has run for governor. Making a strong race, she was not elected, but was defeated by Fob James. She was an effective state senator representing Mobile County and, like Lucy, is an attractive, intelligent person. She is considering a race for mayor of Mobile.

There may be other ladies in these two races but I mention these two because of their statewide prominence and other attributes.

You already see "I love Lucy" signs out over the state. Although she has not made a firm commitment to run for governor, it is very plain that she fully intends to do so. She will run on the Democratic ticket, as she has been a lifelong member of this party.

No one can say at this time whether Mrs. Baxley will be victorious but it can be safely said that she will make a big splash and if anyone beats her, they will most likely be governor. Both Lucy and Ann have children and have thus "rocked the cradle."

Each is above 50 years of age. Lucy admits to being 67, Ann is, so far, quiet on the subject.

Of course Ann will have strong opposition, but as mentioned about Lucy, the person who beats her will probably be mayor of Mobile for the next four years.

Ladies have played prominent parts in Baldwin County politics. The recent death of Mary Frances Stewart ended a successful career, as she was an active, effective member of the Baldwin County Commission. She is being missed.

We also have three effective lady members of the Baldwin County Board of Education. They are Denise Schmidt of Daphne, Stacey Roberts of Spanish Fort, and Margaret Long of Orange Beach. Ruth Underwood, who had served with great distinction for several terms on the same board, retired last year.

Of course we have other lady political office holders, including Judge Lyn Stuart, Associate Justice of the Alabama Supreme Court, and Circuit Clerk Jody Wise, who replaced Jackie Calhoun after she retired. We also have District Judge Carmen Bosch.

There are several elected ladies serving on city councils and other offices in Baldwin.

If it's not a woman's world, I don't know whose it is.

June 2, 2005

GREAT PEOPLE VISIT MY OFFICE

For the past 68 years, thousands of people have visited my offices on 102 West 2nd Street, one half block from the court house or around the corner from *The Baldwin Times* building.

Among them have been prominent people, but mostly average folk like me who are kind enough to visit. Many come by to get my opinions, but I have noticed over the years that most of them give me theirs. All this is fine. Interestingly, some drop by without an appointment. I am able to see them and hopefully visitors will continue to drop by. Recently, two VIP friends dropped in and gave me interesting information, which was appreciated. I always like to see people come, particularly friends.

The first was Ron Creel. Most of you probably do not remember Ron but he was a member of the State Board of Education for one term (1979-83.) It was during this time that he was instrumental in helping select Dr. Gary Branch to become president of Baldwin's community college. We should all be thankful because he has made a great record in developing the school. It was during this period, that Ron met the lovely Shirley McKissack and later married her. Everybody loves Shirley and she was well known because she had been secretary to several of our county's superintendents of education. She is the daughter of Vesta Caprara of the Pine Grove community and the mother of Dr. Randy McKissack, a prominent surgeon in Fairhope and Bay Minette. The other son is Steven, who has a successful landscape and lawn business in Birmingham.

Ron is President and CEO of Alabama Sports Festival at the headquarters in Montgomery where he has lived all his life, and since he married Shirley that is their home. He has worked with the youth of Alabama where he holds a sports tournament in Mobile every year with 7,000 or more in attendance. Shirley has been seriously ill but is now better, according to her mother and Ron.

Ron often stops in to say howdy but this time he had a special message to give me. He said, "In my opinion, Judge Moore will definitely be a candidate for governor." He should know because he is one of Judge Moore's right hand men and is working hard for his interests. Naturally, he thinks the Judge will be our next governor and will easily defeat our present incumbent governor, Governor Riley.

Ron also wanted to tell and invite me to Judge Moore's upcoming Baldwin rally, "For the Love of God and Country Rally" featuring Judge Roy Moore, which will take place Friday, June the 3rd at Oak Hollow Farm, 14210 Greeno Road, Fairhope.

Of course everybody is invited to attend, free fish fry, blue grass music, etc. Doubt if I'll be able to make the rally but you can bet your bottom dollar there will be a huge crowd there.

The other delightful visitor was John McMillan. John is well known in this county, being the twin brother of Steve McMillan, who has been representing Baldwin in the legislature for the past 20 years. Their father was John Murphy McMillan of Stockton where their mother still lives and who recently celebrated her 94th birthday. John is married to the beautiful Katherine Turner, whose father was the county agent in Baldwin County for many years. Her sister Jane and brother Frank Jr. still live in Bay Minette.

Great people visit my office

John served as a Baldwin County Commissioner for one term and one term in the state legislature but resigned to become the Executive Vice President of the Alabama Forestry Association, headquartered in Montgomery. He has held this position for over 20 years but expects to retire in the next year.

Not surprisingly, John is considering running for some local or statewide office. Since being known statewide, he could make a formidable race for such an office as Alabama Commissioner of Agriculture and Industries. He would make a dandy. He might also have his eye on some legislative office such as state senator. If he chooses to run for the senate, living in Stockton, he would be in the same district as Pat Lindsey, which covers some seven counties. At this time it is not known whether Pat will run again, but it can safely be assumed that he will.

This district includes part of northwest and north Baldwin.

John has done an excellent job with the Forestry Commission and I hate to see him retire, but time passes on and things change.

June 16, 2005

RIDING MOTORCYCLE FUN WAY TO SEE COUNTRY

Flying has been a favorite way to see the world for a long time. You fly to a destination, rent a car and head out any direction you wish.

It has been my privilege to enjoy such travel for a long time, all the way from Maine, New York, Canada, California, Mexico and the entire west. Now I've learned the new wrinkle on how to fly and ride. Instead of renting a car, you have a motorcycle waiting for you.

There are a lot of "hogs" in Baldwin, other than the variety that makes pork. They are a Harley Davidson organization group.

Recently, the following six men from Baldwin and Mobile flew to Phoenix, Arizona, with Harley Davidsons awaiting them in Scottsdale, Arizona. These cycles cost $25,000 or more but rent for $100.00 a day.

They spent about eight days from the time they left flying to Phoenix and returning home.

Those making the trip were all dedicated Harley Davidson owners as follows: Dr. Gary Branch, President Faulkner State Community College, Bay Minette; Mr. Phil Law, Regional Pharmaceutical Representative, Daphne; Dr. Don Sanders, Medical Internist, Mobile; Mr. Thomas Steiner, Director of Springhill Nursing Home, Mobile; Mr. Hunter McDonald, Owner of The Locker Room (a men's clothing establishment), Montgomery; and Mr. David Howell, Sales Manager for Harley Davidson, Mobile.

I always get fun out of my own trips and as remembered, have never used this column to tell about any trips made by other people. However, this is so interesting I thought you would enjoy it.

In the main, the following is mostly in their own exciting words. Saturday, May 21st, they picked up their Harleys at the Scottsdale Dealership (Scottsdale is a suburb of Phoenix). The ride was arranged through the Harley Davidson Fly and Ride Program. It's a special program that allows people to fly into major cities, be picked up by shuttle and taken to a local Harley Davidson dealership to get motorcycles for the ride. After the tour or ride, the riders are returned to the airport by shuttle.

The group left Phoenix and rode to the south rim of the Grand Canyon where they enjoyed a sunset and spent the night. The next morning they experienced an equally gorgeous sunrise and headed out again. The Grand Canyon was Dr. Branch's favorite part of the trip. They visited the Painted Desert, Monument Valley, and the Valley of the Gods.

On one particular day, they started out through the desert, the temperature climbing to 103 degrees. By that evening, they had reached the top of Bryce Canyon and rode into snow, sleet and a temperature of 31 degrees.

The riders' tour included: Arches National Park, Utah; Bryce Canyon National Park, Utah; Canyon Lands, Utah; Capital Reef National Park, Utah; and Zion National Park, Utah. They visited Four Corners where Arizona, New Mexico, Colorado and Utah meet. Dr. Branch particularly enjoyed the towns of Telluride, Colorado, Ouray, Colorado, and an old gold mining town (where the group spent the night) Durango, Colorado, and Sedona, Arizona. His favorite state was Colorado.

A special treat for the group was traveling a section of Historic Route 66 where the movie "Easy Rider" was filmed in 1969. Dr. Branch brought back a treasured souvenir, a piece of pavement from the famous road.

He said there was a scene in the movie in which the characters Captain America (Peter Fonda), Billy (Dennis Hopper), and George Hanson (Jack Nicholson) were not allowed to spend the night in a motel because they were "motorcycle riders." He noted this hotel is now deserted.

Dr. Branch verified that "out west" you should buy gas anytime you see a service station. You can actually travel 100 miles without seeing another station. They stopped for gas in Norton, Colorado, and found one service station with two pumps. However, the small town did have three bars and two liquor stores.

The ride covered over 2,000 miles through four states: Arizona, Utah, Colorado and New Mexico. The group returned their motorcycles to Scottsdale on Friday, May 27.

The men thoroughly enjoyed the time they spent riding and viewing these western states and the "great wide open." Dr. Branch observed that it reminded him anew of what a beautiful country we live in and the awesome creative power of God.

August 4, 2005

L. D. Owen's contribution to area immeasurable

L. Dick Owen, Jr., was a mountain of a man and spent 86 years proving it.

Comparatively, he lived a quiet life during his last 20 or 25 years, but was virtually a ball of fire earlier in life.

He had so many it would be difficult to tell which of his accomplishments was the greatest.

He had a great war record in World War II. He received his bachelor's degree from the University of Alabama and immediately went into the service as a reserve officer. He got out of the service in 1945 after receiving many honors for bravery in the European sector.

A native of Bay Minette, he enlisted in the army and served as a paratrooper in the 82nd Airborne Division. Later, he was called back to active duty during the Korean War and retired as Lieutenant Colonel in the U.S.

Army Reserve in 1963. While serving as a paratrooper in the European sector, and being involved in several dangerous battles, he received six bronze stars and several other medals.

It was not my privilege to be close to Dick until we both got out of the war in 1945. However, I was quite involved with the Owen family prior to this. Arriving here in 1936, I was soon elected mayor and his father, L. D. Owen, Sr., "Big Dick" he was called, became mayor pro tem. Then when I volunteered into the Army Air Corps, he became mayor. Later, little Dick served on the city council and also served as mayor pro tem.

Dick was a close friend of Governor George Wallace and worked for him throughout the United States in Wallace's presidential efforts. Because of his friendship and following the death of Probate Judge W.R. Stuart, Governor Wallace appointed Dick probate judge of the county. However, he lost the election for a new term.

Following this, it occurred to me that he was too good a man to dry up, so to speak, here in Bay Minette. He was too able and too needful not to be of political service. With this view, I went to him and practically begged him to run for a vacancy in the state legislature, which was caused when Telfair J. Mashburn was elected circuit judge. I told Dick if he would run, I would raise the money for his race, which at that time, he needed only $2,000.00. At first he was reluctant, but finally agreed to it—he did and I did. Following this, he served six years in the legislature and then eight years in the State Senate.

In the Senate, he received many honors, among which was "Most Effective Senator" by the Alabama Press Association, and was chairman of the powerful Senate Finance and Taxation Committee. I don't recall any other senator from Baldwin County ever achieving this powerful position.

A strong Democrat, he was later defeated for re-election to the Senate when the Republicans sort of took over the county and Perry Hand took his place.

During the past few years, he could always be found at the corner of Courthouse Square in the renowned Builder's Hardware and Supply Company. This company was previously owned by his father and J.C. Burns. Burns was mayor prior to my term. He did not want to run again and unbelievably asked me if I would seek his position. I was 23 and he was in his late sixties. I was humbled and honored and did what he suggested. Upon his death, L. D. Owen, Dick's daddy, "Big Dick," bought the hardware store and it is still in the Owen family.

Dick could always be found in the store serving as a proprietor, clerk, janitor, or whatever came to be needed. He would greet people, including me, as "Hello Boss, what can I do for you?" or "What good news do you have?" He was friendly and had thousands of friends who would drop by to see him, not only locally, but from the entire state. He seemed to always have time to chat.

Dick loved his family, his city, state, county, and country. He was extremely patriotic and although he served in two wars, would have gone again had he been called. I doubt if many people knew it, but Dick disliked the United Nations and told me many times it should be abolished. Sometimes I agree with him.

Dick played a big part in obtaining a two-year college for Baldwin County. It happened something like this: In 1963, legislation was passed making it possible for two-year colleges to be built in Alabama. It was one of George Wallace's main accomplishments and originally they were supposed to build eight. Probably intended to put one in each of the nine Alabama Board of Education districts.

Early on, the one for this area was placed in Monroeville because they had a member on the Board of Education. Also, one was promised to Brewton.

Although Bay Minette got started late, a meeting was called and I was asked to be chairman of the group to obtain a school for us. Even though many made fun of us because they thought we were too late, I did agree to it provided Dick would agree to be co-chairman. He did and because of his friendship to George Wallace and others throughout the state, we were successful.

He was also active in seeing that the school was named after me. Later, with my cooperation, we were able to get the fine new auditorium at the college named the L. D. Owen, Jr., Performing Arts Center.

Owen had two brothers, Robert, who died last year, and his other,

Jimmy, is three years younger than Dick and retired as a General in the Army Reserve.

His only son is L. D. Owen, III, a local attorney. He is attorney for the City of Bay Minette.

Everybody wonders what is going to happen to Builder's Hardware. Hopefully it will remain open. No doubt, his lovely wife, Annie Ruth, will have something to say about this.

October 27, 2005

BALDWIN COUNTY'S FIRST LADY OF EDUCATION

Louise Baggett Hollinger worked with the Baldwin County Department of Education for almost a half century before her death on October 13. With full admiration and agreement by thousands who knew her, we are on this date recognizing her as "Baldwin County's First Lady of Education."

I asked one of her longtime acquaintances if the above title was accurate and he readily replied, "No one else is close."

My first meeting was when she worked with Mr. S. M. Tharp, Baldwin County Superintendent of Education. Five superintendents of Baldwin were fortunate enough to have her working with them for the benefit of the students of this great county. They were, in addition to Mr. Tharp, Mr. Candler McGowan, Dr. Aubrey McVay, Mr. Leslie Smith and Dr. J. Larry Newton.

Her last employer and one of her great admirers was Dr. Newton. I asked him to please give me more detailed information about this lady that I admired so much. I appreciated his assistance and here are some of his notes:

"Louise Baggett Hollinger was born in Uriah, Alabama. Her mother died when she was approximately three weeks old from childbirth complications, and she was raised by her grandmother. Louise attended and graduated from J. U. Blacksher High School. She attended Athens College, in Alabama, for a period of time but had to drop out due to financial reasons.

"She was employed at Brookley Field during World War II and afterwards she went to work for Morrison's. She was employed by the Baldwin County Board of Education in 1946 while Mr. Tharp was Superintendent, and she served as Secretary for the Veterans Program. This program was for GI's returning home after the war, who wanted to return to high school to complete their education.

"She worked her way up to become Treasurer/Comptroller of the Baldwin County School System. She retired in 1987 after 41 years of service, but continued on a part-time basis until 1994.

"In 1995, she was appointed as a member of the Baldwin County Board of Education to fill the unexpired term of Dr. L. E. Rockwell.

"In 1947, she married her childhood sweetheart, Adam Lavaughn Hollinger, a World War II veteran who was a POW. Adam had spent 15 months in a German prison camp. The marriage lasted 57 years, until her death. They had two children, Peggy and Faron.

"Each child continued the educational legacy of their mother. Peggy is presently serving as a counselor at L. E. Rockwell Elementary School, and Dr. Faron Hollinger, Superintendent of the Baldwin County Public School System. Faron's wife, Marsha, is a Librarian at Davidson High School, Mobile, and one of the grandchildren, Jeremy, teaches Special Education in Mobile. I would not be surprised to see the other grandchild, Jonathon, enter the teaching profession.

"The Louise Hollinger Award is given annually to the outstanding secretary in the Baldwin County School System.

"My personal opinion of Louise Hollinger: Our Sunday School teacher asked the class one day if we thought angels were still active today. I told him I was sure they were because I worked with one every day, Louise Hollinger. She was just a wonderful Christian lady."

Adam is a very talented musician who played lead guitar for Hank Williams, Sr., on radio station WSFA in Montgomery in 1941 before Hank became famous. He was associated with the Alabama Department of Veterans Affairs as Service Officer for Baldwin County for over 20 years.

See you again soon, I hope.

From left, celebrating Dr. James H. "Jimmy" Faulkner's 90th birthday March 1, 2006, are Dr. Billy D. Hilyer, president of Faulkner University, Montgomery; Dr. Faulkner; and Dr. Gary L. Branch, president of Faulkner State Community College, Bay Minette. Both institutions are namesakes of Dr. Faulkner. (Photo by John C. Lewis of The Gallery)

INDEX

52, 90

Baldwin County Potato Tour
Association   76, 77, 128

Baldwin County Republican Executive
Committee   9, 10

Baldwin County Savings and Loan
Association   397

Baldwin County Sesquicentennial
195, 196

Baldwin County Singing Convention
49

Baldwin Times   xi, xii, xv, xvi, 3, 68,
113, 173, 197, 235, 266, 273, 274,
293, 330, 356, 357, 367, 397, 398,
420, 428, 429, 433, 438, 447

Baldwin, Clayton   23

Baldwin, M. W.   396

Baldwin, Michael W.   396

Bama Postmaster 179

Bank of Fairhope   102

Bankhead, John H.   417

Barchard, Frank, Sr.   9, 10

Barnes, J. F.   91

Barnett, Ross   234

Barnhill, David   212, 235

Barnwell Farmers Club   25

Barrow, J. L.   xv, 44, 191

Barry, Gene   347

Bauer, John   189

Baxley, Lucy   445, 446

Bay Manufacturing Co., Inc.   158

Bay Minette Chamber of Commerce
36, 42, 112, 263

Bay Minette Coffee Drinkers
Association   36

Bay Minette hit by tornado   344, 345

Bay Minette Hospital   129, 130, 137,
138, 139

Bay Minette Hunting Club   91

Bay Minette Land Company   11, 358,
359

Bay Minette Production Credit

Association   28, 77, 368

Bay Minette, Alabama   4, 5, 7, 8, 10,
11, 12, 16, 17, 283, 290, 291, 298,
299, 301

Beach, Rex   5

Beard, Leonard   229

Beasley, Mr. and Mrs. N. P.   100

Beasley, Wilson   208, 245, 246

Becker, Ina Mae   224, 323, 324

Bedsole, Ann   445, 446

Bedsole, J. L.   400, 401

Beebe, John P.   xv

Beebe, Mrs. W. C.   303

Beebe, W. C. (Bill)   4, 38, 57, 73,
155, 199, 200

Bellingrath Gardens   262, 263

Benik, Al   128

Bennett, Chris   215

Bennett, James H.   154, 160, 166,
215

Bennett, Mrs. James H.   154, 215

Bennett, J. Jefferson   215

Benson, Ezra Taft   170

Benton, Thomas   390

Beveridge, Bruce   30, 40, 52, 54, 91,
138

Beveridge, Bruce, Jr.   130, 132, 133,
134

Beveridge, Mrs. Bruce   40

Bianco, Cyril   190

Bigby, Felix   191

Biggs, Leon   126, 127

Biggs, Mr. and Mrs. J. Henry   126,
127

Bilbo, Senator   319

Biles, Dr. Bayless Edward   376. 377

Bill, Harry   xv

Birmingham News   81, 182, 262, 326

Birmingham Post Herald   328

Birmingham Southern College   28,
368

Bisha, R. E.   141

Bishop, T. V. 181
Black Issues in Higher Education
420
Black, Hugo 4
Blackburn, Ann 40
Blackburn, J. B. xv, 5, 38, 283, 291,
433
Blackburn, Joe 39
Blackmon, John 437
Blair, Dr. John C. 236
Blakeley 5, 6, 401
Blakeley, Josiah 402
Blatckford, Larry 158
Blount, Red 412
Bloxham, Carl 20, 96
Blue Angels 249, 250
Blue Cross and Blue Shield Association
xvi
Bodden, C. A. 283
Boller, Charlie 23
Bonner, J. Miller 340
Bonner, Jo 427
Boone, Mrs. W. A. 70
Boone, W. A. 70
Booth, Mrs. T. A. 71
Booth, T. A. 71
Borman, Frank 349
Bosch, Carmen 346, 446
Boseck, Carl 21
Boutwell, Albert 229
Boykin, Frank 143, 226
Bracey, Frank 34
Bradley, J. T. 172
Brady, Phil 79
Branch, Dr. Gary L. 447, 448, 449,
450, 451, 456
Brannan, L. W., Jr. 116, 140, 141,
177, 275, 296, 297, 324
Breedlove, Linda 429
Breedlove, Mike 429
Breitling, Frank W. 302, 303
Brewer, Albert 352, 355

Brewton Standard 63
Brisbane, Arthur 232
Bristow, Julian 147
Broadus, J. M. (Matt) 84, 85
Bronner, Dr. David George 430, 431,
432
Brookley Air Force Base 249, 250
Brooks, Bill 63, 64
Brothers, E. H. 106
Brown, Carol Anne 435, 436
Brown, George 212
Brown, George A. 405, 406
Brown, James Graham 432, 433, 434
Brown, Julian 59
Brown, Lyle 59
Brown, Orvis M. 22, 45
Brown, Otto 49, 59
Brummel, Bo 365
Brunson, Paul 334, 335
Bryan, Tom 307
Bryant, A. C. 417
Bryant, Dr. and Mrs. P. A. 100
Bryant, Dr. Percy A. 63, 109, 336
Bryant, M. E. 211, 212
Bryant, P. A. 417
Bryant, Paul (Bear) 232, 287, 297,
303, 307, 312, 332, 415
Bryars, A. B. 51
Bryars, Brown 69
Bryars, Harold 265
Bryars, Henry 41, 51, 69, 109, 122,
260, 433
Bryars, Henry, Jr. 42
Bryars, Mrs. Henry 260
Bryars, Rudolph 69
Bryars, Tom 52
Buchanan, Congressman 408
Buck, Virgil 166
Builders Hardware and Supply
Company 209, 210, 452, 453, 454
Bullington, Mr. and Mrs. Doug 100
Burns, G. H. 20

Hodgson, W. M., Jr. 270, 293, 294, 307, 308, 355, 357, 394, 395
Hodgson, W. M., Sr. 35, 57, 71, 72, 189, 307, 308, 354, 355, 394, 395
Hoffman, Frank 417
Hollinger, Adam Lavaughn 455
Hollinger, Dr. Faron 455
Hollinger, Louise Baggett 454, 455, 456
Hollinger, Marsha 455
Hollinger, Peggy 455
Holmes, Dr. W. C. 57, 68, 121, 122
Holmes, Frank 5, 101, 102, 131, 132
Holmes, Hilary Herbert xv
Holmes, S. F. 17, 55, 93
Honey Chile 34
Hooker, Jane Troy 226, 227
Hooks, Bob 172
Hooper, Bill 26
Hooper, L. J. 13, 26, 40
Hooper, Leonard J. 81
Hooper, Mrs. L. J. 40
Hooper, Mrs. L. J., Sr. 26, 81
Hopper, Dennis 450
House, Dot 288
House, Jack 236, 250, 273, 274, 288, 289
Howard, Ralph O. 167
Howell, David 449, 450, 451
Howell, E. M. (Sparky) 243, 244, 248, 270, 379, 428, 429
Humphrey, Hubert M. 256, 347
Humphries, G. Mac 304, 305, 365, 366, 367, 370, 371
Humphries, Judge 20, 174
Hybart, Charlie 417

I

Ingram, Bob 230
International Paper Company, Container Division 295, 296
Inzer, Clarence 340

Irwin, (Tramp) xv
Irwin, Ella Stewart 218, 219
Irwin, Evelyn xvi
Irwin, Florence 29, 40
Irwin, J. S. 219
Irwin, S. J. 152
Irwin, Wade 219

J

James, Fob 440, 441, 445
James Graham Brown Foundation 432, 433, 434
James, H. T. 167
James, Lowell 383, 384
Japan 16
Jenkins, Amelia 160, 161, 162, 163
Jenkins, Hilliard 160, 161, 162, 163, 164
Jenkins, John Wesley 162, 163
Jenkins, Samuel 163
Jenkins, Shelly 163
Johnson, Amelia 396
Johnson, Bufred 273, 274
Johnson, Dixie 160
Johnson, Emery 84, 85, 205
Johnson, Lyndon B. 205, 211, 247, 254, 256, 259, 279, 363
Johnson, Martin 325, 326
Johnson, Mrs. Emery 205
Johnson, Oscar xv, 395, 396, 397
Johnson, Vance 404
Johnson, W. H. 26
Jones, Adolphus 176
Jones, E. J. 285, 286
Jones, Leland 225
Jones, Lonnie 393
Jordan, Dr. 68
Jordan, Green 116
Jordan, James V. 266
Jordan, Leroy 387
Jordan, Ralph (Shug) 287, 306, 307, 339, 340

K

Kahalley, A. 280

Kahalley, Jameal 116

Kaiser Aluminum & Chemical
  Corporation 317, 320, 369

Kaiser, John 112, 144

Kaiser, Mike 111, 112, 113

Kaiser, Mike, Jr. 112, 113

Kaiser, Paul 20

Kaiser, Paul, Jr. 112

Keeney, R. C. 74, 75, 150

Kendall, Robert 352

Kendrick, Calvin, Jr. 396

Kennedy, Bobby 218, 256, 344, 391

Kennedy, H. 96

Kennedy, Jackie 214, 218, 219, 227

Kennedy, Joe 216, 391

Kennedy, John 211, 214, 216, 221,
  223, 235, 259, 391

Kennedy, Ted 391

Khrushchev 223

Kilborn, Vincent F., Jr. 413

Killcrease, Roland 42

Killcrease, Wallace 32, 42, 89, 91

King, Martin Luther 266

Kinniard, Jan 249

Kinsey, Dan 390

Kinsey, Elmer 211

Kirk, Claude, Jr. 342

Klumpp, T. J., Sr. 84, 86, 148

Koehler, Frieda 11

Kucera, Ben 43

L

LaFayette Sun 225

Lambert, Dr. xv

Lambert, Mr. and Mrs. G. M. 100

Lampshire, Wayne 424

Landon, Alf 219

Langham, Tommy 437

Larrimore, B. B. 65, 83, 85

Lassitter, John K. 396

Latham, Woodrow 91

Law, Phil 449, 450, 451

Lawrenz, Max 97

Leak, Lauda 30

Leak, Major xv

Ledlow, John Wesley 413

Ledlow, Mrs. Willie Scott 413

Lee, M. O. 221

LeMay, General 346

Lemler, Sherman 85, 405

LeNoir, Frank 173

Liberty 5

Life 31, 34

Lincoln, Abraham 415

Lindoffer, L. 24

Lindsey, Pat 448

Lisenby, Dr. 68

Liston, Sonny 272

Little River Hunting Club 90, 91

Little, Morgan 155

Lodge, Henry Cabot 211, 247

Long, Huey 264

Long, Margaret 446

Loper, Graham Brown 432, 433, 434

Loper, Mary Frances 432, 433, 434

Loper, Ray E. 432, 433, 434

Louis, Joe 34, 162

Lowell, Mac 404

Lowery, J. S. 141, 142

Loyal American Life Insurance xvi,
  440

M

Mabry, N. M. 91

Malbis Plantation 262, 263, 285

Malbis, Jason 262, 263, 285

Malone, Lawrence L. 188

Manci, Frank 169

Manci, O. J. xv, 14, 251

Manci, O. J., Jr. 60

Marinos, George 145

Marker, Harry 106

454

P

Page, G.K. 32, 36, 70
Page, George K. 52, 213, 214
Page, Mr. and Mrs. G. K. 213
Page, Vivian Reed 213, 214
Palmer, James 396
Panzarella, Frank 317
Patterson, John 225, 329, 330
Pearl Harbor, Hawaii 16
Pearson, R. G. 276, 396
Pepperman, Ed 357
Pepperman, Hazel Robertson 357
Perdido, Alabama 13
Perioux, Ronnie 426
Perkins, Carl 362
Perkins, Jerry 437
Perrin, George 20
Persons, Gordon 165, 276, 321
Peterson, H. C. 74, 75
Peterson, J. D. 176
Phillips, Albert 24
Phillips, E. L. 91
Phillips, Thomas E. 91
Pickens, S. W. (Pick) 21
Pickett, Wingate 75
Pilgrim, J. A., Sr. 97
Pill, Howard E. 167
Pitt, W. M. 232, 257
Pittman, Alec 49
Plash, Melvin 54
Pleet, E. J. 167
Plunkett, George Washington 171, 175, 182, 378
Poland 12
Pollard, Dr. 214
Postma, Freddy 115
Powell, Adam Clayton 318, 319
Prescott, Perry 255, 256
Presley, Elvis 185
Pridgen, Charles 409

Pridgen, Phil 437
Progressive Farmer 153
Pruett, W. G. 168
Pruette, Sam C. 283, 293, 294
Purvis, Mr. 169

Q

Quinley, Mr. and Mrs. Edward 66
Quarles, Francis 196

R

Raddcliffe, Dale A. 205
Randall, Jack xv
Rankin, Allen 162
Ray E. Loper Lumber Company 91, 96, 432, 433, 434
Ray, A. A. xv
Reagan, Maureen 347
Reagan, Ronald 347
Red Eagle 5
Reed, Dr. J. M. 48, 213
Reed, Jeannie 249, 250
Reed, Ray 173
Reid, Ed E. 86, 110
Reid, M. D., (Max) 82, 83, 85 147
Reynolds, H. T. 123
Rhodes, L. T. 27, 42, 206, 207
Rhodes, Marion 11
Rhodes, Mr. and Mrs. L. T., Sr. 100
Rhodes, Mrs. L. T. 20
Rhodes, Virgil 437
Rhodes, V.V. 206, 207
Richerson, W. M. 20
Richerson, Wilbur 172
Rickarby, E. G., Jr. 45, 73
Riemer, Gust 28
Riley, Bob 448
Riviera Utilities 85
Robert Trent Jones Golf Courses 430
Roberts, Dr. 396
Roberts, Perry S. 188
Roberts, Stacey 446

Robertsdale, Alabama 10, 20, 22, 23, 65, 110, 128, 129, 139, 140, 207, 331, 332, 395, 396, 397
Robertson, Billy 173
Robertson, Cleveland 339
Robertson, G. W. xiii, xv, 20, 238, 241, 338, 339, 355, 356, 357
Robertson, G. W. (Billy), Jr. 355, 356, 357
Robertson, Jack 20, 173
Robertson, Jack, Jr. 339
Robertson, Jim 339
Robertson, Mary Frances 339
Robertson, Mrs. G. W. 100, 338, 339
Robertson, R. J. (Jack) 116, 211, 338, 339, 355, 356, 357
Robinson, Clarence 34
Robinson, Elizabeth 34
Rockefeller, Governor 254, 343, 344
Rockwell, Dr. L. E. 455
Rodgers, E. N., Jr. 70
Rodgers, Ed N. 57, 251, 353, 386
Rodgers, Gerry 42
Rodgers, Mr. and Mrs. Ed 42
Rogers, C. M. A., III 413
Rogers, Roy 188
Rogers, Will 225
Romeo, Mr. and Mrs. 75, 78, 79
Roosevelt, Franklin D. xi, xiii, 235, 242, 266
Roosevelt, Teddy 210
Rosinton, Alabama 20
Rose, Frank A. 215
Rountree, Asa 306
Rowland, Wm. L. 167
Ruge, Howard 17, 84, 86
Rundquist, Axel 65
Ruple, Leroy 109
Ruple. W. M. 29

S

Sanders, Dr. Don 449, 450, 451

Sanders, Frank 102
Saunders, Thomas 70
Schenk, John H. 418
Schlich, Carl L., Jr. 417
Schmidt, Denise 446
Schuelke, Susan 435, 436
Scott, (Farmer) xv
Scott, Hazel 34
Selden, Armistead 342
Selden, Mrs. Armistead 342
Sellers, J. D. (Josh) 83, 84, 85, 110, 139, 140, 147, 311, 331, 332, 336, 337, 395, 396, 397
Seminole, Alabama 20
Shakespeare, William S. 244, 245
Shambo, J. N. 44, 100
Shambo, Mrs. J. N. 44
Sharretts, Harlow S., Sr. 149
Shaw, George Bernard 185
Shelley, George 285, 286
Sherman, Dr. Charles 130
Shores, Janie 413, 414
Shores, Jim 413, 414
Sibert, Dr. L. N. 298, 375
Silverhill, Alabama 65, 85, 106, 205, 396
Simmons, Lilla 310
Simms, Roy 11
Simpson, Robert T., Jr. 413, 414
Sims, Ben 32
Sims, Berlin 437
Sims, C. T. 56, 77, 78
Sims, Harold 56
Sims, J. O. 418
Slaughter, Carl 52
Slaughter, H. W. (Boy) 71
Slaughter, H. W. 71
Slaughter, Jesse 70
Smelley, Mr. 184
Smith, Cly T. 13, 23, 36, 40, 51, 179, 245, 246
Smith, Embree 70

Smith, Fred 66
Smith, H. E. 70
Smith, H. E., Jr. 55
Smith, Hector 20
Smith, J. H. H. xvi
Smith, Jesse M. xv, 47, 90, 91, 174
Smith, Jewel 41, 51, 69, 109
Smith, John 51, 69
Smith, Leslie 454
Smith, Mr. and Mrs. Lee 100
Smith, Mrs. Abner J. 10
Smith, Mrs. Cly T. 40
Smith, Mrs. Lee 40
Smith, Robert A. 96
Smith, Sidney 180
Smith, Walter 437
Snook, John McClure 155, 422, 423
Snook, Marjorie Younce 422, 423
Snook, Ward H. 422, 423
Snyder, Alford W. 102
Snyder, Charles W. 102
Sokol, Phil 429
South Alabamian 367, 398, 429
Southern Bell Telephone and Telegraph
    Company 10, 423
Soviet Russia 12
Sparkman, John 136, 148, 308
Sparks, Chauncey 43, 238, 353, 386
Stacey, Dr. J. H. 20, 31, 40, 54, 251
Stacey, Johnny 20, 283
Stacey, Mrs. J. H. 40, 251
Stage Coach Café 435
Stallings, Dr. xv
Stamps, Jeannie 249
Standard Furniture Manufacturing
    Co., Inc. 270, 307, 308, 334, 335,
    357, 394, 395, 443
Stanley, Glenn 46, 47, 53, 54, 75,
    102, 103, 271, 272, 324, 325
Stanley, James Bernley 271, 272
Stanley, Webb 102, 103
Stanton, Mrs. Frank 24

Staples, Mrs. I. T. 70
Stapleton Civic Club 47
Stapleton, W. D. 104
State Bank of Elberta 102, 381
Staurou, Jimmy 145, 146
Steele, Bernie 437
Steele, Clyde 121, 217
Steele, Thomas L. 418
Steele, Tom, Jr. 417
Steele, W. E. 79
Steiner, Thomas 449, 450, 451
Stenzel, Art 173
Stephenson, P. M. 61, 62
Stevenson, Adali 148
Stewart, Bill 30, 165, 367, 397, 398,
    429
Stewart, James E. 167, 244, 248, 270
Stewart, Mary Frances 440, 441, 442,
    446
Still, Harry 75, 283
Still, Joe 52
Still, Mrs. Joe 40
Stimpson, Gordon G. 13, 24, 61
Stimpson, Mrs. Gordon G. 13, 61
Stockton, Alabama 6, 392, 393, 394
Stoddard, Bill xv
Stone, Frank xv, 71
Stone, Norborne xv
Stough, George 32, 36
Stough, Sabra 114
Strack, Bruno 437
Strong, Charles W. 280, 283
Strong, Dr. Quentin 396
Strong, George A. 396
Stuart, Derrill 159
Stuart, George 109
Stuart, Harold 245. 246
Stuart, Lyn 446
Stuart, Mr. and Mrs. W. Ramsey, Jr.
    55
Stuart, W. R. xv, 43, 452
Stuart, W. Ramsey 55, 57, 238, 239

W

Wakeford, Amelia 24
Wakeford, Charley 54
Walker, Clint 347
Wall Street Journal 150
Wallace, George C. 232, 252, 254,
258, 260, 261, 265, 266, 289, 298,
303, 310, 311, 326, 337, 338, 342,
345, 346, 347, 382, 386, 402, 452,
453
Wallace, Lurleen 310, 311, 327, 342,
343, 445
Wang Caiwen (Seven) 442, 443, 444
Wang Win 444
Wang Yi 444
Ward, Mr. 91
Wasdin, Al 409
Washington, Booker T. 34
Washington, George 182
Waters, Eva 173
Waters, Homer S. 70
Waters, John 173
Watson, Rowe xv
Weatherford, John 418
Weaver, A. G. 91, 179
Webb, Douglas S. 201, 202
Weekley, Mrs. Clyde O. 13
Weekley, Roy 12
Weekly, Mrs. 24
West, H. I. 153, 316, 317
West, Harry, Jr. 60
Wharton, (game warden) 53
Wharton, Kirby 17, 102, 141, 142
WHEP 167, 248
White, Alan 438, 439
White, Bob 437
White, C. L. 32
White, Clint 13, 40, 54
White, Doug 36
White, John (Judge) 341
White, Lloyd 70
White, Mamie 396

White, Mrs. Clint 40
Wilkins, M. H. xv, 44, 71, 193, 351,
352, 353
Wilkins, Marion 351, 352, 353, 386
Wilkins, Mildred Mayo 353
Wilkins, Taylor 22, 44, 52, 59, 71,
116, 249, 346, 351, 352, 353
William Green Veterans Retirement
Home 431
Williams, Charlie Frank 91
Williams, Hank, Sr. 455, 456
Williams, Wallace R. (Pinky) 293
Wilson, J. R. 16, 36, 40, 52, 138
Wilson, Johnny 115
Wilson, Mrs. J. R. 40
Wilson, Woodrow 266
Wilters, Harry J., Jr. 45, 119, 220,
244, 249
Wilters, Harry, Sr. 23, 179, 235, 395,
396, 397
Windham, Frank 273, 274
Wise, Jody 446
Wood, Fred 158
Wooley, Belle H. 104
Wooley, Gene 403, 404
World War I 15, 16
World War II xvi, 15,16,17
Wurst, J. A. 205, 283, 291

Y

Yearout, Tommy 409
York, Joe 60
Young, John 172

Z

Zarr, Bob 424, 425
Zarr, Perry 424, 425

www.ingramcontent.com/pod-product-compliance
Lightning Source LLC
Chambersburg PA
CBHW020407100426
42812CB00001B/240